VISUAL QUICKSTART GUIDE

MICROSOFT WORD 2004 FOR MAC OS X

Maria Langer

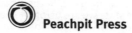

Peachpit Press

Visual QuickStart Guide
Microsoft Word 2004 for Mac OS X
Maria Langer

Peachpit Press
1249 Eighth Street
Berkeley, CA 94710
510-524-2178 • 800-283-9444
510-524-2221 (fax)

Find us on the World Wide Web at: http://www.peachpit.com/

Peachpit Press is a division of Pearson Education

Editors: Ted Waitt, Nancy Davis
Indexer: Julie Bess
Cover Design: The Visual Group
Production: Maria Langer, David Van Ness

Colophon

This book was produced with Adobe InDesign CS and Adobe Photoshop 7 on a dual processor Power Macintosh G5 running Mac OS X 10.3. The fonts used were Utopia, Meta Plus, and PIXymbols Command. Screenshots were created using Snapz Pro X 1.0 on a G4 eMac.

Notice of Rights

Notice of Liability

Trademarks

ISBN 0-321-30457-8

9 8 7 6 5 4 3 2 1

Printed and bound in the United States of America.

Dedication

To Ted Waitt

with best wishes
for the future
at Peachpit Press

This Book Is Safari Enabled

The Safari® Enabled icon on the cover of your favorite technology book means the book is available through Safari Bookshelf. When you buy this book, you get free access to the online edition for 45 days.

Safari Bookshelf is an electronic reference library that lets you easily search thousands of technical books, find code samples, download chapters, and access technical information whenever and wherever you need it.

To gain 45-day Safari Enabled access to this book:

- Go to http://www.peachpit.com/safarienabled
- Complete the brief registration form
- Enter the coupon code 62CH-UH1E-Y2H6-O9EM-IDO1

If you have difficulty registering on Safari Bookshelf or accessing the online edition, please e-mail customer-service@safaribooksonline.com.

Thanks!

To Ted Waitt and Nancy Davis, for their guidance and thorough review work. Without them, a lot of my i's wouldn't be dotted and t's wouldn't be crossed. And let's not even talk about prepositions!

To David Van Ness, for cheerfully helping to fine-tune the book's layout and appearance. And for not making me fix every single widow.

To Julie Bess, for producing another fine index. Maybe someday she'll be able to index a book for me that isn't about a Microsoft product.

To Jessica Sommer at Microsoft Corporation, for helping me get the materials I needed to write this and other Office 2004 books. Also to Warner Wang of Microsoft Office Online Support, for answering a question for me via e-mail when I could not find the information I needed online.

To Microsoft Corporation, for continuing to revise and improve the world's best word processor for Macintosh users.

And to Mike, for the usual reasons.

The Flying M

www.marialanger.com

Table of Contents

Introduction to Word 2004

Introduction

Microsoft Office Word 2004 is the latest version of Microsoft's powerful word processing application for Mac OS X users. Now more powerful than ever, Word enables users to create a wide variety of documents, ranging in complexity from simple, one-page letters to complex, multi-file reports with figures, table of contents, and index.

This Visual QuickStart Guide will help you learn Word 2004 by providing step-by-step instructions, plenty of illustrations, and a generous helping of tips. On these pages, you'll find everything you need to know to get up and running quickly with Word—and more!

This book was designed for page flipping. Use the thumb tabs, index, or table of contents to find the topics for which you need help. If you're brand new to Word or word processing, however, I recommend that you begin by reading at least the first two chapters. **Chapter 1** provides basic information about Word's interface while **Chapter 2** introduces word processing concepts and explains exactly how they work in Word.

If you've used other versions of Word and are interested in information about new Word 2004 features, be sure to browse through this **Introduction**. It'll give you a good idea of the new things Word has in store for you.

New & Improved Features in Word 2004

Word 2004 includes a number of brand new features, as well as improvements to some existing features. Here's a list.

New features

◆ **Paste Options button.** When you paste text or an object into a document, Word displays the Paste Options button, which you can click to display a menu of options for the pasted content (**Figure 1**).

◆ **Notebook Layout view.** The new Notebook Layout view (**Figure 2**) makes it easy to take notes and keep them organized.

◆ **Audio notes.** You can now record sounds, including spoken notes, directly into Word. This feature works hand-in-hand with Notebook Layout view.

◆ **Office Toolbox.** The new Office Toolbox is a palette with four panes of useful tools:

  ▲ **Scrapbook** (**Figure 3**), which replaces the old Office Clipboard, enables you to store multiple selections of text or other objects for use in any Office document.

  ▲ **Reference Tools** (**Figure 4**) includes a dictionary and thesaurus and buttons for searching Encarta Encyclopedia and MSN online.

  ▲ **Compatibility Report** enables you to see how compatible your document will be with other versions of Word for Macintosh or Windows.

  ▲ **Projects** offers access to the Project Center feature of Entourage.

◆ **AutoCorrect Options button.** Each time Word's AutoCorrect feature is activated, you can point to the correction to display a menu of options for it (**Figure 5**).

Figure 1
The Paste Options button displays a menu of options.

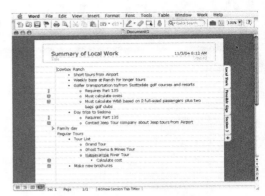

Figure 2 Notebook Layout view is great for taking notes and organizing ideas.

Figures 3 & 4 The Scrapbook (above) and Reference Tools (right) panes of the new Office Toolbox.

Figure 5
The AutoCorrect Options button displays a menu.

NEW & IMPROVED FEATURES IN WORD 2004

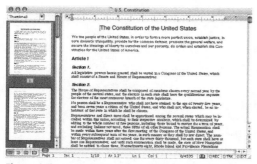

Figure 6 The navigation pane includes a thumbnails view.

Figure 7
You can now use the Formatting Palette to apply and work with styles.

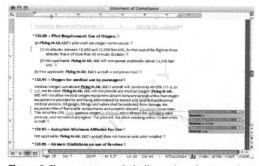

Figure 8 Changes appear in balloons in a document's margins.

Improved features

◆ **Navigation pane.** Word's Document Map feature has been improved to offer two navigation views: the Document Map and Thumbnails (**Figure 6**).

◆ **Styles.** Styles now appear in the Styles area on the Formatting Palette (**Figure 7**). This makes it easier to apply, modify, and add styles.

◆ **Change tracking.** Word now displays changes in comment balloons that appear in the margins beside text (**Figure 8**).

NEW & IMPROVED FEATURES IN WORD 2004

The Word Workplace

Meet Microsoft Word

Microsoft Word is a full-featured word processing application that you can use to create all kinds of text-based documents—letters, reports, form letters, mailing labels, envelopes, flyers, and even Web pages.

Word's interface combines common Mac OS screen elements with buttons, commands, and controls that are specific to Word. To use Word effectively, you must have at least a basic understanding of these elements.

This chapter introduces the Word workplace by illustrating and describing the following elements:

◆ The Word screen, including window elements.

◆ Menus, shortcut keys, toolbars, palettes, and dialogs.

◆ Views and document navigation techniques.

◆ Word's onscreen Help feature.

✔ Tip

■ If you've used previous versions of Word, browse through this chapter to learn about some of the interface elements that are new to this version of Word.

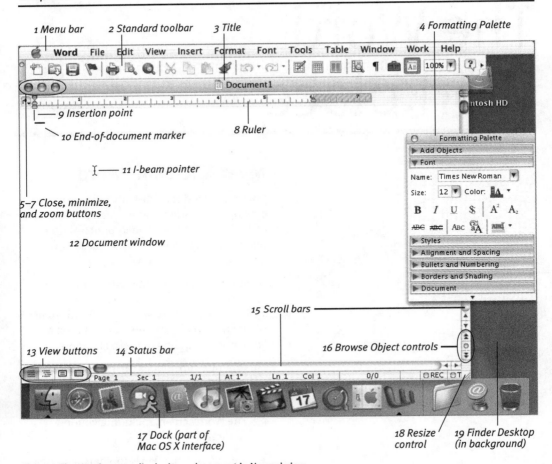

Figure 1 The Word screen displaying a document in Normal view.

Key to the Word screen

1 Menu bar

The menu bar appears at the top of the screen and offers access to Word's commands.

2 Standard toolbar

The Standard toolbar offers buttons for basic Word commands. This toolbar is very similar in other Microsoft Office applications.

3 Title bar

The title bar displays the document's title. You can drag the title bar to move the window.

4 Formatting Palette

The Formatting Palette offers buttons and other controls for applying formatting to document contents.

5 Close button

The close button offers one way to close the window.

6 Minimize button

The minimize button enables you to collapse the window into the Dock. To display the window again, click its icon in the Dock.

7 Zoom button

The zoom button enables you to toggle the window's size from full size to a custom size that you create with the resize control.

8 Ruler

Word's ruler enables you to set paragraph formatting options such as tabs and indents.

9 Insertion point

The blinking insertion point indicates where text will appear when typed or inserted with the Paste command.

10 End-of-document marker

The end-of-document marker indicates the end of the document. It only appears in Normal and Outline views.

11 I-beam pointer

The I-beam pointer enables you to position the insertion point or select text. This pointer, which is controlled by the mouse, turns into various other pointers depending on its position and the Word view.

12 Document window

The document window is where you create, edit, and view Word documents.

13 View buttons

View buttons enable you to switch between various Word views.

14 Status bar

The status bar displays information about the document, such as the current page number and section and insertion point location.

15 Scroll bars

Scroll bars enable you to shift the window's contents to view different parts of the document.

16 Browse Object controls

These buttons enable you to navigate among various document elements.

17 Dock

The Dock, which is part of the Mac OS X interface, offers quick access to commonly used programs and minimized windows.

18 Resize control

The resize control enables you to resize the window to a custom size.

19 Finder Desktop

The Finder Desktop appears in the background as you work with Word. Clicking the Desktop switches you to the Finder.

✔ Tips

- **Figure 1** shows the Word screen in Normal view. Other elements that appear in other views are discussed later in this chapter and throughout this book. Word's views are covered later in this chapter.

- Standard Mac OS window elements are not discussed in detail in this book. For more information about how to use the close button, minimize button, zoom button, resize control, and scroll bars, consult the documentation that came with your computer or Mac OS help.

The Mouse

As with most Mac OS programs, you use the mouse to select text, activate buttons, and choose menu commands.

Mouse pointer appearance

The appearance of the mouse pointer varies depending on its location and the item to which it is pointing. Here are some examples:

◆ In the document window, the mouse pointer usually looks like an I-beam pointer (**Figure 1**).

◆ On a menu name, the mouse pointer appears as an arrow pointing up and to the left (**Figure 2**).

◆ In the selection bar between the left edge of the document window and the text, the mouse pointer appears as an arrow pointing up and to the right (**Figure 3**).

◆ On selected text, the mouse pointer appears as an arrow pointing up and to the left (**Figure 4**).

To use the mouse

There are four basic mouse techniques:

◆ **Pointing** means to position the mouse pointer so that its tip is on the item to which you are pointing (**Figure 2**).

◆ **Clicking** means to press the mouse button once and release it. You click to position the insertion point or to activate a button.

Figure 2
Pointing to a menu name.

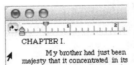

Figure 3
The mouse pointer in the selection bar.

Figure 4
The mouse pointer pointing to selected text.

◆ **Double-clicking** means to press the mouse button twice in rapid succession. You double-click to open an item or to select a word.

◆ **Dragging** means to press the mouse button down and hold it while moving the mouse. You drag to resize windows, select text, choose menu commands, or draw shapes.

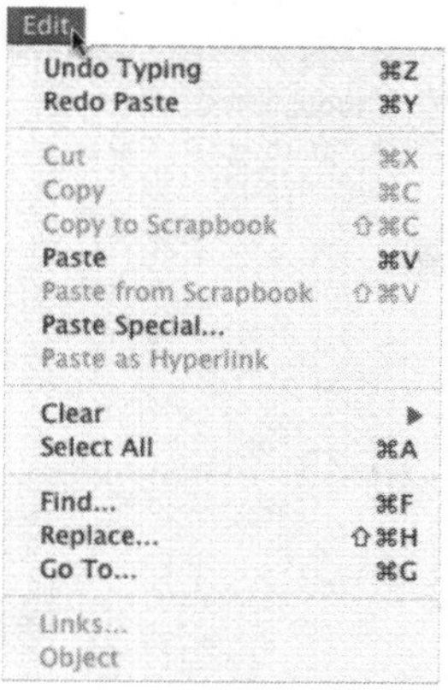

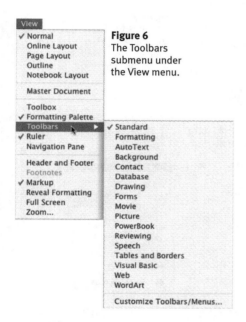

Figure 5
The Edit menu.

Figure 6
The Toolbars submenu under the View menu.

Menus

All of Word's commands are accessible through its menus. Word has two types of menus:

- **Standard menus** appear on the menu bar near the top of the window. **Figures 5** and **6** show examples of standard Word menus.

- **Shortcut or contextual menus** appear at the mouse pointer. **Figure 9** on the next page shows an example of a shortcut menu.

Here are some rules to keep in mind when working with menus:

- A menu command that appears in gray cannot be selected.

- A menu command followed by an ellipsis (…) displays a dialog.

- A menu command followed by a triangle has a submenu. The submenu displays additional commands when the main command is highlighted (**Figure 6**).

- A menu command followed by one or more keyboard characters can be chosen with a shortcut key.

- A menu command preceded by a check mark has been "turned on" (**Figure 6**). To toggle the command from on to off or off to on, choose it from the menu.

✔ Tips

- The above menu rules apply to the menus of most Mac OS programs, not just Word.

- Dialogs and shortcut keys are covered later in this chapter.

- In Mac OS, menus are translucent—you can see right through them. Although I try to minimize menu backgrounds in screenshots throughout this book, **Figure 9** shows an example of menu translucency.

To choose a menu command

1. Click the name of the menu from which you want to choose the command. The menu appears (**Figure 5**).

2. Click the command you want (**Figure 7**).

   or

   If the command is on a submenu, click on the submenu to display it (**Figure 6**) and then click on the command you want (**Figure 8**).

   The command may blink before the menu disappears, confirming that it has been successfully selected.

✔ Tip

■ This book uses the following notation to indicate menu commands: *Menu Name > Submenu Name* (if necessary) *> Command Name*. For example, "choose View > Toolbars > Drawing" instructs you to choose the Drawing command from the Toolbars submenu under the View menu (**Figure 8**).

To use a shortcut menu

1. Point to the item on which you want to use the shortcut menu.

2. Hold down [Control] and press the mouse button down. The shortcut menu appears (**Figure 9**).

3. Choose the command that you want.

✔ Tip

■ The shortcut menu only displays the commands that can be applied to the item to which you are pointing.

Figure 7
Choosing the Paste command from the Edit menu.

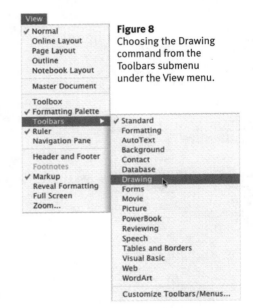

Figure 8
Choosing the Drawing command from the Toolbars submenu under the View menu.

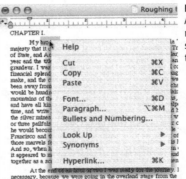

Figure 9
A shortcut menu for selected text.

Shortcut Keys

Shortcut keys are combinations of keyboard keys that, when pressed, choose a menu command without displaying the menu. For example, the shortcut key for the Paste command under the Edit menu (**Figures 5** and **7**) is ⌃⌘V. Pressing this key combination chooses the command.

✔ Tips

■ All shortcut keys use at least one of the following modifier keys:

Key Name	Keyboard Key
Command	⌃⌘
Shift	Shift
Option	Option
Control	Control

■ A menu command's shortcut key appears to its right on the menu (**Figure 7**).

■ Many shortcut keys are standardized from one application to another. The Save and Print commands are good examples; they're usually ⌃⌘S and ⌃⌘P.

■ Mac OS X introduced several new standard shortcut keys, including ⌃⌘H (Hide application) and ⌃⌘M (Minimize Window). Keep this in mind if you're a longtime Word user and used these shortcuts to access the Change and Indent commands in Word.

■ **Appendix A** includes a list of Word's shortcut keys.

To use a shortcut key

1. Hold down the modifier key for the shortcut (normally ⌃⌘).

2. Press the letter or number key for the shortcut.

For example, to choose the Paste command, hold down ⌃⌘ and press the V key.

Toolbars & Palettes

Word includes a number of toolbars and palettes for various purposes. Each one includes buttons or menus that activate menu commands or set options.

Figure 10 The Standard toolbar.

By default, Word automatically displays a toolbar and a palette when you launch it:

◆ The **Standard toolbar** (**Figure 10**) offers buttons for a wide range of commonly used commands.

◆ The **Formatting Palette** (**Figure 11**) offers buttons and menus for formatting selected items.

✔ Tips

■ The options that appear on the Formatting Palette (**Figure 11**) vary depending on what is selected.

■ You can expand or collapse the Formatting Palette by clicking a triangle beside a tool category heading (**Figure 11**).

■ Other toolbars may appear automatically depending on the task you are performing with Word.

■ Buttons with faint icon images (for example, Cut in **Figure 10**) cannot be selected.

■ A button that appears in a gray box with rounded edges is "turned on." The Formatting Palette button in **Figure 10** is a good example.

■ A toolbar can be **docked** or **floating**. A docked toolbar is positioned against the top or bottom of the screen and the document window automatically resizes and repositions around it. A floating toolbar can be moved anywhere onscreen and, when positioned on top of the document window, "floats" above the window's contents.

Close button

Click here to show or hide tools in this area.

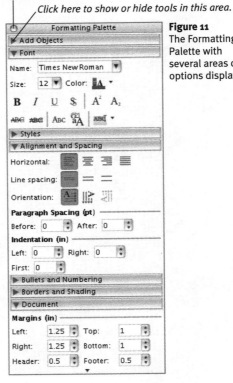

Figure 11
The Formatting Palette with several areas of options displayed.

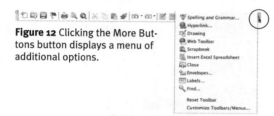

Figure 12 Clicking the More Buttons button displays a menu of additional options.

Figure 13
A ScreenTip appears when you point to a button.

Figure 14
Click the triangle beside the menu to display the menu.

Figure 15 Select the current value...

Figure 16 ...enter a new value, and press Return.

To view more buttons

Click the More Buttons button at the far-right end of the toolbar. Additional buttons for the toolbar appear in a menu (**Figure 12**).

To view ScreenTips

Point to a toolbar or palette button. A tiny yellow box containing the name of the button appears (**Figure 13**).

To use a toolbar button

1. Point to the button for the command or option that you want (**Figure 13**).

2. Click once.

To use a toolbar menu

1. Click on the triangle beside the menu to display the menu and its commands (**Figure 14**).

2. Click a command or option to select it.

✔ Tip

- Menus that display text boxes (**Figure 14**) can be changed by typing a new value into the box. Just click the contents of the box to select it (**Figure 15**), then type in the new value and press Return (**Figure 16**).

USING TOOLBARS & TOOLBAR MENUS

To turn a menu into a floating palette

1. Click the arrow beside a toolbar button to display its menu (**Figure 17**).

2. If the menu displays a dotted move handle along its top edge (**Figure 17**), click the move handle (**Figure 18**) to turn the menu into a floating palette (**Figure 19**).

✔ Tips

- In step 2, if the menu does not display a dotted move handle along its top edge (**Figure 14**), it cannot be turned into a floating palette.

- You can move a floating palette by dragging its title bar.

- To close a floating palette, click its close button.

To display or hide a toolbar

Choose the name of the toolbar that you want to display or hide from the Toolbars submenu under the View menu (**Figure 8**).

If the toolbar name has a check mark beside it, the toolbar is currently displayed and selecting the toolbar name will hide it.

Or

If the toolbar name does not have a check mark beside it, the toolbar is hidden and selecting the toolbar name will display it.

✔ Tip

- You can also hide a floating toolbar by clicking its close button (**Figure 20**).

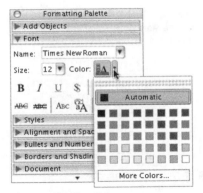

Figure 17 The Font Color menu appears when you click the triangle beside the Font Color button.

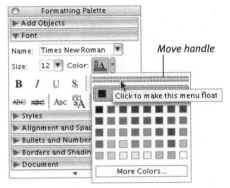

Figure 18 When you click a menu's move handle...

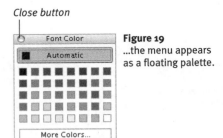

Figure 19
...the menu appears as a floating palette.

Figure 20 The close button and move handle for a toolbar normally appear on its far-left end.

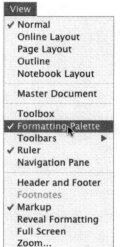

Figure 21
Display or hide the Formatting Palette by choosing its command from the View menu.

Figure 22 Drag the lower-right corner of a toolbar to resize it...

Figure 23
...to almost any dimensions.

To display or hide the Formatting Palette

Choose View > Formatting Palette (**Figure 21**).

If the Formatting Palette command has a check mark beside it, the Formatting Palette is currently displayed and selecting the command will hide it.

Or

If the Formatting Palette command does not have a check mark beside it, the Formatting Palette is hidden and selecting the command will display it.

✔ Tips

■ You can also display or hide the Formatting Palette by clicking the Formatting Palette button on the Standard toolbar.

■ You can also hide the Formatting Palette by clicking its close button (**Figure 11**).

To move a toolbar or palette

Drag the move handle for the toolbar (**Figure 20**) or title bar for the palette to reposition it onscreen.

To resize a toolbar

Drag the resize control in the lower-right corner of the toolbar (**Figures 22** and **23**).

Dialogs

Like most other Mac OS programs, Word uses *dialogs* to communicate with you.

Word can display many different dialogs, each with its own purpose. There are two basic types of dialogs:

◆ Dialogs that simply provide information (**Figure 24**).

◆ Dialogs that offer options to select (**Figure 25**) before Word completes the execution of a command.

✔ Tip

■ Often, when a dialog appears, you must dismiss it by clicking OK, Cancel, or its close button before you can continue working with Word.

Anatomy of a Word dialog

Here are the components of many Word dialogs, along with information about how they work.

◆ **Pane buttons (Figure 25)**, which appear at the top of some dialogs, let you move from one group or pane of dialog options to another. To switch to another group of options, click its button.

◆ **Text boxes** or **entry fields (Figures 25 and 26)** let you enter information from the keyboard. You can press Tab to move from one box to the next or click in a box to position the insertion point within it. Then enter a new value.

◆ **Scrolling lists (Figure 25)** offer a number of options to choose from. Use the scroll bar to view options that don't fit in the list window. Click an option to select it; it becomes highlighted and appears in the text box.

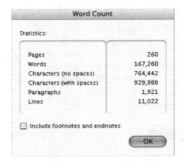

Figure 24 The Word Count dialog just displays information.

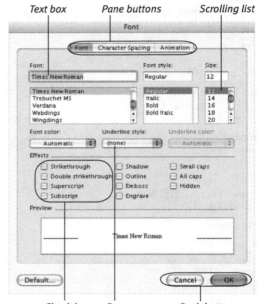

Figure 25 The Font dialog.

Radio buttons

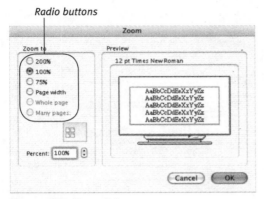

Figure 26 The Zoom dialog.

Figure 27
Displaying a
pop-up menu.

◆ **Check boxes** (**Figure 25**) let you turn options on or off. Click in a check box to toggle it. When a check mark or X appears in the check box, its option is turned on.

◆ **Radio buttons** (**Figure 26**) let you select only one option from a group. Click on an option to select it; the option that was selected before you clicked is deselected.

◆ **Pop-up menus** or **drop-down lists** (**Figure 25**) also let you select one option from a group. Click the triangles or arrows on a pop-up menu to display it (**Figure 27**), then choose the option that you want.

◆ **Preview areas** (**Figures 25** and **26**), when available, illustrate the effects of your changes before you finalize them by clicking the OK button.

◆ **Push buttons** (**Figures 24, 25,** and **26**) let you access other dialogs, accept the changes and close the dialog (OK), or close the dialog without making changes (Cancel). To choose a button, click it once.

✔ Tips

■ When the contents of a text box are selected, whatever you type will replace the selection.

■ Word often uses text boxes and scrolling lists together (**Figure 25**). You can use either one to make a selection.

■ You can turn on any number of check boxes in a group, but you can select only one radio button in a group.

■ A pulsating blue push button is the default button; you can usually "click" it by pressing [Return] or [Enter].

■ You can usually "click" the Cancel button by pressing [Esc] or [⌘][.].

■ A *dialog sheet* is a dialog that is attached to a specific document window.

DIALOGS

Views

Word offers several different ways to view the contents of a document window.

◆ **Normal view (Figure 28)**, which is the view you'll see in most screenshots throughout this book, shows continuously scrolling text. It is the fastest view for entering and editing text but does not show page layout elements.

◆ **Online Layout view (Figure 29)** displays the contents of a document so they are easier to read onscreen. Text wraps to fit the window rather than margins or indentations.

◆ **Page Layout view (Figure 30)** displays the objects on a page positioned as they will be when the document is printed. This is a good view for working with documents that include multiple column text or positioned graphics, such as a newsletter or flyer.

◆ **Outline view (Figure 31)** displays the document's structure—headings and body text—in a way that makes it easy to rearrange the document. Headings can be collapsed to hide detail and simplify the view. Working with Outline view is discussed in **Chapter 12**.

◆ **Notebook Layout view (Figure 32)**, which is new in Word 2004, displays the document in a special format designed for taking and organizing notes. Working with Notebook Layout view is covered in **Chapter 13**.

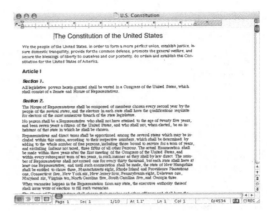

Figure 28 Normal view.

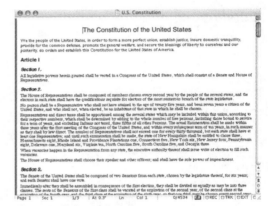

Figure 29 Online Layout view.

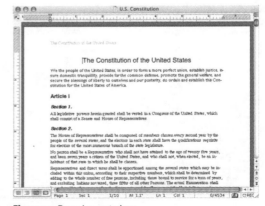

Figure 30 Page Layout view.

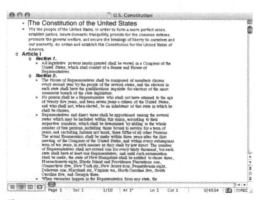

Figure 31 Outline view.

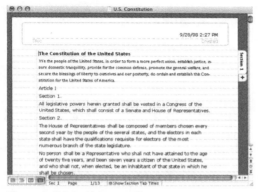

Figure 32 Notebook Layout view.

✔ Tips

■ Although each view is designed for a specific purpose, you can work with a document in any view.

■ The illustrations throughout this book display windows in Normal view, unless otherwise indicated.

To switch to another view

Choose the desired option from the View menu (**Figure 33**).

Or

Click the appropriate view button at the bottom of the window (**Figure 34**).

Figure 33
The View menu.

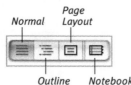

Figure 34 View buttons at the bottom of the document window. The currently selected option is blue.

SWITCHING VIEWS

Document Navigation

Word offers a variety of ways to view different parts of a document.

◆ Use **scroll bars** to shift the contents of the document window.

◆ Use the **Go To command** to view a specific document element, such as a certain page.

◆ Use **Browse Object buttons** to browse a document by its elements.

◆ Use the Navigation Pane's **Document Map** to move quickly to a specific heading, or **Thumbnails** to move quickly to a specific page.

✔ Tips

■ Although some keyboard keys change the portion of the document being viewed, they also move the insertion point. I tell you about these keys in **Chapter 2**.

■ In previous versions of Word, there was no Thumbnails feature. Instead, the Navigation Pane was called the Document Map and enabled you to navigate by headings only.

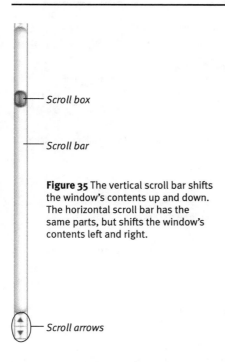

Figure 35 The vertical scroll bar shifts the window's contents up and down. The horizontal scroll bar has the same parts, but shifts the window's contents left and right.

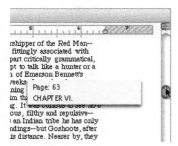

Figure 36 When you drag the scroll box, a yellow box with the page number and heading appears.

To scroll the contents of the document window

Use one of the following techniques:

◆ Click the scroll arrow (**Figure 35**) for the direction that you want to view. For example, to scroll down to view the end of a document, click the down arrow.

◆ Drag the scroll box (**Figure 35**) in the direction that you want to view. As you drag, a yellow box appears onscreen (**Figure 36**). It indicates the page and, if applicable, the heading that you are scrolling to.

◆ Click in the scroll bar above or below the scroll box (**Figure 35**). This shifts the window contents one screenful at a time.

✔ Tips

■ Having trouble remembering which scroll arrow to click? Just remember this: Click up to see up, click down to see down, click left to see left, and click right to see right.

■ **Figure 35** shows a scroll bar as it appears with default Mac OS X settings. If you changed your computer's Appearance preferences to display scroll arrows at the top and bottom of scroll bars, the scroll arrows will appear at either end of the scroll bars rather than together.

To use the Go To command

1. Choose Edit > Go To (**Figure 5**). The Find and Replace dialog appears with its Go To options displayed (**Figure 37**).

2. In the Go to what scrolling list, select the type of document element that you want to view.

3. Enter the appropriate reference in the text box.

4. Click the Next button to go to the next reference.

5. When you're finished, click the dialog's close button to dismiss it.

For example, to go to page 5 of a document, select Page in step 2 and enter the number 5 in step 3.

To browse a document by its elements

1. Point to the Select Browse Object button (**Figure 38**).

2. Click to display the Select Browse Object pop-up menu (**Figure 39**).

3. Choose the element by which you want to browse.

4. Use the Next and Previous navigation buttons (**Figure 38**) to view the next or previous element.

✔ Tips

■ The name of the object that a button represents appears at the top of the Select Browse Object pop-up menu when you point to the button (**Figure 39**).

■ Some of the buttons on the Select Browse Object pop-up menu (**Figure 39**) display dialogs that you can use for browsing.

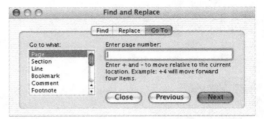

Figure 37 The Go To options of the Find and Replace dialog.

Figure 38 The Browse Object buttons at the bottom of the vertical scroll bar.

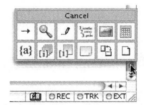

Figure 39 This menu pops up when you click the Select Browse Object button.

GO TO COMMAND & DOCUMENT ELEMENTS

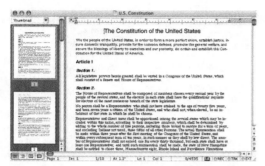

Figure 40 The Navigation Pane showing Thumbnails.

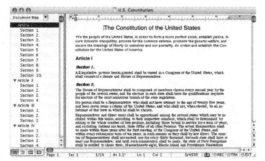

Figure 41 The Navigation Pane showing the Document Map.

Figure 42 Clicking a heading in the Document Map shifts the document view to display that part of the document.

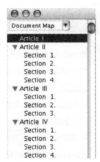

Figure 43
Click a triangle beside a heading to hide or show its subheadings.

To use the Navigation Pane

1. Choose View > Navigation Pane (**Figure** 33) or click the Navigation Pane button on the Standard toolbar.

   The Navigation Pane appears on the left side of the window (**Figure** 40).

2. Choose an option from the pop-up menu at the top of the Navigation Pane:

   ▲ **Thumbnails** (**Figure** 40) displays thumbnail images of a document's pages.

   ▲ **Document Map** (**Figure** 41) displays a document's headings.

3. In the Navigation Pane, click the heading or page that you want to view. The main window pane's view shifts to show the heading (**Figure** 42) or page that you clicked.

✔ Tips

■ Thumbnails are especially useful when working with documents that have a variety of page layouts.

■ The Document Map is a good way to navigate documents that use Word's heading styles. I explain how to use headings in **Chapter** 12 and styles in **Chapter** 4.

■ Clicking a thumbnail or heading in the Navigation Pane also moves the insertion point. Moving the insertion point is discussed in **Chapter** 2.

■ You can collapse and expand headings in the Document Map by clicking the triangles to the left of the heading names (**Figure** 43).

■ To hide the Navigation Pane, choose View > Navigation Pane or double-click the border between the Navigation Pane and the main window pane.

USING THE NAVIGATION PANE

Windows

Word allows you to open more than one document window at a time. You work with windows using commands on the Window menu (**Figure 44**):

◆ **Zoom Window** toggles a window between its full size and a custom size. This is the same as clicking the window's zoom button.

◆ **Minimize Window** reduces the window to an icon and places it in the Dock. This is the same as clicking the window's minimize button. To restore a minimized window, click its icon in the Dock.

◆ **Bring All to Front** displays all Microsoft Word windows on top of other open applications' windows.

◆ **New Window** opens another window with the same contents as the active window. A number after a colon (:) in the title bar (**Figure 45**) indicates that multiple windows are open for a single document. If you edit the contents of one window, those changes are also displayed in the other window(s) for that document.

◆ **Arrange All** resizes and repositions all open windows so you can see into each one (**Figure 46**).

◆ **Split** splits the active document window horizontally (**Figure 47**) so you can scroll the top and bottom halves independently.

◆ *Document Window Name* activates and displays a specific document window.

✔ Tip

■ **Chapter 2** explains how to open and create documents.

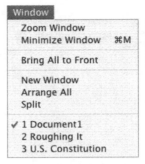

Figure 44
The Window menu with three document windows open.

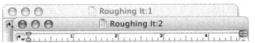

Figure 45 When more than one window is open for a document, the window number appears in the window's title bar.

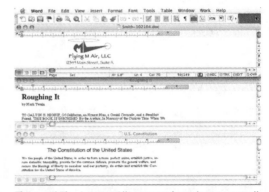

Figure 46 The Arrange All command neatly arranges all windows so you can see inside them.

Figure 47 Splitting a window makes it possible to scroll top and bottom halves independently so you can see two parts of a document at once.

WINDOWS

Figure 48 When multiple windows are open, the active window is the one on top of the stack with the colored buttons in the title bar.

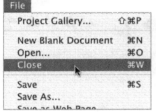

Figure 49
The Close command on the File menu closes the active window.

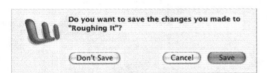

Figure 50 When you close a window that contains unsaved changes, a dialog like this appears.

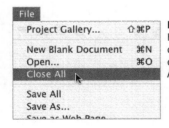

Figure 51
Holding down (Shift) changes the Close command to a Close All command.

To activate a different window

Choose the name of the window that you want to view from the list on the bottom of the Window menu (**Figure 44**). That window comes to the front (**Figure 48**) as the active window.

To close a window

1. If necessary, activate the window that you want to close.

2. Choose File > Close (**Figure 49**), press ⌃⌘W, or click the window's close button.

✔ Tips

■ If the document contains unsaved changes, Word warns you and gives you a chance to save it (**Figure 50**). Saving documents is covered in **Chapter 2**.

■ Hold down (Shift) and display the File menu to change the Close command to the Close All command (**Figure 51**). This command closes all open windows.

To neatly arrange windows

Choose Window > Arrange All (**Figure 44**).

The windows are resized and repositioned so you can see into each one (**Figure 46**).

To split a window

1. Choose Window > Split (**Figure 44**).

2. A split bar appears across the document window (**Figure 47**).

3. Click in the top or bottom half of the window to activate it. You can then use the scroll bars to scroll in that half of the window.

4. When you are finished working with the split window, double-click the split bar to remove it.

Word Help

Word has an extensive onscreen help feature that provides information about using Word to complete specific tasks. You access the Word Help feature with Word's Help menu (**Figure 52**) or the Office Assistant (**Figure 53**).

This part of the chapter explains how to use Word Help to answer your Word questions.

✔ Tips

- Other commands on the Help menu offer access to online help on Microsoft's Web site, as well as other features to help you keep Word up-to-date.

- Have an idea for improving Word? Choose Help > Send Feedback on Word (**Figure 52**) and use the Web-based form that appears to make a suggestion online.

To use Word Help

1. Choose Help > Word Help. The Microsoft Office Help window appears (**Figure 54**).

2. Enter a word, phrase, or question for which you want help in the What are you searching for? box (**Figure 55**) and click Search.

3. Word displays search results in a list below the Search button. Click a blue underlined topic name in this list to display information about the topic in the right side of the window (**Figure 56**).

4. Read the information in the Microsoft Office Help window to learn about the topic.

    or

    Click links in the Microsoft Office Help window to display other topics in the window.

Figure 52
Word's Help menu.

Figure 53
The Office Assistant offers an alternative interface for accessing Word help.

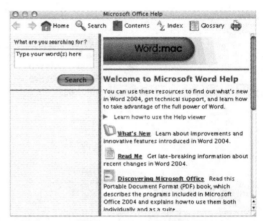

Figure 54 The Microsoft Office Help window.

Figure 55 Enter a search word or phrase in the box.

Figure 56 Click an underlined link to learn about its topic.

Figure 57 Clicking the Office Assistant displays a balloon prompt for you to enter a help request.

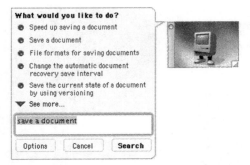

Figure 58 When you click Search, the Office Assistant displays a list of possible help topics.

5. Repeat steps 2 through 4 to explore the information in Help topics that interest you.

6. When you are finished exploring Microsoft Office Help, click the window's close button to dismiss it.

To use the Office Assistant

1. If necessary, choose Help > Use the Office Assistant (**Figure 52**) to display the Office Assistant window (**Figure 53**).

2. Click the Office Assistant to display a yellow balloon like the one in **Figure 57**.

3. Enter a search word or phrase in the box and click Search.

4. The Office Assistant displays another balloon full of search results (**Figure 58**). Click the topic that interests you to display information in the Microsoft Office Help window (**Figure 56**).

5. Repeat steps 3 and 4 to explore information in help topics that interest you.

6. When you are finished exploring Microsoft Office Help, click the window's close button to dismiss it.

USING WORD HELP

To use Help contents

1. Choose Help > Word Help (**Figure 52**) to display the Microsoft Office Help window (**Figure 54**).

2. Click the Contents button to display a list of main categories (**Figure 59**).

3. Click triangles to expand the list of topics and subtopics (**Figure 60**).

4. Click the blue underlined link for the topic that interests you (**Figure 61**).

To use the Help index

1. Choose Help > Word Help (**Figure 52**) to display the Microsoft Office Help window (**Figure 54**).

2. Click the Index button to display a list of letters (**Figure 62**).

3. Click a letter for the topic that interests you. A list of topics beginning with that letter appears (**Figure 63**).

4. Click triangles to expand the list of topics until you find the one you want (**Figure 64**).

5. Click the blue underlined link for the topic that interests you.

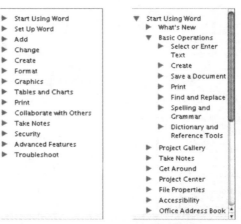

Figure 59 Clicking the Contents button displays a list of main categories.

Figure 60 Click triangles to expand the topic list and display subtopics.

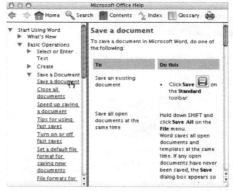

Figure 61 Click a topic to display its information.

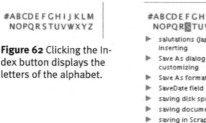

Figure 62 Clicking the Index button displays the letters of the alphabet.

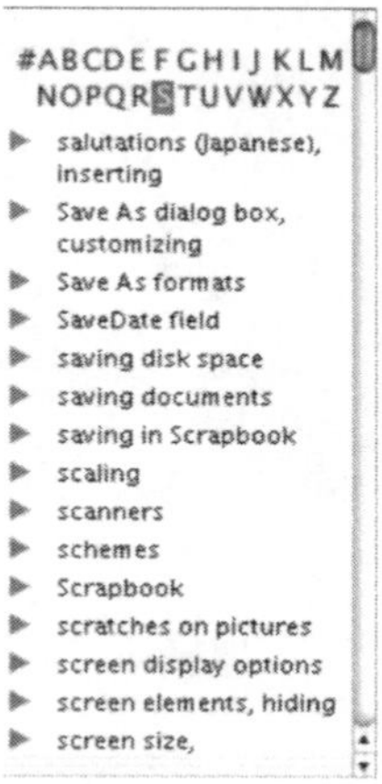

Figure 63 Click a letter to display a list of main topics.

Figure 64 Click triangles to display subtopics.

Word Basics

Word Processing Basics

Word processing software has revolutionized the way we create text-based documents. Rather than committing each character to paper as you type—as you would do with a typewriter—word processing enables you to enter documents onscreen, edit and format them as you work, and save them for future reference or revision. Nothing appears on paper until you use the Print command.

If you're brand new to word processing, here are a few concepts you should understand before you begin working with Microsoft Word or any other word processing software:

◆ Words that you type that do not fit at the end of a line automatically appear on the next line. This feature is called *word wrap*.

◆ Do not press ⌈Return⌉ at the end of each line as you type. Doing so inserts a character that signals the end of a paragraph, not the end of a line. Press ⌈Return⌉ only at the end of a paragraph or to skip a line between paragraphs.

◆ Do not use ⌈Spacebar⌉ to indent text or position text in simple tables. Instead, use ⌈Tab⌉ in conjunction with tab settings on the ruler.

◆ Text can be inserted or deleted anywhere in the document.

I tell you more about all of these concepts in this chapter and throughout this book.

Opening Word

To use Word, you must open the Word program.

To open Word by opening its application icon

1. In the Finder, locate the Microsoft Word application icon (**Figure 1**). It should be in the Microsoft Office 2004 folder in your Applications folder.

2. Double-click the icon.

   The Word splash screen appears briefly (**Figure 2**), then the Project Gallery window appears (**Figure 3**).

✔ Tip

■ You can disable the display of the Project Gallery window at startup. I explain how in **Chapter 20**.

To open Word by opening a Word document

1. In the Finder, locate the icon for the document that you want to open (**Figure 4**).

2. Double-click the icon.

   The Word splash screen appears briefly (**Figure 2**), and then a document window containing the document you opened appears (**Figure 5**).

Microsoft Word

Figure 1 The Word application icon.

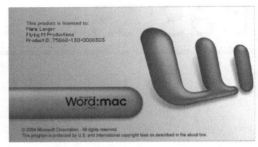

Figure 2 The Word splash screen.

Figure 3 When you open Word by opening its application icon, it displays the Project Gallery window.

Hound of the Baskervilles

Figure 4 A Word document icon.

Figure 5 When you open Word by opening a Word document, it displays the document you opened.

Figure 6
Word's Word menu.

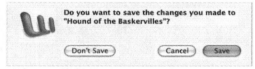

Figure 7 A dialog like this appears if a document with unsaved changes is open when you quit Word.

Quitting Word

When you're finished using Word, you should use the Quit command to close the program. This makes more of the computer's resources available for other applications that you use so your computer can work more efficiently.

✔ Tip

- Quitting Word also instructs Word to save preference settings and any changes to the Normal template.

To exit Word

Choose Word > Quit Word (**Figure 6**) or press ⌃⌘Q.

Here's what happens:

▲ If any documents are open, they close.

▲ If an open document contains unsaved changes, a dialog appears (**Figure 7**) so you can save the changes. Saving documents is discussed later in this chapter.

▲ The Word program closes.

✔ Tip

- As you've probably guessed, Word automatically quits when you restart or shut down your computer.

QUITTING WORD

Word Documents, Templates, & Wizards

The documents you create and save using Word are Word document files. These files contain all the information necessary to display the contents of the document as formatted using Microsoft Word.

All Word document files are based on *templates*. A template is a collection of styles and other formatting features that determines the appearance of a document. Templates can also include default text, macros, and custom toolbars.

For example, you can create a letterhead template that includes your company's logo and contact information or is designed to be printed on special paper. The template can include styles that utilize specific fonts. It can also include custom toolbars with buttons for commands commonly used when writing letters.

Wizards take templates a step further. They are special Word document files that include Microsoft Visual Basic commands to automate the creation of specific types of documents. Word comes with a few wizards that you can explore on your own.

Figure 8
A Word template icon.

Letter-Whimsy

Figure 9
A Word wizard icon.

Brochure Wizard

✔ Tips

- A Word document icon (**Figure 4**), template icon (**Figure 8**), and wizard icon (**Figure 9**) are very similar in appearance.

- Word can open and save files in formats other than Word document format. I tell you more about file formats later in this chapter.

- When no other template is specified for a document, Word applies the default template, *Normal*.

- I cover styles in **Chapter 4**, macros and Visual Basic in **Chapter 19**, and custom toolbars in **Chapter 20**.

Figure 10
The File menu.

The Project Gallery

The Project Gallery (**Figure 3**) offers an easy way to create documents with Microsoft Office applications.

To open the Project Gallery

Choose File > Project Gallery (**Figure 10**) or press Shift ⌃ ⌘ P.

✔ Tip

■ By default, the Project Gallery automatically appears when you open Word by opening its application icon.

To display templates & wizards in a specific category

1. On the left side of the window, click the triangle beside a category you want to view. A list of subcategories appears beneath it (**Figure 11**).

2. Click on the name of a subcategory to display previews of the templates or wizards within it (**Figure 12**).

To show only specific document types

Choose an option from the Show pop-up menu to display only specific types of Office documents (**Figure 13**).

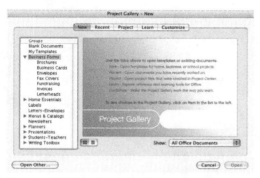

Figure 11 Click the triangle beside a category you want to view to display subcategories within it.

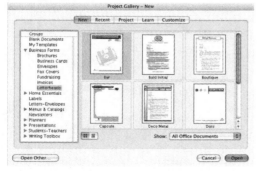

Figure 12 When you click a subcategory, previews of the items within it appear.

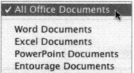

Figure 13
The Show pop-up menu enables you to show a specific type of Office document.

Creating Documents

You can create a new document with the Project Gallery or with the New Blank Document command.

To create a blank document

1. If the Project Gallery is not displayed, choose File > Project Gallery (**Figure 10**) to display it (**Figure 3**).

2. In the Category list, select Blank Documents.

3. In the Preview area, select Word Document.

4. Click Open.

Or

Press ⌃ ⌘ N.

Or

Click the New Blank Document button on the Standard toolbar.

A blank document based on the Normal template appears (**Figure 14**).

✔ Tip

■ The Blank Documents category of the Project Gallery (**Figure 3**) enables you to create other types of Word documents, including Web pages and Word Notebook files. I cover Web pages in **Chapter 18** and Word's Notebook Layout view feature in **Chapter 13**.

Figure 14 A blank document window based on the Normal template. Note that this document is displayed in Normal view; you can click the Normal view button at the bottom of the window to switch to this view.

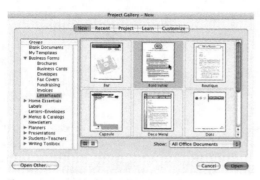

Figure 15 Select the template you want to use.

Figure 16 A new document based on a template.

To create a document based on a template other than Normal

1. If the Project Gallery is not displayed, choose File > Project Gallery (**Figure 10**) to display it (**Figure 3**).

2. In the Category list, select a category.

   or

   In the Category list, click the triangle beside a category to display subcategories and select one of those subcategories (**Figure 12**).

3. In the Preview area, select the icon for the template you want to use (**Figure 15**).

4. Click Open.

   A document based on the template that you selected appears (**Figure 16**).

5. Follow the instructions in the template to replace placeholder text with your text.

CREATING DOCUMENTS BASED ON TEMPLATES

To create a document based on a recently opened document

1. If the Project Gallery is not displayed, choose File > Project Gallery (**Figure 10**) to display it (**Figure 3**).

2. Click the Recent button at the top of the window. The view changes to display recently opened documents (**Figure 17**).

3. If necessary, select an option in the Date column so the file list in the middle of the dialog changes to show the document you want to use.

4. In the file list, select the document you want to use. A preview of the document may appear in the Preview area (**Figure 18**).

5. Click Open As Copy.

   The document opens as an untitled document (**Figure 19**).

✔ Tips

- Creating a document based on an existing document can save time when creating a document that is almost identical to one that already exists.

- Because the new document opens in an untitled window, it is virtually impossible to overwrite the existing document with the changes you make to the new document.

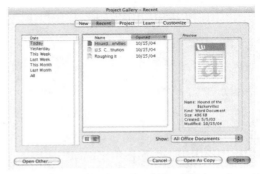

Figure 17 By default, the Recent button displays documents you've opened today.

Figure 18 Select the document you want to base the new document on.

Figure 19 Although this document might look exactly like the original, it is indeed new.

View buttons

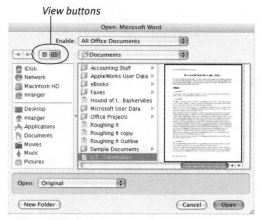

Figure 20 The Open dialog in column view, with a document selected.

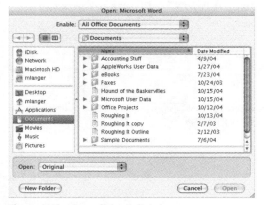

Figure 21 The Open dialog in list view.

Figure 22 Use this pop-up menu to backtrack through the file hierarchy or open recently opened folders.

Figure 23 The Enable pop-up menu includes file formats that can be read by Word.

Opening Documents

Once a document has been saved, you can reopen it to read it, modify it, or print it.

To open an existing document

1. Choose File > Open (**Figure 10**), press ⌘O, or click the Open button on the Standard toolbar.

2. Use the Open dialog that appears (**Figure 20**) to locate the file you want to open:

   ▲ Click a view button to display the list of files and folders in list (**Figure 21**) or column (**Figure 20**) view.

   ▲ Click an item in the Sidebar to display the contents of that item.

   ▲ Use the pop-up menu above the list of files (**Figure 22**) to backtrack through the file hierarchy or open a recently opened folder.

   ▲ Double-click a folder to open it.

3. Select the file you want to open and click the Open button.

   or

   Double-click the file you want to open.

✔ Tips

- To view only specific types of files in the Open dialog, select a format from the Enable pop-up menu at the top of the dialog (**Figure 23**).

- If you select All Documents from the Enable pop-up menu (**Figure 23**), you can open any kind of document file. Be aware, however, that a document in an incompatible format may not appear the way you expect when opened.

- You can open a recent file by selecting it from the list of recently opened files at the bottom of the File menu (**Figure 10**).

Entering Text

In most cases, you will enter text into a Word document using the keyboard.

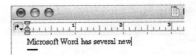

Microsoft Word has several new|

Figure 24 Text characters appear at the blinking insertion point as you type.

✔ Tip

■ A wavy red or green line appearing beneath the text you type indicates that the text has a possible spelling or grammar error. Spelling and grammar checking are covered in **Chapter 7**.

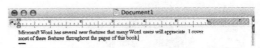

Microsoft Word has several new features that many Word users will appreciate. I cover most of these features throughout the pages of this book.|

Figure 25 Word wrap automatically occurs when the text you type won't fit on the current line.

To type text

Type the characters, words, or sentences that you want to enter into the document. Text appears at the blinking insertion point as you type it (**Figure 24**).

✔ Tips

■ I explain how to move the insertion point a little later in this chapter.

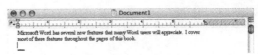

Microsoft Word has several new features that many Word users will appreciate. I cover most of these features throughout the pages of this book.
|

Figure 26 Press Return to start a new paragraph.

■ Do not press Return at the end of a line. A new line automatically begins when a word can't fit on the current line (**Figure 25**).

To start a new paragraph

At the end of a paragraph, press Return. This inserts a paragraph break that ends the current paragraph and begins a new one (**Figure 26**).

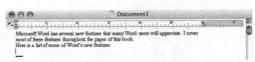

Microsoft Word has several new features that many Word users will appreciate. I cover most of these features throughout the pages of this book.
Here is a list of some of Word's new features:
|

Figure 27 Press Shift Return to start a new line in the same paragraph.

To start a new line

To end a line without ending the current paragraph, press Shift Return. This inserts a line break character (**Figure 27**).

✔ Tip

■ Use a line break instead of a paragraph break to begin a new line without beginning a new paragraph. This makes it easy to apply paragraph formatting to multiple lines that belong together. I cover paragraph formatting in **Chapters 3** and **4**.

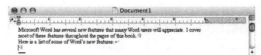

Figure 28 Text with nonprinting characters displayed. This example shows space, paragraph, and line break characters.

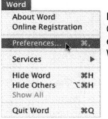

Figure 29 Choose Preferences from the Word menu.

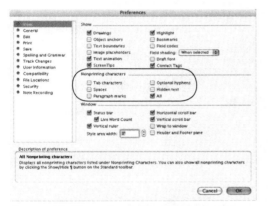

Figure 30 The View options of the Preferences dialog.

✔ Tips

■ To display all formatting marks, turn on the All check box in step 3.

■ Word's Preferences dialog is discussed in detail in **Chapter 20**.

Nonprinting Characters

Every character you type is entered into a Word document—even characters that normally can't be seen, such as space, tab, return, line break, and optional hyphen characters.

Word enables you to display these *nonprinting characters* (**Figure 28**), making it easy to see all the characters in a document.

✔ Tips

■ Nonprinting characters are sometimes referred to as *formatting marks* or *invisible characters*.

■ By displaying nonprinting characters, you can get a better understanding of the structure of a document. For example, **Figure 28** clearly shows the difference between the return and line break characters entered in **Figure 27**.

To show or hide nonprinting characters

Click the Show/Hide ¶ button on the Standard toolbar. This toggles the display of nonprinting characters.

To specify which nonprinting characters should be displayed

1. Choose Word > Preferences (**Figure 29**).

2. Click the View item in the Preferences dialog that appears (**Figure 30**).

3. Turn on the check boxes in the Nonprinting characters area of the dialog to specify which characters should appear.

4. Click OK.

The Insertion Point

The blinking insertion point indicates where the information you type or paste will be inserted. There are two main ways to move the insertion point: with the keyboard and with the mouse.

✔ Tip

- The insertion point also moves when you use the Navigation Pane to navigate within a document. The Navigation Pane is discussed in **Chapter 1**.

To move the insertion point with the keyboard

Press the appropriate keyboard key(s) (**Table 1**).

✔ Tip

- There are additional keystrokes that work within cell tables. I tell you about them in **Chapter 8**, where I discuss tables.

To move the insertion point with the mouse

1. Position the mouse's I-beam pointer where you want to move the insertion point (**Figure 31**).

2. Click once. The insertion point moves (**Figure 32**).

✔ Tips

- Simply moving the I-beam pointer is not enough. You must click to move the insertion point.

- Do not move the mouse while clicking. Doing so will select text.

Table 1

Keystrokes for Moving the Insertion Point	
Press:	To move the insertion point:
→	one character to the right
←	one character to the left
↑	one line up
↓	one line down
⌃ ⌘ →	one word to the right
⌃ ⌘ ←	one word to the left
⌃ ⌘ ↑	one paragraph up
⌃ ⌘ ↓	one paragraph down
End	to the end of the line
Home	to the beginning of the line
⌃ ⌘ End	to the end of the document
⌃ ⌘ Home	to the beginning of the document
Page Up	up one screen
Page Down	down one screen
⌃ ⌘ Page Up	to the top of the previous page
⌃ ⌘ Page Down	to the top of the next page
⌃ ⌘ Option Page Up	to the top of the window
⌃ ⌘ Option Page Down	to the bottom of the window
Shift F5	to the previous edit

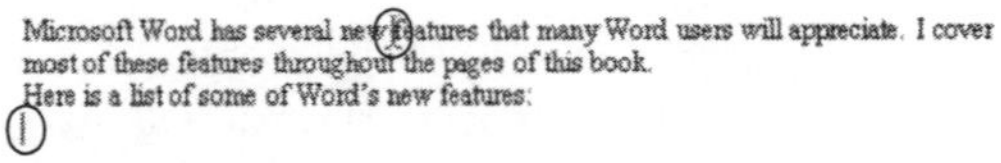

Microsoft Word has several new features that many Word users will appreciate. I cover most of these features throughout the pages of this book.
Here is a list of some of Word's new features:

Figure 31 Position the mouse's I-beam pointer where you want the insertion point to move.

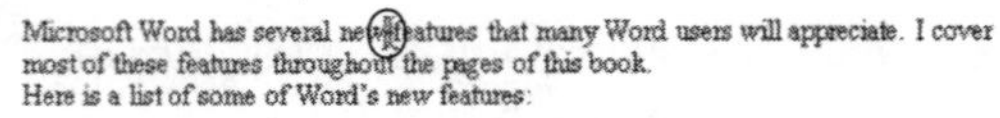

Microsoft Word has several new features that many Word users will appreciate. I cover most of these features throughout the pages of this book.
Here is a list of some of Word's new features:

Figure 32 Click to move the insertion point.

Figure 33 Position the insertion point.

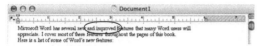

Figure 34 Type the text you want to insert.

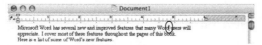

Figure 35 Position the insertion point to the right of the character(s) you want to delete.

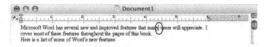

Figure 36 Press Delete to delete the characters.

Inserting & Deleting Text

You can insert or delete characters at the insertion point at any time.

◆ When you insert characters, any text to the right of the insertion point shifts to the right to make room for new characters (**Figures** 33 and 34).

◆ When you delete text, any text to the right of the insertion point shifts to the left to close up space left by deleted characters (**Figures** 35 and 36).

◆ When you insert or delete text, word wrap adjusts if necessary to comfortably fit characters on each line (**Figures** 34 and 36).

To insert text

1. Position the insertion point where you want to insert the text (**Figure** 33).

2. Type the text you want to insert (**Figure** 34).

✔ Tip

■ You can also insert text by pasting the contents of the Clipboard at the insertion point. Using the Clipboard to copy and paste text is covered later in this chapter.

To delete text

1. Position the insertion point to the right of the character(s) you want to delete (**Figure** 35).

2. Press Delete to delete the character to the left of the insertion point (**Figure** 36).

Or

1. Position the insertion point to the left of the character(s) you want to delete.

2. Press Del to delete the character to the right of the insertion point.

✔ Tip

■ You can also delete text by selecting it and pressing Delete. Selecting text is discussed a little later in this chapter.

Click and Type

Click and Type is a feature that makes it easier to position text in a blank area of a page. You simply double-click with the Click and Type pointer (**Figure 37**) and enter the text you want to appear there. Word automatically applies necessary formatting to the text to position it where you want it.

✔ Tip

- Click and Type works only in Page Layout and Online Layout views. Word's views are discussed in **Chapter 1**.

To enter text with Click and Type

1. If necessary, switch to Page Layout or Online Layout view.

2. Position the mouse pointer in an empty area of the document window. The mouse pointer should turn into a Click and Type pointer (**Figure 38**).

3. Double-click. The insertion point appears at the mouse pointer (**Figure 39**).

4. Type the text you want to enter (**Figure 40**).

✔ Tips

- The appearance of the Click and Type pointer indicates how it will align text at the insertion point. For example, the pointer shown in **Figures 37** and **38** indicates that text will be centered (**Figure 40**). I tell you more about alignment, including how to change it, in **Chapter 3**.

- There are some limitations to where you can use the Click and Type feature. Generally speaking, if the Click and Type pointer does not appear, you cannot use it to position text.

Figure 37
The Click and Type pointer.

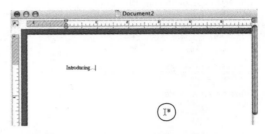

Figure 38 Position the Click and Type pointer where you want to enter text.

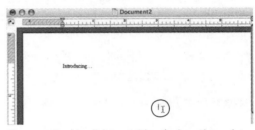

Figure 39 Double-click to position the insertion point.

Figure 40 Type the text you want to appear.

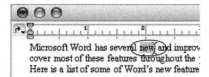

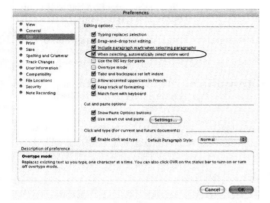

Figure 41 Drag over text to select it.

Figure 42 The Edit options of the Preferences dialog.

Selecting Text

You can select one or more characters to delete, replace, copy, cut, or format. Selected text appears with a colored background or in inverse type.

✔ Tips

■ There are many ways to select text. This section provides just a few of the most useful methods.

■ Word enables you to select multiple blocks of text. To do this, hold down ⌃ ⌘ while selecting each block, using any of the techniques discussed in this chapter.

To select text by dragging

1. Position the mouse I-beam pointer at the beginning of the text.

2. Press the mouse button down and drag to the end of the text you want to select (**Figure 41**).

3. Release the mouse button.

   All characters between the starting and ending points are selected.

✔ Tips

■ This is the most basic text selection technique. It works for any amount of text.

■ By default, Word automatically selects entire words when you drag through more than one word. To disable this feature, choose Word > Preferences (**Figure 29**), click Edit in the Preferences dialog that appears (**Figure 42**), and turn off the check box for When selecting, automatically select entire word.

SELECTING TEXT

To select text by clicking

Click as instructed in **Table 2** to select specific amounts of text.

✔ Tips

- You can combine techniques in **Table 2** with dragging to select multiple lines and paragraphs.

- When you select an entire word by double-clicking it, Word also selects any spaces after it.

To make multiple selections

1. Use any technique to select text.

2. Hold down ⌘ ⌘ while making another selection (**Figure 44**).

3. Repeat step 2 until all selections are made.

✔ Tip

- This ability to select *non-contiguous* blocks of text makes it easy to format multiple blocks of text at once.

To select the contents of a document

Choose Edit > Select All (**Figure 45**) or press ⌘ ⌘ A.

Table 2

Techniques for Selecting Text by Clicking	
To select:	**Do this:**
a word	double-click the word
a sentence	hold down ⌘ ⌘ and click in the sentence
a line	click in the selection bar to the left of the line (**Figure 43**)
a paragraph	triple-click in the paragraph or double-click in the selection bar to the left of the paragraph
the document	hold down ⌘ ⌘ and double-click in the selection bar to the left of any line
any text	position the insertion point at the beginning of the text, then hold down Shift and click at the end of the text

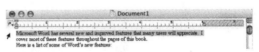

Figure 43 Click in the selection bar beside a line to select the line.

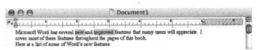

Figure 44 Here's an example of two non-contiguous selections.

Figure 45 The Edit menu.

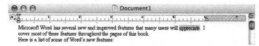

Figure 46 Select the text you want to replace.

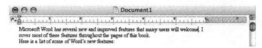

Figure 47 The text you type replaces the selected text.

Editing Selected Text

Once you select text, you can delete it or replace it with other text.

To delete selected text

Press [Delete] or [Del]. The selected text disappears.

To replace selected text

With text selected (**Figure 46**), type the replacement text. The selected text disappears and the replacement text is inserted in its place (**Figure 47**).

Copying & Moving Text

Word offers two ways to copy or move text:

◆ Use the Copy, Cut, and Paste commands (or their shortcut keys) to place text on the Clipboard and then copy it from the Clipboard to another location.

◆ Use drag-and-drop editing to copy or move selected text.

You can copy or move text to:

◆ A different location within the same document.

◆ A different document.

◆ A document created with a program other than Word.

✔ Tips

■ Copying and moving text make it possible to reuse text and reorganize a document without a lot of retyping.

■ The Clipboard is a place in your computer's memory that is used to temporarily store selected items that are copied or cut. Word supports two of these storage spaces:

　▲ The *Mac OS Clipboard* is shared among all Mac OS applications that support the copy and paste commands.

　▲ The *Scrapbook* is shared among all Microsoft Office applications. It offers additional features, which are discussed later in this chapter.

■ Text you copy or cut remains on the Clipboard until you use the Copy or Cut command again or restart your computer. This makes it possible to use Clipboard contents over and over in any document.

■ These techniques also work with objects such as graphics. I tell you more about working with objects in **Chapter 10**.

Figure 48 Select the text that you want to copy.

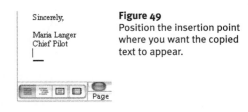

Figure 49
Position the insertion point where you want the copied text to appear.

Figure 50
When you use the Paste command, the contents of the Clipboard appear at the insertion point, along with the Paste Options button.

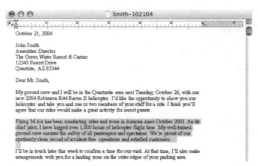

Figure 51 Select the text that you want to move.

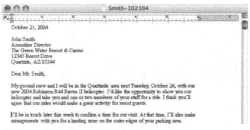

Figure 52 The text you cut disappears.

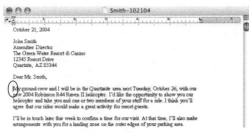

Figure 53 Position the insertion point where you want the cut text to appear.

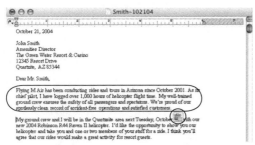

Figure 54 The contents of the Clipboard appear at the insertion point, along with the Paste Options button.

To copy text with Copy & Paste

1. Select the text that you want to copy (**Figure 48**).

2. Choose Edit > Copy (**Figure 45**), press ⌃⌘C, or click the Copy button on the Standard toolbar.

   The selected text is copied to the Clipboard. The document does not change.

3. Position the insertion point where you want the text copied (**Figure 49**).

4. Choose Edit > Paste (**Figure 45**), press ⌃⌘V, or click the Paste button on the Standard toolbar.

   The text in the Clipboard is copied into the document at the insertion point (**Figure 50**).

To move text with Cut & Paste

1. Select the text that you want to move (**Figure 51**).

2. Choose Edit > Cut (**Figure 45**), press ⌃⌘X, or click the Cut button on the Standard toolbar.

   The selected text is copied to the Clipboard and removed from the document (**Figure 52**).

3. Position the insertion point where you want the cut text to appear (**Figure 53**).

4. Choose Edit > Paste (**Figure 45**), press ⌃⌘V, or click the Paste button on the Standard toolbar.

   The text in the Clipboard is copied into the document at the insertion point (**Figure 54**).

USING THE COPY, CUT, & PASTE COMMANDS

To copy text with drag-and-drop editing

1. Select the text that you want to copy (**Figure 48**).

2. Position the mouse pointer on the selected text (**Figure 55**).

3. Hold down Option, press the mouse button, and drag. As you drag, a tiny box and vertical line move with the mouse pointer, which has a plus sign beside it to indicate that it is copying (**Figure 56**).

4. When the vertical line at the mouse pointer is where you want the text copied, release the mouse button and Option. The selected text is copied (**Figure 50**).

To move text with drag-and-drop editing

1. Select the text that you want to move (**Figure 51**).

2. Position the mouse pointer on the selected text (**Figure 57**).

3. Press the mouse button down and drag. As you drag, a box and vertical line move with the mouse pointer (**Figure 58**).

4. When the vertical line at the mouse pointer is where you want the text moved, release the mouse button. The selected text is moved (**Figure 54**).

Flying M Air has b
chief pilot, I have l
ground crew ensure
spotlessly clean rec

Figure 55 Point to the selection.

Maria Langer
Chief Pilot
| Flying M Air

Figure 56 Hold down Option and drag to copy the selection.

My ground crew and I will be in the Quartzsite area next Tuesday, October 26, with our new 2004 Robinson R44 Raven II helicopter. I'd like the opportunity to show you our helicopter and take you and one or two members of your staff for a ride. I think you'll agree that our rides would make a great activity for resort guests.

Flying M Air has been conducting rides and tours in Arizona since October 2001. As its chief pilot, I have logged over 1,000 hours of helicopter flight time. My well-trained ground crew ensures the safety of all passengers and spectators. We're proud of our spotlessly clean record of accident-free operations and satisfied customers.

I'll be in touch later this week to confirm a time for our visit. At that time, I'll also make arrangements with you for a landing zone on the outer edges of your parking area.

I look forward to seeing you next week!

Figure 57 Point to the selection.

Flying M Air has been conducting rides and tours in Arizona since October 2001. As its chief ground crew and I will be in the Quartzsite area next Tuesday, October 26, with our ground new 2004 Robinson R44 Raven II helicopter. I'd like the opportunity to show you our spotl helicopter and take you and one or two members of your staff for a ride. I think you'll agree that our rides would make a great activity for resort guests.

Flying M Air has been conducting rides and tours in Arizona since October 2001. As its chief pilot, I have logged over 1,000 hours of helicopter flight time. My well-trained ground crew ensures the safety of all passengers and spectators. We're proud of our spotlessly clean record of accident-free operations and satisfied customers.

I'll be in touch later this week to confirm a time for our visit. At that time, I'll also make arrangements with you for a landing zone on the outer edges of your parking area.

I look forward to seeing you next week!

Figure 58 Drag to move the selection.

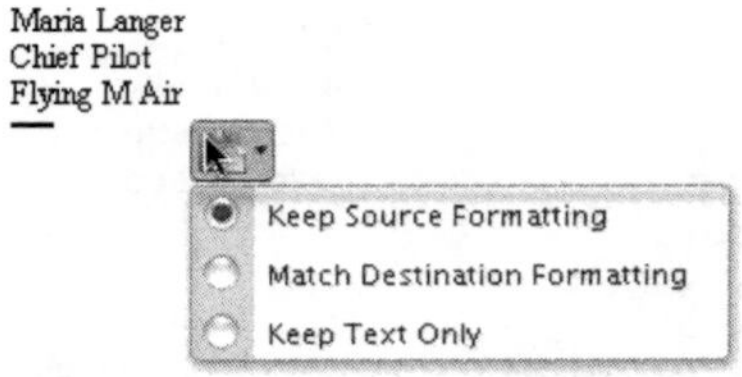

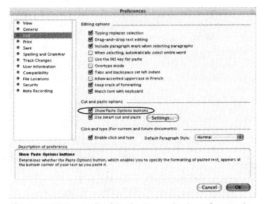

Figure 59 Clicking the Paste Options button displays a menu of formatting options for the pasted item.

Figure 60 You can disable the Paste Options feature in the Edit options of the Preferences dialog.

Paste Options

When you use the Paste command or drag and drop text to copy or move it, the Paste Options button appears (**Figures 50** and **54**). Clicking this icon displays a menu of formatting options (**Figure 59**):

◆ **Keep source formatting** retains the formatting applied to the original item.

◆ **Match destination formatting** changes the formatting to match the new location.

◆ **Keep text only** removes all formatting.

✔ Tips

■ You do not have to use the Paste Options feature when you copy or move text. Use it only when the formatting of the text you copied or moved needs to be changed.

■ The Paste Options button automatically disappears as you work with Word.

■ Formatting text is discussed in detail in **Chapters 3** and **4**.

To set formatting options with Paste Options

1. Click the Paste Options button to display the Paste Options menu (**Figure 59**).

2. Click to select the option you want.

To disable Paste Options

1. Choose Word > Preferences (**Figure 29**).

2. Click Edit in the Preferences dialog that appears (**Figure 60**).

3. Turn off the check box for Show Paste Options buttons.

4. Click OK.

The Scrapbook

The Scrapbook enables you to "collect and paste" multiple items. You simply display the Scrapbook (**Figure 61**), then use the Copy to Scrapbook command to copy selected text or other objects to the Scrapbook rather than to the Clipboard. You can then use the Paste from Scrapbook command to paste a selected Scrapbook item into your Word document.

Figure 61
The Scrapbook, with two items already added.

✔ Tips

- The Scrapbook was referred to as the *Office Clipboard* in Word X.

- The Scrapbook works with all Microsoft Office applications—not just Word—so you can store items from different types of Office documents.

To display the Scrapbook

Choose Tools > Scrapbook (**Figure 62**). The Scrapbook appears in a palette beside the document window.

To add an item to the Scrapbook

1. If necessary, display the Scrapbook (**Figure 61**).

2. Select the text or object you want to copy (**Figure 51**).

3. Choose Edit > Copy to Scrapbook (**Figure 63**) or press Shift ⌃ ⌘ C. The selection appears in the Scrapbook (**Figure 64**).

Figure 62
Choose Scrapbook from the Tools menu.

Figure 63
Choose Copy to Scrapbook from the Edit menu.

Figure 64
The item you selected is copied to the Scrapbook.

Figure 65 Position the insertion point where you want the item to appear, then select the item in the Scrapbook.

Figure 66
Choose Paste from Scrapbook from the Edit menu.

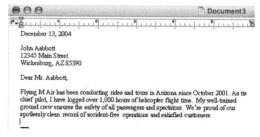

Figure 67 The item you pasted or dragged appears at the insertion point.

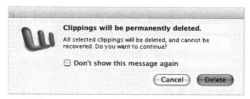

Figure 68 Click Delete in this dialog to remove the item from the Scrapbook.

To use Scrapbook items

1. If necessary, display the Scrapbook.

2. In the document window, position the insertion point where you want to place the Scrapbook item (**Figure 65**).

3. In the Scrapbook, select the item you want to paste into the document (**Figure 65**).

4. Click the Paste button in the Scrapbook, choose Edit > Paste from Scrapbook (**Figure 66**), or press ⇧⌘V.

Or

1. If necessary, display the Scrapbook.

2. Drag the item you want to use from the Scrapbook into the document window.

The item you pasted or dragged appears in the document window (**Figure 67**).

To remove Scrapbook items

1. In the Scrapbook window, select the item you want to remove (**Figure 65**).

2. Click the Delete button in the Scrapbook.

3. A dialog like the one in **Figure 68** appears. Click Delete.

The item is removed from the Scrapbook.

USING & REMOVING SCRAPBOOK ITEMS

Undoing, Redoing, & Repeating Actions

Word offers a trio of commands that enable you to undo, redo, or repeat the last thing you did.

◆ **Undo** reverses your last action. Word supports multiple levels of undo, enabling you to reverse more than the last action.

◆ **Redo** reverses the Undo command. This command is only available if the last thing you did was use the Undo command.

◆ **Repeat** performs your last action again. This command is only available when your last action was anything other than using the Undo or Redo command.

✔ Tips

■ The exact wording of these commands on the Edit menu varies depending on the last action performed. The Undo command is always the first command under the Edit menu; the Redo or Repeat command (whichever appears on the menu) is always the second command under the full Edit menu. **Figures 69**, **70**, and **71** show some examples.

■ The Redo and Repeat commands are never both available at the same time.

■ Think of the Undo command as the *Oops!* command—anytime you say "Oops!" you'll probably want to use it.

■ The Repeat command is especially useful for applying formatting to text scattered throughout your document. I tell you more about formatting in **Chapters 3** and **4**.

Figures 69, 70, & 71
Some examples of how the Undo, Redo, and Repeat commands can appear on the Edit menu.

Figure 72 Use the Undo pop-up menu to select actions to undo.

Figure 73 Use the Redo pop-up menu to select actions to redo.

To undo the last action

Choose Edit > Undo (Figure 69, 70, or 71), press ⌃ ⌘ Z, or click the Undo button on the Standard toolbar.

To undo multiple actions

Choose Edit > Undo (Figure 69, 70, or 71) or press ⌃ ⌘ Z repeatedly.

Or

Click the triangle beside the Undo button on the Standard toolbar to display a pop-up menu of recent actions. Drag down to select all the actions that you want to undo (**Figure 72**). Release the mouse button to undo all selected actions.

To reverse the last undo

Choose Edit > Redo (Figure 69), press ⌃ ⌘ Y, or click the Redo button on the Standard toolbar.

To reverse multiple undos

Choose Edit > Redo (Figures 69 and 70) or press ⌃ ⌘ Y repeatedly.

Or

Click the triangle beside the Redo button on the Standard toolbar to display a pop-up menu of recently undone actions. Drag down to select all the actions that you want to redo (**Figure 73**). Release the mouse button to reverse all selected undos.

To repeat the last action

Choose Edit > Repeat (**Figure 71**) or press ⌃ ⌘ Y.

UNDOING, REDOING, & REPEATING ACTIONS

Find & Replace

Word has a very powerful find and replace feature. With it, you can search a document for specific text strings and, if desired, replace them with other text.

✔ Tip

- By default, the Find and Replace commands search the entire document, beginning at the insertion point.

To find text

1. Choose Edit > Find (**Figure 45**) or press ⌃⌘F to display the Find options of the Find and Replace dialog (**Figure 74**).

2. Enter the text that you want to find in the Find what box.

3. Click the Find Next button. One of two things happens:
   - ▲ If Word finds the search text, it selects the first occurrence that it finds (**Figure 75**). Repeat this step to find all occurrences, one at a time. When the last occurrence has been found, Word tells you with a dialog (**Figure 76**).
   - ▲ If Word does not find the search text, it tells you with a dialog (**Figure 77**). Repeat steps 2 and 3 to search for different text.

4. When you're finished, dismiss the Find and Replace dialog by clicking its close button.

✔ Tips

- To search only part of a document, select the text you want to search, then follow the above instructions.

- If desired, you can fine-tune search criteria. I tell you how a little later in this chapter.

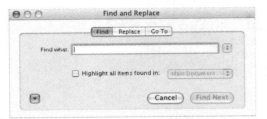

Figure 74 The Find options of the Find and Replace dialog.

Figure 75 Word selects each occurrence of the text that it finds.

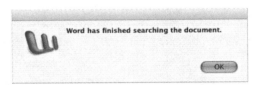

Figure 76 When Word has finished showing all occurrences of the search text, it tells you.

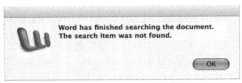

Figure 77 Word also tells you when it can't find the search text at all.

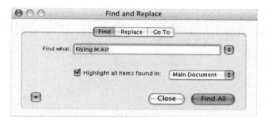

Figure 78 Use the check box and the pop-up menu beside it to select all occurrences of a text string.

Figure 79 Word can select all occurrences of the search text at once.

Figure 80 When text is selected, you can use the pop-up menu to specify what should be searched.

To select all occurrences of a text string

1. Choose Edit > Find (**Figure 45**) or press ⌃⌘F to display the Find options of the Find and Replace dialog (**Figure 74**).

2. Enter the text you want to find in the Find what box.

3. Turn on the Highlight all items found in check box and choose Main Document from the pop-up menu beside it (**Figure 78**).

4. Click the Find All button. One of two things happens:

   ▲ If Word finds the search text, it selects all occurrences (**Figure 79**).

   ▲ If Word does not find the search text, it tells you (**Figure 77**).

5. When you're finished, dismiss the Find and Replace dialog by clicking its close button.

✔ Tips

■ The ability to use the Find dialog to select all occurrences of a text string is a great way to apply special formatting to multiple blocks of text all at once.

■ You can also use this technique to select all occurrences of a text string in selected text—for example, to select all occurrences of the word *helicopter* in the body of the letter in **Figure 79**. Before starting, select the text you want to search. Then, in step 3, choose Current Selection from the pop-up menu (**Figure 80**).

To replace text

1. Choose Edit > Replace (**Figure 45**) or press (Shift)(⌃)(⌘)(H). The Replace pane of the Find and Replace dialog appears (**Figure 81**).

2. Enter the text that you want to find in the Find what box.

3. Enter the text that you want to replace the found text with in the Replace with box.

4. Click the Find Next button to start the search. One of two things happens:

   ▲ If Word finds the search text, it selects the first occurrence that it finds (**Figure 82**). Continue with step 5.

   ▲ If Word does not find the search text, it tells you with a dialog (**Figure 77**). You can repeat steps 2 and 4 to search for different text.

5. Do one of the following:

   ▲ To replace the selected occurrence and automatically find the next occurrence, click the Replace button. Word replaces the text and selects the next occurrence (**Figure 83**). Repeat this step for all occurrences (**Figure 76**).

   ▲ To replace all occurrences, click the Replace All button. Word tells you how many changes it made (**Figure 84**).

   ▲ To skip the current occurrence and move on to the next one, click the Find Next button. You can repeat this step until Word has found all occurrences (**Figure 76**).

6. When you're finished, dismiss the Find and Replace dialog by clicking its close button.

✔ Tip

■ If desired, you can fine-tune search criteria. I tell you how on the next page.

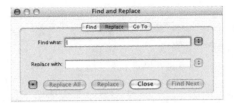

Figure 81 The Replace pane of the Find and Replace dialog.

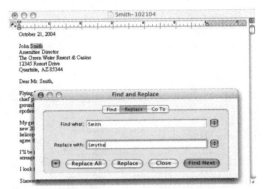

Figure 82 Word selects each occurrence of the search text it finds.

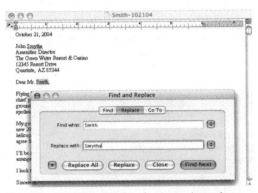

Figure 83 Clicking the Replace button replaces the selected occurrence and finds the next one.

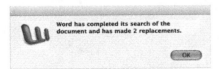

Figure 84 Clicking the Replace All button replaces all occurrences. Word tells you how many replacements it made when it's finished.

REPLACING TEXT

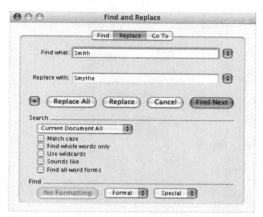

Figure 85 The Replace tab of the Find and Replace dialog expanded to show additional search and replace criteria options.

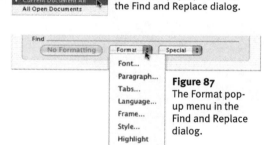

Figure 86
The Search pop-up menu in the Find and Replace dialog.

Figure 87
The Format pop-up menu in the Find and Replace dialog.

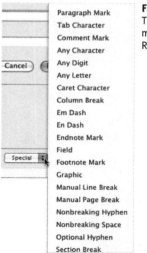

Figure 88
The Special pop-up menu in the Find and Replace dialog.

To fine-tune criteria

1. In the Find (**Figure** 74) or Replace (**Figure** 81) options of the Find and Replace dialog, click the triangle button in the lower-left corner. The dialog expands to show additional search criteria options (**Figure 85**).

2. Click in the Find what or Replace with text box to indicate which criterion you want to fine-tune.

3. Set search criteria options as desired:

   ▲ The **Search** pop-up menu (**Figure 86**) lets you specify whether you want to search the current document or all documents and which direction you want to search.

   ▲ The **Match case** check box exactly matches capitalization.

   ▲ The **Find whole words only** check box finds the search text only when it is a separate word or phrase.

   ▲ The **Use wildcards** check box lets you include wildcard characters (such as ? for a single character and * for multiple characters).

   ▲ The **Sounds like** check box finds homonyms—words that sound alike but are spelled differently.

   ▲ The **Find all word forms** check box searches for all verb, noun, or adjective forms of the search text.

4. Set search or replace criteria options as desired:

   ▲ The **Format** pop-up menu (**Figure 87**) lets you specify formatting options. Choosing one of these options displays the corresponding dialog. I explain how to use these dialogs in **Chapters 3** and 4.

   ▲ The **Special** pop-up menu (**Figure 88**) lets you find and replace special characters.

FINE-TUNING SEARCH CRITERIA

Saving Documents

When you save a document, you put a copy of it on disk. You can then open it at a later time to edit or print it.

✔ Tips

■ Until you save a document, its information is stored only in your computer's memory (RAM). Your work on the document could be lost in the event of a power outage or system crash.

■ It's a good idea to save documents frequently as you work. This ensures that the most recent versions are always saved to disk.

■ Opening files is covered near the beginning of this chapter.

To save a document for the first time

1. Choose File > Save or File > Save As (**Figure 10**), press ⌃⌘⑤, or click the Save button on the Standard toolbar.

2. Use the Save As dialog that appears (**Figure 89**) to navigate to the folder in which you want to save the file:

   ▲ Click a view button to display the list of files and folders in list (**Figure 89**) or column view.

   ▲ Click an item in the Sidebar to display the contents of that item.

   ▲ Use the pop-up menu above the list of files (**Figure 90**) to backtrack through the file hierarchy or open a recently opened folder.

View buttons

If necessary, click here to display the file list.

Figure 89 The Save As dialog.

Figure 90
The pop-up menu near the top of the Save As dialog.

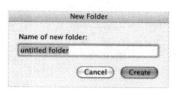

Figure 91 The New Folder dialog.

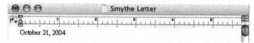

Figure 92 The name you give a document appears in its title bar after you save it.

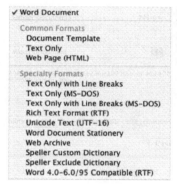

Figure 93
You can use the Format pop-up menu to specify a file format.

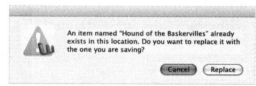

Figure 94 This dialog appears when you attempt to save a file with the same name and same disk location as another file.

▲ Double-click a folder to open it.

▲ Click the New Folder button to create a new folder within the current folder. Enter the name for the folder in the New Folder dialog (**Figure 91**) and click Create.

3. Enter a name for the file in the Save As box.

4. If the document will be opened by a Windows user, turn on the Append file extension check box to enhance compatibility. The characters *.doc* appear at the end of the file name.

5. Click Save.

The file is saved to disk. Its name appears on the window's title bar (**Figure 92**).

✔ Tips

■ You can use the Format pop-up menu in the Save As dialog (**Figure 93**) to specify a different format for the file. This enables you to save the document in a format that can be opened and read by other versions of Word or other applications.

■ If you save a file with the same name and same disk location as another file, a dialog with two buttons appears (**Figure 94**):

▲ **Cancel** redisplays the Save As dialog box so you can change the name or location of the file you are saving.

▲ **Replace** replaces the file already on disk with the file you are saving.

To save changes to a document

Choose File > Save (**Figure 10**), press ⌃⌘S, or click the Save button on the Standard toolbar.

The document is saved with the same name in the same location on disk.

To save a document with a different name or in a different disk location

1. Choose File > Save As (**Figure 10**).

2. Follow steps 2 and/or 3 in the section titled "To save a document for the first time" to select a new disk location and/or enter a different name for the file.

3. Click the Save button.

To save a document as a template

1. Choose File > Save As (**Figure 10**).

2. Enter a name for the file in the Save As box.

3. Choose Document Template from the Format pop-up menu (**Figure 93**). The file list portion of the dialog automatically displays the contents of the My Templates folder (**Figure 95**).

4. Click the Save button.

   The file is saved as a template. Its name appears in the document title bar.

✔ Tips

- To begin using a template right after you created it, close it, then follow the instructions near the beginning of this chapter to open a new file based on a template. The template appears in the My Templates area of the Project Gallery dialog (**Figure 96**).

- I tell you more about templates in the beginning of this chapter.

Figure 95 The Save As dialog when you save a document as a template.

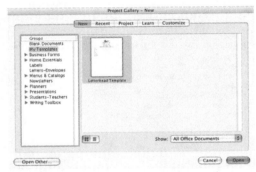

Figure 96 When a file has been saved as a template, it appears in the Project Gallery dialog.

SAVING DOCUMENTS

Text Formatting Basics

Figure 1 A document with no formatting.

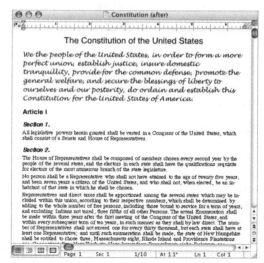

Figure 2 The same document with font and paragraph formatting applied.

Text Formatting Basics

Microsoft Word offers a wide range of text formatting options that you can use to make your documents more interesting and readable. Most text formatting can be broken down into two types:

◆ **Font** or **character formatting** applies to individual characters of text. Examples include bold, italic, underline, and font color. The actual font or typeface used to display characters is also a part of font formatting.

◆ **Paragraph formatting** applies to entire paragraphs of text. Examples are indentation, justification, line spacing, bullets, and numbering.

This chapter introduces text formatting using basic formatting techniques. **Chapter 4** continues the discussion of text formatting by covering advanced formatting techniques.

✔ Tips

■ When properly applied, formatting can make the document easier to read, as illustrated in **Figures 1** and **2**.

■ Don't get carried away with formatting—especially font formatting. Too much formatting distracts the reader, making the document difficult to read.

■ *Page formatting*, which enables you to format document pages or sections, is covered in **Chapter 5**.

Font Formatting

Font formatting, which is sometimes referred to as *character formatting,* can be applied to individual characters of text. Word offers a wide variety of options.

◆ **Font (Figure 3)** is the typeface used to display characters.

◆ **Font style (Figure 4)** is the appearance of font characters: regular, italic, bold, or bold italic.

◆ **Size (Figure 5)** is the size of characters, expressed in points.

◆ **Font color** is the color applied to text characters.

◆ **Underline style (Figure 6)** options allow you to apply a variety of underlines beneath characters.

◆ **Underline color** is the color of the applied underline.

◆ **Effects (Figure 7)** are special effects that change the appearance of characters. Options include strikethrough, double strikethrough, superscript, subscript, shadow, outline, emboss, engrave, small caps, all caps, or hidden.

◆ **Scale (Figure 8)** determines the horizontal size of font characters. Scale is specified as a percentage of normal character width.

◆ **Spacing (Figure 9)** determines the amount of space between each character of text. Spacing can be normal or can be expanded or condensed by the number of points you specify.

◆ **Position (Figure 10)** determines whether text appears above or below the baseline. Position can be normal or can be raised or lowered by the number of points you specify.

Arial
Bookman Old Style
Century Gothic
Courier New
Forte
Garamond
Impact
Συμβολ
Verdana
Times New Roman
✺◉▢❖✦✳✴■✖✦✧✦▼▲

Figure 3
Some font examples using some of the fonts installed on my system. Your system's fonts may differ.

Regular
Bold
Italic
Bold Italic

Figure 4
The font styles offered by Word.

10 points
12 points
14 points
18 points
24 points
36 points

Figure 5
Examples of font sizes. This illustration is not at actual size.

No underline
Words Only
Underline Example
Underline Example
Underline Example
Underline Example
Underline Example
Underline Example
Underline Example
Underline Example
Underline Example
Underline Example
Underline Example
Underline Example
Underline Example
Underline Example
Underline Example

Figure 6
Examples of underlines offered by Word.

Strikethrough
Double Strikethrough
Superscript
Subscript
Shadow
Outline
Emboss
Engrave
SMALL CAPS
ALL CAPS

Figure 7
Examples of effects.

Characters at 200% Scale
Characters at 150% Scale
Characters at 100% Scale
Characters at 75% Scale
Characters at 50% Scale

Figure 8 Examples of various scale settings.

Spacing Expanded by 2 points
Spacing Expanded by 1 point
Spacing Set to Normal
Spacing Condensed by 1 point
Spacing Condensed by 2 points

Figure 9 Examples of various spacing settings.

An example of text raised by 3 points
An example of text neither raised nor lowered
An example of text lowered by 3 points

Figure 10 Examples of various position settings.

We Talk
We Talk

Figure 11 Example of text with kerning turned off (top) and turned on (bottom). Note the way the lowercase e and a tuck under the uppercase W and T.

◆ **Kerning (Figure 11)** determines how certain combinations of letters "fit" together.

◆ **Animations** are special animated effects that alter the appearance of font characters when viewed onscreen.

✔ Tips

■ Although some fonts come with Microsoft Office, Word enables you to apply *any* font that is properly installed in your system.

■ A *point* is 1/72 inch. The larger the point size, the larger the characters.

■ Hidden characters do not show onscreen unless nonprinting characters are displayed. Nonprinting characters are discussed in **Chapter 2**.

■ Don't confuse character position with superscript and subscript. Although all three of these font formatting options change the position of text in relation to the baseline, superscript and subscript also change the size of characters.

■ The effect of kerning varies depending on the size and font applied to characters for which kerning is enabled. Kerning is more apparent at larger point sizes and requires that the font contain *kerning pairs*—predefined pairs of letters to kern. In many instances, you may not see a difference in spacing at all.

Applying Font Formatting

Font formatting is applied to selected characters or, if no characters are selected, to the characters you type at the insertion point after setting formatting options. Here are two examples:

◆ To apply a bold font style to text that you have already typed, select the text (**Figure 12**), then apply the formatting. The appearance of the text changes immediately (**Figure 13**).

◆ To apply a bold font style to text that you have not yet typed, position the insertion point where the text will be typed (**Figure 14**), apply (or "turn on") the bold formatting, and type the text. The text appears in bold (**Figure 15**). You must remember, however, to "turn off" bold formatting before you continue to type (**Figure 16**).

Word offers several methods of applying font formatting:

◆ The Font area of the Formatting Palette (**Figure 17**) enables you to apply font, size, some font styles, and font color formatting.

◆ Shortcut keys enable you to apply some font formatting.

◆ The Font dialog (**Figures 26**, **27**, and **28**) enables you to apply all kinds of font formatting.

✔ Tips

■ In my opinion, it's easier to type text and apply formatting later than to format as you type.

■ I explain how to select text in **Chapter 2**.

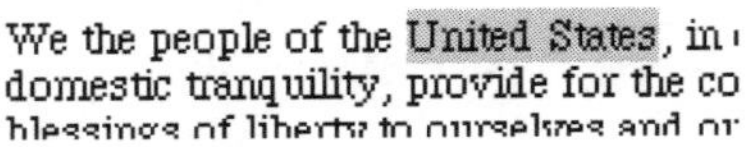

We the people of the United States, in domestic tranquility, provide for the co blessings of liberty to ourselves and or

Figure 12 Select the text that you want to format...

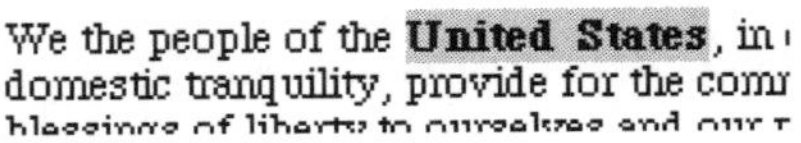

We the people of the **United States**, in domestic tranquility, provide for the comr blessings of liberty to ourselves and our r

Figure 13 ...then apply the formatting.

We the people of the |

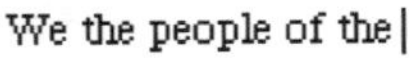

Figure 14 Position the insertion point where you want the formatted text to appear...

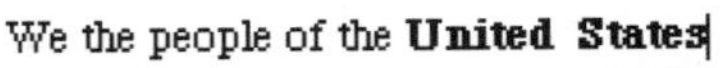

We the people of the **United States**|

Figure 15 ...then "turn on" the formatting and type the text.

We the people of the **United States**, in order to|

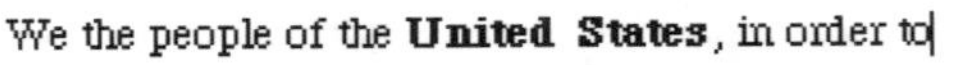

Figure 16 Be sure to "turn off" the formatting before continuing to type.

Click here to display or hide Font formatting options.

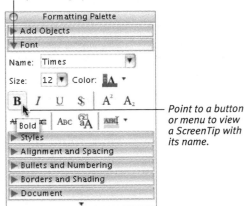

Point to a button or menu to view a ScreenTip with its name.

Figure 17 You can use the Formatting Palette to apply some font formatting.

Figure 18
The Font menu on the Formatting Palette.

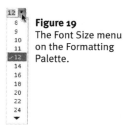

Figure 19
The Font Size menu on the Formatting Palette.

Figure 20 Select the contents of the Font box.

Figure 21 Enter the name of the font that you want to apply.

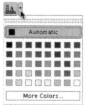

Figure 22 The Font Color menu on the Formatting Palette.

Figure 23 The Highlight Color menu on the Formatting Palette.

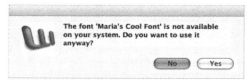

Figure 24 Word tells you when you've entered a font that isn't installed.

To apply font formatting with the Formatting Palette

Choose the font or size that you want to apply from the Font or Font Size menu (**Figures 18** and **19**).

Or

1. Click the Font (**Figure 20**) or Font Size text box to select its contents.

2. Enter the name of the font (**Figure 21**) or the size that you want to apply.

3. Press Return.

Or

Click the button for the font style you want to apply: Bold, Italic, Underline, Shadow, Superscript, Subscript, Strikethrough, Double Strikethrough, Small Caps, or All Caps.

Or

Click the Font Color button to apply the currently selected color or choose another color from the Font Color menu (**Figure 22**).

Or

Click the Highlight button to apply the currently selected color or choose another color from the Highlight Color menu (**Figure 23**).

✔ Tips

■ Font names appear on the Font menu in their typefaces (**Figure 18**).

■ Recently applied fonts appear at the top of the Font menu (**Figure 18**).

■ If you enter the name of a font that is not installed on your system, Word warns you (**Figure 24**). If you use the font anyway, the text appears in the default paragraph font until either the specified font is installed on your system or the document is opened on a system on which the font is installed.

USING THE FORMATTING PALETTE

To apply font formatting with shortcut keys

Press the shortcut key combination (**Table 1**) for the formatting that you want to apply.

✔ Tips

■ The shortcut key to change the font requires that you press the first key combination, enter the name of the font desired, then press [Return]. This command activates the Font box on the Formatting Palette (**Figure 20**).

■ The Reset Character shortcut key ([Ó ⌘][Shift][Z]) clears all font formatting applied to a selection.

Table 1

Shortcut Keys for Font Formatting	
Formatting	**Keystroke**
Font	[Ó ⌘][Shift][F] *Font Name* [Return]
Grow font	[Ó ⌘][Shift][.]
Grow font 1 point	[Ó ⌘][]]
Shrink font	[Ó ⌘][Shift][,]
Shrink font 1 point	[Ó ⌘][[]
Bold	[Ó ⌘][B] or [Ctrl][Ó ⌘][B]
Italic	[Ó ⌘][I] or [Ctrl][Ó ⌘][I]
Underline	[Ó ⌘][U] or [Ctrl][Ó ⌘][U]
Word underline	[Ó ⌘][Shift][W]
Double underline	[Ó ⌘][Shift][D]
Superscript	[Ó ⌘][Shift][=]
Subscript	[Ó ⌘][=]
All caps	[Ó ⌘][Shift][A]
Small caps	[Ó ⌘][Shift][K]
Hidden	[Control][Shift][H]
Reset Character	[Ó ⌘][Shift][Z]

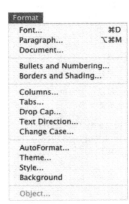

Figure 25
The Format menu.

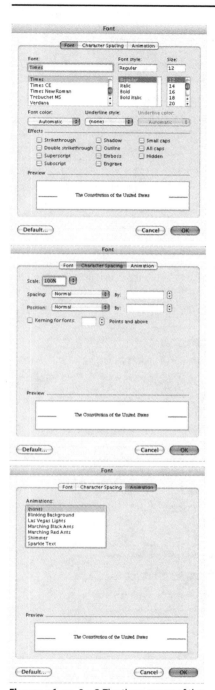

Figures 26, 27, & 28 The three panes of the Font dialog: Font (top), Character Spacing (middle), and Animation (bottom).

To apply font formatting with the Font dialog

1. Choose Format > Font (**Figure 25**) or press ⌃ ⌘ D.

2. Click the button for the type of font formatting you want to set:

   ▲ **Font** (**Figure 26**) enables you to set basic font formatting options, including font, size, style, color, underline, and effects.

   ▲ **Character Spacing** (**Figure 27**) enables you to set font scale, spacing, position, and kerning options.

   ▲ **Animation** (**Figure 28**) enables you to set animation options.

3. Set formatting options as desired.

4. Repeat steps 2 and 3 for each type of formatting you want to set.

5. Click OK.

✔ Tip

■ The Preview area of the Font dialog illustrates what text will look like with the selected formatting applied.

Paragraph Formatting

Paragraph formatting is applied to entire paragraphs of text. Word offers a variety of paragraph formatting options:

◆ **Alignment** (**Figure 29**) is the way lines of text line up between the indents.

◆ **Indentation** (**Figure 30**) is the spacing between text and margins. Word allows you to set left and right margins, as well as special indentations for first line and hanging indents.

◆ **Orientation** determines whether text should read across or down the page.

◆ **Bullets** (**Figure 31**) combines hanging indentation and bullet characters.

◆ **Numbering** (**Figure 32**) combines hanging indentation and automatic numbering.

◆ **Line spacing** (**Figure 33**) is the amount of space between lines.

◆ **Paragraph spacing** (**Figure 34**) is the amount of space before and after the paragraph.

◆ **Pagination** options, including Widow/ Orphan control, Keep lines together, Keep with next, and Page break before, determine how automatic page breaks occur in the document.

◆ **Line numbering** and **hyphenation** options determine whether the paragraph should be excluded from line numbering and hyphenation.

✔ Tip

■ Tabs are also a paragraph formatting option. Because of their relative complexity, however, I discuss them separately later in this chapter.

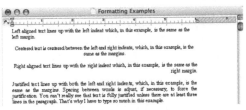

Figure 29 Examples of alignment options.

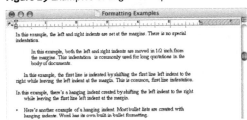

Figure 30 Examples of indentation options. The ruler in this illustration shows the indent markers set for the first sample paragraph.

Figure 31 Example of bullet formatting.

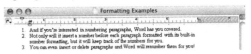

Figure 32 Example of numbering format.

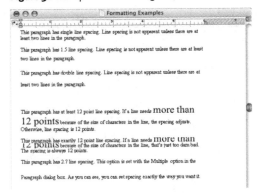

Figure 33 Example of line spacing options.

Figure 34 Example of paragraph spacing options.

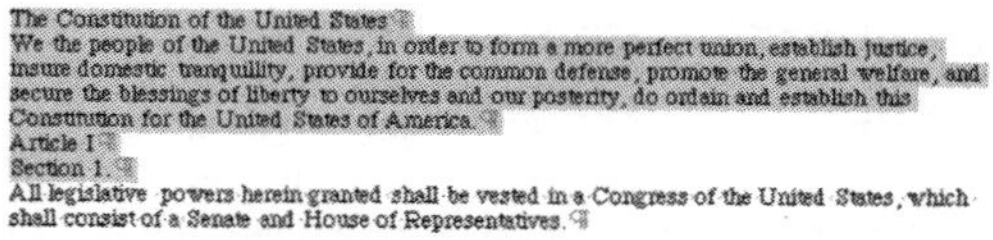

The Constitution of the United States ¶
We the people of the United States, in order to form a more perfect union, establish justice, insure domestic tranquillity, provide for the common defense, promote the general welfare, and secure the blessings of liberty to ourselves and our posterity, do ordain and establish this Constitution for the United States of America. ¶
Article I ¶
Section 1. ¶
All legislative powers herein granted shall be vested in a Congress of the United States, which shall consist of a Senate and House of Representatives. ¶

Figure 35 In this example, the first four paragraphs are completely selected and will be affected by any paragraph formatting applied.

The Constitution of the United States ¶
We the people of the United States, in order to form a more perfect union, establish justice, insure domestic tranquillity, provide for the common defense, promote the general welfare, and secure the blessings of liberty to ourselves and our posterity, do ordain and establish this Constitution for the United States of America. ¶
Article I ¶
Section 1. ¶
All legislative powers herein granted shall be vested in a Congress of the United States, which shall consist of a Senate and House of Representatives. ¶

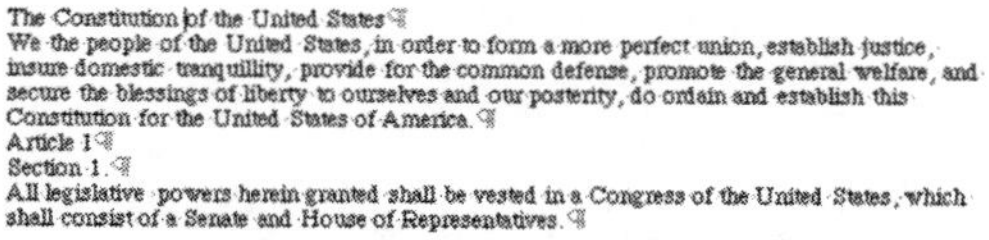

Figure 36 In this example, the insertion point is in the first paragraph. That entire paragraph will be affected by any paragraph formatting applied.

The Constitution of the United States ¶
We the people of the United States, in order to form a more perfect union, establish justice, insure domestic tranquillity, provide for the common defense, promote the general welfare, and secure the blessings of liberty to ourselves and our posterity, do ordain and establish this Constitution for the United States of America. ¶
Article I ¶
Section 1. ¶
All legislative powers herein granted shall be vested in a Congress of the United States, which shall consist of a Senate and House of Representatives. ¶

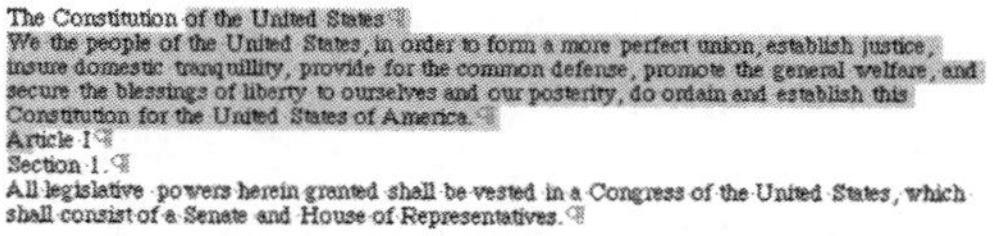

Figure 37 In this example, only part of the first paragraph and part of the third paragraph are selected, along with all of the second paragraph. All three paragraphs will be affected by any paragraph formatting applied.

Applying Paragraph Formatting

Paragraph formatting is applied to selected paragraphs (**Figure 35**) or, if no paragraphs are selected, to the paragraph in which the insertion point is blinking (**Figure 36**).

Word offers several methods of applying paragraph formatting:

◆ The Formatting Palette (**Figure 38**) enables you to apply some paragraph formatting.

◆ Shortcut keys enable you to apply some paragraph formatting.

◆ The ruler enables you to apply indentation and tab formatting.

◆ The Paragraph dialog enables you to apply most kinds of paragraph formatting.

◆ The Bullets and Numbering dialog enables you to apply bullet and numbering formats.

✔ Tips

■ Paragraph formatting applies to the entire paragraph, even if only part of the paragraph is selected (**Figure 37**).

■ A *paragraph* is the text that appears between paragraph marks. You can see paragraph marks when you display Nonprinting characters (**Figures 35 through 37**). Nonprinting characters are discussed in **Chapter 2**.

■ When you press Return, the paragraph formatting of the current paragraph is carried forward to the new paragraph.

■ Selecting paragraphs is explained in **Chapter 2**.

To apply paragraph formatting with the Formatting Palette

Set options in the Formatting Palette (**Figure 38**) to apply formatting to selected paragraphs as desired:

◆ To set horizontal alignment, click Align Left, Center, Align Right, or Justify.

◆ To set line spacing, click Single Space, 1.5 Space, or Double Space.

◆ To set orientation, click one of the Change Text Direction buttons.

◆ To set paragraph spacing, enter a value (in points) in the Before and After boxes.

◆ To set indentation, enter a value (in inches) in the Left, Right, and First boxes.

◆ To enable automatic bullets or numbering, click Bullets or Numbering. If you enable bullets, you can choose an option from the Bullet Style menu beneath the Bullets button to choose a style of bullets. If you enable numbering, you can enter a starting value in the Start box.

To apply paragraph formatting with shortcut keys

Press the shortcut key combination (**Table 2**) for the formatting that you want to apply.

✔ Tip

■ The Reset Paragraph shortcut key (⌃ ⌘ Option Q) clears all paragraph formatting applied to a selection.

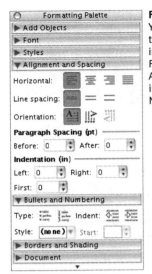

Figure 38
You can apply formatting with options in two areas of the Formatting Palette: Alignment and Spacing and Bullets and Numbering.

Table 2

Shortcut Keys for Paragraph Formatting	
Formatting	Keystroke
Align left	⌃ ⌘ L
Center	⌃ ⌘ E
Align right	⌃ ⌘ R
Justify	⌃ ⌘ J
Indent	Control Shift M
Unindent	⌃ ⌘ Shift M
Hanging indent	⌃ ⌘ T
Unhang indent	⌃ ⌘ Shift T
Single line space	⌃ ⌘ 1
1.5 line space	⌃ ⌘ 5
Double line space	⌃ ⌘ 2
Open/Close Up Paragraph	⌃ ⌘ 0 (zero)
Reset Paragraph	⌃ ⌘ Option Q

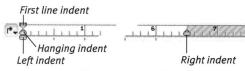

First line indent

Hanging indent

Left indent

Right indent

Figure 39 Indent markers on the ruler.

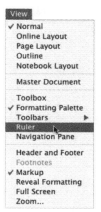

Figure 40
To display the ruler, choose Ruler from the View menu.

To set indentation with the ruler

Drag the indent markers (**Figure 39**) to set indentation as desired:

◆ **First Line Indent** sets the left boundary for the first line of a paragraph.

◆ **Hanging Indent** sets the left boundary for all lines of a paragraph other than the first line. (Dragging this marker also moves the Left Indent marker.)

◆ **Left Indent** sets the left boundary for all lines of a paragraph. (Dragging this marker also moves the First Line Indent and Hanging Indent markers.)

◆ **Right Indent** sets the right boundary for all lines of a paragraph.

✔ Tips

■ If the ruler is not showing, choose View > Ruler (**Figure 40**) to display it.

■ Dragging the First Line Indent marker to the right creates a standard indent.

■ Dragging the Hanging Indent marker to the right creates a hanging indent.

SETTING INDENTATION WITH THE RULER

To apply paragraph formatting with the Paragraph dialog

1. Choose Format > Paragraph (**Figure 25**) to display the Paragraph dialog.

2. Click the Indents and Spacing button to display its options (**Figure 41**). Then set options as desired:

   ▲ **Alignment** (**Figure 42**) sets paragraph alignment.

   ▲ **Outline Level** applies a style corresponding to one of Word's outline levels. (Styles are covered in **Chapter 4**; outlines are covered in detail in **Chapter 12**.)

   ▲ **Left** sets the left indentation. Enter a measurement in inches.

   ▲ **Right** sets the right indentation. Enter a measurement in inches.

   ▲ **Special** (**Figure 43**) applies First line or Hanging indentation. If you choose an option other than (none), you can enter a value (in inches) in the box beside the menu to set the indentation spacing.

   ▲ **Before** sets the amount of space before the paragraph. Enter a measurement in points.

   ▲ **After** sets the amount of space after the paragraph. Enter a measurement in points.

   ▲ **Line spacing** (**Figure 44**) sets the spacing between lines in the paragraph. If you choose At least, Exactly, or Multiple, enter a value in inches in the box beside the menu.

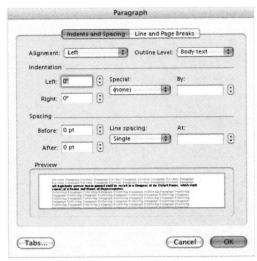

Figure 41 The Indents and Spacing options of the Paragraph dialog.

Figure 42
Use the Alignment menu to set paragraph alignment.

Figure 43
Use the Special menu to apply first line or hanging indentation.

Figure 44
Use the Line spacing menu in the Paragraph dialog to set line spacing for the paragraph.

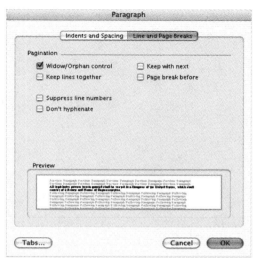

Figure 45 The Line and Page Breaks options of the Paragraph dialog.

3. Click the Line and Page Breaks button to display its options (**Figure 45**). Then set options as desired:

   ▲ **Widow/Orphan control** prevents a page break from occurring right after the first line in a paragraph or right before the last line in a paragraph.

   ▲ **Keep lines together** prevents a page break from occurring within the selected paragraph, thus keeping all lines of the paragraph together on the same page.

   ▲ **Keep with next** prevents a page break from occurring between the selected paragraph and the next paragraph.

   ▲ **Page break before** puts a page break before the selected paragraph.

   ▲ **Suppress line numbers** excludes the paragraph from line numbering when line numbering is enabled.

   ▲ **Don't hyphenate** excludes the paragraph from hyphenation when the document is manually or automatically hyphenated.

4. Click OK to save your settings and dismiss the Paragraph dialog.

✔ Tips

■ The Preview area of the Paragraph dialog illustrates what text will look like with formatting applied.

■ I tell you more about page formatting, including how to insert manual page breaks, in **Chapter 5**.

USING THE PARAGRAPH DIALOG

To apply bulleted list formatting with the Bullets and Numbering dialog

1. Choose Format > Bullets and Numbering (**Figure 25**).

2. In the Bullets and Numbering dialog that appears, click the Bulleted button to display its options (**Figure 46**).

3. Click the box that displays the type of bullet character that you want.

4. Click OK.

✔ Tips

- Clicking the Bullets button on the Formatting Palette applies the last style of bullets you set in the Bullets and Numbering dialog (**Figure 46**) or Customize bulleted list dialog (**Figure 47**).

- To further customize a bullet list, after step 3 above, click the Customize button in the Bullets and Numbering dialog (**Figure 46**). Set options in the Customize bulleted list dialog that appears (**Figure 47**), and click OK.

- You can also use pictures for bullets. Click the Picture button in the Customize bulleted list dialog (**Figure 47**). Then select one of the pictures in the Choose a Picture dialog that appears (**Figure 48**) and click Insert. Word automatically uses the same picture for all bullets in the list.

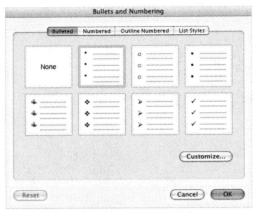

Figure 46 The Bulleted options of the Bullets and Numbering dialog.

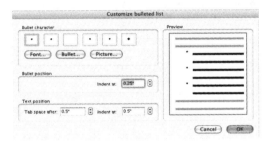

Figure 47 The Customize bulleted list dialog.

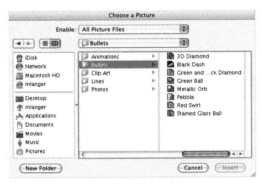

Figure 48 Use the Choose a Picture dialog to select a picture to use for all bullets in a bulleted list.

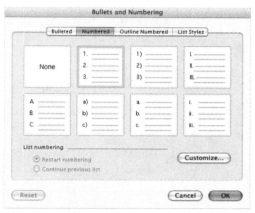

Figure 49 The Numbered options of the Bullets and Numbering dialog.

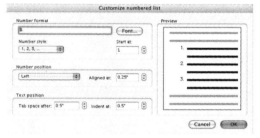

Figure 50 The Customize numbered list dialog.

To apply numbered list formatting with the Bullets and Numbering dialog

1. Choose Format > Bullets and Numbering (**Figure 25**).

2. In the Bullets and Numbering dialog that appears, click the Numbered button to display its options (**Figure 49**).

3. Click the box that displays the numbering format that you want.

4. Click OK.

✔ Tips

■ Clicking the Numbering button on the Formatting Palette applies the last style of numbering you set in the Bullets and Numbering dialog (**Figure 49**) or Customize numbered list dialog (**Figure 50**).

■ To further customize a numbered list, after step 3 above, click the Customize button in the Bullets and Numbering dialog (**Figure 49**). Set options in the Customize numbered list dialog that appears (**Figure 50**), and click OK.

■ If your document already includes a numbered list, you can use the radio buttons at the bottom of the Numbered options of the Bullets and Numbering dialog (**Figure 49**) to determine whether Word should restart numbering or continue the previous list's numbering. These options are only available if the document contains multiple numbered lists.

■ I tell you about the Outline Numbered options of the Bullets and Numbering dialog in my discussion of Word's outlining feature in **Chapter 12**.

USING THE BULLETS & NUMBERING DIALOG

To remove bulleted or numbered list formatting

1. Choose Format > Bullets and Numbering (**Figure 25**).

2. In the Bullets and Numbering dialog (**Figure 46** or **49**), click the None box.

3. Click OK.

Or

To remove bulleted list formatting from a selected paragraph, click the Bullets button on the Formatting Palette (**Figure 38**).

Or

To remove numbered list formatting from a selected paragraph, click the Numbering button on the Formatting Palette (**Figure 38**).

Tab marker menu

Figure 51 Default tab stops appear as tiny gray lines on the ruler.

Figure 52 Word's five tab stops in action. In order, they are: right, bar, left, center, decimal. Examine the ruler to see how they're set.

Figure 53 Word's tab leader options: none, dotted, dashed, and underscore.

Figure 54 Displaying nonprinting characters enables you to see the tab characters.

Tabs

Tab stops determine the horizontal position of the insertion point when you press [Tab].

By default, a blank document includes tab stops every half inch. They appear as tiny gray marks on the bottom of the ruler (**Figure 51**). You can use the ruler or Tabs dialog to set tabs that override the defaults.

Word supports five kinds of tabs (**Figure 52**):

◆ **Left tab** aligns tabbed text to the left against the tab stop.

◆ **Center tab** centers tabbed text beneath the tab stop.

◆ **Right tab** aligns tabbed text to the right against the tab stop.

◆ **Decimal tab** aligns the decimal point (or period) of tabbed numbers beneath the tab stop. When used with text, a decimal tab works just like a right tab.

◆ **Bar tab** is a vertical line that appears beneath the tab stop.

Word also supports four types of *tab leaders* (**Figure 53**)—characters that appear in the space otherwise left by a tab: none, periods, dashes, and underscores.

✔ Tips

■ Tabs are a type of paragraph formatting; they apply to an entire paragraph.

■ Tabs are often used to create simple tables.

■ When trying to align text in a simple table, use tabs instead of spaces. Tabs always align to tab stops. Text positioned with space characters may not align properly due to the size and spacing of characters in a font.

■ It's a good idea to display nonprinting characters when working with tabs (**Figure 54**) so you can distinguish tabs from spaces. Nonprinting characters are discussed in **Chapter 2**.

TABS

To set tab stops with the ruler

1. Use the tab marker menu at the far-left end of the ruler (**Figure 55**) to choose the type of tab stop that you want to set.

2. Click on the ruler where you want to position the tab stop to set it there.

3. Repeat steps 1 and 2 until all desired tab stops have been set (**Figure 52**).

✔ Tip

■ When you set a tab stop, all default tab stops to its left disappear (**Figures 52 and 54**).

To move a tab stop with the ruler

1. Position the mouse pointer on the tab stop that you want to move.

2. Press the mouse button and drag the tab stop to its new position. When you release the mouse button, the tab stop is moved.

✔ Tip

■ Don't click on the ruler anywhere except on the tab stop that you want to move. Doing so will set another tab stop.

To remove a tab stop from the ruler

1. Position the mouse pointer on the tab stop that you want to remove.

2. Press the mouse button and drag the tab stop down into the document. Then you release the mouse button, the tab stop disappears.

Figure 55
Use the tab stop menu, which is new in Word 2004, to choose the type of tab you want to set.

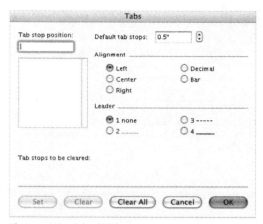

Figure 56 The Tabs dialog.

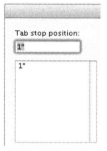

Figure 57 When you add a tab, it appears in the list in the Tabs dialog.

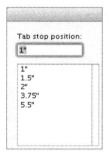

Figure 58 The tab stop settings for **Figure 52**.

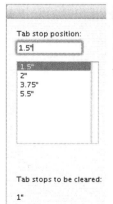

Figure 59 When you click Clear to remove a tab stop, it is removed from the tab list.

To open the Tabs dialog

Use one of the following techniques:

◆ Choose Format > Tabs (**Figure 25**).

◆ Click the Tabs button in the Paragraph dialog (**Figures 41** and **45**).

◆ Choose Tabs from the tab stop menu on the ruler (**Figure 55**).

To set tab stops with the Tabs dialog

1. Open the Tabs dialog (**Figure 56**).

2. In the Alignment area, select the type of tab that you want.

3. In the Leader area, select the type of leader that you want the tab stop to have.

4. Enter a ruler measurement in the Tab stop position box.

5. Click Set. The tab stop is added to the tab list (**Figure 57**).

6. Repeat steps 2 through 5 for each tab stop that you want to set (**Figure 58**).

7. Click OK.

To remove tab stops with the Tabs dialog

1. In the Tabs dialog, select the tab stop that you want to remove.

2. Click Clear. The tab stop is removed from the list and added to the list of Tab stops to be cleared in the dialog (**Figure 59**).

3. Repeat steps 1 and 2 for each tab stop that you want to remove.

4. Click OK.

✔ Tip

■ To remove all tab stops, click the Clear All button (**Figure 56**) and then click OK.

SETTING TAB STOPS WITH THE TABS DIALOG

To change the default tab stops

1. In the Tabs dialog (**Figure 56**), enter a new value in the Default tab stops box.

2. Click OK.

✔ Tip

■ Remember, tab stops that you set manually on the ruler or with the Tabs dialog override default tab stops to their left.

To create a simple table with tab stops

1. Position the insertion point in the paragraph in which you set tabs (**Figure 60**).

2. To type at a tab stop, press (Tab), then type (**Figure 61**).

3. Repeat step 2 to type at each tab stop.

4. Press (Return) or (Shift)(Return) to end the paragraph or line and begin a new one. The tab stops in the paragraph are carried forward (**Figure 62**).

5. Repeat steps 2 through 4 to finish typing your table (**Figure 54**).

✔ Tips

■ You can move tabs at any time—even after you have begun using them. Be sure to select all of the paragraphs that utilize the tab stops before you move them. Otherwise, you may only adjust tabs for part of the table.

■ Another way to create tables is with Word's table feature, which is far more flexible than using tab stops. I tell you about it in **Chapter 8**.

Figure 60 Position the insertion point in the paragraph for which you have set tab stops.

Figure 61 Press (Tab) to type at the first tab stop, then type. In this example, text is typed at a right-aligned tab stop.

Figure 62 When you are finished typing a line, press (Return) to start a new paragraph with the same tab stops.

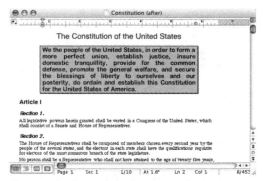

Figure 63 Borders and shading can emphasize text.

Borders & Shading

Borders and shading are two separate features that can work together to emphasize text:

◆ **Borders** enables you to place lines above, below, to the left, or to the right of selected characters or paragraphs (**Figure 63**).

◆ **Shading** enables you to add color or shades of gray to selected characters or paragraphs (**Figure 63**).

✔ Tips

■ How borders or shading are applied depends on how text is selected:

▲ To apply borders or shading to characters, select the characters.

▲ To apply borders or shading to a paragraph, click in the paragraph or select the entire paragraph.

▲ To apply borders or shading to multiple paragraphs, select the paragraphs.

■ When applying borders to selected text characters (as opposed to selected paragraphs), you must place a border around each side, creating a box around the text.

■ I tell you about page borders, which can be applied to entire pages, in **Chapter 5**.

To apply text borders with the Formatting Palette

1. Select the text to which you want to apply borders.

2. If necessary, display the Borders and Shading options in the Formatting Palette (**Figure 64**).

3. Choose an option from the Border Type pop-up menu (**Figure 65**) to set the type of border.

4. Choose an option from the Line Style pop-up menu (**Figure 66**) to set the line style for the border lines.

5. Choose an option from the Border Color pop-up menu (**Figure 67**) to set the color for the border lines.

6. Choose an option from the Line Weight pop-up menu (**Figure 68**) to set the thickness of the border lines.

✔ Tips

- You can apply more than one border to selected paragraphs. For example, if you want a top and bottom border, choose the top border option and then choose the bottom border option. Both are applied.

- Some border options apply more than one border. For example, the outside border option (top left button) applies the outside border as well as the top, bottom, left, and right borders.

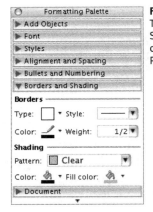

Figure 64
The Borders and Shading options of the Formatting Palette.

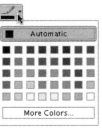

Figure 65 The Border Type pop-up menu.

Figure 66
The Line Style pop-up menu.

Figure 67 The Border Color pop-up menu.

Figure 68 The Line Weight pop-up menu.

APPLYING TEXT BORDERS

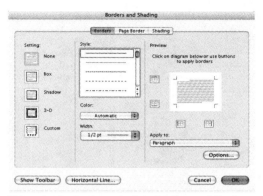

Figure 69 The Borders tab of the Borders and Shading dialog.

Figure 70 If necessary, use the Apply to menu in the Borders and Shading dialog to specify what the border or shading settings should apply to.

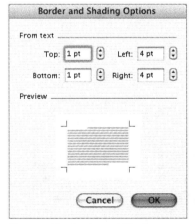

Figure 71 The Border and Shading Options dialog.

To apply text borders with the Borders and Shading dialog

1. Select the text you want to apply borders to.

2. Choose Format > Borders and Shading (**Figure 25**).

3. Click the Borders button in the Borders and Shading dialog that appears to display its options (**Figure 69**).

4. Click a Setting icon to select the type of border. All options except None and Custom place borders around each side of the selected text.

5. Click a style in the Style list box to select a line style.

6. Choose a line color from the Color pop-up menu. (This menu is similar to the one in **Figure 67**.) Automatic applies the color that is specified in the paragraph style applied to the text.

7. Choose a line thickness from the Width pop-up menu. (This menu is similar to the one in **Figure 68**.)

8. If necessary, choose an option from the Apply to pop-up menu (**Figure 70**). The Preview area changes accordingly.

9. To apply custom borders, click the buttons in the Preview area to add or remove lines using the settings in the dialog.

10. When the Preview area illustrates the border you want to apply, click OK.

✔ Tips

- You can repeat steps 5 through 7 and 9 to customize each line of a custom border.

- You can further customize a paragraph border by clicking the Options button to display the Border and Shading Options dialog (**Figure 71**). Set options and click OK.

To remove text borders

1. Select the text from which you want to remove borders.

2. In the Formatting Palette, choose No Border from the Border Type pop-up menu (**Figure 72**).

Or

1. Select the text from which you want to remove borders.

2. Choose Format > Borders and Shading (**Figure 25**) and click the Borders button in the Borders and Shading dialog that appears (**Figure 69**).

3. Click the None icon.

4. Click OK.

To apply shading with the Formatting Palette

1. Select the text to which you want to apply shading.

2. If necessary, display the Borders and Shading options in the Formatting Palette (**Figure 64**).

3. Choose an option from the Shading pop-up menu (**Figure 73**) to set the percent or pattern for the shading.

4. Choose an option from the Pattern Color pop-up menu (**Figure 74**) to set the foreground color for the shading.

5. Choose an option from the Shading Color pop-up menu (**Figure 75**) to set the background color for the shading.

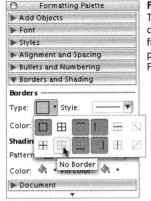

Figure 72
To remove borders, choose No Borders from the Border Type pop-up menu in the Formatting Palette.

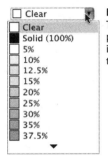

Figure 73
The Shading pop-up menu in the Formatting Palette.

Figure 74 Pattern Color sets the foreground color of the pattern.

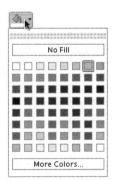

Figure 75 Shading Color sets the background color of the pattern.

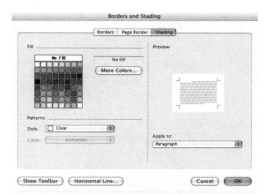

Figure 76 The Shading options of the Borders and Shading dialog.

Figure 77
The Colors dialog enables you to use a standard Mac OS color picker to choose a custom color.

To apply shading with the Borders and Shading dialog

1. Select the text you want to apply shading to.

2. Choose Format > Borders and Shading (**Figure 25**).

3. Click the Shading tab in the Borders and Shading dialog to display its options (**Figure 76**).

4. Click a Fill color or shade to select it. (This becomes a background color, if you choose a pattern in step 5.)

5. To create a pattern, choose an option from the Style drop-down list (similar to **Figure 73**) and then choose a foreground color from the Color pop-up menu (similar to **Figure 67**).

6. If necessary, choose an option from the Apply to drop-down list (**Figure 70**). The Preview area changes accordingly.

7. When the Preview area shows the shading that you want to apply, click OK.

✔ Tips

■ Use text shading with care. If the pattern is too dark or "busy," the shaded area may be impossible to read!

■ Clicking the More Colors button in the Borders and Shading dialog displays the Colors dialog (**Figure 77**), which you can use to select different colors.

APPLYING SHADING

To remove shading

1. Select the text from which you want to remove shading.

2. In the Formatting Palette, choose Clear from the Shading pop-up menu (**Figure 73**).

Or

1. Select the text from which you want to remove shading.

2. Choose Format > Borders and Shading (**Figure 25**) and click the Shading button in the Borders and Shading dialog that appears (**Figure 76**).

3. Click the No Fill button.

4. Click OK.

Drop Caps

A drop cap is an enlarged and/or repositioned character at the beginning of a
paragraph. Word supports two types of
drop caps (**Figure 78**):

◆ **Dropped** enlarges the character and
wraps the rest of the text in the paragraph
around it.

◆ **In Margin** enlarges the character and
moves it into the margin.

✔ Tips

■ Word creates drop caps using frames,
a feature that enables you to precisely
position text on a page or in relation to
a paragraph. Frames is an advanced
feature of Word that is beyond the scope
of this book.

■ To see drop caps, you must be in Print
Layout view or Print Preview. A drop cap
appears as an enlarged character in its own
paragraph in Normal view (**Figure 79**).

■ A drop cap can consist of more than just
the first letter of a paragraph (**Figure 80**).

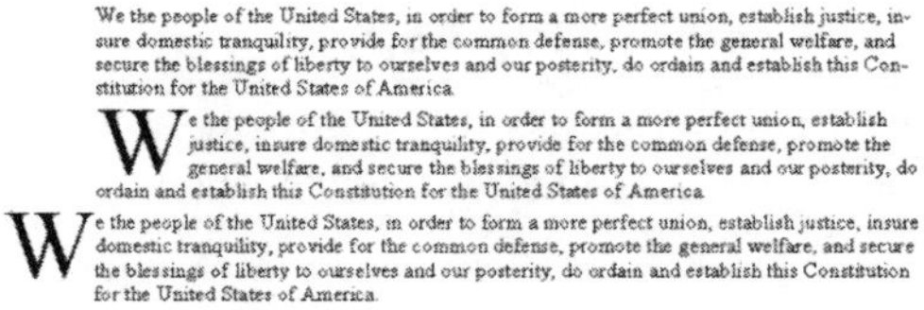

We the people of the United States, in order to form a more perfect union, establish justice, insure domestic tranquility, provide for the common defense, promote the general welfare, and
secure the blessings of liberty to ourselves and our posterity, do ordain and establish this Constitution for the United States of America.

We the people of the United States, in order to form a more perfect union, establish
justice, insure domestic tranquility, provide for the common defense, promote the
general welfare, and secure the blessings of liberty to ourselves and our posterity, do
ordain and establish this Constitution for the United States of America.

We the people of the United States, in order to form a more perfect union, establish justice, insure
domestic tranquility, provide for the common defense, promote the general welfare, and secure
the blessings of liberty to ourselves and our posterity, do ordain and establish this Constitution
for the United States of America.

Figure 78 The same paragraph three ways: without a
drop cap (top), with a drop cap (middle), and with an in
margin drop cap (bottom).

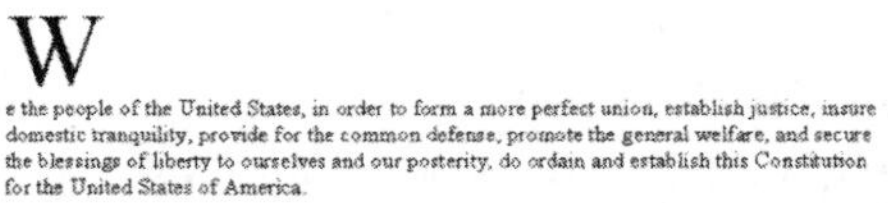

W

e the people of the United States, in order to form a more perfect union, establish justice, insure
domestic tranquility, provide for the common defense, promote the general welfare, and secure
the blessings of liberty to ourselves and our posterity, do ordain and establish this Constitution
for the United States of America.

Figure 79 A paragraph with a drop cap when viewed
in Normal view.

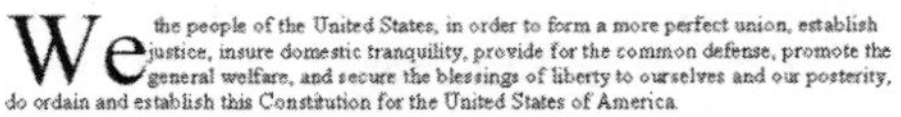

We the people of the United States, in order to form a more perfect union, establish
justice, insure domestic tranquility, provide for the common defense, promote the
general welfare, and secure the blessings of liberty to ourselves and our posterity,
do ordain and establish this Constitution for the United States of America.

Figure 80 A drop cap can consist of more than just one
character.

To create a drop cap

1. Position the insertion point anywhere in the paragraph for which you want to create a drop cap.

2. Choose Format > Drop Cap (**Figure 25**).

3. In the Drop Cap dialog that appears (**Figure 81**), click the icon for the type of drop cap that you want to create.

4. Choose a font for the drop cap from the Font drop-down list.

5. Enter the number of lines for the size of the drop cap character in the Lines to drop box.

6. Enter a value for the amount of space between the drop cap character and the rest of the text in the paragraph in the Distance from text box.

7. Click OK.

✔ Tip

■ To create a drop cap with more than one character (**Figure 80**), select the characters that you want to appear as drop caps, then follow steps 2 through 7 above. You cannot select more than one word to include in drop caps.

To remove a drop cap

Follow steps 1 and 2 above, select the icon for None in step 3, and click OK.

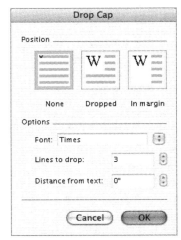

Figure 81 Use the Drop Cap dialog to enter settings for a drop cap.

Advanced Text Formatting

Advanced Text Formatting Techniques

Microsoft Word offers a number of formatting techniques that go beyond the basics discussed in **Chapter 3**:

- ◆ **Reveal Formatting** enables you to get information about the formatting applied to selected text.

- ◆ **Format Painter** enables you to copy font and paragraph formats from one selection to another.

- ◆ **Styles** enables you to define and apply named sets of formatting options for individual characters or paragraphs.

- ◆ **Themes** and the **Style Gallery** enable you to apply predefined sets of styles to a document.

- ◆ **AutoFormat** instructs Word to automatically format text you type.

This chapter covers these advanced formatting techniques and shows you how they can help you format your documents more quickly, effectively, or consistently.

✔ Tip

- ■ It's a good idea to have a solid understanding of the concepts covered in **Chapter 3** before you read this chapter.

Revealing Formatting

Word offers an easy way to see what kind of formatting is applied to text: the Reveal Formatting command (**Figure 1**). This command displays a window with formatting details for the text you click (**Figures** 3 and 4).

To reveal formatting

1. Choose View > Reveal Formatting (**Figure 1**). The mouse pointer turns into the Reveal Formatting pointer (**Figure 2**).

2. To learn about the formatting applied to text, click on the text (**Figures** 3 and 4).

3. Repeat step 2 for any text for which you want to reveal formatting.

4. When you are finished revealing formatting, press [Esc]. The mouse pointer turns back into a regular pointer.

Figure 1
The View menu.

Figure 2
The Reveal Formatting pointer.

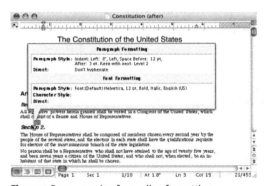

Figure 3 One example of revealing formatting.

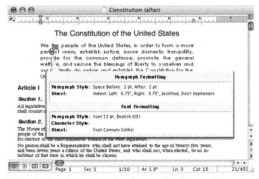

Figure 4 Another example of revealing formatting.

REVEALING FORMATTING

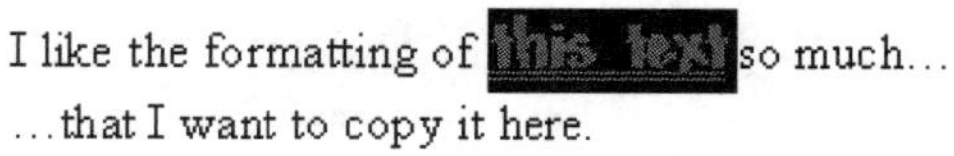

I like the formatting of ▮▮▮▮▮▮▮ so much...

...that I want to copy it here.

Figure 5 Select the text with the formatting you want to copy.

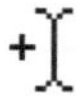

+⌓ **Figure 6** When you click the Format Painter button, the mouse pointer turns into a Format Painter pointer.

I like the formatting of this text so much...

...that I want to copy it here⌓

Figure 7 Use the Format Painter pointer to select the text you want to apply the formatting to.

I like the formatting of this text so much...

...that I want to copy it here.

Figure 8 When you release the mouse button, the formatting is applied.

The Format Painter

The Format Painter enables you to copy the font or paragraph formatting of selected text and apply it to other text. This can save time and effort when applying the same formatting in multiple places throughout a document.

✔ Tip

■ Another way to apply the same formatting in various places throughout a document is with styles. I begin my discussion of Word's styles feature on the next page.

To use the Format Painter

1. Select the text whose formatting you want to copy (**Figure 5**).

2. Click the Format Painter button on the Standard toolbar. The Format Painter button becomes selected and the mouse pointer turns into an I-beam pointer with a plus sign beside it (**Figure 6**).

3. Use the mouse pointer to select the text to which you want to copy the formatting (**Figure 7**). When you release the mouse button, the formatting is applied (**Figure 8**) and the mouse pointer returns to normal.

✔ Tips

■ To copy paragraph formatting, be sure to select the entire paragraph in step 1, including the paragraph formatting mark (¶) at the end of the paragraph. I tell you about formatting marks in **Chapter 2**.

■ To copy the same formatting to more than one selection, double-click the Format Painter button. The mouse pointer remains a Format Painter pointer (**Figure 6**) until you press (Esc) or click the Format Painter button again.

Styles

Word's styles feature enables you to define and apply sets of paragraph and/or font formatting to text throughout a document. This offers two main benefits over applying formatting using the basic techniques covered so far:

◆ **Consistency.** All text with a particular style applied will have the same formatting (**Figure 9**)—unless additional formatting has also been applied.

◆ **Flexibility.** Changing a style's definition is relatively easy. Once changed, the change automatically applies to all text formatted with that style (**Figure 10**).

Word supports four kinds of styles:

◆ **Character styles** affect the formatting of text characters.

◆ **Paragraph styles** affect the formatting of entire paragraphs. The default paragraph style is called *Normal*.

◆ **Table styles** affect the formatting of tables.

◆ **List styles** affect the formatting of bulleted and numbered lists.

✔ Tips

■ Like font or paragraph formatting, you can apply styles as you type or to text that has already been typed. Check **Chapter 3** for details.

■ Styles are sometimes known as *style sheets*.

■ Word includes a number of predefined styles that you can apply to text.

■ Word's outline feature automatically applies predefined Heading styles as you create an outline. You can learn more about outlines in **Chapter 12**.

■ Tables are covered in **Chapter 8**.

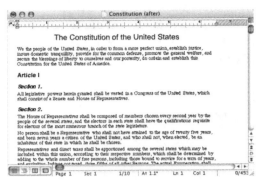

Figure 9 In this example, styles are applied to all text for consistent formatting.

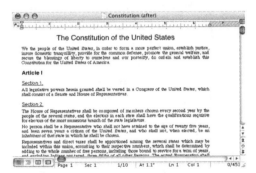

Figure 10 When two of the styles are modified, the formatting of text with those styles applied changes automatically. In this example, Normal style's paragraph formatting was changed from align left to justified and Heading 2 style's font formatting was changed from bold italic to regular with underline.

STYLES

Name of style currently applied to selected text.

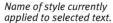

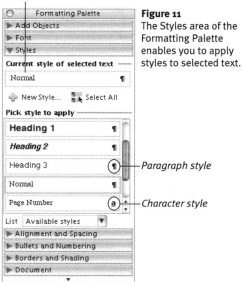

Figure 11
The Styles area of the Formatting Palette enables you to apply styles to selected text.

—Paragraph style

—Character style

Figure 12
Choose All styles from the List drop-down list to see more styles.

Figure 13
When you point to a style name, a menu arrow and a description of the style appear.

To apply a style

1. If necessary, display the Styles area in the Formatting Palette (**Figure 11**).

2. Select one of the styles in the Pick style to apply scrolling list.

✔ Tips

- By default, the Pick style to apply scrolling list (**Figure 11**) displays only some of the styles available to apply in the document. You can choose All styles from the List drop-down list in the bottom of the Styles area (**Figure 12**) to display all styles used in the document as well as all styles pre-programmed into Word.

- The Pick style to apply scrolling list displays each style name using the formatting of that style (**Figure 11**).

- You can distinguish between character styles and paragraph styles in the Pick style to apply scolling list by the symbol to the right of the style name (**Figure 11**).

- Selecting the Clear Formatting option at the top of the Pick style to apply scrolling list (**Figure 13**) removes all applied formatting from selected text, leaving just the formatting that's part of the applied style.

- When you point to the name of a style in the Pick style to apply scrolling list, two things happen (**Figure 13**):
  - ▲ A menu arrow appears. Clicking the arrow displays a menu (**Figure 14**).
  - ▲ A box with a description of the style appears.

To modify a style

1. If necessary, display the Styles area in the Formatting Palette (**Figure 11**).

2. Point to the name of the style you want to modify, and then choose Modify style from its menu (**Figure 14**). The Modify Style dialog appears (**Figure 15**).

3. To change the style's name, enter a new name in the Name box.

4. To change basic style formatting options, use the menus and buttons in the Formatting area.

5. To change other formatting options, choose a type of formatting from the dialog's Format menu (**Figure 16**). Each option displays the appropriate formatting dialog. Make changes as desired in the dialog that appears and click OK.

6. Repeat step 5 as necessary to make all desired formatting changes.

7. To add the revised style to the template on which the document is based, turn on the Add to template check box.

8. To instruct Word to automatically update the style's definition whenever you apply manual formatting to text with the style applied, turn on the Automatically update check box.

9. Click OK.

✔ Tip

- The options that appear in the Modify Style dialog vary depending on the type of style you are modifying.

Figure 14
Clicking the arrow beside a style's name displays a menu of options for that style.

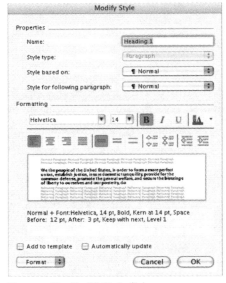

Figure 15 The Modify Style dialog.

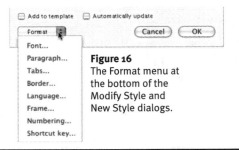

Figure 16
The Format menu at the bottom of the Modify Style and New Style dialogs.

MODIFYING STYLES

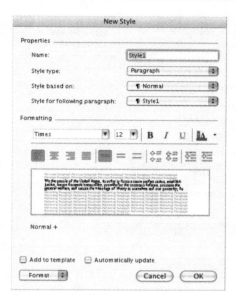

Figure 17 The New Style dialog when creating a paragraph style. The options in this dialog vary depending on the type of style you are creating.

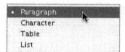

Figure 18
The Style type pop-up menu.

To create a new style

1. If necessary, display the Styles area in the Formatting Palette (**Figure 11**).

2. Click the New Style button to display the New Style dialog (**Figure 17**).

3. Enter a name for the style in the Name box.

4. Choose the type of style that you want to create from the Style type pop-up menu (**Figure 18**).

5. To base the style on an existing style, choose the style from the Style based on pop-up menu. This menu includes all styles of the type you selected in step 4 that are included in the template on which the document is based.

6. If you chose Paragraph in step 4, choose a style from the Style for following paragraph drop-down list. This tells Word what style to apply to the next paragraph when you press Return.

7. To set basic style formatting options, use the menus and buttons in the Formatting area.

8. To set other formatting options, choose a type of formatting from the dialog's Format menu (**Figure 16**). Each option displays the appropriate formatting dialog. Set options as desired in the dialog that appears and click OK.

9. Repeat step 8 as necessary to set all desired formatting options.

10. To add the new style to the template on which the document is based, turn on the Add to template check box.

CREATING NEW STYLES

Continued on next page...

Continued from previous page.

---

11. If you chose Paragraph in step 4, to instruct Word to automatically update the style whenever you apply manual formatting to text with the style applied, turn on the Automatically update check box.

12. Click OK.

✔ Tips

■ The options that appear in the New Style dialog vary depending on the type of style you are creating.

■ I tell you more about list formatting in **Chapter 2** and about tables in **Chapter 8**.

To delete a style

1. If necessary, display the Styles area in the Formatting Palette (**Figure 11**).

2. Point to the name of the style you want to delete, and then choose Delete from its menu (**Figure 19**).

3. In the confirmation dialog that appears (**Figure 20**), click Yes.

✔ Tips

■ When you delete a paragraph style, the default style (Normal) is applied to any text to which the deleted style was applied.

■ Not all styles can be deleted. For example, you cannot delete the Normal style or the Heading styles that are predefined by Word. That's why the Delete command appears gray in **Figure 14**.

Figure 19
Choose Delete from a style's menu to delete that style.

Figure 20 Word confirms that you want to delete a style.

Templates & Styles

As discussed in **Chapter 2**, each Word document is based on a template. The most commonly used template is Normal—the one that's used when you create a Blank new document—but Word comes with a variety of other templates and you can create your own.

Templates can include styles, as well as other Word features. The styles that are part of a template make it possible to create consistently formatted documents. Simply create the document based on the template and apply its styles as you build the document.

But what if you didn't create your document based on the template with the styles you want to use? That's where the Style Gallery, Templates and Add-ins, and Organizer dialogs can help.

Word's Style Gallery enables you to copy styles from another template to the currently open document. You can then apply those styles to the document. If the document has already been formatted using the original template's styles, it will be automatically reformatted using the style definitions of any copied styles that have the same style name as originally applied styles.

The Templates and Add-ins dialog goes a step further by enabling you to attach a different template to an existing file. This replaces all of the original template's elements—which can also include custom AutoText entries, toolbars, and macros—with the newly applied template's elements.

Finally, the Organizer dialog enables you to copy specific template elements, such as styles, from one document to another. This is particularly handy if the styles you'd like to use have already been created and saved in another Word document.

To use the Style Gallery

1. Choose Format > Theme (**Figure 21**).

2. In the Theme dialog that appears, click the Style Gallery button to display the Style Gallery dialog (**Figure 22**).

3. Click the name of a template in the Template list to select it. An example of the document with the template's styles applied appears in the Preview area of the dialog (**Figure 23**).

4. To copy and apply the styles of a selected template to the current document, click OK.

   or

   To close the Style Gallery dialog without copying styles, click Cancel.

✔ Tips

- I tell you about Word's Themes feature in **Chapter 18**.

- If the template you select in step 3 has not yet been installed, a message will appear at the top of the Preview area. Click OK to install the template and apply it to your document. You cannot preview a template or its styles unless it has been installed.

- You can use the Preview option buttons at the bottom of the Style Gallery dialog to change the display within the dialog:

   ▲ **Document** (**Figure 23**) shows the current document with the template's styles applied.

   ▲ **Example** shows an example document with the template's styles applied.

   ▲ **Style samples** shows each of the documents' styles with the style's formatting applied.

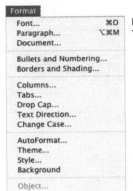

Figure 21
The Format menu.

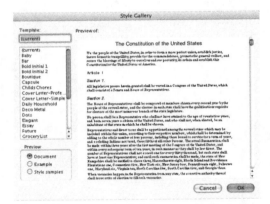

Figure 22 The Style Gallery dialog starts by displaying the document with its current styles.

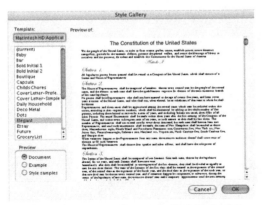

Figure 23 Clicking a template name displays the document with that template's styles applied.

Figure 24
Word's Tools menu.

To attach a template to a document with the Templates & Add-Ins dialog

1. Choose Tools > Templates and Add-Ins (**Figure 24**) to display the Templates and Add-ins dialog (**Figure 25**).

2. To update the current document's styles with styles from the template you are attaching, turn on the Automatically update document styles check box.

3. Click the Attach button.

4. Use the Choose a File dialog that appears (**Figure 26**) to locate, select, and open the template you want to attach to the document.

5. Back in the Templates and Add-ins dialog, click OK.

Figure 25
The Templates and Add-ins dialog.

✔ Tips

- You can attach any Word template to a Word document—not just one of the templates that came with Microsoft Word.

- When you attach a template to a document, you make all the styles stored in the template available for use in the document.

- Attaching a template to a document is a good way to get an existing document to use standard formatting stored in a template file, even if the template was not available when the document was originally created.

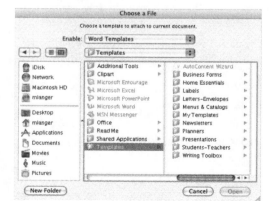

Figure 26 The Choose a File dialog.

ATTACHING TEMPLATES TO DOCUMENTS

To copy styles from one document to another with the Organizer

1. Choose Tools > Templates and Add-Ins (**Figure 24**) to display the Templates and Add-ins dialog (**Figure 25**).

2. Click the Organizer button to display the Organizer dialog.

3. If necessary, click the Styles button to display its options. As shown in **Figure 27**, the dialog shows the styles in the active document on the left and the styles in the attached template on the right.

4. To select a different document or template on either side of the dialog, use one or both of the following techniques:

   ▲ Choose a different document or template from the Styles available in pop-up menu.

   ▲ Click the Close File button to remove the document or template from the dialog, then click the Open File button that appears in its place (**Figure 28**) and use the Choose a File dialog that appears (**Figure 29**) to locate, select, and open the template or document you want.

   When you're finished, two different file names should appear at the top of the scrolling lists in the dialog. **Figure 30** shows an example.

5. Select the style you want to copy from one file to the other (**Figure 30**) and click the Copy button. The style is copied (**Figure 31**).

6. Repeat steps 4 and 5 for each style you want to copy.

7. Click Close to dismiss the Organizer dialog.

Figure 27 The Styles options of the Organizer dialog starts off by listing the styles in the active document and the template on which it is based.

Figure 28 When you click a Close File button, the contents of its scrolling list disappear and the button turns into an Open File button.

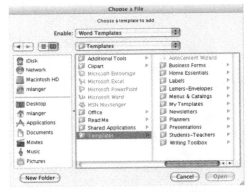

Figure 29 Use the Choose a File dialog to locate and open a template or Word document containing the styles you want to copy.

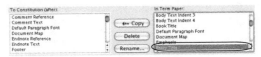

Figure 30 Select the style you want to copy.

Figure 31 Click Copy to copy it to the other document.

Figure 32
The Edit menu.

Reformatting with Find and Replace

The Find and Replace dialog, which I discuss in **Chapter 2**, offers yet another way to change the formatting of a document. Although this dialog is used primarily to find and replace document text, it can also be used to find and replace document formatting, whether the formatting is directly applied or applied with styles.

To change formatting with the Find and Replace dialog

Figure 33 The Replace options of the Find and Replace dialog, expanded to show all options.

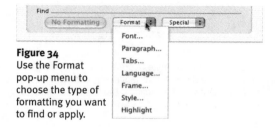

Figure 34
Use the Format pop-up menu to choose the type of formatting you want to find or apply.

1. Choose Edit > Replace (**Figure 32**) or press Shift ⌃ ⌘ H to display the Replace options of the Find and Replace dialog.

2. If necessary, click the triangle button to expand the dialog so it looks like **Figure 33**.

3. To change the formatting of specific text, enter the text in both the Find what and Replace with boxes.

   or

   To change the formatting of any text, make sure the Find what and Replace with boxes are empty.

4. Position the insertion point in the Find what box.

5. Use the Format pop-up menu (**Figure 34**) to select the type of formatting you want to find. The appropriate dialog appears. **Figure 35** shows an example of what the Find Font dialog might look like. Change settings as desired and click OK.

6. Repeat step 5 for each type of formatting that you expect to find. Remember, Word will find text with all the formatting settings you specify.

Continued on next page...

Continued from previous page.

7. Position the insertion point in the Replace with box.

8. Use the Format pop-up menu (**Figure 34**) to select the type of formatting you want to apply to found text. The appropriate dialog appears. Change settings as desired and click OK.

9. Repeat step 8 for each type of formatting that you want to apply to found text. Remember, Word will apply all of the formatting you specify. **Figure 36** shows an example of how the Find and Replace dialog might look when you're finished.

10. Use the Replace or Replace All buttons as discussed in **Chapter 2** to replace formatting occurrences, thus reformatting text.

✔ Tips

- As shown in **Figure 35**, formatting dialog boxes that are accessed from the Find and Replace dialog do not indicate any formatting settings—nothing is selected and check boxes have dashes in them, indicating that an option is neither selected nor deselected. Your settings in these dialogs should indicate the type of formatting you expect to find. For example, to find any text that was underlined, no matter what font, size, or other formatting option is applied, you'd select just the Underline style option you expect to find. Making changes for other options includes those options in your settings.

- If you're not familiar with the Find and Replace dialog, read about it in **Chapter 2** before following the instructions here.

- To clear formatting options, position the insertion point in the Find what or Replace with box and click the No Formatting button.

Figure 35 The Find Font dialog. When you first display this dialog, nothing is selected, indicating that Word will find any font formatting.

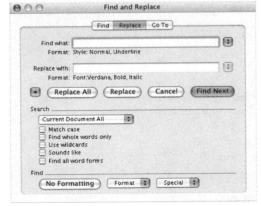

Figure 36 In this example, Word will find any text that's underlined and has the Normal paragraph style applied and replace it with the same text formatted with bold, italic, Verdana font.

REFORMATTING WITH FIND AND REPLACE

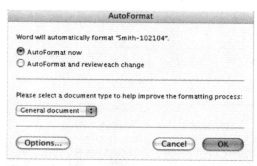

Figure 37 The AutoFormat dialog.

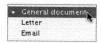

Figure 38 Use this pop-up menu to tell Word what kind of document it must format.

AutoFormat

Word's AutoFormat feature can automatically format a document either as you type or when the document is finished.

Word formats documents by applying appropriate styles to text based on how it is used in the document—for example, as titles, lists, headings, or body text. Word can also format Internet addresses as hyperlinks and replace typed symbols (such as --) with actual symbols (such as —).

✔ Tips

- AutoFormat As You Type is automatically turned on when you first use Word.

- I tell you more about Internet addresses and hyperlinks in **Chapter 18** and about symbols in **Chapter 9**.

To use AutoFormat on a completed document

1. Choose Format > AutoFormat (**Figure 21**) to display the AutoFormat dialog (**Figure 37**).

2. Select one of the two radio buttons:
   ▲ **AutoFormat now** formats the document without giving you an opportunity to review changes as they are made.
   ▲ **AutoFormat and review each change** gives you an opportunity to review each change as it is made.

3. Select the appropriate type of document from the pop-up menu (**Figure 38**).

Continued on next page...

USING AUTOFORMAT

Continued from previous page.

4. Click OK to begin the AutoFormat process.

   ▲ If you selected the AutoFormat now option in step 2, Word formats the document and displays the changes. The AutoFormat process is complete; the rest of the steps do not apply.

   ▲ If you selected the AutoFormat and review each change option in step 2, Word formats the document. Continue with step 5.

5. A different AutoFormat dialog appears (**Figure 39**). Click one of its four buttons to proceed:

   ▲ **Accept All** accepts all changes to the document. The AutoFormat process is complete; the rest of the steps do not apply.

   ▲ **Reject All** rejects all changes to the document. The AutoFormat process is reversed; the rest of the steps do not apply.

   ▲ **Review Changes** enables you to review the changes one by one. The Review AutoFormat Changes dialog appears (**Figure 40**). Continue with step 6.

   ▲ **Style Gallery** displays the Style Gallery dialog (**Figure 22**) so you can select a different template's styles. I tell you how to use the Style Gallery earlier in this chapter. When you are finished using the Style Gallery, you will return to this dialog; click one of the other buttons to continue.

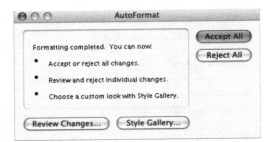

Figure 39 This AutoFormat dialog appears when Word has finished the AutoFormat process and is waiting for you to review its changes.

USING AUTOFORMAT

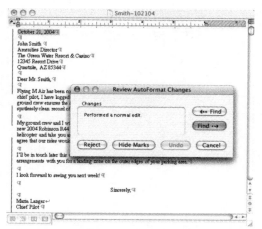

Figure 40 The Review AutoFormat Changes dialog lets you accept or reject each change as it is selected in the document window.

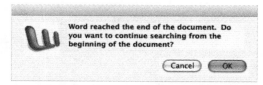

Figure 41 Word tells you when you reach the end of a document.

6. In the Review AutoFormat Changes dialog (**Figure 40**), review the information in the Changes area and click the appropriate button:

   ▲ To accept a change, click a Find button to display the next change.

   ▲ To reject a change and move to the next change, click the Reject button.

7. Repeat step 6 until you have reviewed every change.

8. Word displays a dialog like the one in **Figure 41** when you reach the end of the document. Click Cancel to dismiss it.

9. Click Cancel again to return to the Auto-Format dialog (**Figure 39**).

10. Click Accept All to accept all changes that you did not reject.

To set AutoFormat options

1. Choose Format > AutoFormat (**Figure 21**) to display the AutoFormat dialog (**Figure 37**).

2. Click Options. The AutoFormat options of the AutoCorrect dialog appears (**Figure 42**).

3. Set options as desired:

   ▲ **Headings** applies Word's Heading styles to heading text.

   ▲ **Lists** applies list and bullet styles to numbered, bulleted, and other lists.

   ▲ **Automatic bulleted lists** applies bulleted list formatting to paragraphs beginning with *, o, or - followed by a space or tab.

   ▲ **Other paragraphs** applies other styles such as Body Text, Inside Address, and Salutation.

   ▲ **"Straight quotes" with "smart quotes"** replaces plain quote characters with curly quote characters.

   ▲ **Ordinals (1st) with superscript** formats ordinals with superscript. For example, 1st becomes 1st.

   ▲ **Symbol characters (- -) with symbols** (—) replaces characters commonly used to represent symbols with corresponding symbol characters.

   ▲ ***Bold* and _italic_ with real formatting** formats text enclosed within asterisk characters (*) as bold and text enclosed within underscore characters as italic. For example, *hello* becomes **hello** and _goodbye_ becomes *goodbye*.

   ▲ **Internet paths with hyperlinks** formats e-mail addresses and URLs as clickable hyperlink fields.

   ▲ **Styles** prevents styles already applied in the document from being changed.

4. Click OK to save your settings.

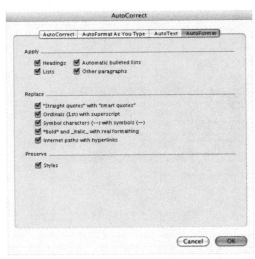

Figure 42 The AutoFormat options of the AutoCorrect dialog.

✔ Tip

■ I tell you about hyperlinks and other Internet-related features in **Chapter 18**.

SETTING AUTOFORMAT OPTIONS

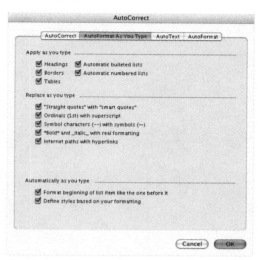

Figure 43 The AutoFormat As You Type options of the AutoCorrect dialog.

✔ Tips

- I tell you about borders and list formatting in **Chapter 3**, about styles earlier in this chapter, and about tables in **Chapter 8**.

- All AutoFormatting As You Type options are turned on by default. The only way to disable this feature is to turn off all options in the AutoFormat As You Type options of the AutoCorrect dialog (**Figure 43**).

To set automatic formatting options

1. Choose Tools > AutoCorrect (**Figure 24**) to display the AutoCorrect dialog.

2. Click the AutoFormat As You Type button to display its options (**Figure 43**).

3. Set options as desired. Most of the options are the same as those in the AutoFormat tab, which is discussed on the previous page. Here are the others:

   ▲ **Borders** automatically applies paragraph border styles when you type three or more hyphens, underscores, or equal signs.

   ▲ **Tables** creates a table when you type a series of hyphens with plus signs to indicate column edges, such as +----------+-----+.

   ▲ **Automatic numbered lists** applies numbered list formatting to paragraphs beginning with a number or letter followed by a space or tab.

   ▲ **Format beginning of list item like the one before it** repeats character formatting that you apply to the beginning of a list item. For example, if the first word of the previous list item was formatted as bold, the first word of the next list item is automatically formatted as bold.

   ▲ **Define styles based on your formatting** automatically creates or modifies styles based on manual formatting that you apply in the document.

4. Click OK to save your settings.

Page & Section Formatting

Page & Section Formatting

Chapters 3 and **4** provide a wealth of information about formatting text—the types of formatting you can apply and the various methods you can use to apply them. But if your document is destined for the printer, you should also be interested in page formatting.

Page formatting is formatting that is applied to an entire document or section of a document. For example, *margins*, which determine the spacing between the edge of the paper and the text indents, are applied to entire pages—you can't have different margins for different words or paragraphs. *Page borders*, which are another example of page formatting, surround the contents of a page, not just parts of it.

Many types of page formatting can be applied to document *sections* or parts. For example, a *header* is text or other information that appears at the top of each page. Rather than have the same thing appear at the top of every page in a document, you can create different document sections, each with its own custom header. *Multiple-column text* is another example of formatting that can be applied to document sections.

In this chapter, I tell you about the different types of page formatting and explain how you can apply them to entire documents and document sections.

Page, Section, & Column Breaks

As you work with a document, Word automatically sets page breaks based on paper size, margins, and contents. A *page break* marks the end of a page; anything after the page break will appear on the next page when the document is printed. This is easy to see in Page Layout view (**Figure 1**). In Normal view, automatic page breaks appear as dotted lines across the document (**Figure 2**).

Although you cannot change an automatic page break directly, you can change it indirectly by inserting a manual page break before it (**Figure 3**). This forces the page to end where you specify and, in most cases, forces subsequent automatic page breaks in the document to change.

In addition to page breaks, Word also enables you to insert section and column breaks. A *section break* marks the end of a document section. Sections are commonly used to divide a document into logical parts, each of which can have its own settings in the Page Setup dialog. A *column break* marks the end of a column of text. Column breaks are usually used in conjunction with multi-column text.

✔ Tips

- Automatic page breaks do not appear in Online Layout, Outline, or Notebook Layout view.

- As discussed later in this chapter, section breaks may be automatically inserted by Word in a document when you change page formatting settings.

- Columns and multi-column text are discussed a little later in this chapter.

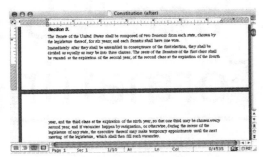

Figure 1 A page break in Page Layout view.

Figure 2 The same page break in Normal view.

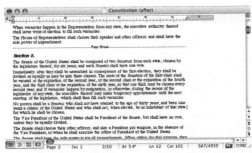

Figure 3 A manual page break adjusts all of the subsequent automatic page breaks.

Figure 4 Position the insertion point where you want the break to occur.

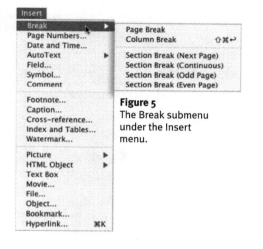

Figure 5
The Break submenu under the Insert menu.

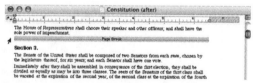

Figure 6 Click in the selection bar to the left of the break to select it.

To insert a break

1. Position the insertion point where you want the break to occur (**Figure 4**).

2. Choose an option from the Break submenu under the Insert menu (**Figure 5**):

   ▲ **Page Break** inserts a page break. **Figure 3** shows an inserted page break.

   ▲ **Column Break** inserts a column break. This forces any text after the break into the next column.

   ▲ **Section Break (Next Page)** inserts a section break that also acts as a page break.

   ▲ **Section Break (Continuous)** inserts a section break in the middle of a page.

   ▲ **Section Break (Odd Page)** inserts a section break that also acts as a page break. The following page will always be odd-numbered.

   ▲ **Section Break (Even Page)** inserts a section break that also acts as a page break. The following page will always be even-numbered.

   or

   Use one of the following shortcut keys:

   ▲ To insert a page break, press Shift Enter.

   ▲ To insert a column break, press Shift ⇧ ⌘ Return.

To remove a break

1. In Normal view, select the break by clicking in the selection bar beside it (**Figure 6**).

2. Press Delete.

The Document Dialog

The Document dialog (**Figures 7** and **8**) enables you to set a number of page and section formatting options. The dialog offers two panes of options:

◆ **Margins** (**Figure 7**) enables you to set margins, gutter, and header and footer locations for a document or document section.

◆ **Layout** (**Figure 8**) enables you to set section start options, header and footer options, and vertical alignment for a document or section.

One very important aspect of the Document dialog is the Apply to pop-up menu (**Figures 9** and **10**) beneath the Preview area in each pane. This menu determines how page formatting options in the dialog are applied to the document. The options on this menu vary depending on what is selected in the document window:

◆ **Whole document** (**Figures 9** and **10**) applies the formatting to all of the pages in the document. This option always appears.

◆ **This point forward** (**Figure 9**) applies the formatting to the document's pages from the insertion point to the end of the document. Choosing this option automatically inserts a section break at the insertion point. This option only appears if no text is selected when you open the Document dialog.

◆ **This section** (**Figure 9**) applies the formatting to the current section—the section in which the insertion point is blinking. This option only appears if the document already contains at least one section break and no text is selected when you open the Document dialog.

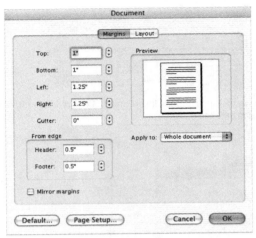

Figure 7 The Margins pane of the Document dialog.

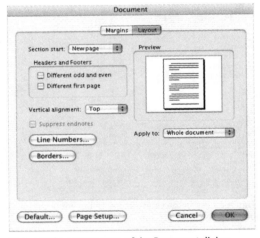

Figure 8 The Layout pane of the Document dialog.

Figures 9 & 10
The Apply to pop-up menu with nothing selected in a multi-section document (top) and with text selected in one section of a multi-section document (bottom).

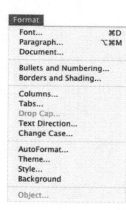

Figure 11
The Format menu.

◆ **Selected text (Figure 10)** applies the formatting to only the text that is selected in the document. Choosing this option automatically inserts a section break before and after the selected text. This option only appears if text is selected when you open the Document dialog.

◆ **Selected sections (Figure 10)** applies the formatting to the currently selected document sections. This option only appears if text in at least once section is selected when you open the Document dialog.

This part of the chapter explains how to set page and section formatting options in the Document dialog.

✔ Tip

■ Some Document options—such as margins, paper size, and orientation—affect the dimensions of a page's printable area. If you plan to use non-standard Document options, consider setting them *before* you create and format your document.

To open the Document dialog

Choose Format > Document (**Figure 11**).

USING THE DOCUMENT DIALOG

To set margin options

1. In the Document dialog, click the Margins button to display its options (**Figure 7**).

2. To set margins, enter values in the Top, Bottom, Left, and Right boxes.

3. To set a gutter width, enter a value in the Gutter box.

4. To set the distance from the top and bottom of the page for the header and footer, enter values in the Header and Footer boxes.

5. To set up the document for double-sided printing and facing pages, turn on the Mirror margins check box. This changes the Left and Right margin options to Inside and Outside options and displays two pages in the Preview area (**Figure 12**).

6. To apply your settings to the entire document, make sure Whole document is selected from the Apply to pop-up menu (**Figures 9** and **10**). Otherwise, choose the desired option from the Apply to pop-up menu.

7. Click OK.

✔ Tips

■ A gutter is additional empty space on one side of a page to accommodate document binding (**Figure 12**).

■ As you make changes in the dialog, the preview area changes accordingly.

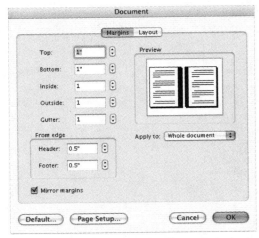

Figure 12 This example shows the Mirror margin check box turned on and gutter set to 1". A setup like this is good for printing double-sided pages that will be bound into a book.

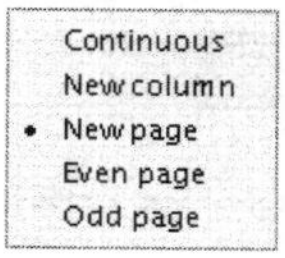

Figure 13
The Section start pop-up menu.

Figure 14
The Vertical alignment pop-up menu.

Figure 15 Examples of vertical alignment: top (left), center (center), and justified (right).

✔ Tips

- I explain how to insert headers and footers later in this chapter.

- Vertical alignment is only apparent on pages that are less than a full page in length.

- On screen, you can only view vertical alignment in Page Layout view and Print Preview.

To set section start options

1. In the Document dialog, click the Layout button to display its options (**Figure 8**).

2. To set options for a section break, choose an option from the Section start pop-up menu (**Figure 13**). These options correspond to the options in the Break submenu under the Insert menu (**Figure 5**), which is discussed earlier in this chapter.

3. To have multiple headers and footers in the document, set options in the Headers and Footers area:

   ▲ **Different odd and even** enables you to specify different headers and footers for odd and even pages of the document or section.

   ▲ **Different first page** enables you to specify a different header and footer for the first page of the document or section.

4. To set vertical alignment for a document page, choose an option from the Vertical alignment pop-up menu (**Figure 14**). **Figure 15** shows print previews of what each option looks like when applied to the same document page.

5. To apply your settings to the entire document, make sure Whole document is selected from the Apply to pop-up menu (**Figures 9** and **10**). Otherwise, choose the desired option from the Apply to pop-up menu.

6. Click OK.

SETTING LAYOUT OPTIONS

To set default page formatting

1. In the Page Setup dialog, set options as desired in the Margins and Layout panes (**Figures 7** and **8**).

2. Click the Default button.

3. Word displays a dialog like the one in **Figure 16**, asking if you want to change the default settings for the template on which the document is based. Click Yes only if you want the settings to apply to all new documents that you create with that template.

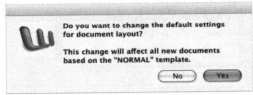

Do you want to change the default settings for document layout?

This change will affect all new documents based on the "NORMAL" template.

No   Yes

Figure 16 This dialog appears when you click the Default button in the Document dialog. Click Yes only if you want to change the default Page Setup settings for the template on which the document is based—in this example, Normal.

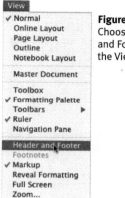

Figure 17
Choose Header and Footer from the View menu.

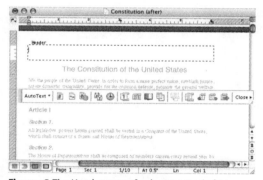

Figure 18 The Header area of a document window.

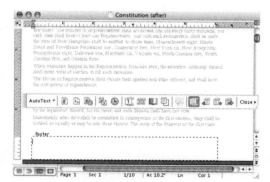

Figure 19 The Footer area of a document window.

Headers & Footers

A header is a part of the document that appears at the top of every page. A footer is a part of the document that appears at the bottom of every page. Headers and footers are commonly used to place page numbers, revision dates, or other document information on document pages.

To display a header or footer

Choose View > Header and Footer (**Figure 17**).

If necessary, Word switches to Page Layout view and displays the Header area of the current document section, as well as the Header and Footer toolbar (**Figure 18**).

◆ To view the footer for the current section, click the Switch Between Header and Footer button on the Header and Footer toolbar. The footer area appears (**Figure 19**).

◆ To view the header or footer for the previous or next section of a multi-section document, click the Show Previous or Show Next button on the Header and Footer toolbar.

✔ Tip

■ In Page Layout view, you can view a header or footer by double-clicking in the Header or Footer area of a page.

To hide a header or footer

Click the Close button on the Header and Footer toolbar.

Or

Double-click anywhere in the document window other than in the header or footer.

The document returns to the view you were in before you viewed the header or footer. The Header and Footer toolbar disappears.

To create a header or footer

1. Display the Header or Footer area (**Figure 18** or **19**) for the header or footer that you want to create.

2. Enter the header (**Figure 20**) or footer (**Figure 21**) information.

3. When you're finished, hide the Header or Footer area to continue working on the document.

✔ Tip

■ You can format the contents of a header or footer the same way that you format any other part of the document. In **Figure 20**, for example, the header text has italic font formatting and a bottom paragraph border applied. You can find detailed text formatting instructions in **Chapters 3 and 4**.

To edit a header or footer

1. Display the Header (**Figure 20**) or Footer (**Figure 21**) area for the header or footer that you want to change.

2. Edit the header or footer information.

3. When you're finished, hide the Header or Footer area to continue working on the document.

To remove a header or footer

1. Display the Header or Footer area for the header or footer that you want to remove.

2. Select its contents and press (Delete). The header or footer is removed.

3. Hide the Header or Footer area to continue working on the document.

Header
The Hound of the Baskervilles

Figure 20 An example of a header with text formatting applied.

Footer
Revised October 22, 1897

Figure 21 A simple footer.

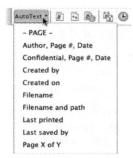

Figure 22
The AutoText pop-up menu on the Header and Footer toolbar.

Insert Page Number
Insert Date

Insert Time
Insert Number of Pages

Figure 23 Word field buttons on the Header and Footer toolbar.

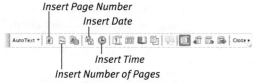

Figure 24 This footer example uses the "Author, Page #, Date" AutoText entry to insert Word fields.

To insert AutoText entries or Word fields in a header or footer

1. Position the insertion point in the Header or Footer area where you want the AutoText entry or field to appear.

2. To insert an AutoText entry, click the Insert AutoText button on the Header and Footer toolbar to display a menu of entries (**Figure 22**). Choose the one that you want to insert.

3. To insert a Word field, click the appropriate button on the Header and Footer toolbar (**Figure 23**) to insert the field:

   ▲ **Insert Page Number** inserts the page number.

   ▲ **Insert Number of Pages** inserts the total number of pages in the document.

   ▲ **Insert Date** inserts the current date.

   ▲ **Insert Time** inserts the current time.

✔ Tips

■ I tell you about AutoText entries and Word fields in **Chapter 9**.

■ To number pages, use the Insert Page Number button on the Header and Footer toolbar or one of the first three options or the last option on the Insert AutoText button's menu (**Figure 22**) to insert a page number in the header or footer. **Figure 24** shows an example using the "Author, Page #, Date" AutoText Entry. In my opinion, using these options is the best way to number pages in a document. Using the Page Numbers command on the Insert menu inserts page numbers in frames that can be difficult to work with. The Page Numbers command is discussed in **Chapter 9**.

INSERTING AUTOTEXT & FIELDS

First Page Header Section 1:

First Page Header Section 2:

Header Section 2:   Same as Previous

First Page Header Section 2:   Same as Previous

Header Section 2:   Same as Previous

Figure 25 Examples of headers for the first three sections of a document with multiple sections and different first page headers and footers. (The first section has only one page.) As you can see, the header and its link status are clearly identified.

To create a different first page or odd and even header and footer

1. Choose Format > Document (**Figure 11**) to display the Document dialog. If necessary, click the Layout button (**Figure 8**).

2. To create a different header and footer on odd- and even-numbered pages of the document, turn on the Different odd and even check box.

3. To create a different header and footer on the first page of the document or document section, turn on the Different first page check box.

4. Click OK.

5. Follow the instructions on the previous pages to create headers and footers as desired. Use the Show Previous and Show Next buttons on the Header and Footer toolbar to display and edit each header and footer.

✔ Tips

- As illustrated in **Figure 25**, the Header or Footer area clearly identifies the current header or footer.

- By default, if your document is set up to have multiple headers or footers, each header and footer is linked to the previous one (**Figure 25**), thus ensuring that they are the same. Use the Link to Previous button on the Header and Footer toolbar to toggle this feature. You must disable this feature to change a header or footer without changing the previous one(s).

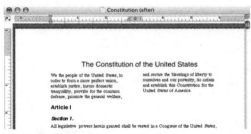

Figure 26 A section of multi-column text in Page Layout view.

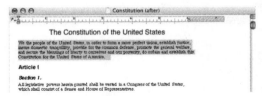

Figure 27 The same document in Normal view.

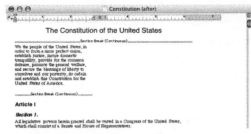

Figure 28 Select the text for which you want to set columns.

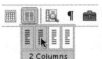

Figure 29 Choose the number of columns from the Columns button menu on the Standard toolbar.

Columns

Word enables you to format text with multiple columns, like those in a newspaper.

✔ Tips

- Although you can edit multi-column text in any view, you must be in Page Layout view (**Figure 26**) to see the columns side by side. In Normal view, the text appears in the same narrow column (**Figure 27**).

- Column formatting applies to sections of text. You can insert section breaks as discussed earlier in this chapter to set up various multi-column sections.

To set the number of columns

1. Select the text for which you want to set the number of columns (**Figure 28**).

2. Click the Columns button on the Standard toolbar to display a menu of columns and choose the number of columns (**Figure 29**).

If you are not in Page Layout view, Word switches to that view. The text is reformatted with the number of columns you specified (**Figure 26**).

✔ Tips

- To set the number of columns for an entire single-section document, in step 1 above, position the insertion point anywhere in the document.

- To set the number of columns for one section of a multi-section document, in step 1 above, position the insertion point anywhere in the section.

- If necessary, Word inserts section breaks to mark the beginning and end of multi-column text (**Figure 27**).

To set column options

1. Position the insertion point in the section for which you want to change column options.

   or

   Select the sections for which you want to change column options.

2. Choose Format > Columns (**Figure 11**) to display the Columns dialog (**Figure 30**).

3. To set the number of columns, click one of the icons in the Presets section or enter a value in the Number of columns box.

4. To set different column widths for each column, make sure the Equal column width check box is turned off, then enter values in the Width boxes for each column. You can also enter values in the Spacing boxes to specify the amount of space between columns.

5. To put a vertical line between columns, turn on the Line between check box.

6. To specify the part of the document that you want the changes to apply to, choose an option from the Apply to pop-up menu (**Figures 9** and **10**).

   or

   To insert a column break at the insertion point, choose This point forward from the Apply to drop-down list (**Figure 9**), then turn on the Start new column check box.

7. Click OK.

✔ Tip

■ You can see the effect of your changes in the Preview area as you change settings in the Columns dialog.

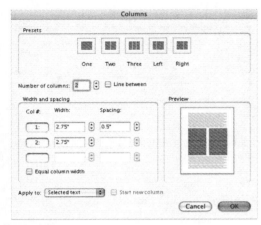

Figure 30 The Columns dialog.

Figure 31 A page border can really dress up a flyer like this one.

Page Borders

Page borders are borders that apply to entire pages of a document. They enable you to, in effect, frame document pages (**Figure 31**).

✔ Tips

- Page borders make it easy to create official-looking certificates and other "suitable for framing" documents.

- Page borders can be applied to all pages in a document or only the pages in a specific document section.

To apply page borders

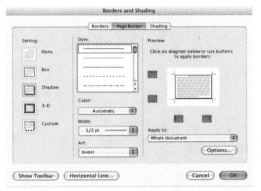

Figure 32 The Page Border pane of the Borders and Shading dialog.

1. If necessary, position the insertion point in the section of the document to which you want to apply page borders.

2. Choose Format > Borders and Shading (**Figure 11**) to display the Borders and Shading dialog.

3. If necessary, click the Page Border button to display its options (**Figure 32**).

4. Click a Setting icon to select the type of border. All options except None and Custom place borders around each side of the page.

5. Click a style in the Style scrolling list to select a line style. Then choose a line color from the Color pop-up menu (**Figure 33**) and a line thickness from the Width pop-up menu (**Figure 34**).

   or

   Select a graphic from the Art pop-up menu (**Figure 35**).

6. If necessary, choose an option from the Apply to pop-up menu (**Figures 9** and **10**).

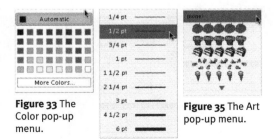

Figure 33 The Color pop-up menu.

Figure 34 The Width pop-up menu.

Figure 35 The Art pop-up menu.

Continued on next page...

APPLYING PAGE BORDERS

Continued from previous page.

7. To apply custom borders, click the buttons in the Preview area to add or remove a line using the settings in the dialog.

8. When the Preview area illustrates the kind of border that you want to apply, click OK.

✔ Tips

■ You can repeat steps 5 and 7 to customize each side of a custom border.

■ You can further customize a border by clicking the Options button in the Borders and Shading dialog to display the Border and Shading Options dialog (**Figure 36**). Set options as desired and click OK to return to the Borders and Shading dialog.

■ I tell you about the other tabs of the Borders and Shading dialog in **Chapter 3**.

To remove page borders

1. Position the insertion point in the section where you want to remove borders.

2. Choose Format > Borders and Shading (**Figure 11**) and click the Page Border button in the Borders and Shading dialog that appears (**Figure 32**).

3. Click the None icon.

4. Click OK.

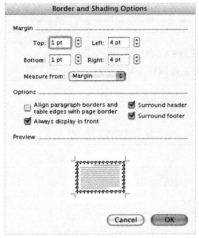

Figure 36 The Border and Shading Options dialog for page borders.

Figure 37 Word enables you to create watermarks using images...

Watermarks

Word's watermark feature enables you to include an image or text in the background of each document page.

For example, you can insert a faded image of your company logo on all letters you write (**Figure 37**) or display the word *DRAFT* on each page of a draft document (**Figure 38**).

Watermarks, when used properly, can make your documents look more polished or professional. They can also provide additional information to document readers.

✔ Tip

■ Watermarks only appear onscreen in Page Layout view and Print Preview. You cannot see watermarks onscreen in Normal view.

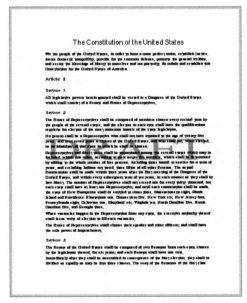

Figure 38 ...or text.

To insert a picture watermark

1. Choose Insert > Watermark (**Figure 39**).

2. In the Insert Watermark dialog that appears, select the Picture radio button (**Figure 40**).

3. Click the Select Picture button.

4. Use the Choose a Picture dialog that appears (**Figure 41**) to locate and select the picture you want to use as a watermark. Click Insert.

   The image you selected appears in the preview area (**Figure 42**).

5. Toggle the Washout check box to adjust the intensity of the image.

6. To manually set the image size, enter a value in the Scale box.

7. Click OK.

   The watermark appears on every page of the document (**Figure 37**).

✔ Tip

- Although an image might be easier to see with Washout turned off (**Figures 37** and 42), text may be difficult to read through the image.

Figure 39
Choose Watermark from the Insert menu.

Figure 40 Select the Picture radio button in the Insert Watermark dialog.

Figure 41 The Choose a Picture dialog.

Figure 42 The Preview area shows what the watermark will look like with sample text over it.

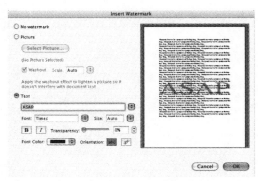

Figure 43 Select the Text button in the Insert Watermark dialog.

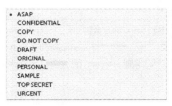

Figure 44 Choose one of the predefined text watermarks from a drop-down list.

Figure 45 The Preview area shows you what the watermark will look like.

To insert a text watermark

1. Choose Insert > Watermark (**Figure 39**).

2. In the Insert Watermark dialog that appears, select the Text radio button (**Figure 43**).

3. Choose an option from the drop-down list at the top of the text area (**Figure 44**).

   or

   Enter the text you want to display as the watermark in the box.

4. Set Font, Size, and other formatting options as desired. The preview area changes accordingly (**Figure 45**).

5. Click OK.

   The watermark appears on every page of the document (**Figure 38**).

✔ Tip

■ Use the Transparency slider in the Insert Watermark dialog (**Figure 43**) to adjust the darkness of the text. The lighter the watermark text, the easier the document text will be to read.

Printing
Documents

Printing Documents

In most cases, when you've finished writing, formatting, and proofreading a document, you'll want to print it. This chapter tells you about the three parts to the printing process:

◆ **Page Setup** enables you to specify information about the paper size, print orientation, and scale.

◆ **Print Preview** enables you to view the document onscreen before you print it. You can also use this view to set page breaks and margins to fine-tune the printed appearance.

◆ **Print** enables you to specify the page range, number of copies, and other options for printing. It then sends the document to your printer.

✔ Tips

■ This chapter assumes that your computer is already set up for printing. If it is not, consult Mac OS Help or the documentation that came with your printer for setup information.

■ Information about printing mailing labels, form letters, and envelopes is provided in **Chapters 14** and **15**.

Page Setup

The Page Setup dialog enables you to set a number of options for printing your document. It is broken down into three groups of settings:

◆ **Page Attributes** settings (**Figure 3**) include the printer, paper size, page orientation, and print scale.

◆ **Custom Paper Size** settings (**Figure 7**) enable you to set up and use a custom paper size and to specify a paper feed method for your printer's manual feed feature.

◆ **Microsoft Word** settings (**Figure 8**) give you access to Word-specific features that affect printing.

✔ Tips

■ Some Page Setup options—such as paper size and orientation—affect a page's margins. If you plan to use non-standard Page Setup options, consider setting them before you create and format your document.

■ You can review all Page Setup settings for a document in the Summary settings pane (**Figure 2**).

To open the Page Setup dialog

Choose File > Page Setup (**Figure 1**).

Or

Click the Page Setup button at the bottom of the Document dialog (**Figure 11**).

Figure 1
Word's File menu.

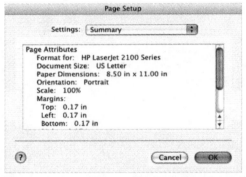

Figure 2 The Summary pane of the Page Setup dialog summarizes all settings for the document.

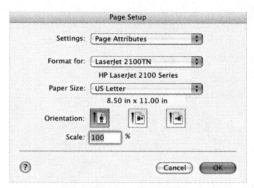

Figure 3 The Page Attributes pane of the Page Setup dialog.

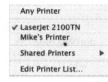

Figure 4
The Format for pop-up menu lists all printers you have access to.

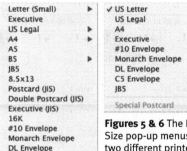

Figures 5 & 6 The Paper Size pop-up menus for two different printers.

To set Page Attributes options

1. Open the Page Setup dialog.

2. If necessary, choose Page Attributes from the Settings pop-up menu to display Page Attributes options (**Figure 3**).

3. Choose the printer you want to print on from the Format for pop-up menu (**Figure 4**).

4. Choose the size of the paper you want to print on from the Paper Size pop-up menu (**Figures 5** and **6**).

5. Click to select an orientation icon. The first icon represents portrait orientation while the other two represent landscape orientation in two different directions.

6. To reduce or enlarge the print size, enter a value in the Scale text box.

7. Click OK to save your settings.

✔ Tips

■ The Format for pop-up menu (**Figure 4**) lists all printers set up and connected to your computer as well as shared printers.

■ As shown in **Figures 5** and **6**, the Paper Size pop-up menu may offer different options, depending on the printer you selected in step 3.

SETTING PAGE ATTRIBUTES

To set Custom Paper Size options

1. Open the Page Setup dialog.

2. If necessary, choose Custom Paper Size from the Settings pop-up menu to display Custom Paper Size options (**Figure 7**).

3. Turn on the Use custom page size check box.

4. Enter dimensions for the paper in the Width and Height boxes.

5. Select an icon corresponding to the Feed Method of your printer's manual paper feed.

6. Select a radio button to indicate whether paper is fed Face up or Face down.

7. Click OK.

✔ Tips

- When the Use custom page size check box is turned on (**Figure 7**), the measurements in the dialog override the option chosen in the Page Attributes settings of the Page Setup dialog (**Figure 3**).

- Clicking the Reset button in the Custom page size area (**Figure 7**) resets Feed Method options.

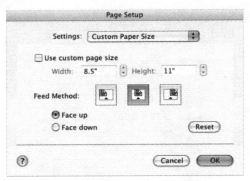

Figure 7 The Custom Paper Size pane of the Page Setup dialog.

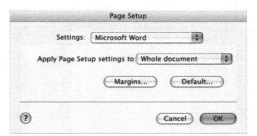

Figure 8 The Microsoft Word pane of the Page Setup dialog.

Figures 9 & 10
The appearance of the Apply Page Setup settings to pop-up menu varies depending on whether text is selected or the document has multiple sections.

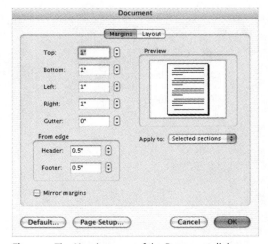

Figure 11 The Margins pane of the Document dialog.

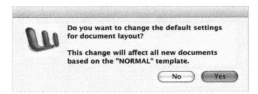

Figure 12 Click Yes in this dialog to make the Page Setup settings the default settings for all documents with the currently applied template.

To set Microsoft Word options

1. Open the Page Setup dialog.

2. If necessary, choose Microsoft Word from the Settings pop-up menu to display Microsoft Word options (**Figure 8**).

3. To apply Page Setup dialog settings to only a part of the document, choose an option from the Apply Page Setup settings to pop-up menu (**Figures 9** and **10**).

4. To set document margins, click the Margins button to display the Margins pane of the Document dialog (**Figure 11**). Set margins as desired and click OK. (You will have to reopen the Page Setup dialog to continue setting options there.)

5. To save the current Page Setup dialog settings as the default settings for all Word documents, click the Default button. Then click Yes in the confirmation dialog that appears (**Figure 12**). (You will have to reopen the Page Setup dialog to continue setting options there.)

6. Click OK to save your settings.

✔ Tips

- Choosing an option other than Whole document from the Apply Page Setup Settings to pop-up menu (**Figures 9** and **10**) may insert section breaks within your document. I tell you about section breaks in **Chapters 5**.

- I explain how to use the Margins tab of the Document dialog to change margins in **Chapter 5**.

Print Preview

Word's Print Preview (**Figure 13**) displays one or more pages of a document exactly as they will appear when printed. It also enables you to make last-minute changes to margins and document contents before printing.

✔ Tip

- Print Preview can save time and paper—it's a lot quicker to look at a document on screen than to wait for it to print, and it doesn't use a single sheet of paper.

To switch to Print Preview

Choose File > Print Preview (**Figure 1**), or click the Print Preview button on the Standard toolbar.

✔ Tip

- The Print Preview toolbar (**Figure 14**) appears automatically at the top of the screen when you switch to Print Preview.

To zoom in or out

1. Select the Magnifier button on the Print Preview toolbar (**Figure 14**).

2. Click on the page. With each click, the view toggles between 100% and the current Zoom percentage on the Print Preview toolbar.

Or

Choose an option from the Zoom drop-down list on the Print Preview toolbar (**Figure 15**).

Or

1. Click in the Zoom box on the Print Preview toolbar.

2. Enter a value.

3. Press (Return).

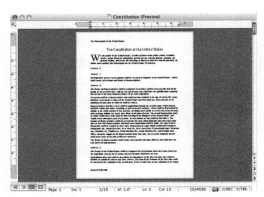

Figure 13 A single page of a document in Print Preview.

Figure 14 The Print Preview toolbar.

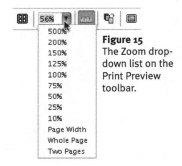

Figure 15
The Zoom drop-down list on the Print Preview toolbar.

Figure 16
Use the Multiple Pages button's menu to choose a layout for displaying multiple document pages in Print Preview.

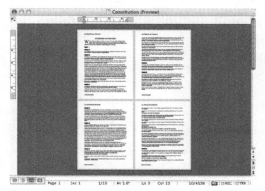

Figure 17 Four pages of a document displayed in Print Preview.

Figure 18
The mouse pointer changes when you position it on a margin on the ruler.

Figure 19
Drag to change the margin.

To view multiple pages

Click the Multiple Pages button on the Print Preview toolbar to display a menu of page layouts and choose the one that you want (**Figure 16**).

The view and magnification change to display the pages as you specified (**Figure 17**).

✔ Tip

■ To return to a single-page view, click the One Page button on the Print Preview toolbar.

To change margins

1. If necessary, click the View Ruler button on the Print Preview toolbar to display the ruler in the Print Preview window (**Figure 13**).

2. Position the mouse pointer on the ruler in the position corresponding to the margin you want to change. The mouse pointer turns into a box with arrows on either end and a yellow box appears, identifying the margin (**Figure 18**).

3. Press the mouse button down and drag to change the margin. As you drag, a dotted line indicates the position of the margin (**Figure 19**). When you release the mouse button, the margin changes.

✔ Tips

■ A better way to change margins is with the Margins tab of the Document dialog (**Figure 11**), which is covered in **Chapter 5**.

■ You can also use the ruler to change indentation for selected paragraphs. **Chapter 3** explains how.

WORKING WITH PRINT PREVIEW

To move from page to page

In Print Preview, click the Previous Page or Next Page button at the bottom of the vertical scroll bar (**Figure 20**).

To edit the document

1. If necessary, zoom in to get a better look at the text you want to edit.

2. Deselect the Magnifier button on the Print Preview toolbar.

3. Click in the document window to position the insertion point.

4. Edit the document as desired.

✔ Tip

■ You may find that your computer responds more quickly when you edit in Page Layout or Normal view than in Print Preview.

To reduce the number of pages

Click the Shrink to Fit button on the Print Preview toolbar.

Word squeezes the document onto one less page by making minor adjustments to font size and paragraph spacing. It then displays the revised document.

✔ Tip

■ This feature is useful for squeezing a two-page letter onto one page when the second page only has a line or two.

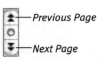

Figure 20 Use the Previous Page and Next Page buttons at the bottom of the vertical scroll bar to move from one page to another.

Full Screen toolbar

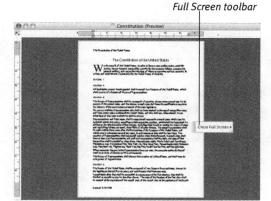

Figure 21 Full Screen view in Print Preview.

To switch to a full-screen view

Click the Full Screen button on the Print Preview toolbar.

The screen redraws to remove the status bar (**Figure 21**). This enables you to get a slightly larger view of the document page(s).

✔ Tip

- To return to a regular Print Preview view, click the Close Full Screen button on the Full Screen toolbar.

To leave Print Preview

Click the Close button on the Print Preview toolbar (**Figure 14**).

The document returns to whatever view you were in before you switched to Print Preview.

WORKING WITH PRINT PREVIEW

Printing

You use the Print dialog to set options for a print job and send it to the printer.

Print dialog options are broken down into a number of settings panes, which vary depending on the type of printer. For example, here are the panes available for my two printers: an HP LaserJet 2100TN and an Epson Stylus Photo 820:

◆ **Copies & Pages** (**Figure 22**) enables you to set the number of document copies and the range of document pages to print.

◆ **Layout** (**Figure 23**) enables you to specify the number of pages per sheet of paper, a layout direction, and border.

◆ **Output Options** (**Figure 24**) enables you to save a document as a PDF or PostScript file.

◆ **Scheduler** (**Figure 25**) enables you to schedule the print job for a specific time in the future.

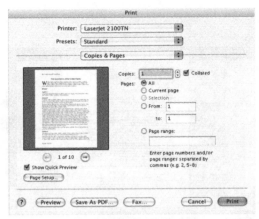

Figure 22 The Copies & Pages pane of the Print dialog for a LaserJet 2100TN printer.

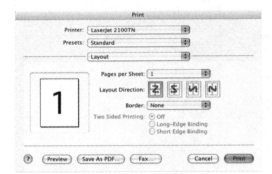

Figure 23 The Layout pane of the Print dialog for a LaserJet 2100TN printer.

Figure 24 The Output Options pane of the Print dialog for a LaserJet 2100TN printer.

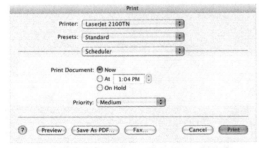

Figure 25 The Scheduler pane of the Print dialog for a LaserJet 2100TN printer.

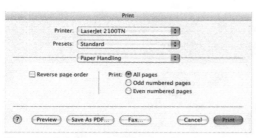

Figure 26 The Paper Handling pane of the Print dialog for a LaserJet 2100TN printer.

Figure 27 The ColorSync pane of the Print dialog for a LaserJet 2100TN printer.

Figure 28 The Cover Page pane of the Print dialog for a LaserJet 2100TN printer.

Figure 29 The Error Handling pane of the Print dialog for a LaserJet 2100TN printer.

◆ **Paper Handling (Figure 26)** enables you to set the print order of pages and print only odd- or only even-numbered pages.

◆ **ColorSync (Figure 27)** enables you to set ColorSync color management options.

◆ **Cover Page (Figure 28)** enables you to print an information page about the print job. This option is useful if you print to a network printer shared with other users.

◆ **Error Handling (Figure 29)** enables you to specify how PostScript and other errors should be handled.

◆ **Paper Feed (Figure 30)** enables you to select paper feed methods or trays.

◆ **Image Quality (Figure 31)** enables you to set printer-specific features.

Continued on next page...

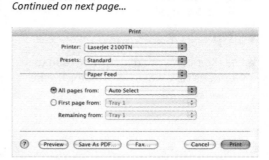

Figure 30 The Paper Feed pane of the Print dialog for a LaserJet 2100TN printer.

Figure 31 The Image Quality pane of the Print dialog for a LaserJet 2100TN printer.

THE PRINT DIALOG

Continued from previous page.

- ◆ **Print Settings** (**Figure 32**) enable you to set options for the type of paper, ink cartridge, print quality, and other print options.

- ◆ **Color Management** (**Figure 33**) enables you to set color options.

- ◆ **Microsoft Word** (**Figure 34**) enables you to specify what part of the Word document you want to print.

- ◆ **Summary** (**Figure 35**) summarizes all Print dialog settings.

After setting options, click the Print button to send the document to the selected printer.

This part of the chapter explains how to set options in the most commonly used Print dialog panes: Copies & Pages (**Figure 22**) and Microsoft Word (**Figure 34**).

✔ Tip

- ■ Remember, Print dialog panes and their options vary greatly depending on the selected printer.

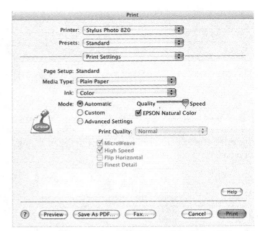

Figure 32 The Print Settings pane of the Print dialog for a Stylus Photo 820 printer.

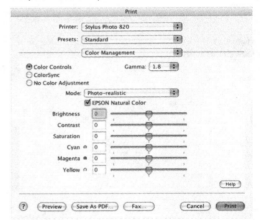

Figure 33 The Color Management pane of the Print dialog for a Stylus Photo 820 printer.

Figure 34 The Microsoft Word pane of the Print dialog for a LaserJet 2100TN printer.

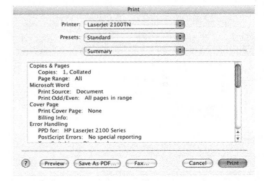

Figure 35 The Summary pane of the Print dialog for a LaserJet 2100TN printer.

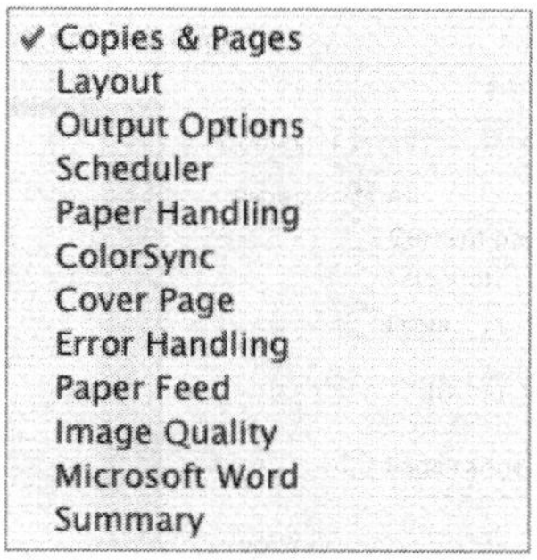

✓ Copies & Pages
Layout
Output Options
Scheduler
Paper Handling
ColorSync
Cover Page
Error Handling
Paper Feed
Image Quality
Microsoft Word
Summary

Figure 36 Use this pop-up menu to display a specific Print dialog pane. The options that appear in this menu on your computer may differ depending on your printer.

To set print options & print

1. Choose File > Print (**Figure 1**) or press ⌘P to display the Print dialog (**Figure 22**).

2. If the Copies & Pages pane is not showing, choose Copies and Pages from the third pop-up menu (**Figure 36**).

3. If more than one printer is available to you, choose a printer from the Printer pop-up menu.

4. Enter the number of copies you want to print in the Copies box.

5. If you are printing more than one copy and you want them to emerge from the printer in collated sets, turn on the Collated check box.

6. Select a Pages option:
   - ▲ **All** prints all pages.
   - ▲ **Current page** prints the currently selected page or the page in which the insertion point is blinking.
   - ▲ **Selection** prints only selected document contents. This option is only available if something is selected in the document window when you open the Print dialog.
   - ▲ **From/to** enables you to enter a starting and ending page number for a single range of pages.
   - ▲ **Page range** enables you to enter one or more page ranges. Separate first and last page numbers with a hyphen; separate multiple page ranges with a comma.

7. Choose Microsoft Word from the third pop-up menu (**Figure 36**).

Continued on next page...

USING THE PRINT DIALOG

Continued from previous page.

8. Choose an option from the Print What drop-down list (**Figure 37**):

    ▲ **Document** prints the Word document.

    ▲ **Document properties** prints information about the document.

    ▲ **Document showing markup** prints the document with any revision marks.

    ▲ **List of markup** prints a list of document markups.

    ▲ **Styles** prints style information.

    ▲ **AutoText entries** prints a list of AutoText entries.

    ▲ **Key assignments** prints a list of shortcut keys available throughout Word.

9. Select a Print radio button:

    ▲ **All pages in range** prints all pages in the range specified in step 6.

    ▲ **Odd pages only** prints only the odd pages in the range specified in step 6.

    ▲ **Even pages only** prints only the even pages in the range specified in step 6.

10. Click Print to send the document to the printer.

✔ Tips

■ Clicking the Print button on the Standard or Print Preview toolbar sends the document directly to the printer without displaying the Print dialog.

■ The options on the Printer menu in step 3 vary depending on the printers set up for your computer.

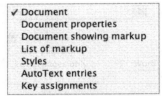

Figure 37 Use this pop-up menu to tell Word what you want to print.

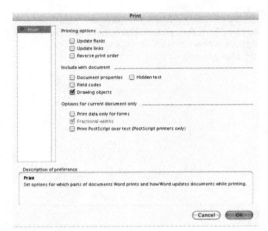

Figure 38 You can set additional printing options in this dialog.

■ Word's revision feature is covered in **Chapter 16**, styles are covered in **Chapter 4**, AutoText is covered in **Chapter 9**, and shortcut keys are covered in **Chapter 1**.

■ Clicking the Word Options button displays Print options (**Figure 38**), which I discuss in **Chapter 20**.

Figure 39 The Presets pop-up menu with two presets defined.

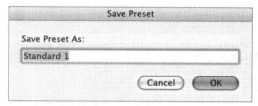

Figure 40 The Save Preset dialog.

To save Print dialog options as a preset

1. In the Print dialog box, set options as desired in any combination of panes (**Figures 22** through **35**).

2. Choose Save As from the Presets pop-up menu (**Figure 39**).

3. In the Save Preset dialog that appears (**Figure 40**), enter a name for the set of print options you are saving.

4. Click OK.

   After a moment, the settings are saved with the name you specified. You can see it listed on the Presets pop-up menu.

To use a Print dialog preset

In the Print dialog box, choose the name of the print settings you want to use from the Presets pop-up menu (**Figure 39**).

All Print dialog settings are restored to those that are part of the preset.

To delete a preset

1. In the Print dialog, choose the preset you want to delete from the Presets pop-up menu (**Figure 39**). That preset setting is restored to the Print dialog.

2. Choose Delete from the Presets pop-up menu (**Figure 39**).

   The preset is immediately removed from the menu.

WORKING WITH PRESETS

To save a document as a PDF file

1. In any pane of the Print dialog (**Figures 22** through **35**), click the Save As PDF button.

2. Use the Save to File dialog that appears (**Figure 41**) to enter a name and specify a disk location for the file.

3. Click Save to save the file to disk.

✔ Tips

■ PDF stands for *Portable Document Format*. PDF files can be opened and read with Preview on Mac OS X or Adobe Acrobat Reader on virtually any computer or operating system.

■ The Save to File dialog works just like the Save As dialog, which is covered in **Chapter 2**.

Figure 41 Use this Save to File dialog to save a document as a PDF file.

Writing Tools

Word's Writing Tools

Microsoft Word includes a number of features that can help you be a better writer. Some of these features can help you find and fix errors in your documents, while other features can help you fine-tune documents for publication.

This chapter covers the following writing tools of interest to most Word users:

◆ The **spelling checker** compares words in your document to words in dictionary files to identify unknown words.

◆ The **grammar checker** checks sentences against a collection of grammar rules to identify questionable sentence construction.

◆ **AutoCorrect** automatically corrects common errors as you type.

◆ The **dictionary** helps you understand the meaning of words in a document.

◆ The **thesaurus** enables you to find synonyms or antonyms for words in your document.

◆ **Hyphenation** automatically hyphenates words based on hyphenation rules.

◆ **Word count** counts the words in a selection or the entire document.

◆ The **Change Case** command changes the capitalization of words you select.

◆ **AutoSummarize** automatically summarizes a document's content.

✔ Tip

■ No proofing tool is a complete substitute for carefully rereading a document to manually check it for errors. Use Word's writing tools to help you find and fix errors, but don't depend on them to find all errors in your documents.

The Spelling & Grammar Checkers

Word's spelling and grammar checkers help you to identify potential spelling and grammar problems in your documents. They can be set to check text automatically as you type or when you have finished typing.

The spelling checker compares the words in a document to the words in its main spelling dictionary, which includes many words and names. If it cannot find a match for a word, it then checks the active custom dictionaries—the dictionary files that you create. If Word still cannot find a match, it flags the word as unknown so you can act on it.

The grammar checker works in much the same way. It compares the structure of sentences in the document with predetermined rules for a specific writing style. When it finds a sentence or sentence fragment with a potential problem, it identifies it for you so you can act on it.

Both the spelling and grammar checkers are highly customizable so they work the way that you want them to.

✔ Tips

- The spelling checker cannot identify a misspelled word if it correctly spells another word. For example, if you type *from* when you meant to type *form*, the spelling checker would not find the error. The grammar checker, on the other hand, might find this particular error, depending on its usage.

- Do not add a word to a custom dictionary unless you *know* it is correctly spelled. Otherwise, the word will never be flagged as an error.

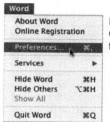

Figure 1
Choose Preferences from the Word menu.

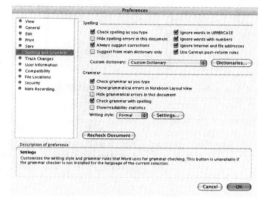

Figure 2 The default settings in the Spelling & Grammar pane of the Preferences dialog.

To enable or disable automatic spelling and/or grammar checking

1. Choose Word > Preferences (**Figure 1**).

2. In the Preferences dialog that appears, click Spelling and Grammar in the left side of the window to display Spelling and Grammar options (**Figure 2**).

3. To enable automatic spelling checking, turn on the Check spelling as you type check box.

   or

   To disable automatic spelling checking, turn off the Check spelling as you type check box.

4. To enable automatic grammar checking, turn on the Check grammar as you type check box.

   or

   To disable automatic grammar checking, turn off the Check grammar as you type check box.

5. Click OK.

✔ Tips

- By default, Word is set up to automatically check spelling and grammar as you type.

- I explain how to set other spelling and grammar preferences in **Chapter 20**.

To check spelling as you type

1. Make sure that the automatic spelling checking feature has been enabled.

2. As you enter text into the document, a red wavy underline appears beneath each unknown word (**Figure 3**).

3. Hold down (Control) and click on a flagged word. The spelling shortcut menu appears (**Figure 4**).

4. Choose the appropriate option:

   ▲ Suggested spellings appear near the top of the shortcut menu. Choosing one of these spellings changes the word and removes the wavy underline.

   ▲ **Ignore All** tells Word to ignore the word throughout the document. Choosing this option removes the wavy underline from all occurrences of the word.

   ▲ **Add** adds the word to the current custom dictionary. The wavy underline disappears and the word is never flagged again as unknown.

   ▲ **AutoCorrect** enables you to create an AutoCorrect entry for the word using one of the suggested spellings (**Figure 5**). The word is replaced in the document and will be automatically replaced with the word you chose each time you type in the unknown word.

   ▲ **Spelling** opens the Spelling dialog (**Figure 6**) for the word.

✔ Tips

■ As shown in **Figure 7**, Word's spelling checker also identifies repeated words and offers appropriate options.

■ AutoCorrect and the Spelling dialog are discussed later in this chapter.

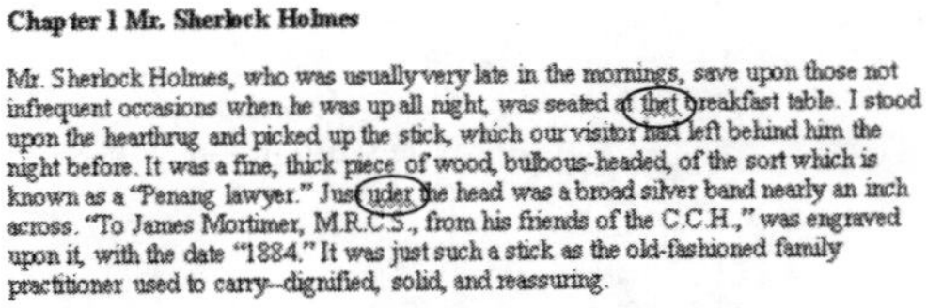

Chapter 1 Mr. Sherlock Holmes

Mr. Sherlock Holmes, who was usually very late in the mornings, save upon those not infrequent occasions when he was up all night, was seated at the breakfast table. I stood upon the hearthrug and picked up the stick, which our visitor had left behind him the night before. It was a fine, thick piece of wood, bulbous-headed, of the sort which is known as a "Penang lawyer." Just under the head was a broad silver band nearly an inch across. "To James Mortimer, M.R.C.S., from his friends of the C.C.H.," was engraved upon it, with the date "1884." It was just such a stick as the old-fashioned family practitioner used to carry--dignified, solid, and reassuring.

Figure 3 Two possible errors identified by the spelling checker.

Figure 4 A shortcut menu displays options to fix a spelling problem.

Figure 5 Choose an option from the AutoCorrect submenu to create an Auto-Correct entry.

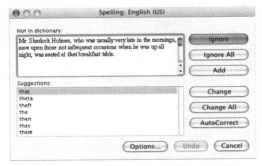

Figure 6 The Spelling dialog offers additional options for dealing with possible spelling errors.

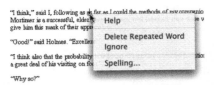

Figure 7 The shortcut menu offers different options for repeated words.

The Constitution of the United States

We the people of the United States, in order to form a more perfect union, establish justice, insure domestic tranquility, provide for the common defense, promote the general welfare, and secure the blessings of liberty to ~~ourselves and our posterity~~, do ordain and establish this Constitution for the United States of America.

Article I

Section 1.

All legislative powers herein granted ~~shall~~ be vested in a Congress of the United States, which shall consist of a Senate and House of Representatives.

Figure 8 Two possible errors identified by the grammar checker.

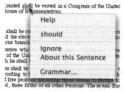

Figures 9 & 10 Using the grammar shortcut menu to correct possible grammar problems.

Order of Words

If you are connecting I, we, me, or us with a noun or another pronoun, place I, we, me, or us last.

• Instead of: I and the student have an appointment.
• Consider: The student and I have an appointment.

• Instead of: Is the dinner for me and you?
• Consider: Is the dinner for you and me?

Figure 11 The Office Assistant can explain grammar rules.

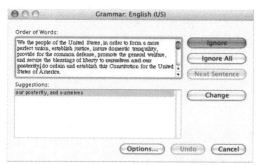

Grammar: English (US)

Order of Words:

We the people of the United States, in order to form a more perfect union, establish justice, insure domestic tranquility, provide for the common defense, promote the general welfare, and secure the blessings of liberty to ourselves and our posterity, do ordain and establish this Constitution for the United States of America.

Suggestions:

our posterity, and ourselves

[Ignore] [Ignore All] [Next Sentence] [Change]

[Options...] [Undo] [Cancel]

Figure 12 The Grammar dialog offers additional options for working with possible grammar problems.

To check grammar as you type

1. Make sure that the automatic grammar checking feature has been enabled.

2. As you enter text into the document, a green wavy underline appears beneath each questionable word, phrase, or sentence (**Figure 8**).

3. Hold down Control and click on a flagged problem. The grammar shortcut menu appears (**Figures 9** and **10**).

4. Choose the appropriate option:

   ▲ Suggested corrections appear near the top of the shortcut menu (**Figure 9**). Choosing a correction changes the text and removes the wavy underline.

   ▲ **Ignore** tells Word to ignore the problem. Choosing this option removes the wavy underline.

   ▲ **About this Sentence** provides information about the grammar rule that caused the sentence to be flagged (**Figure 11**). (The Office Assistant must be displayed for this option to be accessible.)

   ▲ **Grammar** opens the Grammar dialog (**Figure 12**).

✔ Tips

■ I tell you more about the Grammar dialog later in this chapter.

■ Word's grammar checker doesn't always have a suggestion to fix a problem.

■ Don't choose a suggestion without examining it carefully. The suggestion Word offers may not be correct.

To check spelling and grammar all at once

1. Choose Tools > Spelling and Grammar (**Figure 13**) or press Option ⌃ ⌘ L.

   Word begins checking spelling and grammar. When it finds a possible error, it displays the Spelling and Grammar dialog (**Figures 14 and 15**).

2. For a spelling or grammar problem:

   ▲ To ignore the problem, click Ignore.

   ▲ To ignore all occurrences of the problem in the document, click Ignore All.

   ▲ To use one of Word's suggested corrections, select the suggestion and click Change.

   ▲ To change the problem without using a suggestion, edit it in the top part of the Spelling and Grammar dialog. Then click Change.

   For a spelling problem only:

   ▲ To add the word to the current custom dictionary, click Add.

   ▲ To change the word throughout the document to one of the suggested corrections, select the suggestion and click Change All.

   ▲ To create an AutoCorrect entry for the word, select one of the suggestions and click AutoCorrect.

   For a grammar problem only:

   ▲ To skip the current sentence without ignoring it, click Next Sentence.

3. Word continues checking. It displays the Spelling and Grammar dialog for each possible error. Repeat step 2 until the entire document has been checked.

Figure 13
The Tools menu.

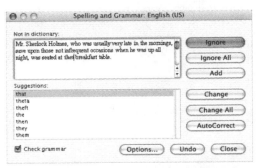

Figure 14 The Spelling and Grammar dialog displaying options for a spelling problem.

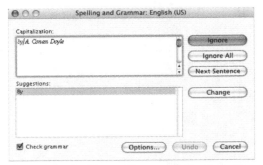

Figure 15 The Spelling and Grammar dialog displaying options for a grammar problem.

Figure 16
If the Office Assistant is displayed, it provides additional information about possible grammar errors.

Capitalization
Capitalize the first word of a sentence.

• Instead of: it usually snows in November.
• Consider: It usually snows in November.

• Instead of: does this book belong to you or to the library?
• Consider: Does this book belong to you or to the library?

✔ Tips

■ The Spelling and Grammar dialog contains elements found in both the Spelling dialog (**Figure 6**) and the Grammar dialog (**Figure 12**).

■ If the Office Assistant is displayed, it will provide additional information (**Figure 16**) about each grammar problem that appears in the Spelling and Grammar dialog (**Figure 15**).

■ To disable grammar checking during a manual spelling check, turn off the Check grammar check box in the Spelling and Grammar dialog (**Figures 14** and **15**).

■ Clicking the Options button in the Spelling and Grammar dialog (**Figures 14** and **15**) displays Spelling & Grammar options (**Figure 2**). I explain how to use these options to customize a spelling and grammar check in **Chapter 20**.

CHECKING SPELLING & GRAMMAR AT ONCE

AutoCorrect

Word's AutoCorrect feature can correct common typographical errors as you make them. You set up AutoCorrect entries by entering the incorrect and correct text in the AutoCorrect dialog (**Figure 17**). Then, each time you make an error for which an Auto-Correct entry exists, Word automatically corrects the error.

✔ Tips

■ Word comes preconfigured with hundreds of AutoCorrect entries based on abbreviations, special symbols, and common errors.

■ AutoCorrect is enabled by default.

To set AutoCorrect options

1. Choose Tools > AutoCorrect (**Figure 13**).

2. The AutoCorrect dialog appears. If necessary, click the AutoCorrect button to display its options (**Figure 17**).

3. Set options as desired:

   ▲ **Correct TWo INitial CApitals** changes the second letter in a pair of capital letters to lowercase.

   ▲ **Capitalize first letter of sentences** capitalizes the first letter following the end of a sentence.

   ▲ **Capitalize names of days** capitalizes the names of the days of the week.

   ▲ **Replace text as you type** enables the AutoCorrect feature for the AutoCorrect entries in the bottom of the dialog.

   ▲ **Automatically use suggestions from the spelling checker** tells Word to replace spelling errors with words from the dictionary as you type.

4. Click OK to save your settings.

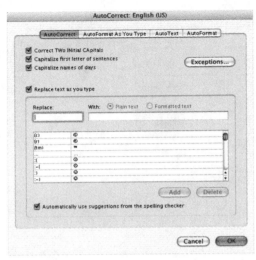

Figure 17 The AutoCorrect options of the AutoCorrect dialog.

✔ Tip

■ To disable AutoCorrect, turn off all check boxes in the AutoCorrect pane of the AutoCorrect dialog (**Figure 17**).

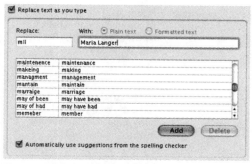

Figure 18 Each AutoCorrect entry has two parts.

To add an AutoCorrect entry

1. Choose Tools > AutoCorrect (**Figure 13**).

2. The AutoCorrect dialog appears. If necessary, click the AutoCorrect button to display its options (**Figure 17**).

3. Type the text that you want to automatically replace in the Replace box.

4. Type the text that you want to replace it with in the With box (**Figure 18**).

5. Click the Add button.

6. Click OK.

✔ Tips

- To add a formatted text entry, enter and format the replacement text in your document. Then select that text and follow the steps above. Make sure the Formatted text radio button is selected before clicking the Add button in step 5.

- As the example in **Figures 18** through **20** illustrates, you can use AutoCorrect to do more than just correct typos and frequent spelling errors. You can also use it to enter lengthy bits of text when you type abbreviations.

To use AutoCorrect

In a document, type the text that appears on the Replace side of the AutoCorrect entries list (**Figure 19**). When you press ⌈Spacebar⌉, ⌈Return⌉, ⌈Shift⌉⌈Return⌉, or some punctuation, the text you typed changes to the corresponding text on the With side of the AutoCorrect entries list (**Figure 20**).

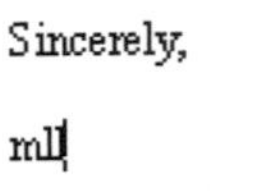

✔ Tip

■ When Word's AutoCorrect feature is activated, it displays a blue underline with an arrow under the entry immediately after it makes a change (**Figure 20**). Pointing to this arrow (or the change after the arrow has disappeared) displays a button for the AutoCorrect Options menu (**Figure 21**). Click the button to access a menu of options for the change (**Figure 22**).

To delete an AutoCorrect entry

1. Choose Tools > AutoCorrect (**Figure 13**).

2. The AutoCorrect dialog appears. If necessary, click the AutoCorrect button to display its options (**Figure 17**).

3. Scroll through the list of AutoCorrect entries in the bottom half of the dialog to find and select the entry that you want to delete.

4. Click the Delete button.

5. Click OK.

Sincerely,

mll

Figure 19
To use an AutoCorrect entry, type the text from the Replace part of the entry...

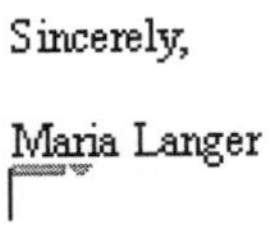

Sincerely,

Maria Langer

Figure 20
...and the With part of the entry appears automatically as you continue typing.

Figure 21 When Word makes an automatic correction, you can point to the change to display a button for the AutoCorrect Options menu.

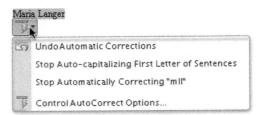

Figure 22 Clicking the button displays a menu of options for working with the change and the AutoCorrect feature.

Click a triangle to display or hide
information in each area.

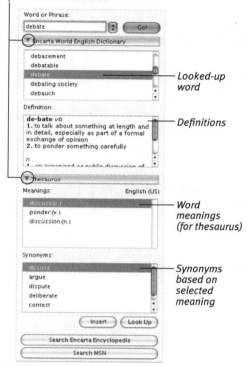

Looked-up word

Definitions

Word meanings (for thesaurus)

Synonyms based on selected meaning

Figure 23 The Reference Tools pane
with the Encarta World English Dictionary and Thesaurus areas displayed.

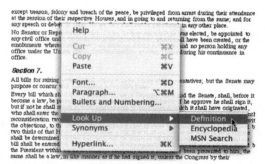

Figure 24 Choose Definition from the Look Up submenu
to display the Reference Tools pane for a specific word
in your document.

Reference Tools

Word includes two built-in reference tools
that can help you use the right words in your
documents:

◆ The **dictionary** enables you to look up
word meanings and usage.

◆ The **thesaurus** enables you to find synonyms and antonyms.

Both of these tools are part of Word's new
Reference Tools pane (**Figure 23**).

✔ Tip

■ The Reference Tools pane also includes
buttons to access the Encarta Encyclopedia and MSN. A discussion of these two
online reference tools is beyond the
scope of this book. If you have an Internet connection, you can explore them on
your own.

To look up a word in a document

1. Hold down Control and click on the word
you want to look up.

2. A shortcut menu appears. Choose
Definition from the Look Up submenu
(**Figure 24**).

Or

1. Select the word you want to look up.

2. Choose Tools > Dictionary (**Figure 13**) or
Tools > Thesaurus (**Figure 13**).

The Reference Tools pane appears (**Figure 23**). The top half of the pane displays
information from the built-in Encarta
World English Dictionary. The bottom
half of the pane displays information
from the built-in thesaurus.

LOOKING UP WORDS

To look up a word that is not in your document

1. If necessary, choose Tools > Reference Tools (**Figure 13**) to display the Reference Tools pane (**Figure 23**).

2. Enter the word you want to look up in the Word or Phrase box at the top of the pane (**Figure 25**).

3. Click Go.

   The word's definition, meanings, and synonyms appear in the Reference Tools pane (**Figure 23**).

To replace a word with a word from the thesaurus

1. Hold down Control and click on the word you want to replace with a synonym.

2. A shortcut menu appears. If the Synonyms option is available, select it to display a submenu of synonyms for the word (**Figure 26**).

3. Choose a replacement word from the submenu.

Or

1. Select the word you want to replace with a synonym.

2. Choose Tools > Thesaurus (**Figure 13**) to display the Reference Tools pane with the word you selected (**Figure 23**).

3. In the Meanings area, select the appropriate meaning for the word.

4. In the Synonyms area, select the synonym you want to replace the selected word with.

5. Click Insert.

The word you originally clicked on or selected is replaced with the new word.

Figure 25 Enter a word in the box at the top of the Reference Tools pane and click Go.

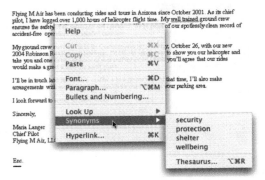

Figure 26 Use the Synonyms submenu to replace a word with a synonym.

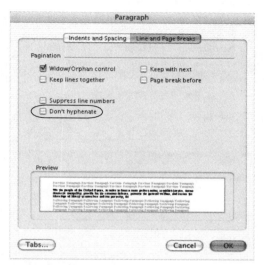

Figure 27 Use the Line and Page Breaks pane of the Paragraph dialog to prevent hyphenation in selected paragraphs.

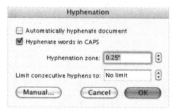

Figure 28 The default settings in the Hyphenation dialog.

✔ Tip

■ To remove hyphenation inserted with the automatic hyphenation feature, turn off the Automatically hyphenate document check box in the Hyphenation dialog (**Figure 28**).

Hyphenation

Word's hyphenation feature can hyphenate words so they fit better on a line. Word can hyphenate the words in your documents automatically as you type or manually when you have finished typing.

✔ Tips

■ Hyphenation helps prevent ragged right margins in left-aligned text and large gaps between words in full-justified text. I tell you about alignment in **Chapter 3**.

■ To prevent text from being hyphenated, select it and then turn on the Don't hyphenate option in the Line and Page Breaks pane of the Paragraph dialog (**Figure 27**). I explain the options in the Paragraph dialog in **Chapter 3**.

To set hyphenation options

1. Choose Tools > Hyphenation (**Figure 13**) to display the Hyphenation dialog (**Figure 28**).

2. Set options as desired:

   ▲ **Automatically hyphenate document** enables automatic hyphenation as you type. (By default, this option is turned off.)

   ▲ **Hyphenate words in CAPS** hyphenates words entered in all uppercase letters, such as acronyms.

   ▲ **Hyphenation zone** is the distance from the right indent within which you want to hyphenate the document. The lower the value you enter, the more words are hyphenated.

   ▲ **Limit consecutive hyphens to** is the maximum number of hyphens that can appear in a row.

3. Click OK.

To manually hyphenate text

1. Follow steps 1 and 2 on the previous page to open the Hyphenation dialog (**Figure 28**) and set options. Be sure to leave the Automatically hyphenate document check box turned off.

2. Click the Manual button. Word begins searching for hyphenation candidates. When it finds one, it displays the Manual Hyphenation dialog (**Figure 29**).

3. Do one of the following:

   ▲ To hyphenate the word at the recommended break, click Yes.

   ▲ To hyphenate the word at a different break, click the hyphen at the desired break and then click Yes. (The hyphen that you click must be to the left of the margin line.)

   ▲ To continue without hyphenating the word, click No.

4. Word continues looking for hyphenation candidates. It displays the Manual Hyphenation dialog for each one. Repeat step 3 until the entire document has been hyphenated.

✔ Tips

■ To hyphenate only part of a document, select the part that you want to hyphenate before following the above steps.

■ You can also manually insert two types of special hyphens within words:

   ▲ Press ⌃ ⌘ − to insert an optional hyphen, which only breaks the word when necessary. Use this to manually hyphenate a word without using the Manual Hyphenation dialog.

   ▲ Press Shift ⌃ ⌘ − to insert a non-breaking hyphen, which displays a hyphen but never breaks the word.

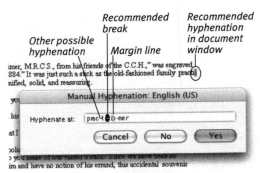

Other possible hyphenation   *Recommended break*   *Margin line*   *Recommended hyphenation in document window*

Figure 29 The Manual Hyphenation dialog.

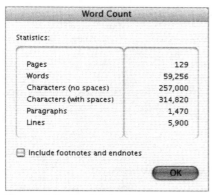

Figure 30 The Word Count dialog.

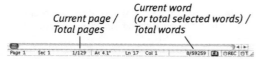

Figure 31 You can find page and word count information at the bottom of the document window.

Word Count

The word count feature counts the pages, words, characters, paragraphs, and lines in a selection or the entire document.

✔ Tip

■ The word count feature is especially useful for writers who often have word count limitations or get paid by the word.

To count pages, words, characters, paragraphs, & lines

1. If necessary, select the text that you want to count.

2. Choose Tools > Word Count (**Figure 13**) to display the Word Count dialog (**Figure 30**).

    After a moment, complete count figures appear.

3. To include footnotes and endnotes in the count, turn on the Include footnotes and endnotes check box.

4. When you are finished working with the count figures, click OK to dismiss the dialog.

✔ Tips

■ If you select text before opening the Word Count dialog, Word only counts the words, characters, etc. in the selection.

■ Word displays word count information in the status bar at the bottom of the document window (**Figure 31**). Clicking this display opens the Word Count dialog.

Change Case

You can use the Change Case dialog (**Figure 32**) to change the case of selected characters. There are five options (**Figure 33**):

◆ **Sentence case** capitalizes the first letter of a sentence.

◆ **lowercase** changes all characters to lowercase.

◆ **UPPERCASE** changes all characters to uppercase.

◆ **Title Case** capitalizes the first letter of every word.

◆ **tOGGLE cASE** changes uppercase characters to lowercase and lowercase characters to uppercase.

✔ Tips

■ You might be wondering: If the Change Case command is under the Format menu, why is it being discussed with features under the Tools menu? Technically speaking, changing the case of characters with the Change Case dialog (**Figure 32**) does *not* format the characters. Instead, it changes the actual characters that were originally entered into the document. To emphasize this point, I decided to discuss it in this chapter, as a writing tool.

■ To change the case of characters without changing the characters themselves, use the All caps or Small caps option in the Font pane of the Font dialog (**Figure 34**). I tell you how in **Chapter 3**.

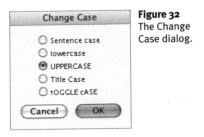

Figure 32
The Change Case dialog.

You can use the Change Case dialog box to change the case of typed characters.
You can use the Change Case dialog box to change the case of typed characters.
you can use the change case dialog box to change the case of typed characters.
YOU CAN USE THE CHANGE CASE DIALOG BOX TO CHANGE THE CASE OF TYPED CHARACTERS.
You Can Use The Change Case Dialog Box To Change The Case Of Typed Characters.
yOU CAN USE THE cHANGE cASE DIALOG BOX TO CHANGE THE CASE OF TYPED CHARACTERS.

Figure 33 Change Case in action—from top to bottom: original text, Sentence case, lowercase, UPPERCASE, Title Case, and tOGGLE cASE.

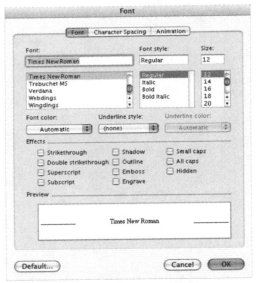

Figure 34 The Font pane of the Font dialog.

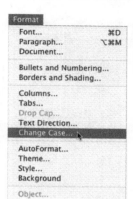

Figure 35
Choosing Change Case from the Format menu.

To change the case of characters

1. Select the characters whose case you want to change.

2. Choose Format > Change Case (**Figure 35**).

3. In the Change Case dialog that appears (**Figure 32**), select the option you want.

4. Click OK.

✔ Tip

■ If you use the Change Case dialog to change the case of characters and get unexpected results, use the Undo command to reverse the action, then try the Change Case dialog again. I cover the Undo command in **Chapter 2**.

AutoSummarize

Word's AutoSummarize feature can automatically summarize a document to identify its key points. It does this by analyzing words and sentences and assigning them a score. More frequently used words get a higher score, identifying them as key points.

✔ Tips

- AutoSummarize works best with documents that are highly structured, such as reports and articles.

- Review a summary before relying on it. It may not be as complete as it needs to be.

To automatically summarize a document

1. Open the document you want to summarize.

2. Choose Tools > AutoSummarize (**Figure 13**) to display the AutoSummarize dialog (**Figure 36**).

3. Select the icon for the type of summary you want. The description beside each icon clearly explains what it does.

4. If desired, use the Percent of original pop-up menu (**Figure 37**) to tell Word how long (or short!) the summary should be.

5. To include the summary in the Summary tab of the Properties dialog, make sure the Update document statistics check box is turned on.

6. Click OK. Word prepares the summary to your specifications. **Figure 38** shows an example.

✔ Tip

- I tell you about the Properties dialog in **Chapter 16**.

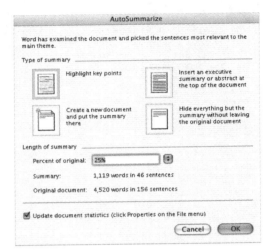

Figure 36 The AutoSummarize dialog.

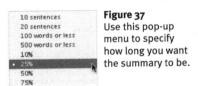

Figure 37
Use this pop-up menu to specify how long you want the summary to be.

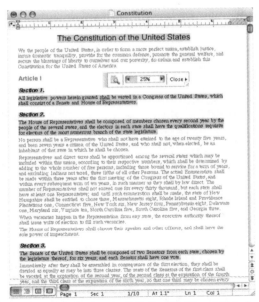

Figure 38 Here's what the U.S. Constitution might look like after Word has highlighted its key points. Note the AutoSummarize toolbar that appears when you summarize with the Highlight key points option.

Tables

Item Name	Description	Item Number	Price
Envelopes, #10	#10 envelopes, 20 lb. white, all-purpose. 500 per box.	ENV10	$15.99/box
Envelopes, #9	#9 envelopes, 20 lb. white, all-purpose. 500 per box.	ENV09	$12.99/box
Permanent Marker, Blue	Mark of Zorro brand permanent marker. 0.5 mm felt tip. Airtight cap. Blue.	MRK01	$2.99 each
Permanent Marker, Red	Mark of Zorro brand permanent marker. 0.5 mm felt tip. Airtight cap. Red.	MRK03	$2.99 each
Laser Paper, White	White, 20 lb. paper, designed for use in laser printers. 8-1/2 x 11 inches. 500 sheets per ream.	PAP05	$5.99/ream
InkJet Paper, White	White, 20 lb. paper, designed for use in inkjet printers. 8-1/2 x 11 inches. 500 sheets per ream.	PAP11	$7.99/ream
Copier Paper, White	White, 20 lb. paper, designed for use in copy machines. 8-1/2 x 11 inches. 500 sheets per ream.	PAP01	$4.99/ream
Shipping Boxes, 9 x 12	9 x 12 inches, corrugated cardboard shipping boxes. White.	BOX05	$10.99/pkg

Figure 1 A four-column, nine-row table with borders. Each box is an individual cell.

Tables

Microsoft Word's table feature enables you to create tables of information.

A table consists of table cells arranged in columns and rows (**Figure 1**). You enter information into each cell, which is like a tiny document of its own. You can put multiple paragraphs of text into a cell and format characters or paragraphs as discussed in **Chapters 3** and **4**.

Table structure and format are extremely flexible and can be modified to meet your needs. A cell can expand vertically to accommodate long blocks of text or graphics; you can also resize it manually as desired. You can format cells, merge cells, and split cells. You can even put a table within a table cell. These capabilities make the table feature a good choice for organizing a wide variety of data.

✔ Tip

- You can also use tab stops and tab characters to create simple tables without cells. **Chapter 3** explains how to do this. This method, however, is not nearly as flexible as using cell tables.

Creating a Table

Word offers four ways to create a table:

- ◆ Use the **Insert Table** command and dialog to create a table at the insertion point.

- ◆ Use the **Insert Table** toolbar button to create a table at the insertion point.

- ◆ Use the **Draw Table** command and toolbar button to draw a table anywhere on a page.

- ◆ Use the **Convert Text to Table** command to convert existing text to a table.

To insert a table with the Insert Table dialog

1. Position the insertion point where you want the table to appear.

2. Choose Table > Insert > Table (**Figure 2**) to display the Insert Table dialog (**Figure 3**).

3. Enter the number of columns and rows for the table in the Number of columns and Number of rows boxes.

4. Choose an AutoFit behavior option:

   ▲ **Initial column width** sets the width of each column regardless of its contents or the window width. If you select this option, enter Auto in the text box to set the table as wide as the print area and divide the table into columns of equal width or enter a value in the text box to specify the width of each column.

   ▲ **AutoFit to contents** sets each column to fit the contents of the widest cell in the column and makes the table as wide as all of the columns combined.

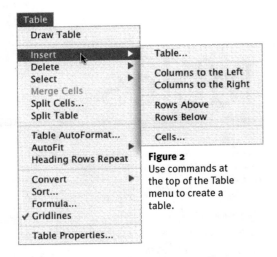

Figure 2
Use commands at the top of the Table menu to create a table.

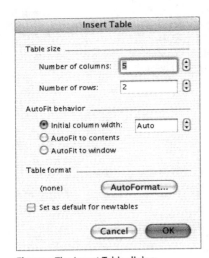

Figure 3 The Insert Table dialog.

Here are some of the tours we offer:

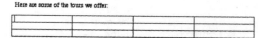

Figure 4 An empty four-column, three-row table inserted after some text.

▲ **AutoFit to window** sets the table's width based on the width of the window and divides the table into columns of equal width.

5. Click OK. The table appears, with the insertion point in the top left cell (**Figure 4**).

✔ Tips

■ You can click the AutoFormat button in the Insert Table dialog (**Figure 3**) to format the table as you create it. Automatically formatting tables is covered later in this chapter.

■ To set the options in the Insert Table dialog (**Figure 3**) as the default options for all new tables you create, turn on the Set as default for new tables check box.

■ You can use this technique to insert a table into a table cell. Just make sure the insertion point is within a table cell before you choose Table > Insert > Table (**Figure 2**).

To insert a table with the Insert Table button

1. Position the insertion point where you want the table to appear.

2. Click the Insert Table button on the Standard toolbar to display a menu of columns and rows.

3. Select the number of columns and rows you want in the table (**Figure 5**).

   The table appears, with the insertion point in the top left cell (**Figure 4**).

✔ Tips

■ This is probably the fastest way to insert an empty table into a document.

■ You can use this technique to insert a table into a table cell. Just make sure the insertion point is within a table cell before you use the Insert Table button's menu.

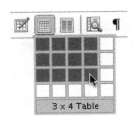

Figure 5
The Insert Table button's menu of columns and rows.

3 x 4 Table

Figure 6 The Tables and Borders toolbar appears when you draw a table.

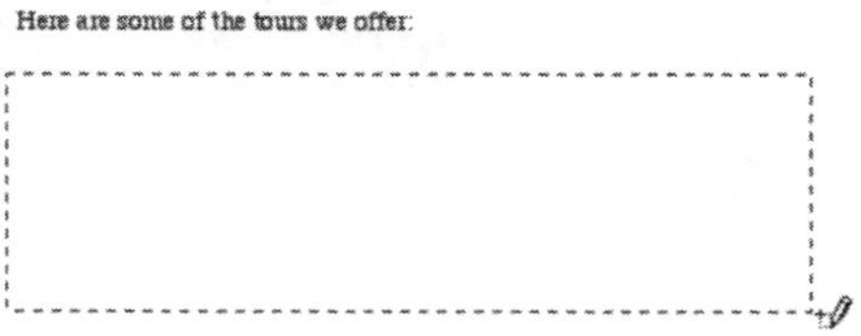

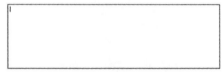

Figure 7 Drag diagonally to draw a box the size and shape of the table you want.

Figure 8 The outside border for a single-cell table appears.

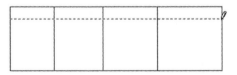

Figure 9 Draw vertical lines for column boundaries...

Figure 10 ...and horizontal lines for row boundaries.

Figure 11 A drawn table.

To draw a table

1. Choose Table > Draw Table (**Figure 2**) or click the Tables and Borders button on the Standard toolbar.

2. If you are not in Page Layout view, Word switches to that view. The Tables and Borders toolbar appears (**Figure 6**). If necessary, click the Draw Table button to select it.

3. Position the Draw Table tool, which looks like a pencil (**Figure 6**), where you want the upper-left corner of the table.

4. Press the mouse button down and drag diagonally to draw a box the size and shape of the table you want (**Figure 7**). When you release the mouse button, the outside border of the table appears (**Figure 8**).

5. Drag the Draw Table tool from the top border of the table to the bottom to draw each column boundary (**Figure 9**).

6. Drag the Draw Table tool from the left border of the table to the right to draw each row boundary (**Figure 10**).

   When you're finished, the table might look something like the one in **Figure 11**.

✔ Tip

- Don't worry if you can't draw column and row boundaries exactly where you want them. Changing column widths and row heights is discussed later in this chapter.

DRAWING TABLES

To convert text to a table

1. Select the text that you want to convert to a table (**Figure 12**).
2. Choose Table > Convert > Convert Text to Table (**Figure 13**).
3. In the Convert Text to Table dialog that appears (**Figure 14**), confirm that the correct separator has been selected and the correct values appear in the text boxes. Make any required changes.
4. Click OK.

   The text turns into a table (**Figure 15**).

✔ Tips

- This method works best with tab- or comma-separated text.
- The AutoFit behavior options in the Convert Text to Table dialog (**Figure 14**) are the same as in the Insert Table dialog. I explain them earlier in this chapter.
- In most instances, Word will correctly "guess" the settings for the Convert Text to Table dialog (**Figure 14**) and no changes will be required in step 3 above.

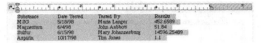

Figure 12 Tab-separated text selected for conversion.

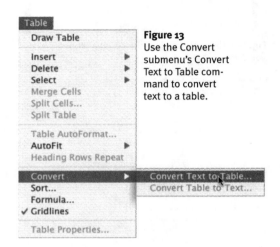

Figure 13 Use the Convert submenu's Convert Text to Table command to convert text to a table.

Figure 14 The Convert Text to Table dialog.

Substance	Date Tested	Tested By	Results
MSG	5/18/98	Maria Langer	452.6589
Magnesium	6/4/98	John Aabbott	51.84
Sulfur	6/15/98	Mary Johannesburg	14596.25489
Aspirin	10/17/98	Tim Jones	1.1

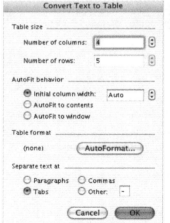

Figure 15 The text in **Figure 12** converted to a table.

Table move handle	End-of-cell mark	End-of-row mark

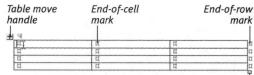

Table resize handle

Figure 16 Table elements include column, row, and cell boundaries, end-of-cell and end-of-row marks, and, in this example, borders.

Figure 17 When a table has no borders, gridlines can identify the boundaries.

Anatomy of a Table

A table includes a variety of elements (**Figure 16**):

◆ **Column boundaries** appear on either side of a column.

◆ **Row boundaries** appear on the top and bottom of a row.

◆ **Cell boundaries** are the portions of column and row boundaries that appear around an individual cell.

◆ **End-of-cell marks** appear within each table cell. They indicate the end of the cell's contents—just like the end-of-document marker marks the end of a Word document.

◆ **End-of-row marks** appear to the right of the last cell in a row. They indicate the end of the row.

◆ **Table move handle** enables you to select the entire table and drag it to a new position in the document.

◆ **Table resize handle** enables you to resize the table by dragging.

◆ **Borders** are lines that can appear on any column, row, or cell boundary. These lines print when the table is printed.

◆ **Gridlines** (**Figure 17**) are lines that appear on any column, row, or cell boundary. Unlike borders, however, gridlines don't print.

Continued on next page...

ANATOMY OF A TABLE

Continued from previous page.

✔ Tips

- To see end-of-cell and end-of-row marks, display nonprinting characters by enabling the Show/Hide ¶ button on the Standard toolbar. I tell you more about nonprinting characters and the Show/Hide ¶ button in **Chapter 1**.

- The table move handle and table resize handle only appear in Page Layout view when the mouse pointer is on the table (**Figure 16**).

- By default, Word creates tables with borders on all column and row boundaries. You can change or remove them using techniques discussed in **Chapter 4**.

- You can only see gridlines on boundaries that do not have borders (**Figure 17**). In addition, the Gridlines option on the Table menu (**Figure 18**) must be enabled for gridlines to appear.

Figure 18
The Table menu.

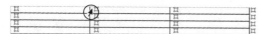

Figure 19 Position the mouse pointer in the cell's selection bar.

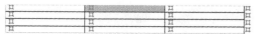

Figure 20 Click to select the cell.

Basic Wickenburg Tour	Circle downtown Wickenburg.	10-15 minutes	$30
Grand Tour of Wickenburg	Our most popular tour offers a complete look at Wickenburg and the surrounding areas, including Vulture Peak, Big Spar Mine, Rancho de los Caballeros, Cemetery Wash, downtown Wickenburg, the Hassayampa River, Box Canyon and the narrow slot canyon beyond, and many of the town's ranches and homes.	20-30 minutes	$75
Ghost Towns and Mines of the Wickenburg Area	Tour the area's hard-to-reach ghost towns and mines. This tour includes sites from Wickenburg to Congress and features Vulture Peak, Vulture City, Big Spar Mine, Mammoth Mine, Dragon Mine, Monte Cristo Mine, Constellation, Gold Bar Mine, Octave, Stanton and Senate Mine.	50-70 minutes	$150

Figure 21 Position the I-beam pointer at the beginning of the cell's contents.

Basic Wickenburg Tour	Circle downtown Wickenburg.	10-15 minutes	$30
Grand Tour of Wickenburg	Our most popular tour offers a complete look at Wickenburg and the surrounding areas, including Vulture Peak, Big Spar Mine, Rancho de los Caballeros, Cemetery Wash, downtown Wickenburg, the Hassayampa River, Box Canyon and the narrow slot canyon beyond, and many of the town's ranches and homes.	20-30 minutes	$75
Ghost Towns and Mines of the Wickenburg Area	Tour the area's hard-to-reach ghost towns and mines. This tour includes sites from Wickenburg to Congress and features Vulture Peak, Vulture City, Big Spar Mine, Mammoth Mine, Dragon Mine, Monte Cristo Mine, Constellation, Gold Bar Mine, Octave, Stanton and Senate Mine.	50-70 minutes	$150

Figure 22 Drag through the cell's contents to select it.

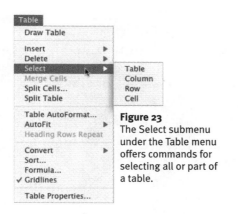

Figure 23
The Select submenu under the Table menu offers commands for selecting all or part of a table.

Selecting Table Cells

In many cases, to format the contents of table cells or restructure a table, you must begin by selecting the cells you want to change. Selecting table cells is very similar to selecting other document text, but Word offers some tricks to make it easier.

To select a cell

1. Position the mouse pointer in the far-left side of the cell so it points to the right (**Figure 19**). This is the cell's selection bar.

2. Click once. The cell becomes selected (**Figure 20**).

Or

1. Position the mouse pointer at the beginning of a cell's contents. The mouse pointer must look like an I-beam pointer (**Figure 21**).

2. Press the mouse button down and drag through the contents of the cell. When you release the mouse button, the cell is selected (**Figure 22**).

Or

1. Position the insertion point anywhere within the cell you want to select.

2. Choose Table > Select > Cell (**Figure 23**).

SELECTING CELLS

To select a row

1. Position the mouse pointer in the selection bar of any cell in the row (**Figure 19**) at the far-left side of the window.

2. Double-click. The entire row becomes selected (**Figure 24**).

Or

1. Click to position the blinking insertion point in any cell in the row (**Figure 25**) or select any cell in the row (**Figure 22**).

2. Choose Table > Select > Row (**Figure 23**). The entire row is selected (**Figure 26**).

To select a column

1. Position the mouse pointer over the top boundary of the column that you want to select. It turns into an arrow pointing down (**Figure 27**).

2. Click once. The column is selected (**Figure 28**).

Or

Hold down Option while clicking anywhere in the column that you want to select.

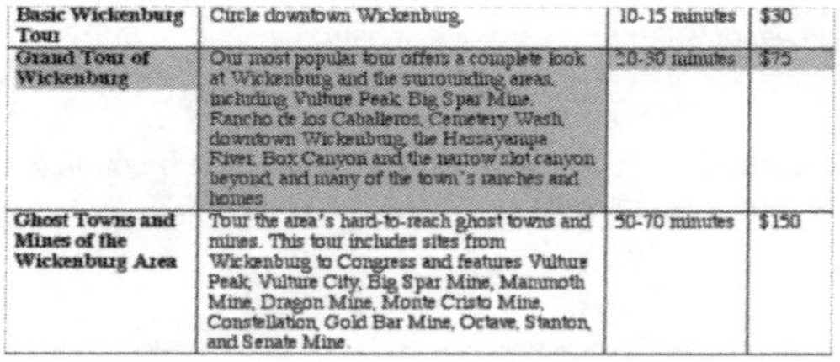

Or

1. Click to position the blinking insertion point in any cell in the column (**Figure 25**) or select any cell in the column (**Figure 22**).

2. Choose Table > Select > Column (**Figure 23**). The entire column is selected (**Figure 29**).

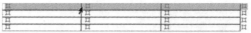

Figure 24 Double-click in a cell's selection bar to select the entire row.

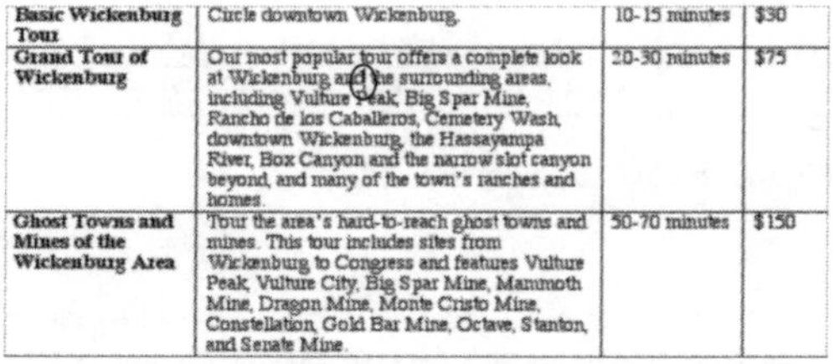

Figure 25 Position the insertion point in any cell in the row.

Figure 26 When you choose Table > Select > Row, the entire row is selected.

Figure 27 Position the mouse pointer over the top boundary of the column.

Figure 28 Click once to select the column.

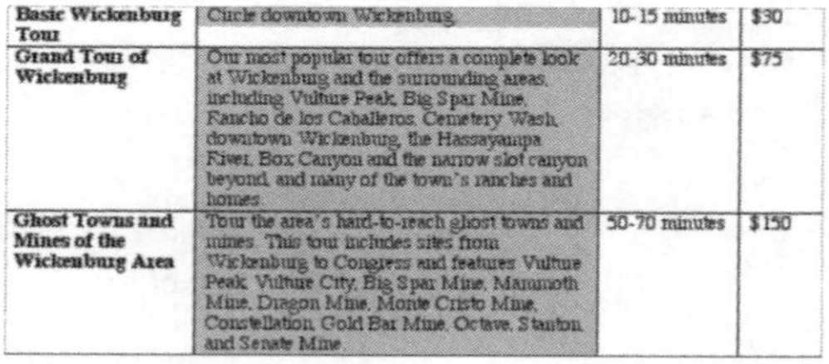

Figure 29 When you choose Table > Select > Column, the entire column is selected.

Figure 30 A selected table.

Basic Wickenburg Tour	Circle downtown Wickenburg	10-15 minutes	$30
Grand Tour of Wickenburg	Our most popular tour offers a complete look at Wickenburg and the surrounding areas, including Vulture Peak, Big Spar Mine, Rancho de los Caballeros, Cemetery Wash, downtown Wickenburg, the Hassayampa River, Box Canyon and the narrow slot canyon beyond, and many of the town's ranches and homes.	20-30 minutes	$75
Ghost Towns and Mines of the Wickenburg Area	Tour the area's hard-to-reach ghost towns and mines. This tour includes sites from Wickenburg to Congress and features Vulture Peak, Vulture City, Big Spar Mine, Mammoth Mine, Dragon Mine, Monte Cristo Mine, Constellation, Gold Bar Mine, Octave, Stanton and Senate Mine.	50-70 minutes	$150

Figure 31 Another selected table.

To select an entire table

Hold down (Option) while double-clicking anywhere in the table. The table is selected (**Figure 30**).

Or

In Page Layout view, click the table move handle (**Figure 16**). The entire table is selected (**Figure 30**).

Or

1. Click to position the blinking insertion point in any cell in the table (**Figure 25**) or select any cell in the table (**Figure 22**).

2. Choose Table > Select > Table (**Figure 23**). The entire table is selected (**Figure 31**).

✔ Tip

■ Although the table move handle's true purpose is to enable you to move a table by dragging it, clicking the move handle automatically selects the entire table.

Entering & Formatting Table Information

You enter text and other information into a table the same way you enter it into any document: type, paste, or drag it in. Then format it as desired using techniques in **Chapters** 3 and 4.

✔ Tips

- Think of each cell as a tiny document window. The cell boundaries are like document margins. You can enter as much information as you like and apply any kind of formatting.

- As you enter information into a cell, the cell expands vertically as necessary to accommodate the text.

- I tell you about copying and moving text with the Cut, Copy, and Paste commands and drag-and-drop text editing in **Chapter 2**.

To enter text into a cell

1. Position the insertion point in the cell (**Figure 32**).

2. Type the text that you want to appear in the cell (**Figure 33**).

   or

   Use the Edit menu's Paste command to paste the Clipboard contents (a previously copied or cut selection) into the cell.

Or

1. Select text in another part of the document (**Figure 34**) or another document.

2. Drag the selected text into the cell in which you want it to appear (**Figure 35**). When you release the mouse button, the text appears in the cell (**Figure 36**).

Figure 32 Position the insertion point in the cell in which you want to enter text.

Basic Tour of Wickenburg			

Figure 33 Type to enter the text.

Basic Tour of Wickenburg			

Circle downtown Wickenburg

Figure 34 Select the text that you want to move into a cell.

Basic Tour of Wickenburg	Circle downtown Wickenburg		

Circle downtown Wickenburg

Figure 35 Drag the selection into the cell.

Basic Tour of Wickenburg	Circle downtown Wickenburg		

Figure 36 When you release the mouse button, the selection moves into the cell.

✔ Tip

- To enter a tab character in a cell, press Control Tab.

Figure 37
You can use the Insert menu to insert special text or objects into a table cell.

Figure 38 Select the object that you want to move into a cell.

Figure 39 Drag the object into the cell.

Figure 40 When you release the mouse button, the object moves.

To enter special text or objects into a cell

1. Position the insertion point in the cell.

2. Choose the appropriate command from the Insert menu (**Figure 37**) to insert special text or objects.

   or

   Use the Edit menu's Paste command to paste the Clipboard contents (a previously copied or cut selection) into the cell.

Or

1. Select special text or objects in another part of the document (**Figure 38**) or another document.

2. Drag the selection into the cell in which you want it to appear (**Figure 39**). When you release the mouse button, it appears in the cell (**Figure 40**).

✔ Tip

■ I tell you about options under the Insert menu in **Chapter 9**.

To move the insertion point from one cell to another

To advance to the next cell in the table, press Tab.

Or

To advance to the previous cell in the table, press Shift Tab.

✔ Tip

■ If you use either of these techniques to advance to a cell that is not empty, the cell's contents become selected. Otherwise, the insertion point appears in the cell.

ENTERING OTHER INFO INTO TABLE CELLS

To format characters or paragraphs in a cell

1. Select the characters that you want to format.

2. Apply font formatting (such as font, font size, and font style) and/or paragraph formatting (such as alignment, indentation, and line spacing) as discussed in **Chapters 3** and **4**.

✔ Tips

- Almost every kind of font or paragraph formatting can be applied to the contents of individual cells.

- I tell you more about formatting tables when I discuss the Table AutoFormat feature later in this chapter.

To align a table

1. Select the entire table (**Figure 41**).

2. Click one of the alignment buttons in the Alignment and Spacing area of the Formatting Palette:

   ▲ **Align Left** or **Justify** shifts the table against the left margin (**Figure 41**). This is the default setting.

   ▲ **Center** shifts the table to center it between the left and right margins (**Figure 42**).

   ▲ **Align Right** shifts the table against the right margin.

✔ Tip

- You will only notice a change in a table's alignment if the table is narrower than the printable area between the document's left and right margins.

Figure 41 Select the table that you want to align.

Figure 42 When you click the Center button on the Formatting Palette, the table centers between the left and right document margins.

Substance	Date Tested	Tested By	Results
MSG	5/18/98	Maria Langer	452.6589
Magnesium	6/4/98	John Aabbott	51.84
Sulfur	6/15/98	Mary Johannesburg	14596.25489
Aspirin	10/17/98	Tim Jones	1.1

Figure 43 Select the column adjacent to where you want to insert a column.

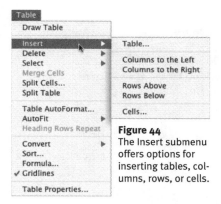

Figure 44
The Insert submenu offers options for inserting tables, columns, rows, or cells.

Substance	Date Tested	Tested By	Results
MSG	5/18/98	Maria Langer	452.6589
Magnesium	6/4/98	John Aabbott	51.84
Sulfur	6/15/98	Mary Johannesburg	14596.25489
Aspirin	10/17/98	Tim Jones	1.1

Figure 45 When you choose Columns to the Left from the Insert submenu, a column is inserted to the left of the selected column.

Substance	Date Tested	Tested By	Results
MSG	5/18/98	Maria Langer	452.6589
Magnesium	6/4/98	John Aabbott	51.84
Sulfur	6/15/98	Mary Johannesburg	14596.25489
Aspirin	10/17/98	Tim Jones	1.1

Figure 46 Select a row adjacent to where you want to insert the row.

Substance	Date Tested	Tested By	Results
MSG	5/18/98	Maria Langer	452.6589
Magnesium	6/4/98	John Aabbott	51.84
Sulfur	6/15/98	Mary Johannesburg	14596.25489
Aspirin	10/17/98	Tim Jones	1.1

Figure 47 When you choose Rows Above from the Insert submenu, a row is inserted above the selected row.

Inserting & Deleting Cells

You can insert or remove columns, rows, or individual cells at any time to change the structure of a table.

To insert a column

1. Select a column adjacent to where you want to insert a column (**Figure 43**).

2. To insert a column to the left of the selected column, choose Table > Insert > Columns to the Left (**Figure 44**) or click the Insert Columns button on the Standard toolbar.

   or

   To insert a column to the right of the selected column, choose Table > Insert > Columns to the Right (**Figure 44**).

   An empty column is inserted (**Figure 45**).

✔ Tip

- To insert multiple columns, select the same number of columns that you want to insert (if possible) in step 1 or repeat step 2 until the number of columns that you want to insert has been inserted.

To insert a row

1. Select a row adjacent to where you want to insert a row (**Figure 46**).

2. To insert a row above the selected row, choose Table > Insert > Rows Above (**Figure 44**) or click the Insert Rows button on the Standard toolbar.

   or

   To insert a row below the selected row, choose Table > Insert > Rows Below (**Figure 44**).

   An empty row is inserted (**Figure 47**).

Continued on next page...

INSERTING COLUMNS & ROWS

Continued from previous page.

Substance	Date Tested	Tested By	Results
MSG	5/18/98	Maria Langer	452.6589
Magnesium	6/4/98	John Aabbott	51.84
Sulfur	6/15/98	Mary Johannesburg	14596.25489
Aspirin	10/17/98	Tim Jones	1.1

Figure 48 Pressing Tab while the insertion point is in the last cell of the table adds a row at the bottom of the table.

✔ Tips

■ Another way to insert a row at the bottom of the table is to position the insertion point in the last cell of the table and press Tab. An empty row is inserted (**Figure 48**).

■ To insert multiple rows, select the same number of rows that you want to insert (if possible) in step 1 or repeat step 2 until the number of rows that you want to insert has been inserted.

Substance	Date Tested	Tested By	Results
MSG	5/18/98	Maria Langer	452.6589
Magnesium	6/4/98	John Aabbott	51.84
Sulfur	6/15/98	Mary Johannesburg	14596.25489
Aspirin	10/17/98	Tim Jones	1.1

Figure 49 Select the cell where you want to insert a cell.

To insert a cell

1. Select the cell at the location where you want to insert a cell (**Figure 49**).

2. Choose Table > Insert > Cells (**Figure 44**) or click the Insert Cells button on the Standard toolbar.

3. In the Insert Cells dialog that appears (**Figure 50**), select an option:

   ▲ **Shift cells right** inserts a cell in the same row and moves the cells to its right to the right (**Figure 51a**).

   ▲ **Shift cells down** inserts a cell in the same column and moves the cells below it down (**Figure 51b**).

   ▲ **Insert entire row** inserts a row above the selected cell.

   ▲ **Insert entire column** inserts a column to the left of the selected cell.

4. Click OK.

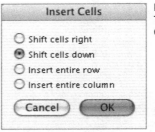

Figure 50 The Insert Cells dialog.

Substance	Date Tested	Tested By	Results	
MSG	5/18/98	Maria Langer		452.6589
Magnesium	6/4/98	John Aabbott	51.84	
Sulfur	6/15/98	Mary Johannesburg	14596.25489	
Aspirin	10/17/98	Tim Jones	1.1	

Substance	Date Tested	Tested By	Results
MSG	5/18/98	Maria Langer	
Magnesium	6/4/98	John Aabbott	452.6589
Sulfur	6/15/98	Mary Johannesburg	51.84
Aspirin	10/17/98	Tim Jones	14596.25489
			1.1

Figures 51a & 51b You can shift cells to the right (top) or down (bottom) when you insert a cell.

✔ Tip

■ To insert multiple cells, select the same number of cells that you want to insert (if possible) in step 1 or repeat steps 2 and 3 until the number of cells that you want to insert has been inserted.

INSERTING CELLS

Substance	Date Tested	Tested By	Results
MSG	5/18/98	Maria Langer	455.6589
Magnesium	6/4/98	John Aabbott	51.84
Sulfur	6/15/98	Mary Johannesburg	14596.25489
Aspirin	10/17/98	Tim Jones	1.1

Figure 52 Select the column that you want to delete.

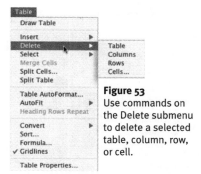

Figure 53
Use commands on the Delete submenu to delete a selected table, column, row, or cell.

Substance	Date Tested	Results
MSG	5/18/98	455.6589
Magnesium	6/4/98	51.84
Sulfur	6/15/98	14596.25489
Aspirin	10/17/98	1.1

Figure 54 The column is deleted.

Substance	Date Tested	Tested By	Results
MSG	5/18/98	Maria Langer	455.6589
Magnesium	6/4/98	John Aabbott	51.84
Sulfur	6/15/98	Mary Johannesburg	14596.25489
Aspirin	10/17/98	Tim Jones	1.1

Figure 55 Select the row that you want to delete.

Substance	Date Tested	Tested By	Results
Magnesium	6/4/98	John Aabbott	51.84
Sulfur	6/15/98	Mary Johannesburg	14596.25489
Aspirin	10/17/98	Tim Jones	1.1

Figure 56 The row is deleted.

Substance	Date Tested	Tested By	Results
MSG	5/18/98	Maria Langer	455.6589
Magnesium	6/4/98	John Aabbott	51.84
Sulfur	6/15/98	Mary Johannesburg	14596.25489
Aspirin	10/17/98	Tim Jones	1.1

Figure 57 Select the cell that you want to delete.

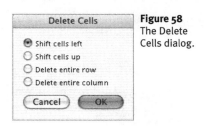

Figure 58
The Delete Cells dialog.

Substance	Date Tested	Tested By	Results
MSG	5/18/98	Maria Langer	
Magnesium	6/4/98	John Aabbott	51.84
Sulfur	6/15/98	Mary Johannesburg	14596.25489
Aspirin	10/17/98	Tim Jones	1.1

Substance	Date Tested	Tested By	Results
MSG	5/18/98	Maria Langer	51.84
Magnesium	6/4/98	John Aabbott	14596.25489
Sulfur	6/15/98	Mary Johannesburg	1.1
Aspirin	10/17/98	Tim Jones	

Figures 59a & 59b You can shift cells to the left (top) or up (bottom) when you delete a cell.

To delete a column, row, or cell

1. Select the column (**Figure 52**), row (**Figure 55**), or cell (**Figure 57**) that you want to remove.

2. Choose the appropriate command from the Table menu's Delete submenu (**Figure 53**) to delete the selected column, row, or cell.

   or

   Press [Delete].

3. If you delete a column, it disappears and the columns to its right shift to the left (**Figure 54**).

   or

   If you delete a row, it disappears and the rows below it shift up (**Figure 56**).

   or

   If you delete a cell, choose an option in the Delete Cells dialog that appears (**Figure 58**):

   ▲ **Shift cells left** deletes the cell and moves the cells to its right to the left (**Figure 59a**).

   ▲ **Shift cells up** deletes the cell and moves the cells below it up (**Figure 59b**).

   ▲ **Delete entire row** deletes the row.

   ▲ **Delete entire column** deletes the column.

   Then click OK.

✔ Tips

- The contents of a column, row, or cell are deleted with it.

- You can select multiple contiguous columns, rows, or cells in step 1 above to delete them all at once.

Merging & Splitting Cells & Tables

You can modify the structure of a table by merging and splitting cells or splitting the table:

◆ Merging cells turns multiple cells into one cell that spans multiple columns or rows.

◆ Splitting a cell turns a single cell into multiple cells in the same column or row.

◆ Splitting a table turns a single table into two separate tables.

To merge cells

1. Select the cells that you want to merge (**Figure 60**).

2. Choose Table > Merge Cells (**Figure 18**). The cells become a single cell (**Figure 61**).

✔ Tip

■ When you merge cells containing text, each cell's contents appear in a separate paragraph of the merged cell (**Figure 61**).

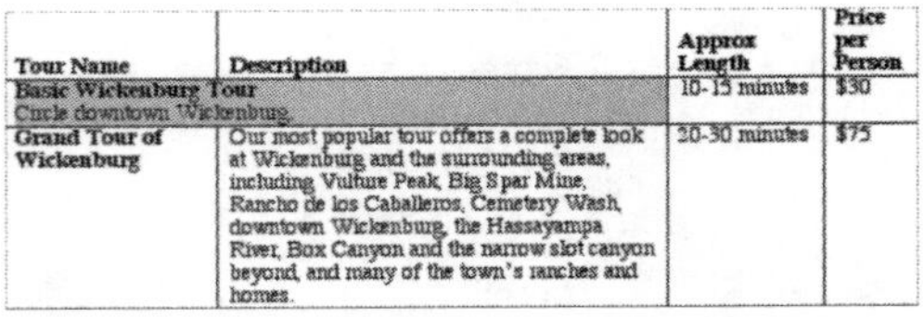

To split cells

1. Select the cell(s) that you want to split (**Figure 62**).

2. Choose Table > Split Cells (**Figure 18**) to display the Split Cells dialog (**Figure 63**).

3. Enter the number of columns and rows for the cell split in the Number of columns and Number of rows text boxes.

4. Click OK. The cell splits as specified (**Figure 64**).

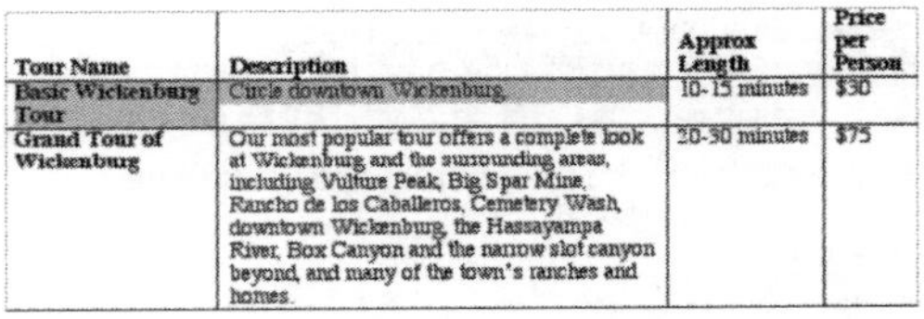

Figure 60 Select the cells that you want to merge.

Figure 61 The cells are merged into one cell.

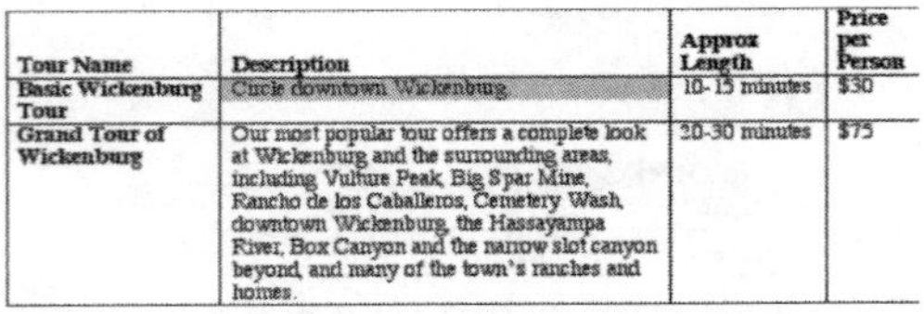

Figure 62 Select the cell that you want to split.

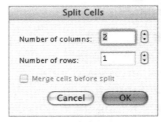

Figure 63 The Split Cells dialog.

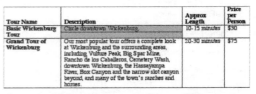

Figure 64 A cell split into one column and two rows.

Figure 65 The cells selected in **Figure 60** after merging and splitting them into one column and three rows.

Figure 66 Position the insertion point in the row below where you want the split to occur.

Figure 67 The table splits above the insertion point.

✔ Tips

■ To split a cell in the middle of its contents, in step 1 position the insertion point where you want the split to occur.

■ To merge and split multiple cells at the same time, in step 1, select all the cells (**Figure 60**). Then, in step 3, make sure the Merge cells before split check box is turned on (**Figure 63**). When you click OK, the cells are merged and split (**Figure 65**).

To split a table

1. Position the insertion point anywhere in the row below where you want the split to occur (**Figure 66**).

2. Choose Table > Split Table (**Figure 18**).

   The table splits above the row you indicated (**Figure 67**).

Resizing Columns & Rows

Word offers two ways to manually change the width of columns or height of rows:

◆ Drag to change column widths and row heights.

◆ Use the Table Properties dialog to change column widths and row heights.

To change a column's width by dragging

1. Position the mouse pointer on the boundary between the column that you want to change and the one to its right. The mouse pointer turns into a double line with arrows (**Figure 68**).

2. Press the mouse button down and drag:

   ▲ Drag to the right to make the column wider.

   ▲ Drag to the left to make the column narrower.

   As you drag, a dotted line indicating the new boundary moves with the mouse pointer (**Figure 69**).

3. Release the mouse button. The column boundary moves to the new position, resizing both columns (**Figure 70**).

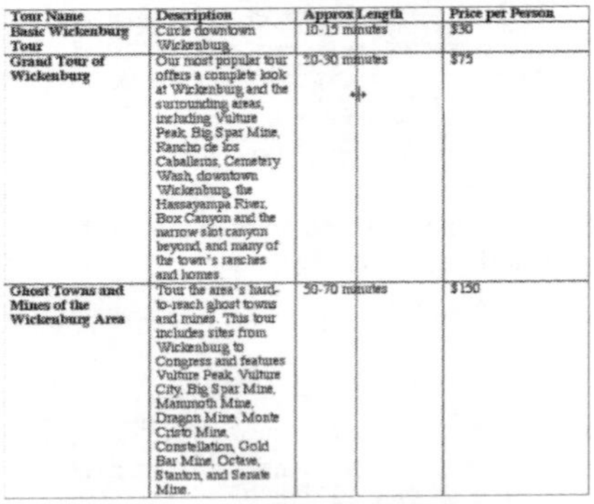

✔ Tips

■ To resize a column without changing the width of other columns, in step 1, position the mouse pointer on the Move Table Column area for the column's right boundary (**Figure 71**). Because this method changes only one column's width, it also changes the width of the table.

■ If a cell is selected when you drag to resize a column, only the selected cell's width changes.

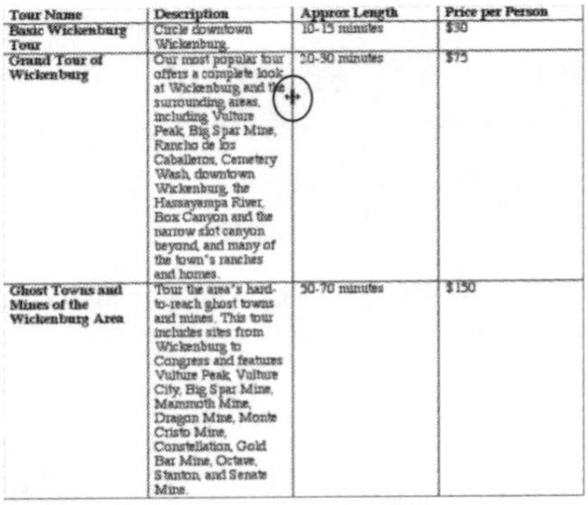

Figure 68 Position the mouse pointer on the column's right boundary.

Figure 69 Drag the column boundary.

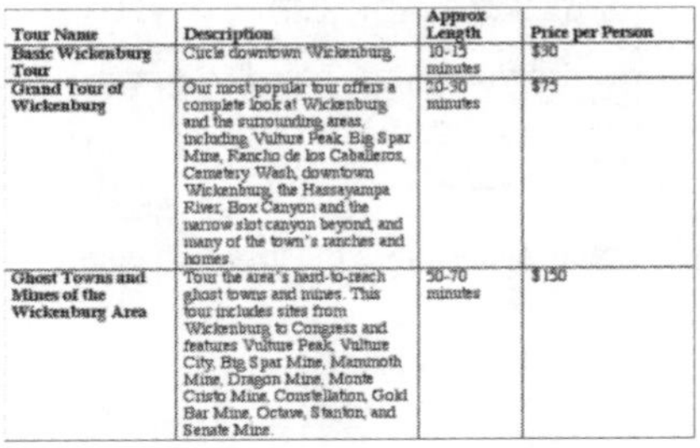

Figure 70 When you release the mouse button, the column and the column to its right resize.

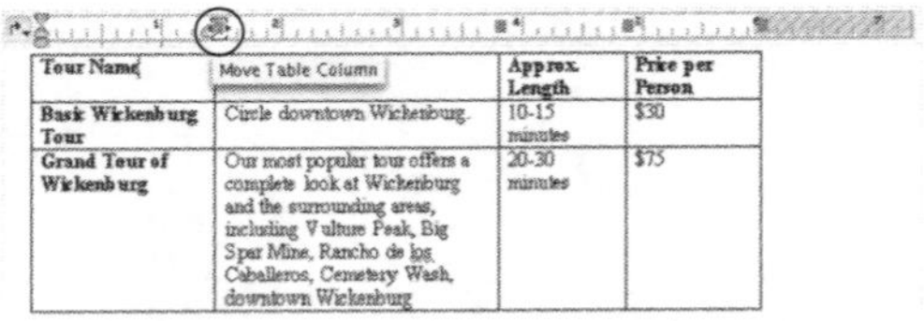

Figure 71 You can also resize a column by dragging the Move Table Column area for the column's right boundary.

Substance	Date Tested	Tested By	Results
MSG	5/18/98	Maria Langer	452.6589
Magnesium	6/4/98	John Aabbott	51.84
Sulfur	6/15/98	Mary Johannesburg	14596.25489
Aspirin	10/17/98	Tim Jones	1.1

Figure 72 Position the mouse pointer on the bottom boundary.

Substance	Date Tested	Tested By	Results
MSG	5/18/98	Maria Langer	452.6589
Magnesium	6/4/98	John Aabbott	51.84
Sulfur	6/15/98	Mary Johannesburg	14596.25489
Aspirin	10/17/98	Tim Jones	1.1

Figure 73 Drag the row boundary.

Substance	Date Tested	Tested By	Results
MSG	5/18/98	Maria Langer	452.6589
Magnesium	6/4/98	John Aabbott	51.84
Sulfur	6/15/98	Mary Johannesburg	14596.25489
Aspirin	10/17/98	Tim Jones	1.1

Figure 74 When you release the mouse button, the boundary moves, changing the row's height.

Figure 75 You can also resize a row by dragging the Adjust Table Row area for the row's bottom boundary.

To change a row's height by dragging

1. If necessary, switch to Page Layout view.

2. Position the mouse pointer on the boundary between the row that you want to change and the one below it. The mouse pointer turns into a double line with arrows (**Figure 72**).

3. Press the mouse button down and drag:
   ▲ Drag up to make the row shorter.
   ▲ Drag down to make the row taller.

   As you drag, a dotted line indicating the new boundary moves with the mouse pointer (**Figure 73**).

4. Release the mouse button. The row boundary moves to the new position. The rows beneath it shift accordingly (**Figure 74**).

✔ Tips

■ Another way to resize a row by dragging is to position the mouse pointer on the Adjust Table Row area of the row's bottom boundary (**Figure 75**). Then follow steps 3 and 4 above.

■ Changing a row's height changes the total height of the table.

■ You can't make a row's height shorter than the height of the text within the row.

To change a table's size by dragging

1. If necessary, switch to Page Layout view.

2. Position the mouse pointer on the table resize handle. The mouse pointer turns into a box with arrows in two corners (**Figure 76**).

3. Press the mouse button down and drag in any direction:

   ▲ Drag to the left to make the table narrower.

   ▲ Drag to the right to make the table wider.

   ▲ Drag up to make the table shorter.

   ▲ Drag down to make the table longer.

   As you drag, a dotted line indicating the new table boundary moves with the mouse pointer (**Figure 77**).

4. Release the mouse button. The table resizes (**Figure 78**).

✔ Tips

■ Dragging the table resize handle to resize a table resizes each column and row proportionally.

■ You cannot make a table any shorter than it needs to be to display table contents.

■ Although you can make a table wider than the page boundaries, the table may be cropped when printed. It's best to keep table width within the page margins. You can change page orientation to landscape (in the Page Setup dialog, as discussed in **Chapter 6**) to print a wide table.

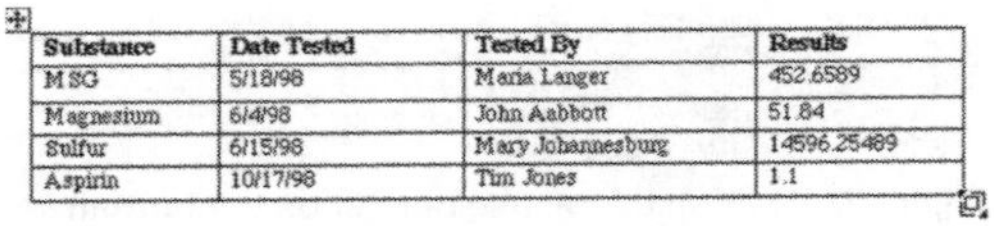

Figure 76 When you position the mouse pointer on the table resize handle, it turns into a resize pointer.

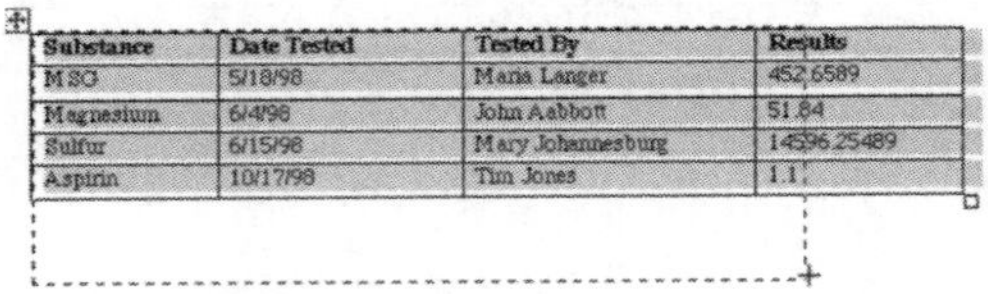

Figure 77 Drag the table resize handle.

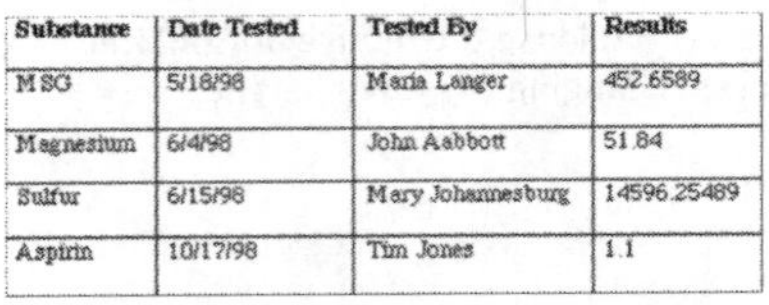

Figure 78 When you release the mouse button, the table is resized.

Figure 79 The Row pane of the Table Properties dialog.

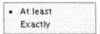

Figure 80 Use this pop-up menu to specify how the row height measurement you enter should be used.

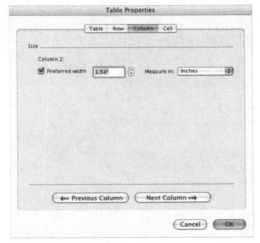

Figure 81 The Column pane of the Table Properties dialog.

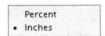

Figure 82 Use this pop-up menu to specify how the column width measurement you enter should be used.

To set row height or column width

1. Select a cell in the row or column for which you want to set height or width.

2. Choose Table > Table Properties (**Figure 18**) to display the Table Properties dialog.

3. To set row height, click the Row button to display its options (**Figure 79**). Turn on the Specify height check box, enter a value in the box beside it, and choose an option from the Row height is pop-up menu (**Figure 80**).

   or

   To set column width, click the Column button to display its options (**Figure 81**). Turn on the Preferred width check box, enter a value in the box beside it, and choose an option from the Measure in pop-up menu (**Figure 82**).

4. Click OK.

✔ Tips

- To set column width and row height at the same time, in step 1, select a cell that is in both the column and row that you want to change. Then follow the remaining steps, including both parts of step 3.

- You can click the Previous Row and Next Row buttons in the Row pane (**Figure 79**) and the Previous Column and Next Column buttons in the Column pane (**Figure 81**) of the Table Properties dialog to cycle through and set values for all the rows and columns in the table.

- The Table Properties dialog also offers a number of advanced features for formatting tables, rows, columns, and cells. Explore them on your own.

Using AutoFit

Table AutoFit options (**Figure 84**) instruct Word to automatically set the column width or row height depending on the table or window width or cell contents. The options are:

◆ **AutoFit to Contents** automatically sizes a column's width based on its contents.

◆ **AutoFit to Window** automatically sizes a table's width to fill the space between the margins.

◆ **Fixed Column Width** locks a column's width so it does not automatically change.

◆ **Distribute Rows Evenly** equalizes the height of rows.

◆ **Distribute Columns Evenly** equalizes the width of columns.

To adjust columns to best fit contents

1. To adjust all table columns, click anywhere in the table (**Figure 83**).

   or

   To adjust just one or more columns, select the column(s).

2. Choose Table > AutoFit > AutoFit to Contents (**Figure 84**).

   The column(s) adjust to minimize word wrap (**Figure 85**).

Figure 83 Position the insertion point anywhere in the table.

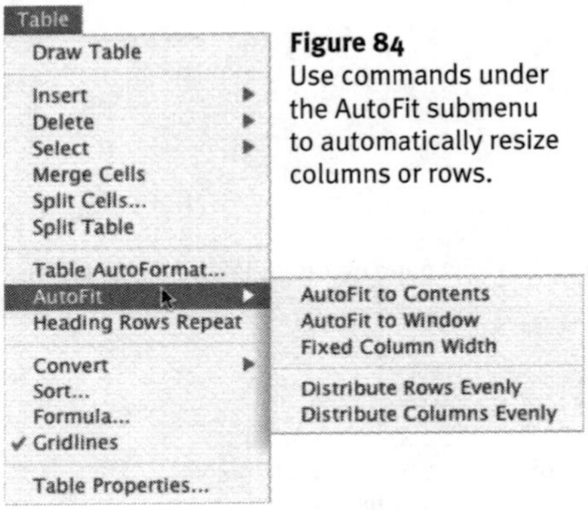

Figure 84 Use commands under the AutoFit submenu to automatically resize columns or rows.

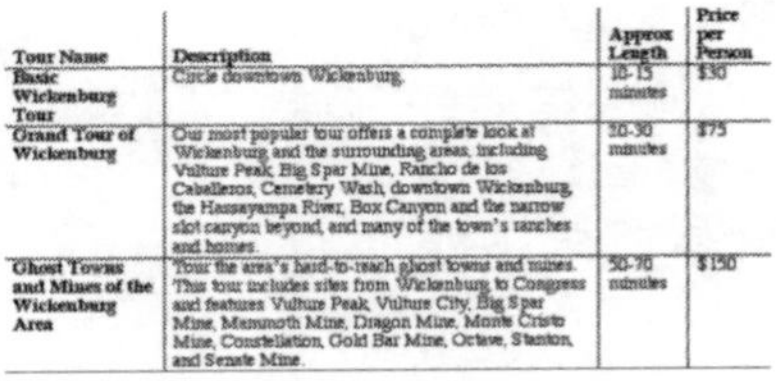

Figure 85 The AutoFit to Contents command minimizes word wrap within cells.

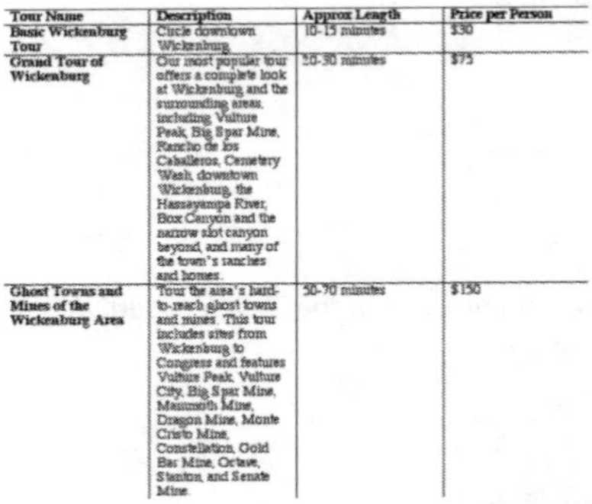

Figure 86 The AutoFit to Window command resizes columns proportionally so the table fits in the space between the margins.

Figure 87 Select the columns for which you want to equalize width.

Figure 88 The space used by the columns is distributed evenly between them.

Figure 89 Select the rows for which you want to equalize height.

Figure 90 The row heights change as necessary so each selected row is the same height.

To adjust a table's width to fill the window

1. Click anywhere in the table (**Figure 83**).

2. Choose Table > AutoFit > AutoFit to Window (**Figure 84**).

   The table's width adjusts to fill the space between the margins (**Figure 86**). Columns are resized proportionally.

To equalize the width of columns

1. Select the columns for which you want to equalize width (**Figure 87**).

2. Choose Table > AutoFit > Distribute Columns Evenly (**Figure 84**). The column widths change to evenly distribute space within the same area (**Figure 88**).

To equalize the height of rows

1. Select the rows for which you want to equalize height (**Figure 89**).

2. Choose Table > AutoFit > Distribute Rows Evenly (**Figure 84**). The row heights change so that all selected rows are the same height (**Figure 90**).

✔ Tip

■ Using the Distribute Rows Evenly command usually increases the height of the table, since all selected rows become the same height as the tallest row.

USING AUTOFIT

Table Headings

A table heading consists of one or more rows that appear at the top of the table. If page breaks occur within a table, the table heading appears at the top of each page of the table (**Figure 91**).

✔ Tip

■ Setting a row as a table heading does not change its appearance. You must manually apply formatting or use the Table AutoFormat command to make headings look different from other data in the table. I tell you about formatting text in **Chapters 3** and **4** and about the Table AutoFormat command on the next page.

To set a table heading

1. Select the row(s) that you want to use as a table heading (**Figure 92**).

2. Choose Table > Heading Rows Repeat (**Figure 93**).

   The selected rows are set as headings.

To remove a table heading

1. Select the row(s) that comprise the heading (**Figure 92**).

2. Choose Table > Heading Rows Repeat (**Figure 93**).

   The headings setting is removed from the selected rows.

✔ Tip

■ Removing the heading feature from selected row(s) does not delete the row(s) from the table.

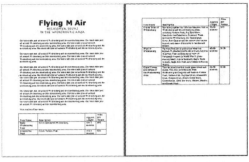

Figure 91 If a page break splits a table into multiple pages, the headings appear at the top of each page of the table.

Tour Name	Description	Approx Length	Price per Person
Basic Wickenburg Tour	Circle downtown Wickenburg.	10-15 minutes	$30
Around the Peak	Circle Vulture Peak.	10-15 minutes	$30
Grand Tour of Wickenburg	Our most popular tour offers a complete look at Wickenburg and the surrounding areas, including Vulture Peak, Big Spar Mine, Rancho de los Caballeros, Cemetery Wash, downtown Wickenburg, the Hassayampa River, Box Canyon and the narrow slot canyon beyond, and many of the town's ranches and homes.	20-30 minutes	$75
West of Wickenburg	Fly west from the airport to see what lies beyond Wickenburg down the old Los Angeles Highway. Tour includes aerial view of Forepaugh Airport (a World War II glider training base), Aguila farmland, Eagle Roost Airpark, Eagle Eye Peak, and Robson's Mining World.	40-50 minutes	$130
Ghost Towns and Mines of the Wickenburg Area	Tour the area's hard-to-reach ghost towns and mines. This tour includes sites from Wickenburg to Congress and features Vulture Peak, Vulture City, Big Spar Mine, Mammoth Mine, Dragon Mine, Monte Cristo Mine, Constellation, Gold Bar Mine, Octave, Stanton, and Senate Mine.	50-70 minutes	$150

Figure 92 Select the row(s) that you want to use as a heading.

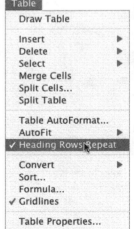

Figure 93 Choose Heading Rows Repeat from the Table menu a second time to remove the heading feature from selected row(s).

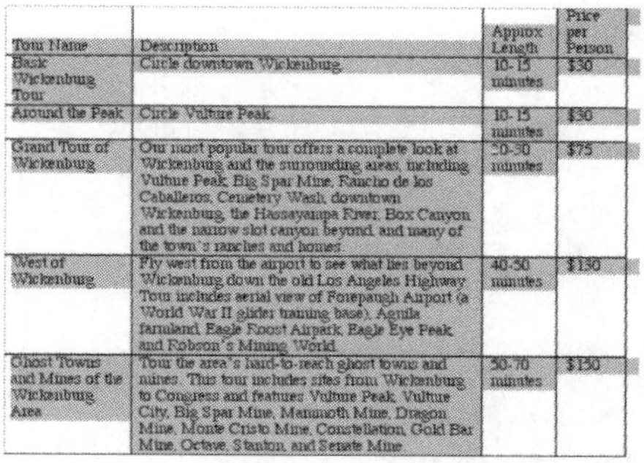

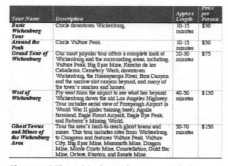

Figure 94 Select the table that you want to format.

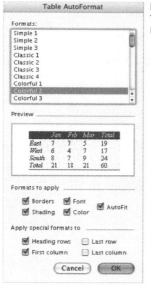

Figure 95
The Table Auto-
Format dialog.

Table AutoFormat

Word's Table AutoFormat feature offers a quick and easy way to combine many formatting options for an entire table.

To use Table AutoFormat

1. Select the table that you want to format (**Figure 94**).

2. Choose Table > Table AutoFormat (**Figure 18**) to display the Table Auto-Format dialog (**Figure 95**).

3. Click to select one of the formats in the scrolling list.

4. Toggle check boxes in the Apply special formats to area to specify which part(s) of the table should get the special formatting.

5. When you're finished setting options, click OK. The formatting for the Auto-Format is applied to the table (**Figure 96**).

✔ Tips

- Each time you make a change in the Table AutoFormat dialog (**Figure 95**), the Preview area changes to show the effect of your changes.

- The Table AutoFormat dialog (**Figure 95**) applies table styles to the selected cells. You can also use this dialog to create new table styles or modify existing ones. Styles are discussed in **Chapter 4**.

- If you don't like the formatting applied by the Table AutoFormat feature, use the Undo command to reverse it. Then try again or format the table manually.

To remove AutoFormatting

Follow steps 1 and 2 above, but select Table Grid in the scrolling list (**Figure 95**) in step 3, and then click OK.

Figure 96 The table from **Figure 91** with the Colorful 2 format applied.

Removing a Table

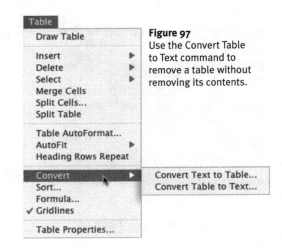

Figure 97
Use the Convert Table to Text command to remove a table without removing its contents.

You can remove a table two ways:

◆ Delete the table, thus removing it and its contents from the document.

◆ Convert the table to text, thus removing the structure of the table from the document but not the table's contents.

To delete a table

1. Select the table that you want to delete.

2. Choose Table > Delete > Table (**Figure 53**).

   or

   Press [Delete].

   The table, and all of its data, is removed from the document.

To convert a table to text

1. Select the table that you want to convert to text.

2. Choose Table > Convert > Convert Table to Text (**Figure 97**).

Figure 98
The Convert Table to Text dialog.

3. In the Convert Table to Text dialog that appears (**Figure 98**), select the radio button for the type of delimiter that you want to use to separate the contents of table cells when the cell boundaries are removed.

4. Click OK.

   The table is converted to text.

Inserting Special Text

Figure 1
The Insert menu.

✔ Tip

- I discuss other Insert menu commands throughout this book:
  - ▲ Break, in **Chapter 4.**
  - ▲ Comment, in **Chapter 16.**
  - ▲ Footnote, Caption, Cross-reference, Index and Tables, and Bookmark, in **Chapter 11.**
  - ▲ Watermark, in **Chapter 5.**
  - ▲ Picture submenu commands, Movie, and Text Box, in **Chapter 10.**
  - ▲ HTML Object submenu commands and Hyperlink, in **Chapter 18.**
  - ▲ Object, in **Chapter 17.**

Special Text

Microsoft Word's Insert menu (**Figure 1**) includes a number of commands that you can use to insert special text into your documents:

- ◆ **AutoText** submenu commands enable you to create and insert AutoText entries, which are commonly used text snippets, such as your name or the closing of a letter.

- ◆ **Field** enables you to insert Word fields, which are pieces of information that change as necessary, such as the date, file size, or page number.

- ◆ **Date and Time** inserts a date or time field than can automatically update to reflect the current date or time.

- ◆ **Page Numbers** inserts a page number field on each page of the document. When viewed onscreen or printed, the field indicates the number of the page on which it appears.

- ◆ **Symbol** enables you to insert symbols and special characters such as bullets, smiley faces, and the registered trade-mark symbol (®).

- ◆ **File** enables you to insert another file into your document.

AutoText & AutoComplete

Word's AutoText feature makes it quick and easy to insert text snippets that you use often in your documents. First, create the AutoText entry that you want to use. Then use one of two methods to insert it:

◆ Use options on the AutoText submenu under the Insert menu (**Figure 3**) to insert the entry.

◆ Begin to type the entry or entry name. When an AutoComplete ScreenTip appears (**Figure 9**), press [Return] to enter the rest of the entry. This feature is known as AutoComplete.

This section explains how to set up and use Word's AutoText and AutoComplete features.

✔ Tips

■ Word comes preconfigured with dozens of AutoText entries.

■ Word's AutoComplete feature also works with contacts from an Entourage contact database. Entourage is part of the Microsoft Office suite of products.

We the people of the(United States)in o:
insure domestic tranquility, provide for 1

Figure 2 Select the text that you want to use as an AutoText entry.

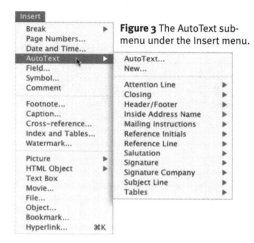

Figure 3 The AutoText sub-menu under the Insert menu.

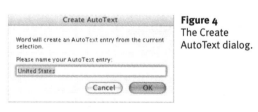

Figure 4 The Create AutoText dialog.

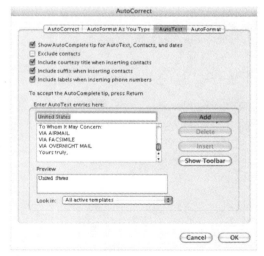

Figure 5 The AutoText pane of the AutoCorrect dialog.

To create an AutoText entry

1. Select the text that you want to use as an AutoText entry (**Figure 2**).

2. Choose Insert > AutoText > New (**Figure 3**).

3. The Create AutoText dialog appears (**Figure 4**). It displays a default name for the entry. If desired, change the name.

4. Click OK.

Or

1. Choose Insert > AutoText > AutoText (**Figure 3**) to display the AutoText pane of the AutoCorrect dialog (**Figure 5**).

2. Enter the text that you want to use as an AutoText entry in the Enter AutoText entries here box.

3. Click Add. The entry appears in the list.

4. Repeat steps 2 and 3, if desired, to add additional entries.

5. When you are finished, click OK.

✔ Tip

■ An AutoText entry can include multiple lines of formatted text (**Figure 6**) and even images. Just select everything you want to include in the entry and use the first set of instructions above.

To delete an AutoText entry

1. Choose Insert > AutoText > AutoText (**Figure 3**) to display the AutoText tab of the AutoCorrect dialog (**Figure 5**).

2. In the scrolling list of AutoText entries, click to select the entry that you want to delete (**Figure 6**). You can confirm that you have selected the correct entry by checking its contents in the Preview area.

3. Click Delete. The entry is removed from the scrolling list.

4. Repeat steps 2 and 3, if desired, to delete other entries.

5. When you are finished, click OK.

To insert an AutoText entry with the AutoText submenu

1. Position the insertion point where you want the AutoText entry to appear.

2. Use your mouse to display the AutoText submenu under the Insert menu (**Figure 3**).

3. Select the submenu option that contains the entry that you want (**Figures 7** and **8**) and select the entry. It is inserted into the document at the insertion point.

✔ Tip

■ The AutoText entries you create appear on the Normal submenu under the AutoText submenu (**Figure 8**).

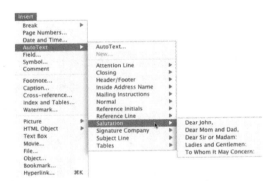

Figure 6 Selecting an AutoText entry.

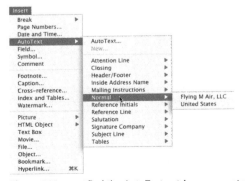

Figure 7 Each submenu on the AutoText submenu contains one or more AutoText entries.

Figure 8 You can find the AutoText entries you create on the Normal submenu.

insure domestic tranquility, provide for the common de
secure the blessin United States ourselves and our pos·
Constitution for the Uni.

Figure 9 When you begin to type text for which there is
an AutoText entry, an AutoComplete ScreenTip appears.

insure domestic tranquility, provide for the common de
secure the blessings of liberty to ourselves and our pos·
Constitution for the United States.

Figure 10 Press [Return] to complete the text you are
typing with the AutoText entry.

Sincerely,

Maria Langer

Figure 11
Word puts a purple dotted
underline beneath contacts
inserted with AutoComplete.

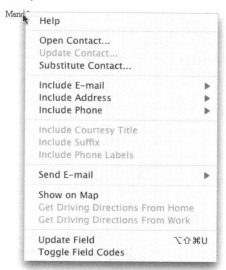

Figure 12 You can display a shortcut menu of options
for inserting additional information for a contact. In
this example, some items are gray and cannot be
selected because they are not available in the contact's
Entourage entry.

To insert an AutoText entry with AutoComplete

1. Type text into your document.

2. When you type the first few characters of an AutoText entry, an AutoComplete ScreenTip appears (**Figure 9**).

3. To enter the text displayed in the Screen-Tip, press [Return]. The text you were typing is completed with the text from the Auto-Text entry (**Figure 10**).

   or

   To ignore the AutoComplete suggestion, keep typing.

✔ Tip

- When you insert a contact from your Entourage contact database with Auto-Complete, Word puts a purple dotted underline beneath it (**Figure 11**). Hold down [Control] and click the contact name to display a shortcut menu of options you can use to insert additional information (**Figure 12**). The dotted underline does not print.

USING AUTOCOMPLETE

To set AutoComplete options

1. Choose Insert > AutoText > AutoText (**Figure 3**) to display the AutoText pane of the AutoCorrect dialog (**Figure 13**).

2. Toggle check boxes in the dialog to set options as desired:

   ▲ **Show AutoComplete tip for AutoText, Contacts, and dates** enables the AutoComplete feature.

   ▲ **Exclude contacts** does not include contacts from your Entourage contact database in AutoComplete.

   ▲ **Include courtesy title when inserting contacts** includes Mr., Ms., etc. when inserting a contact.

   ▲ **Include suffix when inserting contacts** includes Jr., Sr., etc. when inserting a contact.

   ▲ **Include labels when inserting phone numbers** includes identifying labels such as Home, Work, or Mobile when inserting a contact's phone number.

3. Click OK to save your settings.

✔ Tips

- The AutoComplete feature is turned on by default.

- Clicking the Show Toolbar button displays the tiny AutoText toolbar (**Figure 14**), which you can use while you work with Word.

- If you have a lot of contacts in your Entourage contact database, the AutoComplete feature's ScreenTips may drive you crazy by displaying a ScreenTip for any word that you begin to type that matches someone's name. Fortunately, you can turn on the Exclude contacts check box as instructed above to save your sanity. That's what I do.

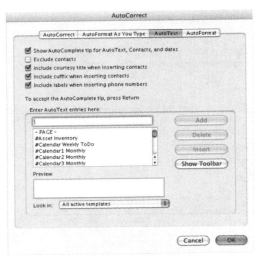

Figure 13 Set AutoComplete options in the top half of the AutoText pane of the AutoCorrect dialog.

Figure 14 The AutoText toolbar.

Word Fields

Word *fields* are special codes that, when inserted in a document, display specific information. But unlike typed text, fields can change when necessary so the information they display is always up-to-date.

For example, the LastSavedBy field displays the name of the last person who saved the document. If someone else saves the document, the contents of the LastSavedBy field will change to that person's name. Similarly, the PrintDate field displays the date the document was last printed. If the document is printed again at a later date, the contents of the PrintDate field will change to reflect the new date.

The Insert menu includes three commands for inserting Word fields:

◆ **Field** enables you to insert any Word field.

◆ **Date and Time** enables you to insert a date or time field.

◆ **Page Number** inserts a page number field in a frame in the document's header or footer. This makes it possible to position a page number anywhere on a page.

This part of the chapter explains how to use these three commands to insert Word fields into your documents. It also explains how to select, update, and delete Word fields.

✔ Tip

■ Word's field feature is a complex and extremely powerful feature of Microsoft Word—one that an entire book could be written about. Although a thorough discussion of Word fields is beyond the scope of this book, the following pages provide the basic information you need to get started using Word fields in your documents.

To insert any Word field

1. Position the insertion point where you want the field to appear (**Figure 15**).

2. Choose Insert > Field (**Figure 1**) to display the Field dialog (**Figure 16**).

3. In the Categories list, select a code category.

4. In the Field names list, select the name of the field you want to insert. A description of the field appears in the bottom half of the Field dialog (**Figure 16**).

5. Click OK. The field is inserted in the document (**Figure 17**).

✔ Tips

■ To set options for the field, after step 4, click the Options button. Then use the Field Options dialog that appears (**Figure 18**) to add field codes for formatting and other options. The options that appear vary depending on the field you are inserting.

■ If field codes appear instead of field contents (**Figure 19**), choose Word > Preferences, click the View options in the Preferences dialog that appears, and turn off the Field codes check box (**Figure 20**).

Aviation Department
Monthly Report

Prepared by: |

Figure 15
Position the insertion point where you want the field to appear.

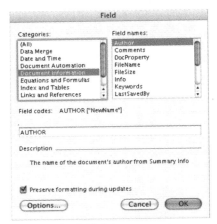

Figure 16 The Field dialog.

Aviation Department
Monthly Report

Prepared by: Maria Langer|

Figure 17
In this example, the Author field was inserted.

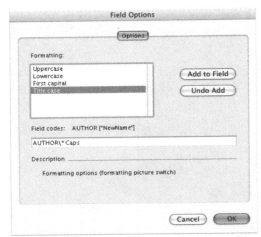

Figure 18 You can use the Field Options dialog to add codes to a field to customize it.

Aviation Department
Monthly Report

Prepared by: { AUTHOR * MERGEFORMAT }|

Figure 19 Here's the same field as **Figure 17** with the field codes rather than the field contents displayed.

Figure 20 Make sure Field codes is turned off in the View pane of the Preferences dialog.

Aviation Department
Monthly Report

Prepared by: Maria Langer
Revision date: |

Figure 21 Position the insertion point where you want the date or time to appear.

Figure 22 The Date and Time dialog.

Aviation Department
Monthly Report

Prepared by: Maria Langer
Revision date: 10/27/2004|

Figure 23 This example shows the Date field inserted in a document.

To insert a date or time field

1. Position the insertion point where you want the field to appear (**Figure 21**).

2. Choose Insert > Date and Time (**Figure 1**) to display the Date and Time dialog (**Figure 22**).

3. Select one of the options in the Available formats list.

4. To insert the date or time as a field that automatically updates when you save or print the document, turn on the Update automatically check box.

5. Click OK. The current date or time is inserted in the document (**Figure 23**).

✔ Tips

■ As shown in **Figure 22**, some of the options in the Available formats list include both the date and the time.

■ If you do not turn on the Update automatically check box in step 4, the current date or time is inserted as plain text rather than as a Word field.

■ If field codes appear instead of field contents (**Figure 19**), choose Word > Preferences, click the View options in the Preferences dialog that appears, and turn off the Field codes check box (**Figure 20**).

INSERTING DATES OR TIMES

To insert a page number

1. Choose Insert > Page Numbers (**Figure 1**) to display the Page Numbers dialog (**Figure 24**).

2. Choose an option from the Position pop-up menu. The options are Top of page (Header) or Bottom of page (Footer).

3. Choose an option from the Alignment pop-up menu (**Figure 25**):

   ▲ **Left** aligns the page number at the left margin of all pages.

   ▲ **Center** centers the page number between margins on all pages.

   ▲ **Right** aligns the page number at the right margin of all pages.

   ▲ **Inside** aligns the page number at the left margin of odd-numbered pages and at the right margin of even-numbered pages.

   ▲ **Outside** aligns the page number at the right margin of odd-numbered pages and at the left margin of even-numbered pages.

4. To include the page number on the first page, make sure the Show number on first page check box is turned on.

5. Click OK. A page number field is inserted in a frame at the location you specified (**Figure 26**).

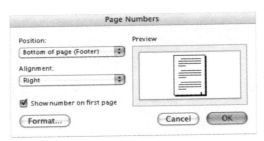

Figure 24 The Page Numbers dialog.

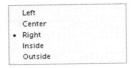

Figure 25 Use the Alignment pop-up menu to set the horizontal position of the page number.

Figure 26 A page number inserted in a footer. In this example, the page number's frame is selected so it's easier to see.

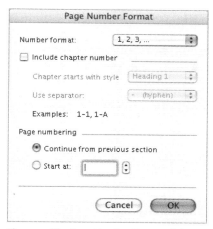

Figure 27 The Page Number Format dialog.

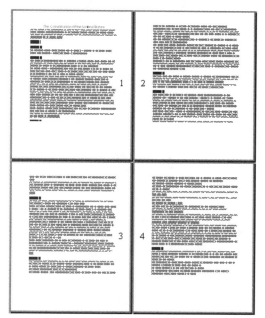

Figure 28 Four pages of a lengthy document in Print Preview. In this example, I used the Page Numbers command to insert a page number in the footer, then formatted the page number and used the Frame dialog to position it in the outside margin.

✔ Tips

- You can click the Format button in the Page Numbers dialog and use the Page Number Format dialog that appears (**Figure 27**) to set number formatting options for the page number.

- To see an inserted page number, choose View > Header and Footer. Then, if necessary, click the Switch Between Header and Footer button on the Header and Footer toolbar to switch to the footer (**Figure 26**). I tell you more about headers and footers in **Chapter 5**.

- The Page Numbers command inserts a page number in a frame. This makes it possible to position the page number *anywhere* on the page (**Figure 28**). Simply drag the frame into position while in Page Layout view or use the Frame dialog to specify precise position settings. I tell you more about working with frames in **Chapter 10**.

- In my opinion, the Page Numbers command is *not* the best way to insert page numbers into a document. A better way is to use the Header and Footer toolbar's Insert Page Number button to insert a page number field in the header or footer, as I explain in **Chapter 5**. This inserts the page number without the frame, which keeps things simple.

To select a field

1. In the document window, click the field once. It turns light gray and the insertion point appears within it (**Figure 29a**).

2. Drag over the field. The field turns dark gray and is selected (**Figure 29b**).

✔ Tip

■ Once you have selected a field, you can format it using formatting techniques discussed in **Chapter 3** or delete it by pressing Delete.

To update a field

1. Hold down the Control key and click on the field to display its shortcut menu (**Figure 30**).

2. Choose Update Field. If necessary, the contents of the field changes.

✔ Tip

■ To ensure that all fields are automatically updated before the document is printed, choose Word > Preferences, click the Print option in the Preferences dialog that appears, and turn on the Update fields check box (**Figure 31**).

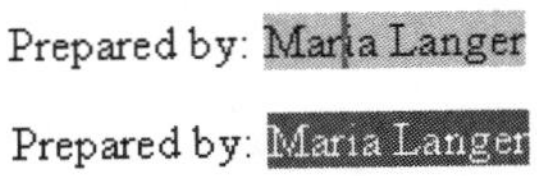

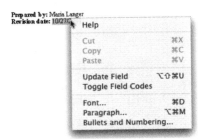

Figures 29a & 29b When you click a field, it turns light gray and the insertion point appears within it (top). When you drag over the field, it turns dark gray or black and is selected (bottom).

Figure 30 A field's shortcut menu includes the Update Field command.

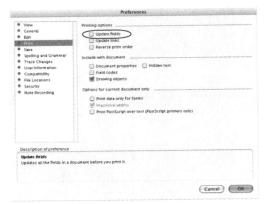

Figure 31 To ensure that all fields are updated before a document is printed, turn on the Update fields check box in the Print pane of the Preferences dialog.

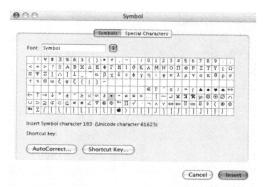

Figure 32 The Symbols pane of the Symbol window.

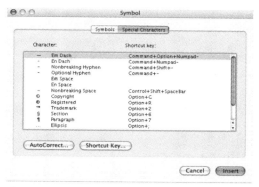

Figure 33 The Special Characters pane of the Symbol window.

Symbols & Special Characters

Symbols are special characters that don't appear on the keyboard. They include special characters within a font, such as ®, ©, ™, or é, and characters that appear only in special "dingbats" fonts, such as ■, ▲, →, and ♣.

Word's Symbol window (**Figures 32** and **33**) makes it easy to insert all kinds of symbols and special characters in your documents.

✔ Tips

- You don't need to use the Symbol window to insert symbols or special characters in your documents. You just need to know the keystrokes and, if necessary, the font to apply. The Symbol window takes all the guesswork out of inserting these characters.

- A *dingbats font* is a typeface that displays graphic characters rather than text characters. Monotype Sorts, Webdings, Wingdings, and Zapf Dingbats are four examples.

- In the Special Characters pane of the Symbol window (**Figure 33**), special characters appear in the current font.

To insert a symbol or special character

1. Position the insertion point where you want the character to appear (**Figure 34**).

2. Choose Insert > Symbol (**Figure 1**).

3. If necessary, click the Symbols button in the Symbol window that appears to display its options (**Figure 32**).

4. Choose the font that you want to use to display the character from the Font drop-down list (**Figure 35**). The characters displayed in the Symbol window change accordingly.

5. Click the character that you want to insert to select it (**Figure 36**).

6. Click Insert. The character that you clicked appears at the insertion point (**Figure 37**).

7. Repeat steps 4 through 6, if desired, to insert additional characters.

8. When you are finished inserting characters, click the Cancel button to dismiss the Symbol window.

✔ Tips

- The (normal text) option on the Font drop-down list (**Figure 35**) uses the default font for the paragraph or character style applied to the text at the insertion point. Styles are discussed in **Chapter 4**.

- When inserting a symbol or special character in the normal font, you may prefer to use the Special Characters tab of the Symbol window (**Figure 33**). The list of special characters includes the shortcut key you can use to type the character without using the Symbol window.

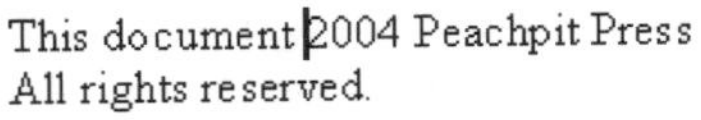

This document 2004 Peachpit Press
All rights reserved.

Figure 34 Position the insertion point where you want the symbol or special character to appear.

Figure 35
The Font drop-down list in the Symbol window lists all fonts installed on your computer that include symbols.

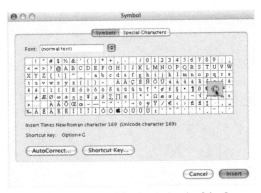

Figure 36 An example of the Symbols tab of the Symbol window being used to insert a special character in the default font.

This document ©2004 Peachpit Press
All rights reserved.

Figure 37 The character you selected appears at the insertion point.

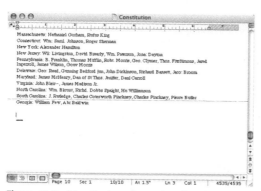

Figure 38 Position the insertion point where you want to insert the file.

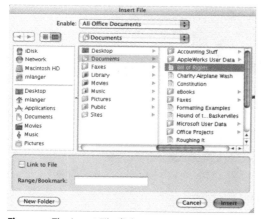

Figure 39 The Insert File dialog.

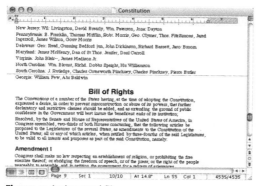

Figure 40 An inserted file.

Files

You can use the File command under the Insert menu to insert one file (the *source* file) within another file (the *destination* file). The source file then becomes part of the destination file.

✔ Tips

- The source file can be in any format that Word recognizes.

- Copy-and-paste and drag-and-drop are two other methods for inserting the contents of one file into another. These techniques are explained in **Chapter 2**.

- A file can be inserted with or without a link. If the source file is linked, when you update the link, the destination file is updated with fresh information from the source file. This means that changes in the source file are reflected in the destination file.

To insert a file

1. Position the insertion point where you want the source file to be inserted (**Figure 38**).

2. Choose Insert > File (**Figure 1**).

3. Use the Insert File dialog that appears (**Figure 39**) to locate and select the file that you want to insert.

4. Click the Insert button. The file is inserted (**Figure 40**).

✔ Tip

- You can use the Enable pop-up menu at the top of the Insert File dialog (**Figure 39**) to view a list of only certain types of files.

INSERTING FILES

To insert a file as a link

Follow all of the steps on the previous page to insert a file. In step 4, turn on the Link to File check box.

✔ Tips

- When you click the contents of a linked file, it turns gray (**Figure 41**).

- Any changes you make in the destination file to the contents of a linked file are lost when the link is updated.

- A linked file is inserted as a field. I tell you about fields earlier in this chapter.

To update a link

1. Hold down Control and click on the linked file to display its shortcut menu (**Figure 42**).

2. Choose Update Field.

   The link's contents are updated to reflect the current contents of the source file.

✔ Tip

- If Word cannot find the source file when you attempt to update a link, it replaces the contents of the source file with an error message (**Figure 43**). There are three ways to fix this problem:

  ▲ Undo the update.

  ▲ Remove the linked file and reinsert it.

  ▲ Choose Edit > Links to fix the link with the Links dialog. (A discussion of the Links dialog is beyond the scope of this book.)

To remove an inserted file

1. Select the contents of the inserted file.

2. Press Delete.

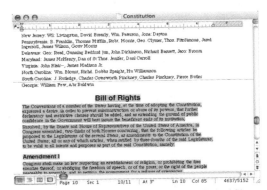

Figure 41 When you click the contents of a linked file, it turns gray.

Figure 42 The shortcut menu for a linked file.

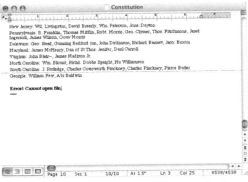

Figure 43 Word displays an error message in the document window when you attempt to update a link and it can't find the source file.

Working
with Graphics

10

Figure 1
The Insert menu.

Working with Graphics

Microsoft Word includes support for inserting and formatting graphic objects, including pictures, line drawings, diagrams, and charts. Graphic elements like these can make your documents more interesting or more informative to readers.

This chapter explores options under the Insert menu (**Figure 1**) and its Picture submenu (**Figure 2**) for inserting graphic elements in your Word documents:

◆ **Picture** submenu options enable you to insert a variety of picture types, including clip art, image files, drawings, AutoShapes, and WordArt.

◆ **Movie** enables you to insert movies in a variety of formats.

◆ **Text Box** inserts a box in which you can enter and format text.

This chapter also provides some basic information for formatting and working with the graphic elements in your Word documents.

✔ Tip

■ I discuss other Insert menu commands throughout this book:

▲ Break, in **Chapter 4**.

▲ Page Numbers, Date and Time, Auto-Text submenu commands, and File, in **Chapter 9**.

▲ Comment, in **Chapter 16**.

▲ Footnote, Caption, Cross-reference, Index and Tables, and Bookmark, in **Chapter 11**.

▲ Watermark, in **Chapter 5**.

▲ HTML Object submenu commands and Hyperlink, in **Chapter 18**.

▲ Object, in **Chapter 17**.

Pictures

Pictures are graphic objects. Word's Picture submenu (**Figure 2**) enables you to insert a variety of picture types:

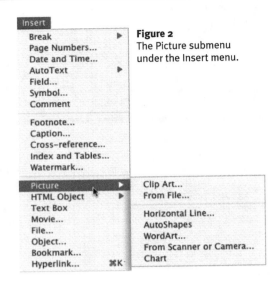

Figure 2
The Picture submenu under the Insert menu.

- ◆ **Clip Art** inserts clip art, pictures, sounds, and videos from the Clip Gallery.

- ◆ **From File** inserts a picture file.

- ◆ **Horizontal Line** inserts a picture file as a horizontal divider.

- ◆ **AutoShapes** displays the AutoShapes and Drawing toolbars, which you can use to draw shapes and lines.

- ◆ **WordArt** inserts stylized text.

- ◆ **From Scanner or Camera** enables you to import images directly from a scanner or digital camera into a Word document.

- ◆ **Chart** inserts a Microsoft Graph chart.

This section introduces all of these options.

✔ Tip

- ■ When a graphic object is inserted into a Word document, it is usually inserted in the *document layer* as an *inline image*—an image that appears on text baselines like any other text. Some graphics, however, can be drawn on or moved to the *drawing layer*. This layer is separate from the text in your Word documents and text can wrap around it.

PICTURES

Figure 3 Position the insertion point where you want the clip art to appear.

Figure 4 Browse Word's clip art by selecting a category.

Figure 5 Clip art that matches your search criteria appears in the Clip Gallery window.

Figure 6 The image is inserted in your document.

To insert clip art

1. Position the insertion point where you want the clip art to appear (**Figure 3**).

2. Choose Insert > Picture > Clip Art (**Figure 2**) to display the Clip Gallery (**Figure 4**).

3. To browse through clip art, select a category on the left side of the window and scroll through the images that appear on the right side of the window.

   or

   To search for clip art by keyword, enter a word or phrase in the Search box at the top of the window and click Search. After a moment, search results appear in the window (**Figure 5**).

4. Select the image you want to insert.

5. Click Insert. The image appears at the insertion point as an inline image (**Figure 6**).

✔ Tip

- If you click the Online button in the Clip Gallery window (**Figure 4**), Word launches your default Web browser and displays the Microsoft Office Clip Art and Media Home Page, where you can search for and download additional clip art.

To insert a picture from a file

1. Position the insertion point where you want the picture to appear.

2. Choose Insert > Picture > From File (**Figure 2**) to display the Choose a Picture dialog (**Figure 7**).

3. Locate and select the file that you want to insert.

4. Click the Insert button.

   The file is inserted as an inline image at the insertion point (**Figure 8**).

✔ Tips

- The Choose a Picture dialog looks and works a lot like the Open dialog. The Open dialog is covered in detail in **Chapter 2**.

- You can use the Enable pop-up menu (**Figure 9**) to specify the type of image file to display in the Choose a Picture dialog.

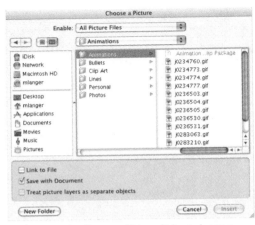

Figure 7 Use the Choose a Picture dialog to insert a picture from a file on disk.

Figure 8 When you insert a picture from a file on disk, it appears at the insertion point.

Figure 9 The Enable pop-up menu lists all kinds of image file formats.

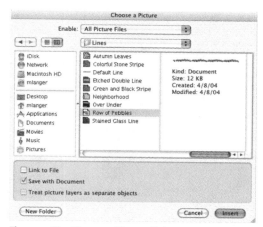

Figure 10 The Choose a Picture dialog automatically looks in the Lines folder for horizontal lines.

Figure 11 The line appears at the insertion point.

To insert a horizontal line

1. Position the insertion point where you want the horizontal line to appear.

2. Choose Insert > Picture > Horizontal Line (**Figure 2**) to display the Choose a Picture dialog (**Figure 10**).

3. Locate and select the line that you want to insert.

4. Click the Insert button.

   The line is inserted as an inline image at the insertion point (**Figure 11**).

✔ Tip

■ As shown in **Figure 10**, the Choose a Picture dialog automatically displays the contents of the Lines folder within the Clipart folder in the Microsoft Office 2004 folder.

INSERTING HORIZONTAL LINES

To display the AutoShapes & Drawing toolbars

Choose Insert > Picture > AutoShapes (**Figure 2**). The AutoShapes and Drawing toolbars appear (**Figure 12**).

✔ Tips

- To display either of these toolbars individually, choose its name from the Toolbars submenu under the View menu. I tell you more about displaying and hiding toolbars in **Chapter 1**.

- The Drawing toolbar has many options you can use to draw lines and shapes or format selected objects—far too many options to cover in this book. Experiment with the toolbar on your own to see how you can use it in your Word documents.

To draw a shape or line

1. Display the AutoShapes toolbar.

2. Click a button to display a pop-up menu of shapes (**Figure 13**) or lines and choose the shape or line that you want to draw.

3. Move the mouse pointer, which becomes a crosshairs pointer (**Figure 14**), into the document window where you want to begin to draw the shape or line.

4. Press the mouse button down and drag. As you drag, the shape (**Figure 15**) or line appears.

5. Release the mouse button to complete the shape (**Figure 16**) or line as an object on the drawing layer.

✔ Tip

- The shape or line pop-up menu that appears when you click an AutoShapes toolbar button (**Figure 13**) can be dragged off the toolbar to create its own toolbar (**Figure 17**).

Drawing toolbar   *AutoShapes toolbar*

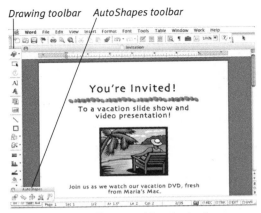

Figure 12 The AutoShapes and Drawing toolbars appear when you choose the AutoShapes command.

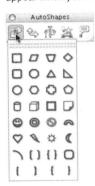

Figure 13 Click a button to display a menu of related shapes or lines.

Figures 14, 15, & 16 Position the crosshairs pointer where you want to begin the shape (left). Press the mouse button and drag; the shape begins to emerge (middle). When you release the mouse button, the shape appears as a selected picture in the document (right).

Figure 17 AutoShapes toolbar pop-up menus can be torn off to form their own toolbars.

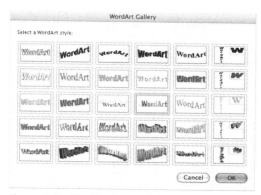

Figure 18 The WordArt Gallery dialog.

Figure 19 The default text in the Edit WordArt Text dialog.

Figure 20 A WordArt image and the WordArt toolbar in a document window.

To insert WordArt

1. Display the Word document in which you want the WordArt image to appear.

2. Choose Insert > Picture > WordArt (**Figure 2**).

3. In the WordArt Gallery dialog that appears (**Figure 18**), click to select a WordArt style.

4. Click OK.

5. In the Edit WordArt Text dialog that appears next (**Figure 19**), change the sample text to the text that you want to display. You can also select a different font and font size and turn on bold and/or italic formatting.

6. Click OK.

   The WordArt image is inserted in your document's drawing layer and the WordArt toolbar appears (**Figure 20**).

✔ Tips

■ Once you have created a WordArt image, you can use buttons on the WordArt toolbar to modify it. The toolbar only appears when the WordArt image is selected.

■ In many instances, the WordArt image will appear right over document text (**Figure 20**). To move a WordArt image, simply drag it to a new position.

To insert a picture from a scanner or a digital camera

1. Make sure the scanner software is properly installed and that the scanner is connected to your computer and turned on. Then place the image you wish to scan on the scanning surface.

   or

   Make sure the digital camera software is properly installed and that the camera is connected to your computer and turned on.

2. In the Word document, position the insertion point where you want the picture to appear.

3. Choose Insert > Picture > From Scanner or Camera (**Figure 2**).

4. The Insert Picture from Scanner or Camera dialog appears (**Figure 21**). Use the drop-down list to choose a device.

5. Click Acquire.

6. Follow the instructions that appear onscreen (**Figure 22**) to scan, select, or capture the image. When you are finished, the image appears in the Word document as an inline image (**Figure 23**).

✔ Tips

- If the Insert Picture from Scanner or Camera dialog (**Figure 21**) does not appear after step 3, your scanner or camera is either not installed correctly or not compatible with Word 2004. (iSight cameras, for example, are not compatible.)

- The procedure in step 6 varies depending on the device you are using. Word may launch your scanner or digital camera software (**Figure 22**) to complete the scan or download an image. If so, consult the device's documentation for instructions.

Figure 21 Use this dialog to select the scanner or camera you want to access.

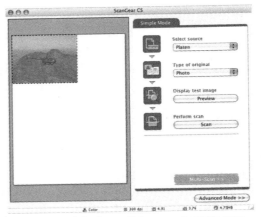

Figure 22 Word displays a dialog you can use to scan, select, or capture the image. In this example, I'm using my Canon scanner to scan a photograph.

Figure 23 The picture appears at the insertion point.

Word document window   Datasheet window   Chart window

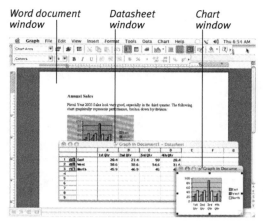

Figure 24 Word inserts a default chart and displays the corresponding Datasheet and Chart windows.

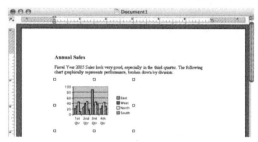

Figure 25 The completed chart appears in the document's drawing layer.

To insert a chart

1. Activate the Word document in which you want the chart to appear.

2. Choose Insert > Picture > Chart (**Figure 2**). Word inserts a chart in the document and displays the corresponding Datasheet and Chart windows (**Figure 24**).

3. Edit the contents of the Datasheet window to reflect the data that you want to chart; the Chart window is updated automatically.

4. When you are finished, choose Graph > Quit & Return to *Document Name*.

   The chart is inserted in the document's drawing layer (**Figure 25**).

✔ Tips

■ You can edit a chart by double-clicking it to display the Datasheet and Chart windows again.

■ You can format a chart by double-clicking its components in the Chart window to display various formatting dialogs.

■ The Graph application that works with Word is very similar to Excel's charting features. If you know Excel, Graph's interface should be very familiar to you.

Movies

The Insert menu's Movie command (**Figure 1**) enables you to insert a movie into a Word document. Word supports a variety of movie formats, including QuickTime, Flash, MPEG, and AVI.

To insert a movie

1. Position the insertion point where you want the movie to appear.

2. Choose Insert > Movie (**Figure 1**) to display the Insert Movie dialog.

3. Locate and select the movie file that you want to insert (**Figure 26**).

4. Click the Choose button. The movie is inserted in the document's drawing layer and the Movie toolbar appears (**Figure 27**).

✔ Tips

- You can use the Movie toolbar (**Figure 27**) to play and set options for a selected movie.

- Click the icon within the movie frame (**Figure 27**) to display the movie's controller (**Figure 28**).

- When you insert a movie, you link it to your document. To open the document with the movie on another computer, the movie must be copied to that computer with the document.

Figure 26 Use this dialog to insert a movie into a Word document.

Figure 27 An inserted QuickTime movie and the Movie toolbar.

Figure 28 An inserted movie with its controller displayed.

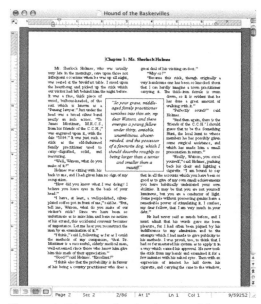

Figure 29 In this example, a text box containing a quote from the document is used as a design element. Text boxes only appear exactly as positioned in Page Layout view (shown here) and Print Preview.

Text Boxes & Frames

Text boxes and *frames* are containers for text and graphics. Word enables you to position them just about anywhere on a page, format them and their contents, and flow text around them (**Figure 29**).

Frames have been a Word feature for as long as I can remember—and I've been using Word since 1990. Text boxes were introduced a few versions ago as part of Word's drawing features. But as Word evolved, Microsoft added more and more functionality to text boxes. In Word X and 2004, you can use a command on the Insert menu (**Figure 1**) to insert a text box in your document; previous versions enabled you to insert a frame instead.

Clearly, Microsoft is encouraging Word users to use text boxes instead of frames. But what's more important is that there are specific instances when you must use one instead of the other.

You must use a text box to do any of the following:

◆ Make text flow from one container to another. This is done by linking text boxes; frames cannot be linked.

◆ Change the orientation of text in a container using the Format menu's Text Direction command.

◆ Format a text container using options on the Drawing toolbar. This includes changing the shape of the text box to one of Word's AutoShapes.

◆ Group text containers and change the alignment or distribution of them as a group.

Continued on next page...

TEXT BOXES & FRAMES

Continued from previous page.

- Create a watermark that appears on document pages when printed. This feature differs from any watermark capabilities that your printer may support.

On the other hand, you must use frames if your text container includes any of the following:

- Inserted comments, which are indicated by comment marks.

- Footnotes or endnotes, which are indicated by note reference marks.

- Certain Word fields, including AUTONUM, AUTONUMLGL, and AUTONUMOUT, which are used for numbering lists and paragraphs in legal documents and outlines, or TC, TOC, RD, XE, TA, and TOA, which are used for various indexes and tables.

This part of the chapter will concentrate on text boxes that are inserted with the Insert menu's Text Box command (**Figure 1**).

✔ Tips

- When you open a document that contains frames created with a previous version of Word, Word keeps the frames.

- You can convert a text box into a frame. I explain how later in this part of the chapter.

- I tell you about footnotes and endnotes in **Chapter 11**. I tell you about Word fields and explain how to insert a page number in a frame in **Chapter 9**.

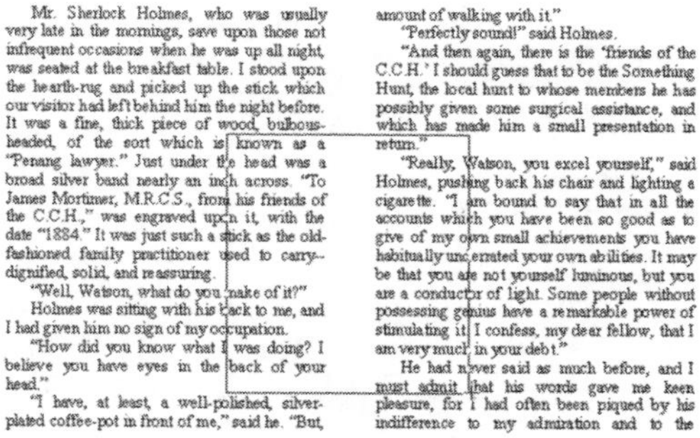

Mr. Sherlock Holmes, who was usually very late in the mornings, save upon those not infrequent occasions when he was up all night, was seated at the breakfast table. I stood upon the hearth-rug and picked up the stick which our visitor had left behind him the night before. It was a fine, thick piece of wood, bulbous-headed, of the sort which is known as a "Penang lawyer." Just under the head was a broad silver band nearly an inch across. "To James Mortimer, M.R.C.S.," from his friends of the C.C.H.," was engraved upon it, with the date "1884." It was just such a stick as the old-fashioned family practitioner used to carry—dignified, solid, and reassuring.

"Well, Watson, what do you make of it?"

Holmes was sitting with his back to me, and I had given him no sign of my occupation.

"How did you know what I was doing? I believe you have eyes in the back of your head."

"I have, at least, a well-polished, silver-plated coffee-pot in front of me," said he. "But,

amount of walking with it."

"Perfectly sound!" said Holmes.

"And then again, there is the 'friends of the C.C.H.' I should guess that to be the Something Hunt, the local hunt to whose members he has possibly given some surgical assistance, and which has made him a small presentation in return."

"Really, Watson, you excel yourself," said Holmes, pushing back his chair and lighting a cigarette. "I am bound to say that in all the accounts which you have been so good as to give of my own small achievements you have habitually underrated your own abilities. It may be that you are not yourself luminous, but you are a conductor of light. Some people without possessing genius have a remarkable power of stimulating it. I confess, my dear fellow, that I am very much in your debt."

He had never said as much before, and I must admit that his words gave me keen pleasure, for I had often been piqued by his indifference to my admiration and to the

Figure 30 Use a crosshairs pointer to draw a text box.

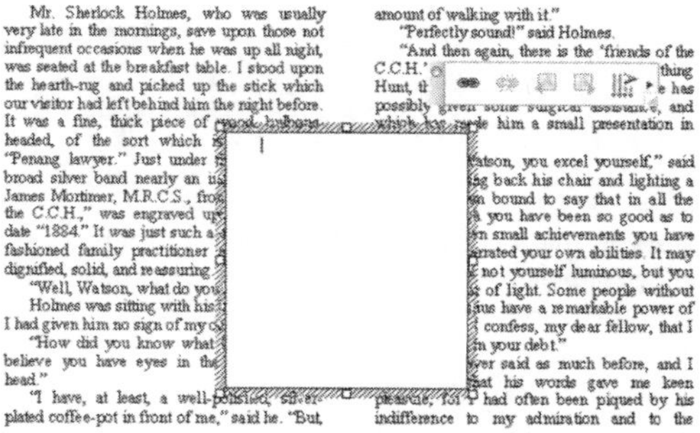

Mr. Sherlock Holmes, who was usually very late in the mornings, save upon those not infrequent occasions when he was up all night, was seated at the breakfast table. I stood upon the hearth-rug and picked up the stick which our visitor had left behind him the night before. It was a fine, thick piece of wood, bulbous-headed, of the sort which "Penang lawyer." Just under broad silver band nearly an James Mortimer, M.R.C.S., from the C.C.H.," was engraved up date "1884." It was just such a fashioned family practitioner dignified, solid, and reassuring.

"Well, Watson, what do you Holmes was sitting with his I had given him no sign of my o

"How did you know what believe you have eyes in the head."

"I have, at least, a well-plated coffee-pot in front of me," said he. "But,

amount of walking with it."

"Perfectly sound!" said Holmes.

"And then again, there is the 'friends of the C.C.H.'

Hunt, th

possibly

which

tson, you excel yourself," said g back his chair and lighting a bound to say that in all the you have been so good as to small achievements you have rated your own abilities. It may not yourself luminous, but you of light. Some people without us have a remarkable power of confess, my dear fellow, that I in your debt."

er said as much before, and I at his words gave me keen had often been piqued by his indifference to my admiration and to the

Figure 31 When you release the mouse button, the text box and the Text Box toolbar appear.

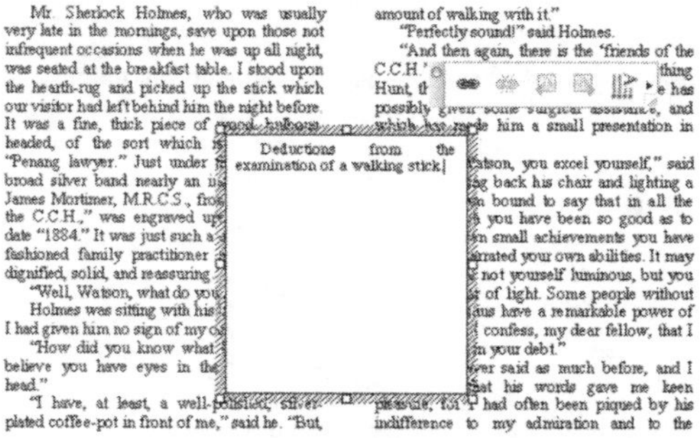

Mr. Sherlock Holmes, who was usually very late in the mornings, save upon those not infrequent occasions when he was up all night, was seated at the breakfast table. I stood upon the hearth-rug and picked up the stick which our visitor had left behind him the night before. It was a fine, thick piece of wood, bulbous-headed, of the sort which "Penang lawyer." Just under broad silver band nearly an James Mortimer, M.R.C.S., from the C.C.H.," was engraved up date "1884." It was just such a fashioned family practitioner dignified, solid, and reassuring.

"Well, Watson, what do you Holmes was sitting with his I had given him no sign of my

"How did you know what believe you have eyes in the head."

"I have, at least, a well-plated coffee-pot in front of me," said he. "But,

amount of walking with it."

"Perfectly sound!" said Holmes.

"And then again, there is the 'friends of the C.C.H.'

Hunt, th

possibly

which

Deductions from examination of a walking stick

tson, you excel yourself," said g back his chair and lighting a bound to say that in all the you have been so good as to small achievements you have rated your own abilities. It may not yourself luminous, but you of light. Some people without us have a remarkable power of confess, my dear fellow, that I in your debt."

er said as much before, and I at his words gave me keen had often been piqued by his indifference to my admiration and to the

Figure 32 You can enter text into a text box by typing or pasting it in.

To insert a text box

1. In an open Word document, choose Insert > Text Box. Two things happen:

   ▲ If the document was in any view other than Page Layout view, it switches to Page Layout view.

   ▲ The mouse pointer appears as a crosshairs pointer.

2. Use the crosshairs pointer to draw a box the approximate size and shape of the text box you want in the location you want it (**Figure 30**).

3. Release the mouse button. The text box appears on the document's drawing layer with selection handles around it and a blinking insertion point within it (**Figure 31**).

4. Enter the text you want to appear in the text box (**Figure 32**).

✔ Tips

- By default, text does not wrap around a text box. I explain how to wrap text around graphic objects, including text boxes, later in this chapter.

- Once text has been entered into a text box, the text can be formatted like any other text. Consult **Chapter 3** for more information about formatting text.

- You can use the Text Box toolbar to change the orientation of text in a text box or link text from one text box to another. Explore the toolbar buttons on your own.

- You can resize a text box like any other graphic object. I explain how later in this chapter.

To select a text box

Click anywhere inside the text box. A thick hashmark border and white selection handles appear around the text box (**Figure 33**).

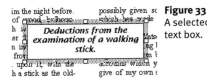

Figure 33 A selected text box.

✔ Tip

■ To select multiple text boxes at the same time, hold down [Shift] while clicking the border of each one.

To delete a text box

1. Select the text box you want to delete (**Figure 33**).

2. Press [Delete]. The text box disappears.

✔ Tip

■ To delete a text box without deleting its contents, first select and copy its contents to another part of the document or to another document.

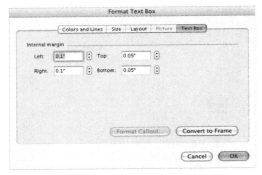

Figure 34 The Text Box tab of the Format Text Box dialog enables you to set text box options or convert a text box to a frame.

To convert a text box to a frame

1. Select the text box you want to convert.

2. Choose Format > Text Box. The Format Text Box dialog appears.

3. Click the Text Box tab to display its options (**Figure 34**).

4. Click the Convert to Frame button.

5. A warning dialog like the one in **Figure 35** appears. Click OK. The text box is converted into a frame (**Figure 36**).

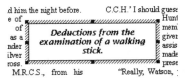

Figure 35 Word warns you before it converts a text box.

✔ Tips

■ By default, text wraps around a frame, as shown in **Figure 36**.

■ You cannot directly convert a frame to a text box. Instead, create a text box, copy the contents of the frame, paste them into the text box, and delete the frame.

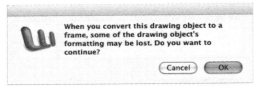

Figure 36 A text box converted to a frame. Note that the selection handles are black and text automatically wraps around a frame. I explain how to wrap text around a text box or other graphic object later in this chapter.

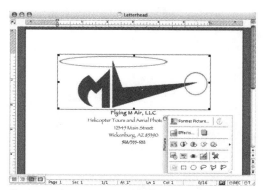

Figure 37 When you click a graphic object in the document layer, a black selection box and handles appear around it and the Picture toolbar appears.

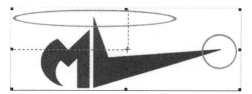

Figure 38 Drag the selection handle toward the center of the picture to make the picture smaller.

Figure 39 When you release the mouse button, the picture resizes.

Working with Graphic Objects

Word includes many powerful image-editing tools that you can use to work with the graphic objects in your Word documents. Although a complete discussion of all of these tools is far beyond the scope of this book, here are some instructions for performing some common layout-related tasks on graphic objects and text boxes in your Word documents.

To move a graphic object

Drag it with the mouse pointer.

◆ A graphic object in the document layer can be moved like a text character.

◆ A graphic object in the drawing layer can be moved anywhere on a page.

To resize a graphic object

1. Click the object to select it. White or black selection handles appear around it (**Figure 37**).

2. Position the mouse pointer on a handle, press the mouse button, and drag as follows:

    ▲ Drag away from the object to make it larger.

    ▲ Drag toward the center of the object to make it smaller (**Figure 38**).

    When you release the mouse button, the object resizes (**Figure 39**).

✔ Tip

■ To resize the object proportionally, drag a corner handle (**Figure 38**).

MOVING & RESIZING GRAPHIC OBJECTS

To wrap text around a graphic object

1. Click the object you want to wrap text around to select it.

2. Choose the last command under the Format menu. As shown in **Figures 40a, 40b**, and **40c**, this command's name changes depending on what is selected.

3. In the Format dialog that appears, click the Layout button to display its options (**Figure 41**).

4. Select one of the Wrapping style options:

   ▲ **In line with text** places the object in the document layer as an inline image. This is the default setting for inline images.

   ▲ **Square** wraps text around all sides of the object with some space to spare.

   ▲ **Tight** wraps text tightly around all sides of the object.

   ▲ **Behind text** places the object behind the document layer. There is no word wrap.

   ▲ **In front of text** places the object in front of the document layer. There is no word wrap. This is the default setting for text boxes.

5. Choose one of the Horizontal alignment options to determine how the object will be aligned in the document window.

6. Click OK.

7. If you selected a Wrapping style option other than In line with text in step 4, the image is moved from the document layer to the drawing layer. Drag it into position in the document and text wraps around it (**Figure 42**).

Figures 40a, 40b, & 40c The last command on the Format menu changes depending on what kind of object is selected in the document window.

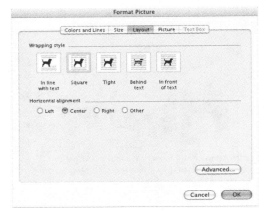

Figure 41 The Layout pane of the Format dialog enables you to set Word wrap options for a selected object.

Figure 42 Once an object is set for text wrapping, text flows around it.

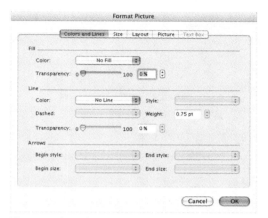

Figure 43 The Colors and Lines tab of the Format Picture dialog.

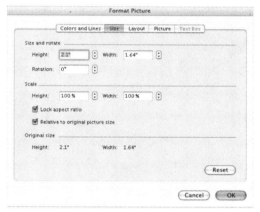

Figure 44 The Size pane of the Format Picture dialog.

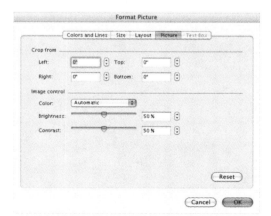

Figure 45 The Picture pane of the Format Picture dialog.

To set advanced formatting options

1. Click the object you want to format to select it.

2. Choose the last command under the Format menu. As shown in **Figures 40a**, **40b**, and **40c**, this command's name changes depending on what is selected.

3. In the Format dialog that appears, click the button for the type of formatting option you want to set:

   ▲ **Colors and Lines** (**Figure 43**) enables you to set options for the object's fill and border color and transparency.

   ▲ **Size** (**Figure 44**) enables you to set size, rotation, and scaling options for the object.

   ▲ **Layout** (**Figure 41**) enables you to set wrapping style and alignment options for the object.

   ▲ **Picture** (**Figure 45**) enables you to set cropping and image control options for the object.

   ▲ **Text Box** (**Figure 34**) enables you to set internal margin options for a text box.

4. Set options in the tab as desired.

5. Repeat steps 3 and 4 for each group of options you want to set.

6. When you are finished setting formatting options, click OK to save your settings. The object changes accordingly.

Continued on next page...

Continued from previous page.

✔ Tips

- The options that are available in each pane of the Format dialog vary, depending on the object you are formatting.

- A complete discussion of all formatting options is far beyond the scope of this book. Experiment with these options on your own. Remember, the Undo command is always available to get you out of trouble if formatting goes wrong.

To remove a graphic object

1. Click the object once to select it.

2. Press (Delete). The object disappears.

Reference Features

Break ▶
Page Numbers...
Date and Time...
AutoText ▶
Field...
Symbol...
Comment

Footnote...
Caption...
Cross-reference...
Index and Tables...
Watermark...

Picture ▶
HTML Object ▶
Text Box
Movie...
File...
Object...
Bookmark...
Hyperlink... ⌘K

Figure 1
The Insert menu.

Reference Features

Microsoft Word includes several features you can use to insert references within a document. These commands can be found on the Insert menu (**Figure 1**):

◆ **Bookmark** enables you to mark a document location for use with the Go To command or other reference features.

◆ **Footnote** inserts a footnote or endnote marker and enables you to enter corresponding reference text.

◆ **Caption** inserts a labeled caption above or below a table, graphic object, or equation.

◆ **Cross-reference** inserts a cross-reference to another part of the document.

◆ **Index and Tables** enables you to create an index or table of contents.

Word's reference features all have one thing in common: They work with Word fields, which I discuss in **Chapter 9**, to create dynamic document content. But instead of requiring you to insert the correct field, the command you use inserts it for you, making the process easier and keeping Word fields out of sight.

This chapter explains how to use each of these reference features in your Word documents.

Bookmarks

A bookmark is an item or location in a document that you identify with a name. You can then reference it by name to jump to the location quickly, create cross-references, and perform other tasks.

For example, suppose you're writing a book about Word and there's a chapter with a section covering captions. You can select all of the text in that section and mark it with a bookmark named *Captions*. You can then use the Go To dialog to quickly display the Captions section. You can also use the bookmark when you create an index, as discussed later in this chapter, to reference all of the pages covering the captions topic.

This part of the chapter explains how to create, modify, and delete bookmarks in Word documents.

To create a bookmark

1. Select the text or item you want to name with a bookmark.

   or

   Position the insertion point where you want to insert the bookmark (**Figure 2**).

2. Choose Insert > Bookmark (**Figure 1**) to display the Bookmark dialog (**Figure 3**).

3. Enter a name for the bookmark in the Bookmark name box.

4. Click Add. The bookmark is created and the dialog disappears.

✔ Tips

- Bookmark names cannot begin with a number or contain nonalphanumeric characters (including spaces) except for the underscore character (_). A bookmark name that begins with an underscore character is hidden.

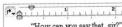

Figure 2
Position the insertion point where you want to insert the bookmark. In this example, the bookmark will be inserted at the beginning of a paragraph.

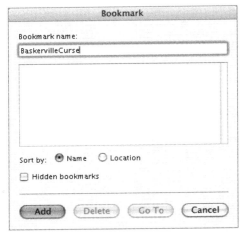

Figure 3 The Bookmark dialog with a bookmark name entered but not yet saved.

- Normally, bookmarks are not visible in a document. I explain how to display them later in this section.

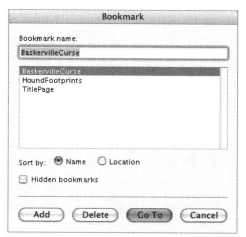

Figure 4 The Bookmark dialog with several book-marks created.

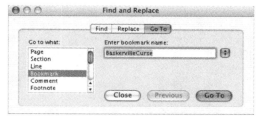

Figure 5 The Go To tab of the Find and Replace dialog.

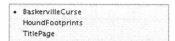

Figure 6 All bookmark names appear on the Enter bookmark name drop-down list in the Go To tab of the Find and Replace dialog.

To go to a bookmark

1. Choose Insert > Bookmark (**Figure 1**).

2. In the Bookmark dialog that appears (**Figure 4**), select the name of the book-mark you want to go to.

3. Click Go To. One of two things happens:
   - ▲ If the bookmark was for a selection, that text or item is selected.
   - ▲ If the bookmark was for a location, the insertion point moves to that location.

Or

1. Choose Edit > Go To or press ⌃⌘G to display the Go To tab of the Find and Replace dialog (**Figure 5**).

2. Select Bookmark in the scrolling list.

3. Choose the bookmark you want to go to from the Enter bookmark name drop-down list (**Figure 6**).

4. Click Go To.

✔ Tips

- ■ If your document contains many book-marks, select a Sort by option in the Bookmark dialog (**Figure 4**) to sort them by name or location.

- ■ No matter which method you use to go to a bookmark, the dialog remains onscreen when you're finished so you can go to another bookmark if desired.

GOING TO BOOKMARKS

To delete a bookmark

1. Choose Insert > Bookmark (**Figure 1**).

2. In the Bookmark dialog that appears (**Figure 4**), select the name of the bookmark you want to delete.

3. Click Delete. The bookmark is removed from the list.

✔ Tip

■ Deleting a bookmark does not delete the text or item that the bookmark refers to.

To display bookmarks

1. Choose Word > Preferences to display the Preferences dialog.

2. Click View to display View Preferences (**Figure 7**).

3. Turn on the Bookmarks check box.

4. Click OK.

   Bookmarks appear in the document as either brackets around a selection (**Figure 8**) or as an I-beam in a location (**Figure 9**).

✔ Tip

■ Although bookmarks may appear onscreen, they don't print.

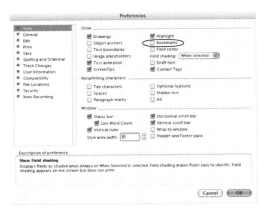

Figure 7 You can make bookmarks visible with the View Preferences dialog.

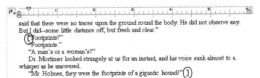

Figure 8 Brackets appear around a bookmark for a selection.

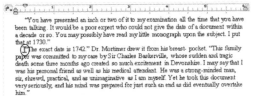

Figure 9 An I-beam appears as a bookmark for a location.

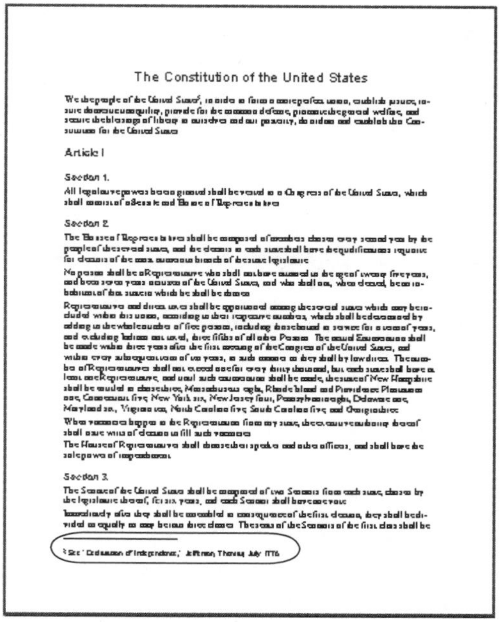
The Constitution of the United States

Article I

Section 1.

Section 2.

Section 3.

Figure 10 A page with a footnote. Word automatically inserts the footnote separator line, too.

Footnotes & Endnotes

Footnotes and endnotes are annotations for specific document text. You insert a marker—usually a number or symbol—right after the text, tell Word where you want the note to go, and enter the note. When you view the document in Page Layout view or Print Preview, or print the document, the note appears where you specified.

The difference between a footnote and an endnote is its position in the document:

- **Footnotes** appear either after the last line of text on the page on which the annotated text appears or at the bottom of the page on which the annotated text appears (**Figure 10**).
- **Endnotes** appear either at the end of the section in which the annotated text appears or at the end of the document.

✔ Tips

- Footnotes and endnotes are commonly used to show the source of a piece of information or provide additional information that may not be of interest to every reader.
- Multiple-section documents are covered in **Chapter 5**.
- Word automatically renumbers footnotes or endnotes, whenever necessary, when you insert or delete a note.
- If you're old enough to remember preparing high school or college term papers on a typewriter, you'll recognize this feature as another example of how easy kids have it today. (Sheesh! I sound like my mother!)

To insert a footnote or endnote

1. Position the insertion point immediately after the text that you want to annotate (**Figure 11**).

2. Choose Insert > Footnote (**Figure 1**) to display the Footnote and Endnote dialog (**Figure 12**).

3. In the Insert area, select the option for the type of note you want to insert.

4. In the Numbering area, select the option for the type of numbering you want. If you select Custom mark, enter a character for the mark in the box beside it.

5. Click OK. Word inserts a marker at the insertion point, then one of two things happens:

   ▲ If you are in Normal or Online Layout view, the window splits to display a footnote or endnote pane with the insertion point blinking beside the marker (**Figure 13**).

   ▲ If you are in Page Layout view, the view shifts to the location of the footnote or endnote where a separator line is inserted. The insertion point blinks beside the marker (**Figure 14**).

6. Enter the footnote or endnote text (**Figure 15**).

✔ Tips

- In step 4, you can click the Symbol button to display the Symbol window (**Figure 16**), click a symbol to select it, and click OK to insert it in the Custom mark box. I explain how to use the Symbol dialog in **Chapter 9**.

- In Normal view, to close the footnote pane, click the Close button at the top of the pane.

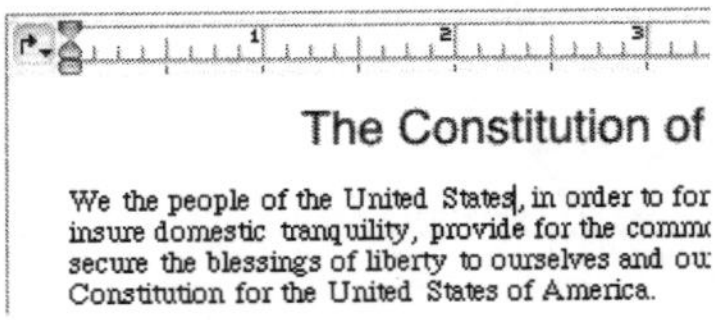

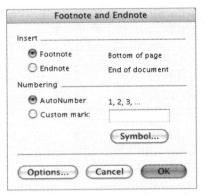

Figure 11 Position the insertion point immediately after the text that you want to annotate.

Figure 12 The Footnote and Endnote dialog.

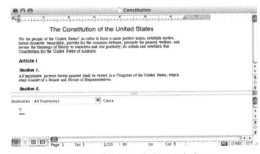

Figure 13 Entering a footnote in Normal view.

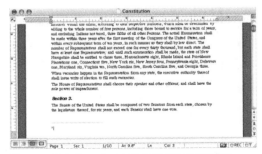

Figure 14 Entering a footnote in Page Layout view.

[1] See "Declaration of Independence," Jefferson, Thomas, July 1776|

Figure 15 Enter Footnote text right after the marker.

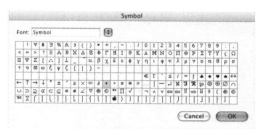

Figure 16 You can use the Symbol window to select a symbol (instead of a number) to use as a marker.

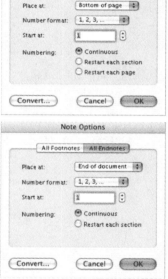

Figures 17 & 18 The Note Options dialog for All Footnotes (top) and All Endnotes (bottom).

To set note options

1. Choose Insert > Footnote (**Figure 1**) to display the Footnote and Endnote dialog (**Figure 12**).

2. Click the Options button to display the Note Options dialog.

3. Click the button for the type of note you want to set options for: All Footnotes (**Figure 17**) or All Endnotes (**Figure 18**).

4. Choose an option from the Place at pop-up menu to determine where the notes should appear.

5. Choose an option from the Number format pop-up menu (**Figure 19**).

6. If you want the notes to start with a number other than 1, enter a different value in the Start at box.

7. Choose a Numbering option to determine how Word should automatically number the notes.

8. Click OK to save your settings.

9. In the Footnote and Endnote dialog, click Close to save your settings without inserting a footnote or endnote.

- 1, 2, 3, ...
  a, b, c, ...
  A, B, C, ...
  i, ii, iii, ...
  I, II, III, ...
  *, †, ‡, §, ...

Figure 19 Use the Number format pop-up menu to choose an automatic numbering option.

SETTING NOTE OPTIONS

To convert notes

1. Choose Insert > Footnote (**Figure 1**) to display the Footnote and Endnote dialog (**Figure 12**).

2. Click the Options button to display the Note Options dialog (**Figure 17 or 18**).

3. Click the Convert button to display the Convert Notes dialog (**Figure 20**).

4. Select the option for the type of conversion that you want to do.

5. Click OK to make the conversion.

6. In the Footnote and Endnote dialog, click Close to save your settings without inserting a footnote or endnote.

✔ Tip

- The options available in the Convert Notes dialog (**Figure 20**) vary depending on the type(s) of notes in the document.

To delete a note

1. In the document window (not the note area or pane), select the note marker (**Figure 21**).

2. Press (Delete). The note marker and corresponding note are removed from the document. If the note was numbered using the AutoNumber option, all notes after it are properly renumbered.

✔ Tip

- If you have trouble selecting the tiny note marker in the document, use the Zoom drop-down list on the Standard toolbar (**Figure 22**) to increase the window's magnification so you can see it better. Zooming a window's view is covered in **Chapter 1**.

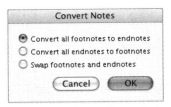

Figure 20 The Convert Notes dialog for a document that contains both footnotes and endnotes.

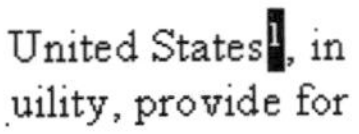

United States , in uility, provide for

Figure 21 To delete a footnote or endnote, begin by selecting the note marker.

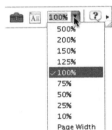

Figure 22 You can use the Zoom drop-down list on the Standard toolbar to increase the window's magnification so you can see the tiny note markers.

CONVERTING & DELETING NOTES

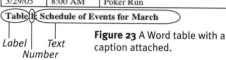

Date	Time	Event Name
3/1/05	9:00 AM	Museum Tour
3/8/05	10:30 AM	Horseback Ride
3/15/05	2:00 PM	Pot Luck Barbeque
3/22/05	10:00 AM	Hummer Tour
3/29/05	8:00 AM	Poker Run

Table 1: Schedule of Events for March

Label | Text
       Number

Figure 23 A Word table with a caption attached.

Captions

A caption is a numbered label that you can attach to a table, graphic, equation, or other item. It consists of three parts (**Figure 23**):

- **Caption label** is text that identifies the type of item. Word comes preconfigured with three caption labels—Equation, Figure, and Table—but you can add others.

- **Caption number** is the number assigned to the caption. This number is dynamic and can change when other labels are inserted or deleted before it.

- **Caption text** is text that you type for the caption. This is optional—a caption can consist of just the label and number.

There are two ways to add captions:

- Manually add captions to items in your document using the Caption command under the Insert menu.

- Set up Word to automatically insert captions when you insert a table, graphic, or equation in your document.

This part of the chapter explains how to manually insert, modify, and delete captions, as well as how to set up Word to automatically insert them for you.

✔ Tips

- Although this book wasn't written in Word, each of its figure captions follows the standard format used by Word. (Unfortunately, I had to number—and renumber—them manually.)

- Note that Word maintains separate numbering for each caption label. For example, if your document contains captions using the Figure and Table labels, Word numbers each type of caption starting with 1 (or A or i).

- Captions are formatted using the Caption style. You can change the formatting of all captions in a document by modifying the Caption style. I explain how to use styles in **Chapter 5**.

To insert a caption

1. Select the item for which you want to insert a caption (**Figure 24**).

   or

   Position the insertion point where you want the caption to appear.

2. Choose Insert > Caption (**Figure 1**) to display the Caption dialog (**Figure 25**).

3. Set basic options for the caption:

   ▲ **Label** is the caption label. The predefined choices are Equation, Figure, or Table.

   ▲ **Position** is the position of the caption in relation to the selected item: above it or below it.

4. To change numbering options for the caption, click the Numbering button. The Caption Numbering dialog (**Figure 26**) appears. Set options and click OK:

   ▲ **Format** is the number format. You can choose among Arabic, alphabetical, and Roman numeral styles (**Figure 27**).

   ▲ **Include chapter number** automatically inserts the chapter number as part of the caption number. If you enable this option, you must choose a heading level from the "Chapter starts with style" pop-up menu and a separator from the Use separator pop-up menu (**Figure 28**).

5. If desired, enter caption text after the caption label and number that appears in the Caption box.

6. Click OK. The caption is inserted to your specifications (**Figure 23**).

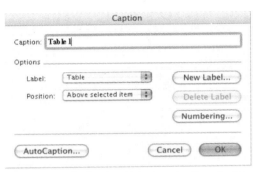

Date	Time	Event Name
3/1/05	9:00 AM	Museum Tour
3/8/05	10:30 AM	Horseback Ride
3/15/05	2:00 PM	Pot Luck Barbeque
3/22/05	10:00 AM	Hummer Tour
3/29/05	8:00 AM	Poker Run

Figure 24 Select the item you want to insert the caption for.

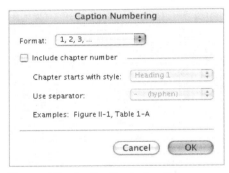

Figure 25 Use the Caption dialog to set options for the captions you insert.

Figure 26 The Caption Numbering dialog.

Figure 27 The Format pop-up menu lets you choose from among number formats.

- 1, 2, 3, ...
- a, b, c, ...
- A, B, C, ...
- i, ii, iii, ...
- I, II, III, ...

Figure 28 The Use separator pop-up menu.

- (hyphen)
. (period)
: (colon)
— (em-dash)
- (en-dash)

INSERTING CAPTIONS

Figure 29 The New Label dialog.

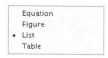

Figure 30 The new label is added to the Label pop-up menu.

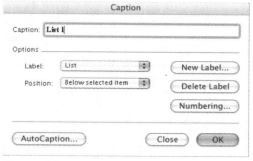

Figure 31 When a custom label is selected from the Label pop-up menu, the Delete Label button can be clicked.

✔ Tips

- In step 3, to create a new label, click the New Label button (**Figure 25**), enter the desired label in the New Label dialog that appears (**Figure 29**), and click OK. The new label appears in the Label pop-up menu (**Figure 30**).

- You can delete a custom label. In the Caption dialog, select the label you want to delete from the Label pop-up menu (**Figure 31**). Click Delete Label. The label is removed from the list. If the deleted label is used in a document caption, it is not deleted where it appears in the document.

- In step 3, if you choose Above selected item from the Position pop-up menu, Word automatically formats the caption so that it stays with the next paragraph. This ensures that the caption and the item to which it applies are always on the same page.

- In step 4 (**Figure 26**), you can only include the chapter number in the caption number if the chapter name and number is formatted with a heading style and you have set up that heading style with automatic numbering.

- If you want a colon or other punctuation to appear between the caption number and the caption text as shown in **Figure 23**, you must type that punctuation as part of the caption text in step 5.

To modify a caption

1. Select the caption you want to modify (**Figure 32**).

2. Choose Insert > Caption (**Figure 1**). The Caption dialog appears with the caption settings displayed (**Figure 33**).

3. Change settings as discussed in the section titled "To insert a caption."

4. Click OK. The caption changes accordingly.

✔ Tip

- You must use this method to change the caption label or number format. You can change the caption text, however, using standard editing techniques right in the document window.

To delete a caption

1. Select the caption you want to delete (**Figure 32**).

2. Press ⌈Delete⌉. The caption disappears.

✔ Tip

- When you delete a caption, subsequent caption numbers may not automatically update. I explain how to update captions and cross-references near the end of this chapter.

Date	Time	Event Name
3/1/05	9:00 AM	Museum Tour
3/8/05	10:30 AM	Horseback Ride
3/15/05	2:00 PM	Pot Luck Barbeque
3/22/05	10:00 AM	Hummer Tour
3/29/05	8:00 AM	Poker Run

Table 1: Schedule of Events for March

Figure 32 When you select an entire caption, it turns black.

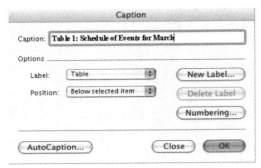

Figure 33 The Caption dialog for the caption selected in **Figure 32**.

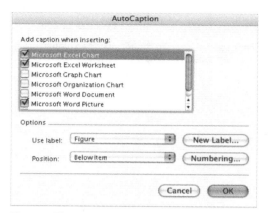

Figure 34 The AutoCaption dialog. In this illustration, the automatic caption feature is enabled for several types of items.

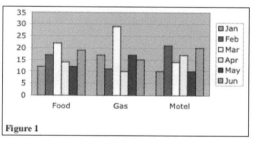

Figure 1

Figure 35 An automatically inserted caption beneath an Excel chart inserted in a Word document.

To automatically insert captions

1. Choose Insert > Caption (**Figure 1**) to display the Caption dialog (**Figure 25**).

2. Click the AutoCaption button to display the AutoCaption dialog (**Figure 34**).

3. Turn on the check box beside a type of item you want to automatically insert captions for.

4. With the item you enabled in step 3 selected, set options in the bottom half of the window:

   ▲ **Use label** enables you to choose a caption label for that type of item.

   ▲ **Position** enables you to specify whether the caption should appear above or below the item.

   ▲ **New Label** displays the New Label dialog (**Figure 29**), which you can use to create a new label. I explain how to use this dialog earlier in this section.

   ▲ **Numbering** displays the Caption Numbering dialog (**Figure 26**), which you can use to set numbering options. I explain how to use this dialog earlier in this section.

5. Repeat steps 3 and 4 for each type of item you want to automatically insert captions for.

6. Click OK. From that point forward, each time you use Insert menu commands to insert a type of item for which you enabled automatic captions, a caption appears for that item (**Figure 35**).

AUTOMATICALLY INSERTING CAPTIONS

Continued on next page...

Continued from previous page.

✔ Tips

- To add caption text to an automatically inserted caption, position the insertion point at the end of the caption in the document window and type the text you want to appear (**Figure 36**).

- To disable the automatic caption feature for a type of item, follow steps 1 and 2 to display the AutoCaption dialog (**Figure 34**), turn off the check box beside the item, and click OK. The automatic caption feature for that item is disabled.

- Changes you make in the AutoCaption dialog are saved in the document template, not the document itself. I tell you more about templates in **Chapter 2**.

Figure 1: Expenses for the first half of 2003.

Figure 36 You can add caption text to an automatically inserted caption by simply typing it in.

Static introductory text

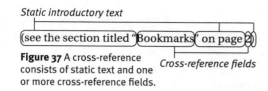

Figure 37 A cross-reference consists of static text and one or more cross-reference fields.

Cross-reference fields

Cross-References

A cross-reference is a reference to an item that appears in another location in a document. "See Table 2 in Chapter 3" and "See the section titled 'Bookmarks' on page 5" are two examples of cross-references. Cross-references are commonly used in technical documents, like computer how-to books. (In fact, if Adobe InDesign had a cross-reference feature like Word's, this book would have a lot more cross-references, complete with page numbers.)

Word's cross-reference feature is extremely powerful. It enables you to create cross-references to headings, footnotes, bookmarks, captions, numbered paragraphs, and other items in your Word documents. If an item moves or is modified, the cross-reference can be easily updated for the change. And if you're creating a document that will be read onscreen, you can take advantage of the hyperlink feature to make cross-references clickable links to the referenced item.

Cross-references are made up of two components (**Figure 37**):

◆ **Static introductory text** is text you type as part of the cross-reference. This text does not change.

◆ **Cross-reference field** is text inserted by the cross-reference feature as a Word field. This text can change if the information it refers to changes.

This part of the chapter explains how to insert and delete cross-references in your Word documents.

To insert a cross-reference

1. Position the insertion point where you want the cross-reference to appear (**Figure 38**).

2. Enter the first part of the static text of the cross-reference (**Figure 39**).

3. Choose Insert > Cross-reference (**Figure 1**) to display the Cross-reference dialog (**Figure 40**).

4. Choose a type of reference from the Reference type pop-up menu (**Figure 41**).

5. Choose an option from the Insert reference to pop-up menu. The options that appear vary based on what you chose in step 4. **Figure 42** shows the options for a Heading reference.

6. To insert the reference as a clickable hyperlink, turn on the Insert as hyperlink check box.

7. To instruct Word to include the word "above" or "below" as part of the reference, turn on the Include above/below check box. (This option is only available for some reference types.)

8. Select the item you want to refer to in the scrolling list. For example, to duplicate the reference that appears in **Figure 37**, I'd select "Bookmarks."

9. Click Insert. The reference is inserted, but the Cross-reference dialog remains active (**Figure 43**).

10. If necessary, click in the document window and position the insertion point where additional static text should appear. Then type in the additional text (**Figure 44**).

Reference Features

Microsoft Word includes several features you can use to insert references within a document. These commands can be found on the Insert menu (**Figure 1**):

- **Bookmark** enables you to mark a document location for use with the Go To command or other reference features.
- **Footnote** inserts a footnote or endnote marker and enables you to enter corresponding reference text.
- **Caption** inserts a labeled caption above or below a table, graphic object, or equation.

Figure 38 Position the insertion point where you want the cross-reference to begin.

- **Bookmark** (see the section titled " enables you to mark a document location for use with the Go To command or other reference features.

Figure 39 Enter the first part of the static text.

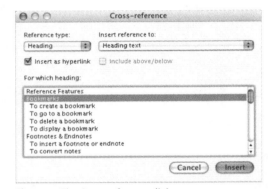

Figure 40 The Cross-reference dialog.

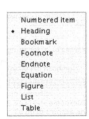

Figure 41
The Reference type pop-up menu.

- Heading text
  Page number
  Heading number
  Heading number (no context)
  Heading number (full context)
  Above/below

Figure 42 The Insert reference to pop-up menu with Heading chosen from the Reference type pop-up menu.

INSERTING CROSS-REFERENCES

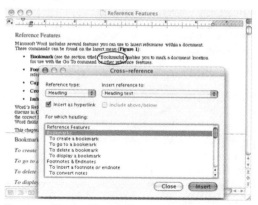

Figure 43 A cross-reference inserted into a document.

• **Bookmark** (see the section titled "Bookmarks" on page 2) enables you to mark a document location for use with the Go To command or other reference features.

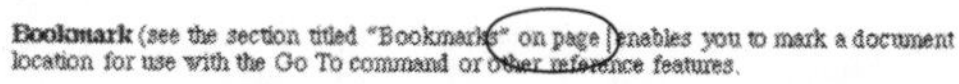

Figure 44 Additional static text inserted after the first cross-reference.

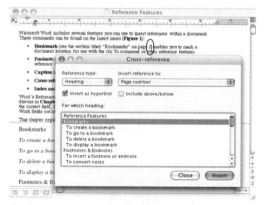

Figure 45 Another cross-reference inserted into a document. In this case, the reference is the page number for a specific heading.

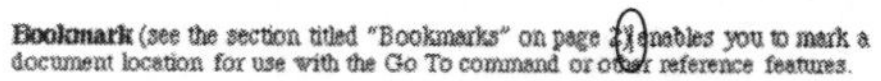

• **Bookmark** (see the section titled "Bookmarks" on page 2) enables you to mark a document location for use with the Go To command or other reference features.

Figure 46 The final bit of static text—a close parenthesis character—inserted into the document. The cross-reference shown in **Figure 37** is now complete.

11. To insert another cross-reference, click the Cross-reference dialog to make it active, then follow steps 4 through 9 to insert it (**Figure 45**).

12. If necessary, repeat steps 10 and 11 for additional static text (**Figure 46**) and/or cross-references.

13. When you're finished with the Cross-reference dialog, click Close to dismiss it.

✔ Tips

■ It is impossible to cover all options available in the Cross-reference dialog, since they vary based on the reference type and the contents of a document. The instructions here provide enough information to get you started exploring the options on your own. Remember, if you insert the wrong cross-reference, you can always delete it and try again.

■ Cross-references can be formatted like any other document text.

To delete a cross-reference

1. In the document window, select the cross-reference you want to delete. It becomes highlighted in black (**Figure 47**).
2. Press Delete. The cross-reference disappears, like any other text.

To change what a cross-reference refers to

1. Select the cross-reference you want to modify. (Do not select any introductory text.) The cross-reference is highlighted in black (**Figure 47**).
2. Choose Insert > Cross-reference (**Figure 1**) to display the Cross-reference dialog (**Figure 48**).
3. Choose options from the Reference type (**Figure 41**) and Insert reference to (**Figure 42**) drop-down lists to set revised cross-reference options (**Figure 48**).
4. Click Insert. The new cross-reference replaces the one that was selected (**Figure 49**).

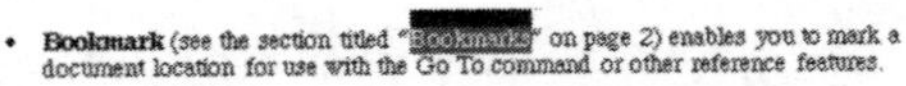

• Bookmark (see the section titled "Bookmarks" on page 2) enables you to mark a document location for use with the Go To command or other reference features.

Figure 47 Select the cross-reference you want to delete or modify.

Cross-reference
Reference type:
Insert reference to:
Heading
Heading text
Insert as hyperlink
Include above/below
For which heading:
Reference Features
Bookmarks
To create a bookmark
To go to a bookmark
To delete a bookmark
To display a bookmark
Footnotes & Endnotes
To insert a footnote or endnote
To convert notes
Close
Insert

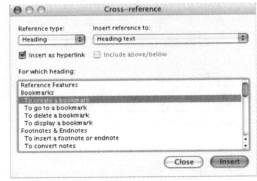

Figure 48 The Cross-reference dialog also enables you to change a selected cross-reference.

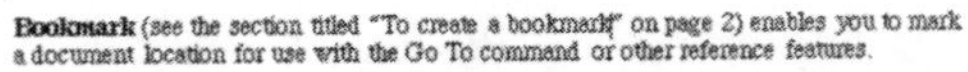

• Bookmark (see the section titled "To create a bookmark" on page 2) enables you to mark a document location for use with the Go To command or other reference features.

Figure 49 The cross-reference you selected is replaced with the new one.

Indexes

An index is an alphabetical list of topics with page references for each topic's location within a document. Word indexes can include two levels of index entries: main entries and subentries. Indexes may also include *See* cross-references to other topics and special formatting of page numbers.

Creating an index in Word is a two-step process:

1. **Mark index entries.** This tells Word what text should be included in the index.

2. **Generate the index.** This gathers together all index entries, alphabetizes them, and displays them with page numbers in index format.

This part of the chapter explains how to create an index in a Word document.

✔ Tips

- The indexing feature can use bookmarks, which I discuss earlier in this chapter, to include ranges of pages in an index entry. If you plan on indexing topic discussions that span multiple pages, it's a good idea to bookmark those topics *before* marking index entries.

- Indexes, like other reference features, are created with Word fields. If pagination or document content changes after an index has been generated, you'll need to update the index before finalizing the document. I explain how to update indexes at the end of this chapter.

To manually mark an index entry

1. In the document window, select the text you want to index (**Figure 50**).

2. Choose Insert > Index and Tables (**Figure 1**) to display the Index and Tables dialog.

3. If necessary, click the Index button to display its options (**Figure 51**).

4. Click the Mark Entry button to display the Mark Index Entry dialog (**Figure 52**).

5. In the Main entry box, enter the text you want to appear in the index. By default, the selected text appears there, but you can enter something else if desired.

6. If the entry should be a subentry under the main entry, enter the text you want to appear as a subentry in the Subentry box. **Figure 53** shows an example.

7. Select one of the Options radio buttons:

   ▲ **Cross-reference** enables you to create a textual cross-reference to another index entry. Since a cross-reference normally appears after the word *See*, that word is entered in italics by default. Enter the cross-reference text in the box after *See*.

   ▲ **Current page** sets the index entry's page reference to the page on which the selected text appears. This is the most commonly used option.

   ▲ **Page range** enables you to choose a bookmark to correspond to the range of pages you want to index. Use the pop-up menu to select the bookmark.

8. To set special formatting for the index entry's page number, turn on one or both of the Page number format check boxes.

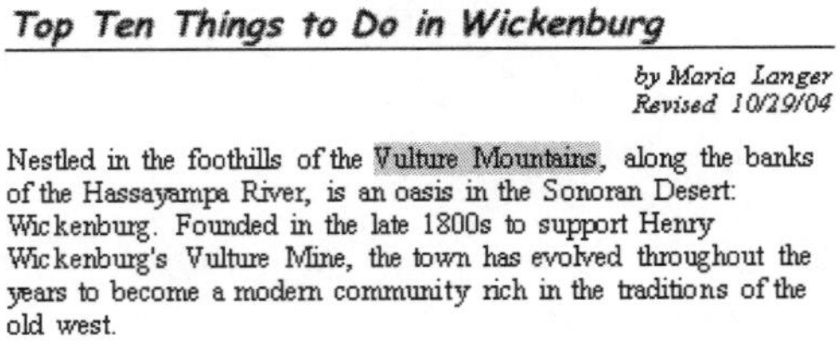

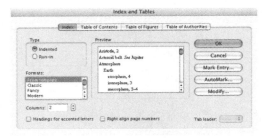

Top Ten Things to Do in Wickenburg

by Maria Langer
Revised 10/29/04

Nestled in the foothills of the Vulture Mountains, along the banks of the Hassayampa River, is an oasis in the Sonoran Desert: Wickenburg. Founded in the late 1800s to support Henry Wickenburg's Vulture Mine, the town has evolved throughout the years to become a modern community rich in the traditions of the old west.

Figure 50 Select the text you want to create an index entry for.

Figure 51 The Index pane of the Index and Tables dialog.

Figure 52 The Mark Index Entry dialog.

Figure 53 An example of an index entry with a main entry and subentry. The subentry text will appear indented beneath the main entry text in the index.

MANUALLY MARKING INDEX ENTRIES

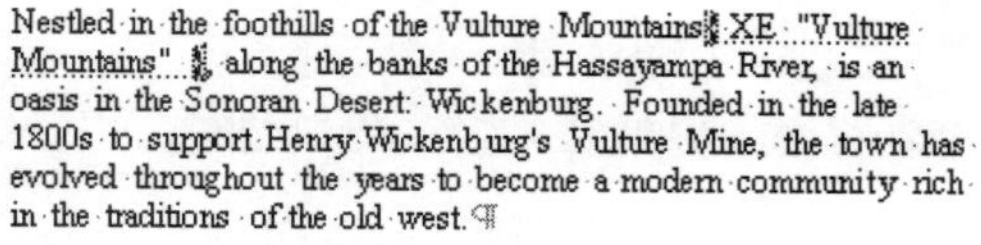

Nestled·in·the·foothills·of·the·Vulture·Mountains.XE·"Vulture·
Mountains"·,·along·the·banks·of·the·Hassayampa·River,·is·an·
oasis·in·the·Sonoran·Desert·Wickenburg.·Founded·in·the·late·
1800s·to·support·Henry·Wickenburg's·Vulture·Mine,·the·town·has·
evolved·throughout·the·years·to·become·a·modern·community·rich·
in·the·traditions·of·the·old·west.¶

Figure 54 If formatting marks are displayed, the field codes for each index entry appear after the text it was inserted for.

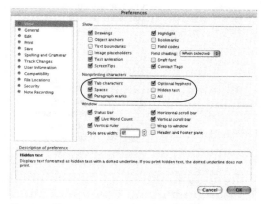

Figure 55 The View options of the Preferences dialog. When Nonprinting characters are set as shown here, all nonprinting characters except hidden text will appear. The field codes for index entries do not appear.

9. **Click Mark.** The index entry is marked with an XE field. If nonprinting characters are displayed, you can see the field codes for the entry (**Figure 54**), which are formatted as hidden text. The Mark Index Entry dialog remains onscreen.

10. To index another entry, follow step 1, then click the Mark Index Entry dialog to activate it and follow steps 5 through 9.

11. Repeat step 10 for every index entry you want to mark.

12. When you are finished marking index entries, click the Mark Index Entry dialog's close button.

✔ Tips

- A quicker way to open the Mark Index Entry dialog (**Figure 52**) is to press ⌘ Option Shift X. By doing this, you can skip steps 2 through 4. (The trick is to remember all the keys you have to press!)

- In step 9, if you click Mark All, Word automatically searches through the document and marks all occurrences of the selected word as an index entry using the options you set in the Mark Index Entry dialog. Although this is a quick way to consistently mark text for indexing, it may create far more index entries for selected text than you need. Use this option with care!

- If you find the index entry fields distracting (I do!), you can hide them by clicking the Show/Hide ¶ button on the Standard toolbar. Or, to show all formatting marks except hidden characters, set options in the Nonprinting characters area of the Preferences dialog's View options (**Figure 55**).

- I cover bookmarks in detail earlier in this chapter.

MANUALLY MARKING INDEX ENTRIES

To automatically mark index entries

1. Choose File > New Blank Document, press ⌃ ⌘ N, or click the New Blank Document button on the Standard toolbar to create a blank Word document.

2. Choose Table > Insert > Table (**Figure 56**) to display the Insert Table dialog (**Figure 57**).

3. Enter 2 in the Number of columns box and 1 in the Number of rows box.

4. Click OK. A two-by-one table appears in the document window (**Figure 58**).

5. In the left cell, enter a word that appears in your document that you want to be automatically marked as an index entry.

6. Press Tab.

7. In the right cell, enter the text you want to appear in the index:

   ▲ If you want just a main entry to appear, enter just the main entry text.

   ▲ If you want a main entry and subentry to appear, enter the main entry followed by a colon (:) and then the subentry.

   Figure 59 shows what a completed entry might look like.

8. To add another entry, press Tab to add another row to the table. Then follow steps 5 through 7 to add entry information.

9. Repeat step 8 for each entry you want to add. When you're finished, you should have a table of indexable words with corresponding index entry text (**Figure 60**).

10. Choose File > Save, press ⌃ ⌘ S, or click the Save button on the Standard toolbar. Then use the Save dialog that appears to save the document.

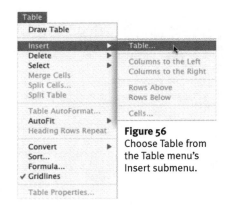

Figure 56
Choose Table from the Table menu's Insert submenu.

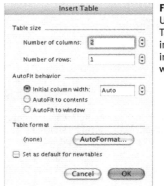

Figure 57
Use the Insert Table dialog to insert a cell table in the document window.

Figure 58 A table in a Word document.

| Henry Wickenburg¤ | Wickenburg:Henry¤ |

Figure 59 A completed concordance file entry.

Henry Wickenburg¤	Wickenburg:Henry¤
ghost town¤	ghost town¤
Vulture Peak¤	Vulture Peak¤
Vulture Mine¤	Vulture Mine¤
Vulture Mountains¤	Vulture Mountains¤
restaurants¤	Wickenburg:dining¤
golf¤	Wickenburg:golf¤
hiking¤	Wickenburg:hiking¤
Box Canyon¤	Box Canyon¤
Hassayampa River¤	Hassayampa River¤
BC Jeep Tours¤	Wickenburg:tours¤
Flying M Air¤	Wickenburg:tours¤

Figure 60 Each entry in a concordance file appears in its own row.

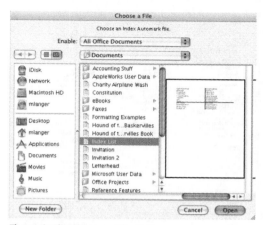

Figure 61 The Choose a File dialog.

Nestled in the foothills of the Vulture Mountains{ XE "Vulture Mountains" }, along the banks of the Hassayampa River{ XE "Hassayampa River" }, is an oasis in the Sonoran Desert. Wickenburg. Founded in the late 1800s to support Henry Wickenburg{ XE "Wickenburg Henry" }'s Vulture Mine{ XE "Vulture Mine" }, the town has evolved throughout the years to become a modern community rich in the traditions of the old west.¶

Figure 62 To select an index entry, select the { and } characters and all text between them.

11. Open or switch to the document you want to index.

12. Choose Insert > Index and Tables (**Figure 1**) to display the Index and Tables dialog.

13. If necessary, click the Index button to display its options (**Figure 51**).

14. Click the AutoMark button to display the Choose a File dialog (**Figure 61**).

15. Locate and select the file you created in step 10. Then click Open.

    Word searches the document for the words you entered in the left column and inserts index entries from the right column (**Figure 62**).

✔ Tips

■ The document you create with steps 1 through 10 is referred to in Word documentation as a *concordance file* or an *Index AutoMark* file.

■ Use this feature with care! If you include a word in the left column that has multiple meanings, all occurrences will be indexed the same way. Is this really what you want?

To delete an index entry

1. Select the entire index entry, including the { and } characters (**Figure 62**).

2. Press (Delete). The entry disappears and will not be included in the index.

To generate an index

1. Position the insertion point where you want the index to appear. Normally, this will be at the end of the document, but it can be anywhere you like.

2. Choose Insert > Index and Tables (**Figure 1**) to display the Index and Tables dialog.

3. If necessary, click the Index button to display its options (**Figure 51**).

4. Select one of the Type options:

   ▲ **Indented** indents each subentry beneath the main entry. This is the type of index used in this book.

   ▲ **Run-in** displays all subentries with the main entry, in the same paragraph.

5. Enter the number of columns the index should occupy on each page in the Columns box.

6. Set other formatting options as desired:

   ▲ **Formats** enables you to select one of several predefined index formats. Click a format to select it; a preview of what it might look like appears in the Preview area.

   ▲ **Headings for accented letters** creates separate headings for entries that begin with accented characters.

   ▲ **Right align page numbers** shifts page numbers to the right side of the column. This option is only available if you chose Indented in step 4.

   ▲ **Tab leader** enables you to choose the characters that appear between the index text and page number reference. This option is only available if you turned on the Right align page numbers check box.

7. Click OK. Word generates the index and inserts it in the document (**Figure 63**).

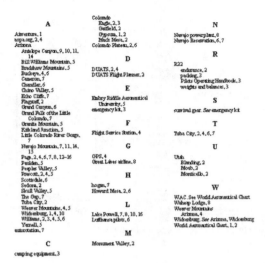

Figure 63 A completed index in Print Preview. This index uses the Indented type, Classic format, and three columns.

GENERATING INDEXES

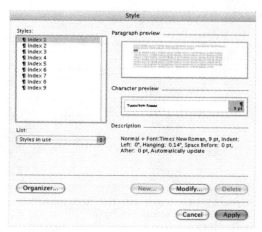

Figure 64 The Style dialog enables you to modify style definitions for index styles.

{ INDEX \h "A" \c "2" \z "1033" }

Figure 65 The index field codes for the index in **Figure 63**.

✔ Tips

■ You can see the effect of changes you make in steps 4 through 6 in the Preview area of the Index and Tables dialog (**Figure 51**).

■ You can further define the appearance of an index by clicking the Modify button in the Index pane of the Index and Tables dialog (**Figure 51**) when From template is selected in the Formats scrolling list. This displays the Style dialog (**Figure 64**), which you can use to modify style definitions for index styles. I tell you more about styles in **Chapter 4**.

■ If you don't like the way an index looks, you can delete it and start over. Just select the entire index and press ⎡Delete⎤, then follow the steps on the previous page to generate a new index.

■ If your index looks more like **Figure 65** than **Figure 63**, View preferences are set to display field codes. To display the index instead, turn off the Field codes option in the Preferences dialog's View options (**Figure 55**).

■ As illustrated in **Figure 65**, an index is created with an index (INDEX) field.

GENERATING INDEXES

Table of Contents

A table of contents lists, in order of appearance, the major headings within a document. The table of contents for this book, for example, lists the chapters and first level headings with their corresponding page numbers. Although not as detailed as an index, a table of contents can help readers find specific content within a lengthy document.

Creating a table of contents for a Word document is a two-step process:

1. **Format document headings for a table of contents.** This tells Word what text should be included in the table of contents. The easiest way to do this is using Word's built-in heading styles, but you can use any style you want.

2. **Generate the table of contents.** This gathers together all table of contents entries (or headings) and displays them with page numbers in table of contents format.

This part of the chapter explains how to create a table of contents in a Word document.

✔ Tips

■ If your document utilizes Word's built-in heading styles, you can view an onscreen table of contents with Word's document map feature. Choose View > Navigation Pane and then choose Document Map from the drop-down list that appears in the upper-left corner of the window (**Figure 66**). I discuss the document map feature in **Chapter 1**.

■ A table of contents is created with Word fields. If pagination or document content changes after a table of contents has been generated, you'll need to update the table of contents before finalizing the document. I explain how to update tables at the end of this chapter.

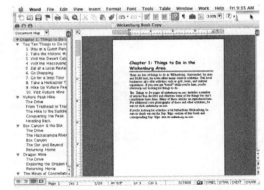

Figure 66 The document map feature displays a table of contents using Word headings in a pane on the left side of the document window.

Top Ten Things to Do in Wickenburg
by Maria Langer
Revised 10/29/04

Nestled in the foothills of the Vulture Mountains, along the banks of the Hassayampa River, is an oasis in the Sonoran Desert: Wickenburg. Founded in the late 1800s to support Henry Wickenburg's Vulture Mine, the town has evolved throughout the years to become a modern community rich in the traditions of the old west.

Figure 67 Position the insertion point anywhere in the heading's paragraph.

Figure 68
Choose a heading style from the Formatting Palette's Style drop-down list.

Top Ten Things to Do in Wickenburg

by Maria Langer
Revised 10/29/04

Nestled in the foothills of the Vulture Mountains, along the banks of the Hassayampa River, is an oasis in the Sonoran Desert: Wickenburg. Founded in the late 1800s to support Henry Wickenburg's Vulture Mine, the town has evolved throughout the years to become a modern community rich in the traditions of the old west.

Figure 69 The heading is formatted with the heading style you choose. (As you can see here, I've customized the heading styles in this document, so they probably don't look exactly as yours do.)

To format headings for a table of contents

1. Make sure the heading is in its own paragraph. To do this, position the insertion point at the end of the heading and press Return.

2. Position the insertion point anywhere in the heading's paragraph (**Figure 67**).

3. Choose a heading style from the Style drop-down list on the Formatting Palette (**Figure 68**). The heading is formatted with the style you applied (**Figure 69**).

4. Repeat steps 1 through 3 for each heading in the document.

✔ Tips

- The easiest way to generate an index based on heading styles is to apply Word's built-in heading styles (Heading 1 through Heading 9). You can, however, apply any style, as long as the styles you use meet the following criteria:

  ▲ The styles are used only for headings.

  ▲ There is a different style for each heading level.

  ▲ The styles are applied consistently to each heading level.

- Another way to format headings for a table of contents is to switch to Outline view and use its tools to convert paragraphs into headings. I discuss outlines in **Chapter 12**.

- If you created your document using Word's outline feature, you can skip this step. Your headings are already formatted and ready to use for a table of contents.

FORMATTING TABLE OF CONTENTS HEADINGS

To generate a table of contents from built-in heading styles

1. Position the insertion point where you want the table of contents to appear. This is usually at the beginning of the document, but it can be anywhere you like.

2. Choose Insert > Index and Tables (**Figure 1**) to display the Index and Tables dialog.

3. If necessary, click the Table of Contents button to display its options (**Figure 70**).

4. Set formatting options as desired:

   ▲ **Formats** enables you to select one of several predefined table of contents formats. Click to select a format and see what it might look like in the Preview area.

   ▲ **Show levels** determines how many heading levels will be included in the table of contents.

   ▲ **Show page numbers** displays the corresponding page number for each heading listed in the table of contents.

   ▲ **Right align page numbers** shifts page numbers to the right side of the page. This option is only available if you turned on the Show page numbers check box.

   ▲ **Tab leader** enables you to choose the characters that appear between the heading text and page number reference. This option is only available if you turned on the Right align page numbers check box.

5. Click OK. Word generates the table of contents and inserts it in the document (**Figure 71**).

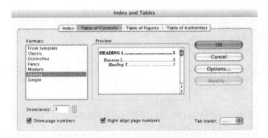

Figure 70 The Table of Contents pane of the Index and Tables dialog.

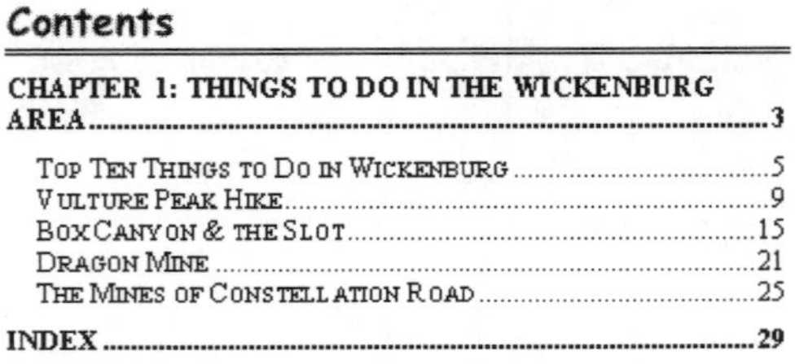

Contents

Figure 71 A table of contents using the Formal format. (Okay, so this book isn't done yet. But I can only write one book at a time!)

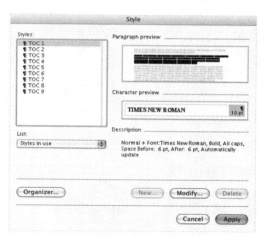

Figure 72 Use the Style dialog to modify the definition of TOC styles.

{TOC \O "1-3" \H \Z \U }

Figure 73 The TOC field codes for the table of contents in **Figure 71**.

✔ Tips

- You can see the effect of changes you make in step 4 in the Preview area of the Index and Tables dialog (**Figure 70**).

- You can further define the appearance of a table of contents by clicking the Modify button in the Table of Contents pane of the Index and Tables dialog (**Figure 70**) when From template is selected from the Formats scrolling list. This displays the Style dialog (**Figure 72**), which you can use to modify style definitions for TOC (table of contents) styles. I tell you more about modifying styles in **Chapter 4**.

- If you don't like the way a table of contents looks, you can delete it and start over. Just select the entire table of contents and press Delete, then follow the steps on the previous page to generate a new table of contents.

- If your table of contents looks more like **Figure 73** than **Figure 71**, View preferences are set to display field codes. To display the table of contents instead, turn off the Field codes option in the Preferences dialog's View options (**Figure 55**).

To generate a table of contents from custom heading styles

1. Follow steps 1 through 4 in the previous section to set basic options for the table of contents.

2. Click the Options button in the Table of Contents pane of the Index and Tables dialog (**Figure 70**) to display the Table of Contents Options dialog (**Figure 74**).

3. Make sure the Styles check box is turned on.

4. Scroll through the list of styles in your document and:

   ▲ Remove numbers in the boxes beside styles that should not be used for table of contents headings.

   ▲ Enter table of contents level numbers in the boxes beside styles that should be used for table of contents headings.

   For example, suppose the document headings used two styles called Main heading and Other heading. You'd remove numbers beside every style except those, enter a 1 beside Main heading, and enter a 2 beside Other heading (**Figure 75**).

5. Click OK to save your settings and dismiss the Table of Contents Options dialog.

6. Click OK in the Index and Tables dialog. Word generates the table of contents and displays it at the insertion point (**Figure 71**).

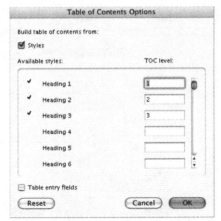

Figure 74 The default settings in the Table of Contents Options dialog.

Figure 75 You can set any style in the document to be used as a table of contents heading.

GENERATING A TABLE OF CONTENTS

Updating Reference Fields

When the content, pagination, or entry fields in a document change, any reference features created with Word fields that are already in the document must be updated to reflect the change.

For example, suppose you wrote a report, complete with bookmarks, cross-references, a table of contents, and an index. You submitted the report to management and although they liked it, they decided to expand the report scope. As a result, you had to write another 20 report pages and insert them in the middle of the report.

As part of the editing process, you created new cross-references, bookmarks, headings, and index entries. The existing references are no longer correct; they omit headings and index entries and have incorrect page references. These references must be manually updated for the revised document.

By "manually" I mean you must take some action to update the fields. Fortunately, updating them is as easy as selecting them and choosing a menu command or pressing a keyboard key. Or you can instruct Word to automatically update the fields that produce indexes and tables before a document prints.

In this part of the chapter, I explain how to update reference fields to ensure that they are accurate in your Word documents.

To manually update indexes & tables

1. Hold down the Control key and click anywhere in the reference field you want to update. A contextual menu like the one in **Figure 76** appears.

2. Choose Update Field from the contextual menu.

3. A dialog like the one in **Figure 77** may appear. Select an option to indicate what you want to update:

   ▲ **Update page numbers only** updates only the page numbers.

   ▲ **Update entire table** recreates the entire table from scratch.

   The reference is updated to reflect current document contents and information.

✔ Tips

■ To update all reference fields in a document, choose Edit > Select All or press ⌘A to select the entire document and press ⌘ Option Shift S. Follow step 3 if necessary to complete the update. This will update all Word fields in the selection.

■ In step 2, choosing Toggle Field Codes displays captions and cross-references as Word field codes. Although you probably won't want to view them this way, you may find it interesting to see how Word tracks this information internally. You can choose the command again to view the references as they will print.

Figure 76 Holding down Control while clicking a reference field like this table of contents displays a contextual menu that enables you to update the field.

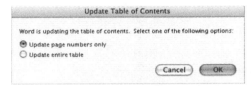

Figure 77 The Update Table of Contents dialog.

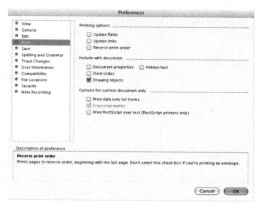

Figure 78 The Print pane in Word's Preferences dialog.

To automatically update indexes & tables before printing

1. Choose Word > Preferences to display the Preferences dialog.

2. Click Print on the left side of the dialog to display Print options (**Figure 78**).

3. Turn on the Update fields check box.

4. Click OK.

   From that point forward, Word updates all Word fields—including reference fields—in the document before you print it.

✔ Tip

■ I recommend enabling this option for any document that contains reference fields. This can prevent you from printing the document with inaccurate information.

AUTOMATICALLY UPDATING REFERENCE FIELDS

Outlines

Figure 1 Part of an outline in Outline view.

Figure 2 The outline in **Figure 1** in Normal view.

✔ Tips

■ Word's outline feature automatically applies the Heading and Normal styles as you work. You can redefine these styles to meet your needs; **Chapter 4** explains how.

Outlines

An outline is a great tool for organizing ideas. By grouping topics and subtopics under main headings, you can set up the logical flow of a lengthy or complex document. A well-prepared outline is like a document "skeleton"—a solid framework on which the document can be built.

An outline has two components (**Figure 1**):

◆ *Headings* are topic names. Various levels of headings (1 through 9) are arranged in a hierarchy to organize and develop relationships among them.

◆ *Body text* provides information about each heading.

Microsoft Word's Outline view makes it easy to build and refine outlines. Start by adding headings that you can set to any level of importance. Then add body text. You can use drag-and-drop editing to rearrange headings and body text. You can also switch to Normal view (**Figure 2**) or another view to continue working with your document.

■ You can distinguish headings from body text in Outline view by the symbols that appear before them. Hollow dashes or plus signs appear to the left of headings while small hollow boxes appear to the left of body text (**Figure 1**).

Building an Outline

Building an outline is easy. Just create a new document, switch to Outline view, and start adding headings and body text.

✔ Tip

■ You can turn an existing document into an outline by simply switching to Outline view and adding headings.

To create an outline

1. Create a new blank document.

2. Choose View > Outline (**Figure 3**).

   or

   Click the Outline View button at the bottom of the document window (**Figure 4**).

   The document switches to Outline view and the Outlining toolbar appears (**Figure 5**).

✔ Tips

■ The Outlining toolbar (**Figure 6**) appears automatically any time you switch to Outline view. If it does not appear, you can display it by choosing View > Toolbars > Outlining. Displaying and hiding toolbars is covered in **Chapter 1**.

■ Remember, you can point to a toolbar's buttons to learn their names.

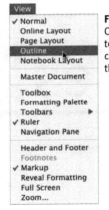

Figure 3
One way to switch to Outline view is to choose Outline from the View menu.

Outline View button

Figure 4 The View buttons at the bottom of the document window.

Figure 5 The document window in Outline view. The Outlining toolbar is right above the window.

Figure 6 The Outlining toolbar.

CREATING OUTLINES

Outlines

Figure 1 Part of an outline in Outline view.

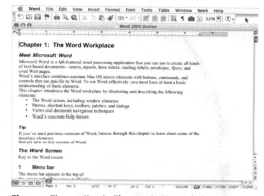

Figure 2 The outline in **Figure 1** in Normal view.

✔ Tips

■ Word's outline feature automatically applies the Heading and Normal styles as you work. You can redefine these styles to meet your needs; **Chapter 4** explains how.

Outlines

An outline is a great tool for organizing ideas. By grouping topics and subtopics under main headings, you can set up the logical flow of a lengthy or complex document. A well-prepared outline is like a document "skeleton"—a solid framework on which the document can be built.

An outline has two components (**Figure 1**):

◆ *Headings* are topic names. Various levels of headings (1 through 9) are arranged in a hierarchy to organize and develop relationships among them.

◆ *Body text* provides information about each heading.

Microsoft Word's Outline view makes it easy to build and refine outlines. Start by adding headings that you can set to any level of importance. Then add body text. You can use drag-and-drop editing to rearrange headings and body text. You can also switch to Normal view (**Figure 2**) or another view to continue working with your document.

■ You can distinguish headings from body text in Outline view by the symbols that appear before them. Hollow dashes or plus signs appear to the left of headings while small hollow boxes appear to the left of body text (**Figure 1**).

Building an Outline

Building an outline is easy. Just create a new document, switch to Outline view, and start adding headings and body text.

✔ Tip

■ You can turn an existing document into an outline by simply switching to Outline view and adding headings.

To create an outline

1. Create a new blank document.

2. Choose View > Outline (**Figure 3**).

   or

   Click the Outline View button at the bottom of the document window (**Figure 4**).

   The document switches to Outline view and the Outlining toolbar appears (**Figure 5**).

✔ Tips

■ The Outlining toolbar (**Figure 6**) appears automatically any time you switch to Outline view. If it does not appear, you can display it by choosing View > Toolbars > Outlining. Displaying and hiding toolbars is covered in **Chapter 1**.

■ Remember, you can point to a toolbar's buttons to learn their names.

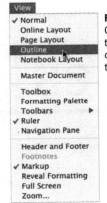

Figure 3
One way to switch to Outline view is to choose Outline from the View menu.

Outline View button

Figure 4 The View buttons at the bottom of the document window.

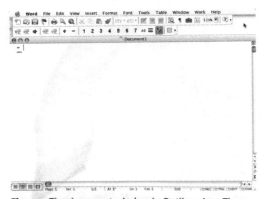

Figure 5 The document window in Outline view. The Outlining toolbar is right above the window.

Figure 6 The Outlining toolbar.

CREATING OUTLINES

- **Introduction to Word**|

Figure 7 Enter the text that you want to use as a heading.

- **Introduction to Word**
- |

Figure 8 When you press (Return), Word creates a new paragraph with the same heading level.

- **Introduction to Word**
- **The Word Workplace**
- |

Figure 9 To create a new heading at the same level, simply type it in.

- **Introduction to Word**
⊕ **The Word Workplace**
   - *Introduction*
   - /

Figure 10 To create a heading at a lower level, click the Demote button before typing it in. When you press (Return), Word creates a new paragraph at the same (lower) heading level.

- **Introduction to Word**
⊕ **The Word Workplace**
   - *Introduction*
- **New and Improved Features in Word**
- |

Figure 11 To create a heading at a higher level, click the Promote button while the insertion point is in the heading. When you press (Return), Word creates a new paragraph at the same (higher) heading level.

Figure 12 You can apply a Heading style to an outline paragraph with the Formatting Palette to assign the corresponding outline level.

To add headings

1. Type the heading text (**Figure 7**).

2. Press (Return). A new paragraph at the same heading level appears (**Figure 8**).

3. Continue using one of these techniques:
   ▲ To add a heading at the same level, repeat steps 1 and 2 (**Figure 9**).
   ▲ To add a heading at the next lower level, press (Tab) or click the Demote button on the Outlining toolbar. Then repeat steps 1 and 2 (**Figure 10**).
   ▲ To add a heading at the next higher level, press (Shift)(Tab) or click the Promote button on the Outlining toolbar. Then repeat steps 1 and 2 (**Figure 11**).

✔ Tips

- By default, the first heading you create is Level 1—the top level.

- When you create a lower level heading beneath a heading, the marker to the left of the heading changes to a hollow plus sign to indicate that the heading has subheadings (**Figure 10**).

- Because outline levels correspond to Word's Heading styles, you can use the Styles area of the Formatting Palette (**Figure 12**) to apply a Heading style to a paragraph, thus assigning the corresponding outline level.

- Don't worry about entering a heading at the wrong level. You can promote or demote a heading at any time—I tell you how next.

To promote or demote a heading

1. Click anywhere in the heading to position the insertion point within it (**Figure 13**).

2. To promote the heading, press Shift Tab or click the Promote button on the Outlining toolbar. The heading shifts to the left and changes into the next higher level heading (**Figure 14**).

   or

   To demote the heading, press Tab or click the Demote button on the Outlining toolbar. The heading shifts to the right and changes into the next lower level heading.

✔ Tips

- You cannot promote a Heading 1 level heading. Heading 1 is the highest level.

- You cannot demote a Heading 9 level heading. Heading 9 is the lowest level.

- To promote or demote multiple headings at the same time, select the headings, then follow step 2 above.

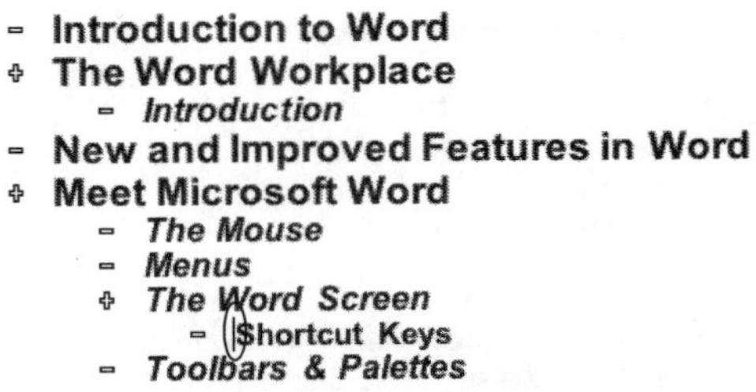

- Introduction to Word
- ✦ The Word Workplace
  - *Introduction*
- New and Improved Features in Word
- ✦ Meet Microsoft Word
  - *The Mouse*
  - *Menus*
  - ✦ *The Word Screen*
    - *Shortcut Keys*
  - *Toolbars & Palettes*

Figure 13 Position the insertion point in the heading that you want to promote or demote.

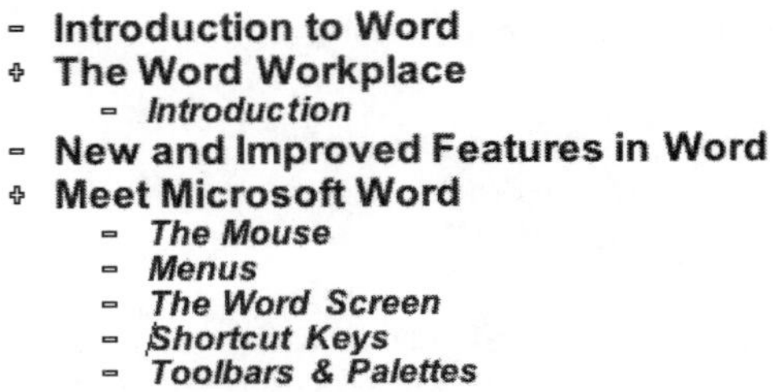

- **Introduction to Word**
- ✦ **The Word Workplace**
  - *Introduction*
- **New and Improved Features in Word**
- ✦ **Meet Microsoft Word**
  - *The Mouse*
  - *Menus*
  - *The Word Screen*
  - *Shortcut Keys*
  - *Toolbars & Palettes*

Figure 14 Clicking the Promote button shifts the heading to the left and changes it to the next higher heading level.

Outlines

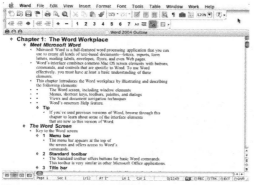

Figure 1 Part of an outline in Outline view.

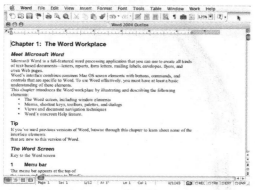

Figure 2 The outline in **Figure 1** in Normal view.

✔ Tips

- Word's outline feature automatically applies the Heading and Normal styles as you work. You can redefine these styles to meet your needs; **Chapter 4** explains how.

Outlines

An outline is a great tool for organizing ideas. By grouping topics and subtopics under main headings, you can set up the logical flow of a lengthy or complex document. A well-prepared outline is like a document "skeleton"—a solid framework on which the document can be built.

An outline has two components (**Figure 1**):

- *Headings* are topic names. Various levels of headings (1 through 9) are arranged in a hierarchy to organize and develop relationships among them.

- *Body text* provides information about each heading.

Microsoft Word's Outline view makes it easy to build and refine outlines. Start by adding headings that you can set to any level of importance. Then add body text. You can use drag-and-drop editing to rearrange headings and body text. You can also switch to Normal view (**Figure 2**) or another view to continue working with your document.

- You can distinguish headings from body text in Outline view by the symbols that appear before them. Hollow dashes or plus signs appear to the left of headings while small hollow boxes appear to the left of body text (**Figure 1**).

Building an Outline

Building an outline is easy. Just create a new document, switch to Outline view, and start adding headings and body text.

✔ Tip

- You can turn an existing document into an outline by simply switching to Outline view and adding headings.

To create an outline

1. Create a new blank document.

2. Choose View > Outline (**Figure 3**).

   or

   Click the Outline View button at the bottom of the document window (**Figure 4**).

   The document switches to Outline view and the Outlining toolbar appears (**Figure 5**).

✔ Tips

- The Outlining toolbar (**Figure 6**) appears automatically any time you switch to Outline view. If it does not appear, you can display it by choosing View > Toolbars > Outlining. Displaying and hiding toolbars is covered in **Chapter 1**.

- Remember, you can point to a toolbar's buttons to learn their names.

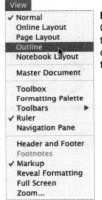

Figure 3
One way to switch to Outline view is to choose Outline from the View menu.

Outline View button

Figure 4 The View buttons at the bottom of the document window.

Figure 5 The document window in Outline view. The Outlining toolbar is right above the window.

Figure 6 The Outlining toolbar.

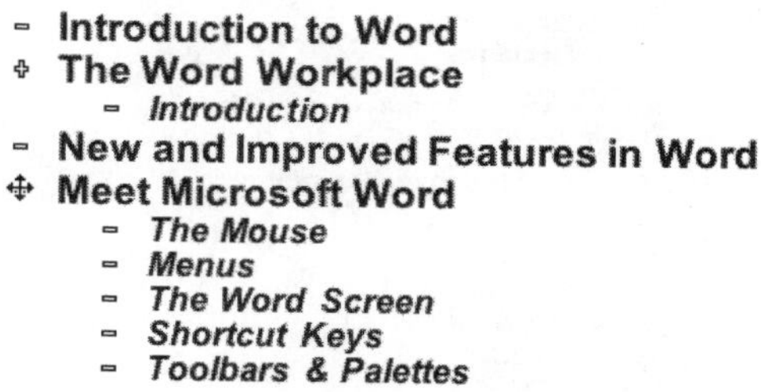

- Introduction to Word
- The Word Workplace
  - *Introduction*
- New and Improved Features in Word
- Meet Microsoft Word
  - *The Mouse*
  - *Menus*
  - *The Word Screen*
  - *Shortcut Keys*
  - *Toolbars & Palettes*

Figure 15 Position the mouse pointer over a heading marker; it turns into a four-headed arrow.

- Introduction to Word
- The Word Workplace
  - *Introduction*
- New and Improved Features in Word
- Meet Microsoft Word
  - *The Mouse*
  - *Menus*
  - *The Word Screen*
  - *Shortcut Keys*
  - *Toolbars & Palettes*

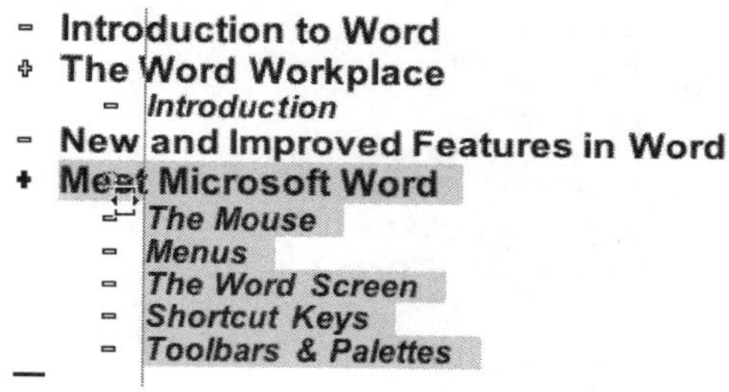

Figure 16 When you drag the heading marker, a line indicates the heading's level when you release the mouse button.

- Introduction to Word
- The Word Workplace
  - *Introduction*
- New and Improved Features in Word
  - *Meet Microsoft Word*
    - The Mouse
    - Menus
    - The Word Screen
    - Shortcut Keys
    - Toolbars & Palettes

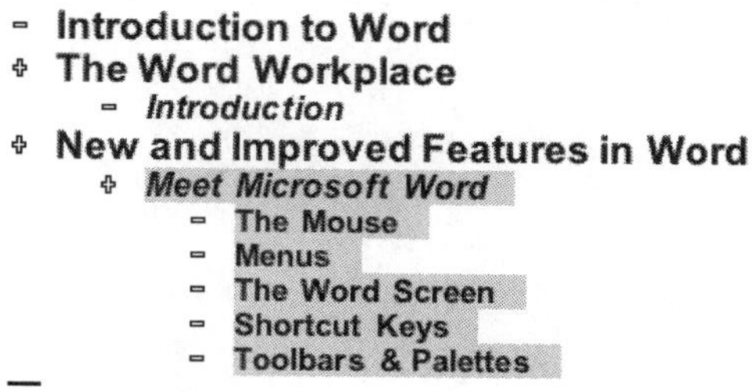

Figure 17 Release the mouse button to change the level of the heading and its subheadings.

To promote or demote a heading with its subheadings

1. Position the mouse pointer over the hollow plus sign to the left of the heading. The mouse pointer turns into a four-headed arrow (**Figure 15**).

2. To promote the headings, press the mouse button and drag to the left.

   or

   To demote the headings, press the mouse button and drag to the right (**Figure 16**).

   The heading and its subheadings are selected. As you drag, a line indicates the level to which the heading will be moved when you release the mouse button. You can see all this in **Figure 16**.

3. Release the mouse button to change the level of the heading and its subheadings (**Figure 17**).

✔ Tips

- You can also use this method to promote or demote a heading with no subheadings. Simply drag the hollow dash as instructed in step 2 to change its level.

- Another way to promote or demote a heading with its subheadings is with the Promote or Demote button on the Outlining toolbar. Just click the hollow plus sign marker (**Figure 15**) to select the heading and its subheadings. Then click the Promote or Demote button to change the selected headings' levels.

PROMOTING & DEMOTING HEADINGS

To add body text

1. Position the insertion point at the end of the heading after which you want to add body text (**Figure 18**).

2. Press [Return] to create a new line with the same heading level (**Figure 19**).

3. Click the Demote to Body Text button on the Outlining toolbar. The marker to the left of the insertion point changes into a small hollow square to indicate that the paragraph is body text (**Figure 20**).

4. Type the text that you want to use as body text (**Figure 21**).

✔ Tips

- Word automatically applies the Normal style to body text. You can modify the style to meet your needs; I tell you how in **Chapter 4**.

- Each time you press [Return] while typing body text, Word creates a new paragraph of body text.

- You can convert body text to a heading by clicking the Promote or Demote button on the Outlining toolbar.

- Introduction to Word
- ◇ The Word Workplace
    - Introduction
    - New and Improved Features in Word
    - Meet Microsoft Word

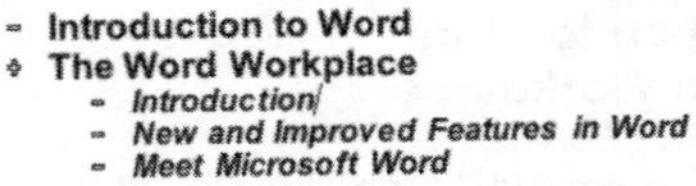

Figure 18 Position the insertion point.

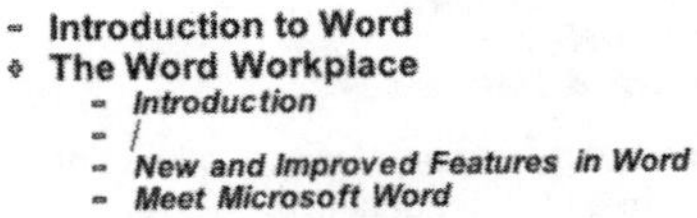

- Introduction to Word
- ◇ The Word Workplace
    - Introduction
    -
    - New and Improved Features in Word
    - Meet Microsoft Word

Figure 19 Press [Return].

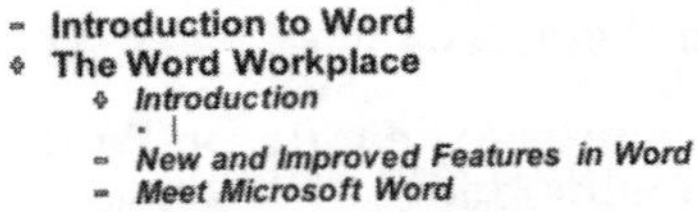

- Introduction to Word
- ◇ The Word Workplace
    - ◇ Introduction
      - ·
    - New and Improved Features in Word
    - Meet Microsoft Word

Figure 20 When you click the Demote to Body Text button, the level changes to body text.

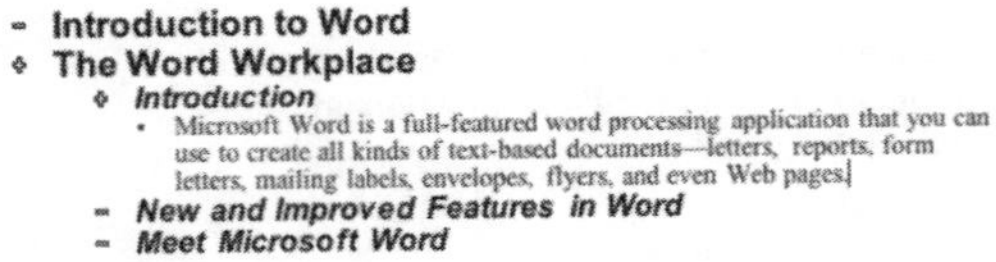

- Introduction to Word
- ◇ The Word Workplace
    - ◇ Introduction
      - · Microsoft Word is a full-featured word processing application that you can use to create all kinds of text-based documents—letters, reports, form letters, mailing labels, envelopes, flyers, and even Web pages
    - New and Improved Features in Word
    - Meet Microsoft Word

Figure 21 Type the text that you want to appear as body text.

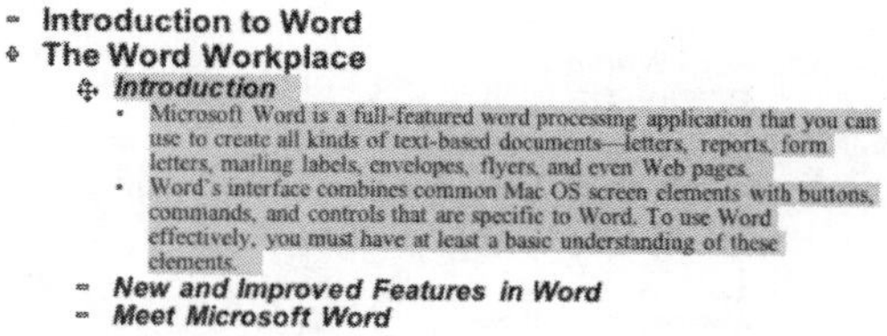

- Introduction to Word
- The Word Workplace
  - *Introduction*
    - Microsoft Word is a full-featured word processing application that you can use to create all kinds of text-based documents—letters, reports, form letters, mailing labels, envelopes, flyers, and even Web pages.
    - Word's interface combines common Mac OS screen elements with buttons, commands, and controls that are specific to Word. To use Word effectively, you must have at least a basic understanding of these elements.
  - *New and Improved Features in Word*
  - *Meet Microsoft Word*

Figure 22 When you click the marker to the left of a heading, Word selects the heading and all of its sub-headings and body text.

To remove outline components

1. To remove a single heading or paragraph of body text, click the hollow dash or small square marker to the left of the heading or body text. This selects the entire paragraph of the heading or body text.

   or

   To remove a heading with its subheadings and body text, click the hollow plus sign marker to the left of the heading. This selects the heading and all of its subheadings and body text (**Figure 22**).

2. Press (Delete). The selection is removed.

✔ Tip

- You can edit an outline in any of Word's views. Just use commands under the View menu to switch to your favorite view and edit the outline as desired.

Rearranging Outline Components

Word's outline feature offers two methods to move selected outline components up or down:

◆ Click the Move Up or Move Down button on the Outlining toolbar.

◆ Drag heading or body text markers.

✔ Tips

■ Rearranging outline components using these methods changes the order in which they appear but not their level of importance.

■ Either of these methods can be used to move a single heading or paragraph of body text, multiple headings, or a heading with all of its subheadings and body text.

To move headings and/or body text with toolbar buttons

1. To move a single heading or paragraph of body text, click to position the insertion point within it (**Figure 23**).

   or

   To move a heading with its subheadings and body text, click the hollow plus sign marker to the left of the heading to select the heading, its subheadings, and its body text (**Figure 22**).

2. To move the heading up, click the Move Up button on the Outlining toolbar. The heading moves one paragraph up.

   or

   To move the heading down, click the Move Down button on the Outlining toolbar. The heading moves one paragraph down (**Figure 24**).

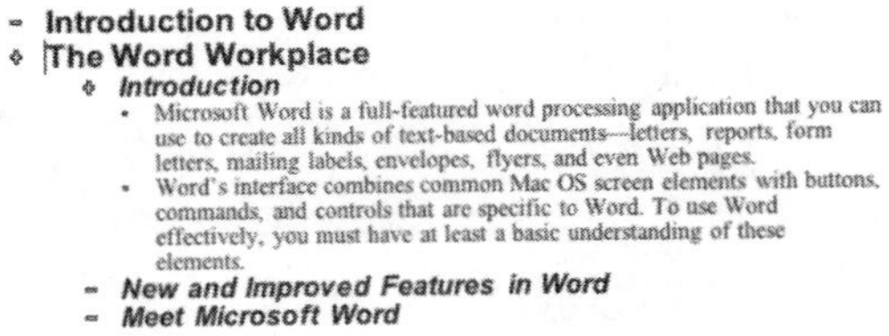

Figure 23 Click to position the insertion point.

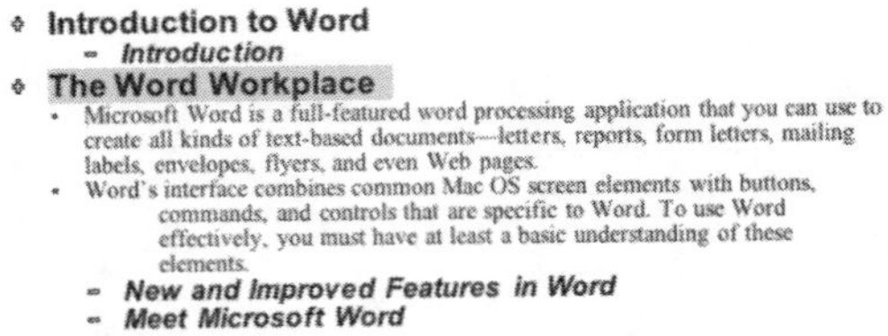

Figure 24 When you click the Move Down button, the heading moves down.

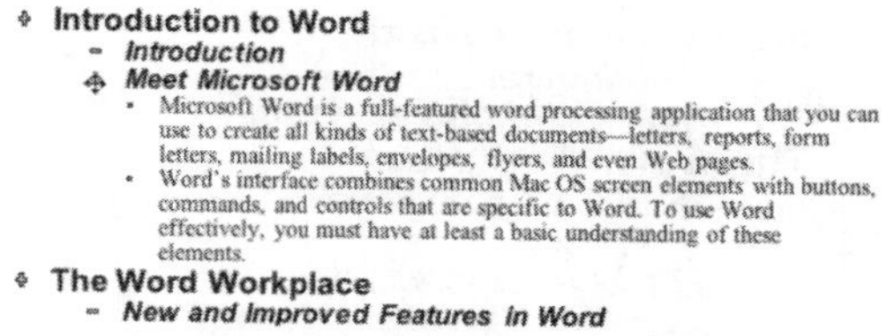

- ◆ **Introduction to Word**
  - – *Introduction*
  - ⊕ *Meet Microsoft Word*
    - • Microsoft Word is a full-featured word processing application that you can use to create all kinds of text-based documents—letters, reports, form letters, mailing labels, envelopes, flyers, and even Web pages.
    - • Word's interface combines common Mac OS screen elements with buttons, commands, and controls that are specific to Word. To use Word effectively, you must have at least a basic understanding of these elements.
- ◆ **The Word Workplace**
  - – *New and Improved Features in Word*

Figure 25 Position the mouse pointer over the heading marker.

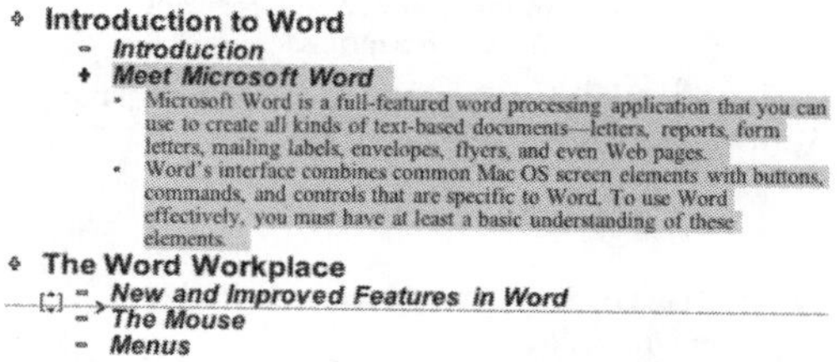

- ◆ **Introduction to Word**
  - – *Introduction*
  - ◆ *Meet Microsoft Word*
    - • Microsoft Word is a full-featured word processing application that you can use to create all kinds of text-based documents—letters, reports, form letters, mailing labels, envelopes, flyers, and even Web pages.
    - • Word's interface combines common Mac OS screen elements with buttons, commands, and controls that are specific to Word. To use Word effectively, you must have at least a basic understanding of these elements.
- ◆ **The Word Workplace**
  - ┈[•]┈▸*New and Improved Features in Word*
    - – *The Mouse*
    - – *Menus*

Figure 26 As you drag, a line indicates the new position when you release the mouse button.

- ◆ **Introduction to Word**
  - – *Introduction*
- ◆ **The Word Workplace**
  - – *New and Improved Features in Word*
  - ◆ *Meet Microsoft Word*
    - • Microsoft Word is a full-featured word processing application that you can use to create all kinds of text-based documents—letters, reports, form letters, mailing labels, envelopes, flyers, and even Web pages.
    - • Word's interface combines common Mac OS screen elements with buttons, commands, and controls that are specific to Word. To use Word effectively, you must have at least a basic understanding of these elements.
    - – *The Mouse*
    - – *Menus*

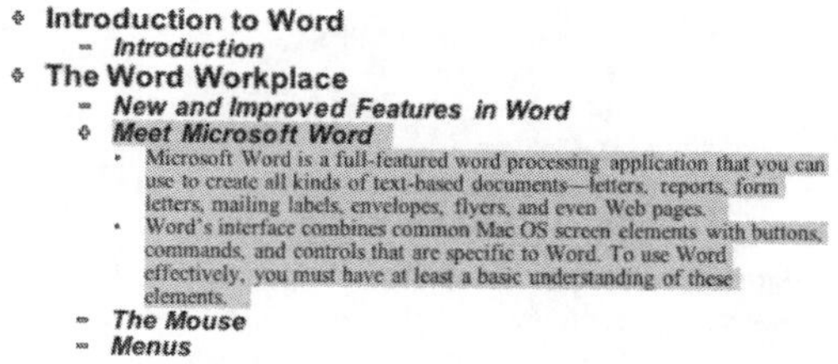

Figure 27 When you release the mouse button, the headings (and their body text, if any) move.

To move headings and/or body text by dragging

1. To move a single heading or paragraph of body text, position the mouse pointer over the hollow dash or small square marker to its left.

   or

   To move a heading with its subheadings and body text, position the mouse pointer on the plus sign marker to its left (**Figure 25**).

   The mouse pointer turns into a four-headed arrow (**Figure 25**).

2. To move the component(s) up, press the mouse button down and drag up (**Figure 26**).

   or

   To move the component(s) down, press the mouse button down and drag down.

   The components are selected. As you drag, a line indicates the location to which they will be moved when you release the mouse button. You can see this in **Figure 26**.

3. Release the mouse button to move the component(s) (**Figure 27**).

REARRANGING OUTLINE COMPONENTS

VIEWING HEADING LEVELS

Viewing Outlines

Buttons on the Outlining toolbar (**Figure 6**) enable you to change your view of an outline:

◆ Collapse headings to hide subheadings and body text.

◆ Expand headings to show subheadings and body text.

◆ Show only specific heading levels.

◆ Show all heading levels.

◆ Show only the first line of text in each paragraph.

◆ Show all lines of text in each paragraph.

◆ Show or hide formatting.

✔ Tip

■ These viewing options do not change the document's content—just your view of it.

To collapse a heading

1. Click the marker to the left of the heading that you want to collapse to select the heading, its subheadings, and its body text (**Figure 28**).

2. Click the Collapse button on the Outlining toolbar. The heading collapses to hide the lowest displayed level (**Figure 29**).

3. Repeat step 2 until only the levels you want to see are displayed (**Figure 30**).

Or

Double-click the marker to the left of the heading that you want to collapse. The heading collapses to its level (**Figure 30**).

✔ Tip

■ When you collapse a heading with sub-headings or body text, a gray line appears beneath it to indicate hidden items (**Figures 29** and **30**).

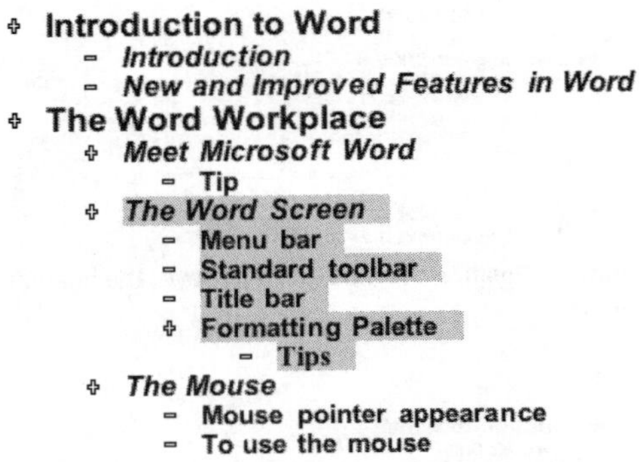

⊕ **Introduction to Word**
  – *Introduction*
  – *New and Improved Features in Word*
⊕ **The Word Workplace**
  ⊕ *Meet Microsoft Word*
    – Tip
  ⊕ *The Word Screen*
    – Menu bar
    – Standard toolbar
    – Title bar
    ⊕ Formatting Palette
      – Tips
  ⊕ *The Mouse*
    – Mouse pointer appearance
    – To use the mouse

Figure 28 Click a heading's marker to select it, along with its subheadings and body text.

⊕ **Introduction to Word**
  – *Introduction*
  – *New and Improved Features in Word*
⊕ **The Word Workplace**
  ⊕ *Meet Microsoft Word*
    – Tip
  ⊕ *The Word Screen*
    – Menu bar
    – Standard toolbar
    – Title bar
    ⊕ Formatting Palette
  ⊕ *The Mouse*
    – Mouse pointer appearance
    – To use the mouse

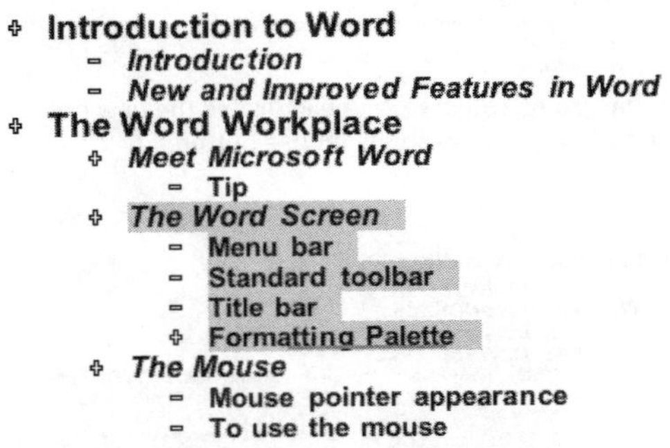

Figure 29 When you click the Collapse button, the lowest displayed level—in this example, Level 4—is hidden.

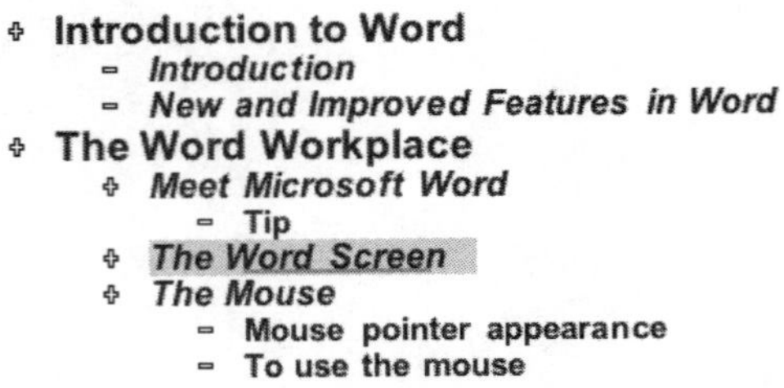

⊕ **Introduction to Word**
  – *Introduction*
  – *New and Improved Features in Word*
⊕ **The Word Workplace**
  ⊕ *Meet Microsoft Word*
    – Tip
  ⊕ *The Word Screen*
  ⊕ *The Mouse*
    – Mouse pointer appearance
    – To use the mouse

Figure 30 You can click the Collapse button repeatedly to hide multiple levels.

- ◆ **Introduction to Word**
  - ‐ *Introduction*
  - ‐ *New and Improved Features in Word*
- ◆ **The Word Workplace**
  - ◆ *Meet Microsoft Word*
    - ‐ Tip
  - ◆ *The Word Screen*
    - ‐ Menu bar
    - ‐ Standard toolbar
    - ‐ Title bar
    - ◆ Formatting Palette
  - ◆ *The Mouse*
    - ‐ Mouse pointer appearance
    - ‐ To use the mouse
  - ◆ *Menus*
    - ‐ To choose a menu command
    - ◆ To use a shortcut menu
  - ◆ *Shortcut Keys*
    - ‐ To use a shortcut key
  - ◆ *Toolbars & Palettes*
    - ‐ To view more buttons
    - ‐ To view ScreenTips
    - ‐ To use a toolbar button
    - ‐ To use a toolbar menu

Figure 31 In this example, the Show Heading 3 button was clicked to display heading levels 1, 2, and 3.

- ◆ **Introduction to Word**
  - ‐ *Introduction*
  - ‐ *New and Improved Features in Word*
- ◆ **The Word Workplace**
  - ◆ *Meet Microsoft Word*
  - ◆ *The Word Screen*
  - ◆ *The Mouse*
  - ◆ *Menus*
  - ◆ *Shortcut Keys*
  - ◆ *Toolbars & Palettes*
  - ‐ *Dialogs*
  - ‐ *Views*
  - ‐ *Document Navigation*
  - ‐ *Windows*
  - ‐ *Word Help*
  - ‐ *The Office Assistant*

Figure 32 In this example, the Show Heading 2 button was clicked to display heading levels 1 and 2.

- ◆ **Introduction to Word**
  - ‐ *Introduction*
  - ‐ *New and Improved Features in Word*
- ◆ **The Word Workplace**
  - ◆ *Meet Microsoft Word*
    - • Microsoft Word is a full-featured word processing application that you can use to create all kinds of text-based documents—letters, reports, form letters, mailing labels, envelopes, flyers, and even Web pages.
    - • Word's interface combines common Mac OS screen elements with buttons, commands, and controls that are specific to Word. To use Word effectively, you must have at least a basic understanding of these elements.
      - ‐ Tip
  - ◆ *The Word Screen*
    - ‐ Menu bar
    - ‐ Standard toolbar
    - ‐ Title bar
    - ◆ Formatting Palette
      - ‐ Tips
  - ◆ *The Mouse*
    - ‐ Mouse pointer appearance
    - ‐ To use the mouse
  - ◆ *Menus*
    - ‐ To choose a menu command
    - ◆ To use a shortcut menu
      - ‐ Tips

Figure 33 Choosing Show All Headings displays all levels of headings and the body text.

To expand a heading

1. Click the marker to the left of the heading that you want to expand to select the heading and all of its subheadings and body text.

2. Click the Expand button on the Outlining toolbar. The heading expands to display the highest hidden level.

3. Repeat step 2 as desired to display all of the levels you want to see.

Or

Double-click the marker to the left of the heading that you want to expand. The heading expands to show all levels.

To view only certain heading levels

On the Outlining toolbar (**Figure 6**), click the button that corresponds to the lowest level of heading that you want to display.

The outline collapses or expands to show just that level (**Figures 31** and **32**).

To view all heading levels

On the Outlining toolbar (**Figure 6**), click the Show All Headings button.

The outline expands to show all headings and body text (**Figure 33**).

VIEWING HEADING LEVELS

To display only the first line of every paragraph

Click the Show First Line Only button on the Outlining toolbar.

The Outline view changes to display only the first line of each heading and paragraph of body text (**Figure 34**).

✔ Tip

- The Show First Line Only button works like a toggle switch. When turned on, only the first line of every paragraph is displayed. When turned off, all lines of every paragraph are displayed. This button is turned off by default.

To hide formatting

Click the Show Formatting button on the Outlining toolbar.

The Outline view changes to display all headings and body text in the default paragraph font for the Normal style (**Figure 35**).

✔ Tip

- The Show Formatting button works like a toggle switch. When turned on, paragraph formatting is displayed. When turned off, all text appears in the default paragraph font for the Normal style. This button is turned on by default.

Figure 34 Turning on the Show First Line Only button displays only the first line of each heading or paragraph of body text.

Figure 35 Turning off the Show Formatting button displays all text in the default paragraph font for the Normal style—in this case, 12-point New Times Roman.

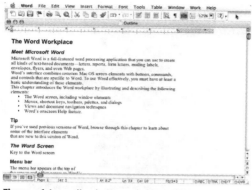

Figure 36 An outline in Normal view...

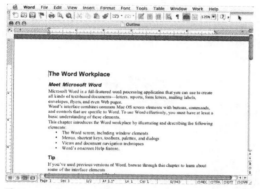

Figure 37 ...Page Layout view...

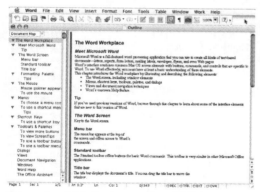

Figure 38 ...and Online Layout view with the Document Map showing.

Working with an Outline in Another View

You can switch to Normal (**Figure 36**), Page Layout (**Figure 37**), or Online Layout (**Figure 38**) view while working with an outline. There's nothing special about an outline except the additional outlining features available in Outline view. It's the same document when you switch to another view.

✔ Tips

- You can switch between any of Word's views at any time.

- I explain how to switch from one view to another in **Chapter 1**.

- Once the structure of a lengthy or complex document has been established in Outline view, you may find it easier to complete the document in Normal or Page Layout view.

- In Normal, Page Layout, and Online Layout views, you can apply the Heading and Normal styles using the Style area of the Formatting Palette. Styles are covered in **Chapter 4**.

- The Document Map lists all of the outline's headings (**Figure 38**). Double-click a heading to move quickly to that part of the document. You can show the Document Map in Normal or Online Layout view. The Document Map is discussed in **Chapter 1**.

Numbering Outline Headings

One of the more tedious aspects of working with a long, structured document is numbering (and renumbering) headings. This is especially cumbersome when dealing with legal documents that have multiple heading levels and strict heading or paragraph numbering requirements. But it can be almost as frustrating when dealing with a simple document that's frequently reorganized.

Fortunately, Word's paragraph numbering feature can automatically number—and renumber—paragraph headings. You can set up this feature as you build your document in Outline or Normal view so you don't have to worry about numbering. As long as you use Word's built-in heading styles, Word can handle all the numbering for you.

This part of the chapter explains how to set up outline numbering so Word can number your headings for you.

To automatically number headings in an outline

1. Select the outline for which you want to number headings (**Figure 39**).

2. Choose Format > Bullets and Numbering to display the Bullets and Numbering dialog.

3. If necessary, click the Outline Numbered button to display its options (**Figure 40**).

4. Select the preview for the numbering format that most closely matches the format you want.

5. Click the Customize button to display the Customize outline numbered list dialog (**Figure 41**).

6. Select a heading level from the Level list.

Figure 39 Select the outline you want to number.

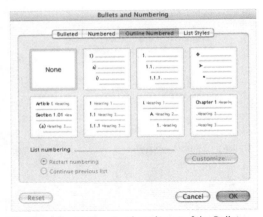

Figure 40 The Outline Numbered pane of the Bullets and Numbering dialog.

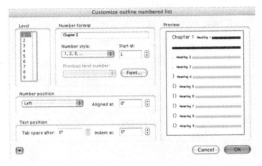

Figure 41 The Customize outline numbered list dialog.

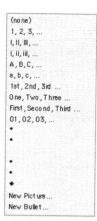

Figure 42
The Number style
pop-up menu.

Figure 43 The Font dialog.

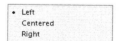

Figure 44 The Number
position pop-up menu.

7. Edit the contents of the Number format box so it includes the text you want to appear with the number. Do not edit the gray highlighted number in the box.

8. Choose an option from the Number style pop-up menu (**Figure 42**). The Number format box changes to reflect the option you chose.

9. If desired, enter a starting number in the Start at box.

10. If you chose a heading level other than 1 in step 6, indicate the previous heading level by choosing an option from the Previous level number pop-up menu. Only those heading levels that are lower than the level you selected in step 6 appear; this option is not available if you chose heading level 1.

11. If desired, click the Font button and use the Font dialog that appears (**Figure 43**) to set the character formatting options for the contents of the Number format box. Click OK to save your settings.

12. To set the heading number position, choose an option from the Number position pop-up menu (**Figure 44**) and enter an indentation setting in the Aligned at box.

13. To set the position of text that appears after the heading number, enter a value in the Indent at box.

14. Repeat steps 6 through 13 for each heading level used in your document.

15. Click OK to save your settings in the Customize outline numbered list dialog.

16. If necessary, click OK in the Bullets and Numbering dialog.

Continued on next page...

AUTOMATICALLY NUMBERING HEADINGS

Continued from previous page.

Figure 45 shows the outline in **Figure 39** with heading numbering set up for heading levels 1 and 2 and all number format options removed for heading 3.

✔ Tips

■ In step 4, if one of the previews indicates the exact formatting you want, you can skip steps 5 through 15.

■ In step 7, be sure to include (or remove) any punctuation you want to appear (or not appear).

■ If you skip step 11, the heading number will appear in the default paragraph font for the heading in which it appears.

■ After step 13, you can click the triangle button in the lower-left corner of the Customize outline numbered list dialog to expand the dialog and offer more options (**Figure 46**).

■ Once heading numbering has been set for an outline, rearranging outline levels automatically renumbers the outline. **Figure 47** shows an example.

◊ **Chapter 1: The Word Workplace**
  ▫ *Section I: Meet Microsoft Word*
  ◊ *Section II: The Word Screen*
    ▫ Title Bar
    ▫ Menu Bar
    ▫ Standard Toolbar
    ▫ Formatting Toolbar
    ▫ Task Pane
    ▫ Ruler
    ▫ Insertion Point
    ▫ End-of-Document Marker
    ▫ I-beam Pointer
    ▫ Document Window
    ▫ View Buttons
    ▫ Status Bar
    ▫ Browse Object Controls
  ◊ *Section III: The Mouse*
    ▫ Mouse Pointer Appearance
    ▫ To use the mouse
  ◊ *Section IV: Menus*
    ▫ To choose a menu command

Figure 45 The outline in **Figure 39** with automatic numbering applied to Level 1 and Level 2 headings.

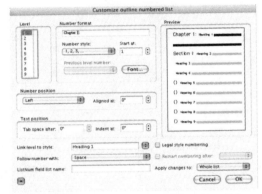

Figure 46 The Customize outline numbered list dialog, expanded to show additional options.

◊ **Chapter 1: The Word Workplace**
  ▫ *Section I: Meet Microsoft Word*
  ◊ *Section II: The Mouse*
    ▫ Mouse Pointer Appearance
    ▫ To use the mouse
  ◊ *Section III: The Word Screen*
    ▫ Title Bar
    ▫ Menu Bar
    ▫ Standard Toolbar
    ▫ Formatting Toolbar
    ▫ Task Pane
    ▫ Ruler
    ▫ Insertion Point
    ▫ End-of-Document Marker
    ▫ I-beam Pointer
    ▫ Document Window
    ▫ View Buttons
    ▫ Status Bar
    ▫ Browse Object Controls
  ◊ *Section IV: Menus*
    ▫ To choose a menu command

Figure 47 When you rearrange an outline, the headings are automatically renumbered.

- Chapter 1: The Word Workplace
  - *Meet Microsoft Word*
  - *The Word Screen*
  - *The Mouse*
  - *Menus*
  - *Shortcut Keys*
  - *Toolbars & Palettes*
  - *Dialogs*
  - *Views*
  - *Document Navigation*
  - *Windows*
  - *Word Help*
  - *The Office Assistant*
- Chapter 2: Word Basics
  - *Word Processing Basics*
  - *Running Word*
  - *Exiting Word*
  - *Word Documents, Templates, & Wizards*
  - *The Project Gallery*
  - *Creating Documents*
  - *Opening Existing Documents*
  - *Entering Text*
  - *Nonprinting Characters*
  - *The Insertion Point*
  - *Inserting & Deleting Text*

Figure 48 Some of the Heading 1 and Heading 2 heads for the first two chapters of this book.

✔ Tips

- A master document can also be used to manage a large document accessible by multiple users over a network. Users can work on different subdocuments at the same time.
- One of the benefits of using master documents to organize components of a lengthy document is that the template of the master document is automatically used by each subdocument. This ensures consistency in formatting and in other elements such as headers and footers.

Master Documents

Very long documents, such as books, can be cumbersome to create. Creating the entire document in one document file can result in a monster file that slows performance when editing or scrolling text. But creating a separate file for each chapter makes it difficult to ensure consistent formatting and review the document as a whole. What's the solution?

Word's master document feature offers the best of both approaches. A *master document* is a Word document that includes a group of related documents called *subdocuments*. Master documents are commonly used to divide a long document into smaller, more manageable pieces.

Master documents normally start as outlines created in Word's Outline view. You can then use the master document feature to set up headings and their subheadings as subdocuments. For example, take the original outline for the first nine chapters of this book, part of which is shown in **Figure 48**. Chapter names are Heading 1 level headings that can be designated as subdocuments. The result is that each chapter becomes a separate document.

Although using outlines may be the best way to create a master document from scratch, you can also turn an existing document into a master document or add existing documents to a master document to make them subdocuments.

In this part of the chapter, I explain how to create and work with master documents.

To convert an outline into a master document

1. Click the Master Document View button on the Outlining toolbar to switch to Master Document view and display the Master Document toolbar (**Figure 49**).

2. In the document window, click an outline symbol to select the heading and associated subheadings that you want to turn into a subdocument (**Figure 50**).

3. Click the Create Subdocument button on the Master Document toolbar.

   A subdocument icon appears near the heading and a gray box appears around the heading and its subheadings (**Figure 51**).

4. Repeat steps 2 and 3 for each heading you want to turn into a subdocument.

5. Save the document. Word automatically creates a separate document file for each subdocument (**Figure 52**).

✔ Tips

- Remember, you can point to a toolbar button to learn its name.

- Word inserts section breaks between each subdocument in a master document. I tell you more about section breaks in **Chapter 5**.

- To convert part of a document into a subdocument, the part of the document you want to convert must begin with a heading style.

CONVERTING OUTLINES TO MASTER DOCUMENTS

Figure 49 The Master Document toolbar.

Figure 50 Click an outline symbol to select a heading and all of its subheadings and body text.

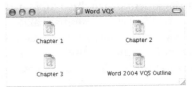

Figure 51 A box appears around each subdocument.

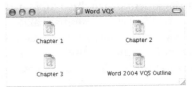

Figure 52 When you save a master document, each of its subdocuments is saved as a separate document file. This example shows the master document's icon ("Word 2004 VQS Outline") and the icons for subdocuments created for the first three chapters in the outline.

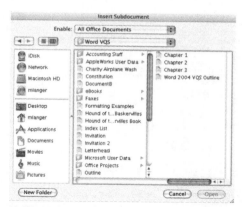

Figure 53 The Insert Subdocument dialog enables you to insert a Word document as a subdocument in a master document.

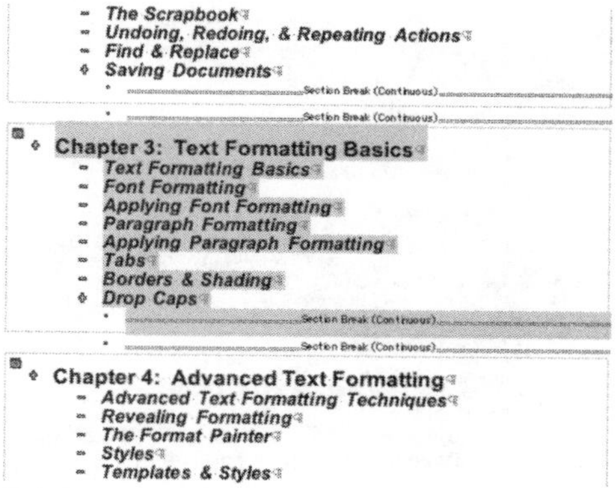

Figure 54 Click the subdocument icon for a subdocument to select it.

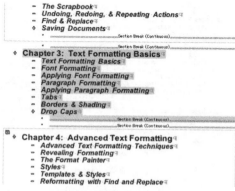

Figure 55 As shown here, removing a subdocument doesn't remove any text. Only the subdocument icon and the box around the text disappear.

To insert a subdocument into a master document

1. Position the insertion point where you want to insert the subdocument.

2. Click the Insert Subdocument button on the Master Document toolbar.

3. In the Insert Subdocument dialog that appears (**Figure 53**), locate and select the document you want to insert as a subdocument and click Open.

   The document is inserted as a subdocument, with a subdocument icon near its heading and a gray box around its contents.

To remove a subdocument

1. In the document window, click the subdocument icon near the first heading for the subdocument to select the entire subdocument (**Figure 54**).

2. Click the Remove Subdocument button on the Master Document toolbar.

   The subdocument icon and gray box around the subdocument disappear. The document becomes part of the master document (**Figure 55**).

✔ Tip

- Clicking the Remove Subdocument button doesn't remove any text from your document. Instead, it converts the subdocument to part of the master document. If the master document had been saved before you removed the subdocument, the subdocument's contents still exist as a separate document file (**Figure 52**).

To merge two or more subdocuments

1. Click the subdocument icon for one of the subdocuments to select the entire subdocument.

2. Hold down Shift and click the subdocument icon for a subdocument you want to merge with the first subdocument. The subdocument is added to the selection (**Figure 56**).

3. Repeat step 2 for each subdocument you want to include in the merge.

4. Click the Merge Subdocument button on the Master Document toolbar.

   The subdocuments are merged into one (**Figure 57**).

To split a subdocument into two subdocuments

1. Position the insertion point where you want the split to occur (**Figure 58**).

2. Click the Split Subdocument button on the Master Document toolbar.

   A new subdocument is created at the insertion point (**Figure 59**).

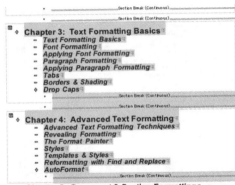

Figure 56 Select the subdocuments you want to merge by holding down Shift and clicking on their subdocument icons.

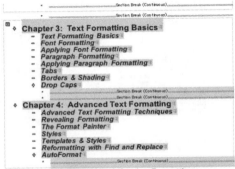

Figure 57 The two subdocuments selected in **Figure 56** after merging them into a single subdocument.

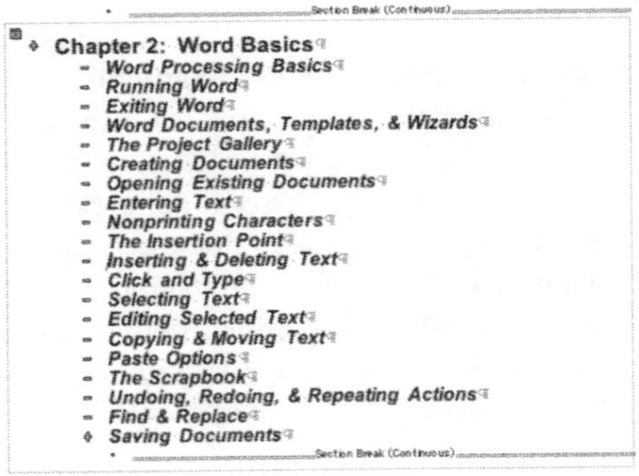

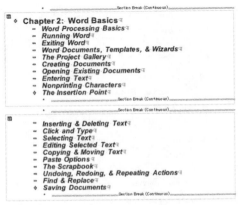

Figure 58 Position the insertion point where you want to split the document.

Figure 59 The subdocument is split into two subdocuments.

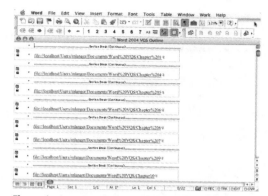

Figure 60 A master document with the subdocuments collapsed.

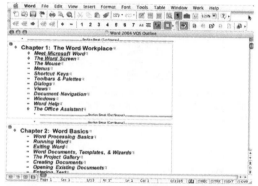

Figure 61 The master document from **Figure 60** with subdocuments expanded.

To collapse subdocuments

Click the Collapse Subdocuments button on the Master Document toolbar.

The subdocuments are replaced with hyperlinks to their respective files (**Figure 60**).

✔ Tips

- When you open a master document, it usually appears in a collapsed view (**Figure 60**).

- Collapsing a master document makes it easy to see a list of all of its subdocuments.

To expand subdocuments

Click the Expand Subdocuments button on the Master Document toolbar.

The subdocuments' hyperlinks are replaced with the contents of their files (**Figure 61**).

To edit a subdocument in its own document window

Double-click the subdocument icon for the subdocument you want to open. Its file opens in its own document window (**Figure 62**).

✔ Tips

■ It doesn't matter whether subdocuments are expanded (**Figure 61**) or collapsed (**Figure 60**) when you double-click a subdocument icon. Either way, the document opens.

■ Saving changes to a subdocument automatically saves changes to that document in the master document.

To prevent a subdocument from being edited

1. Position the insertion point anywhere in the subdocument you want to lock to prevent editing of its contents.

2. Click the Lock Document button on the Master Document toolbar. A padlock icon appears beneath the subdocument icon (**Figure 63**). The document can no longer be edited.

✔ Tips

■ To allow editing of a locked subdocument, position the insertion point in the subdocument and click the Lock Document button on the Master Document toolbar. The document is unlocked.

■ To prevent an unauthorized user from editing a document, you can use Word's document protection features to protect it with a password. I tell you how in **Chapter 16**.

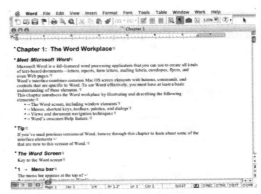

Figure 62 Double-clicking a subdocument icon opens the subdocument in its own document window.

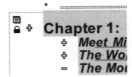

Figure 63 A padlock icon beneath the subdocument icon indicates that the subdocument cannot be edited.

Notebook Layout View

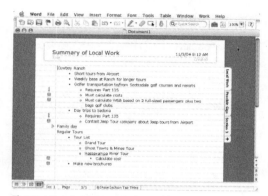

Figure 1 Notebook Layout view, with some notes.

Notebook Layout View

Notebook Layout view (**Figure 1**) is a Macintosh-only feature that is brand new in Word 2004. With "pages" that resemble a ruled notebook, Notebook Layout view is designed to make it easy to take notes and write down your thoughts quickly, in a free-form style that's easy to organize.

In Notebook Layout view, you enter text using an outline-like note structure. You type a note at the top level, then add notes beneath it in indented sublevels. Like Outline view, you can collapse or expand note levels to hide or display details.

In Notebook Layout view, your notes aren't limited to what you can type. You can use the Scribble tool to draw images. You can also use tools on the Audio Notes toolbar to record and play audio notes in a document.

Notebook Layout view includes a few unique organizational tools. For example, you can create named page tabs that identify groups of notes. You can also flag notes for future action or insert check boxes beside notes to check off items for whatever reason you want.

This chapter explains how to get started using Notebook Layout view to take notes with Word.

✔ Tip

- I tell you about Word's Outline view in **Chapter 12**. Because Notebook Layout view and Outline view have some similarities, you may find it helpful to read **Chapter 12** before continuing with this chapter.

Creating a Notebook File

Any Word document can be viewed in Notebook Layout view. The best way to use this feature, however, is to create a Word notebook file. This automatically formats the document for the Notebook Layout feature and displays it in Notebook Layout view.

You can also convert an existing document to Notebook Layout view. Doing so, however, may cause some of the document's formatting to be lost.

To create a Word notebook file

1. Choose File > Project Gallery, or press Shift ⌃ ⌘ P to display the Project Gallery dialog.

2. Click the New button near the top of the Project Gallery dialog to display New document options (**Figure 2**).

3. In the Groups list, select Blank Documents.

4. Select the Word Notebook icon.

5. Click Open.

   Word creates a new document and displays it in Notebook Layout view (**Figure 3**).

✔ Tip

■ Another way to create a Word notebook file is to create a blank new document using any of the techniques covered in **Chapter 2** and switch to Notebook Layout view (as discussed on the next page) before entering any text into the document.

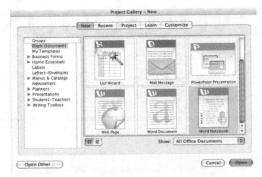

Figure 2 You can use the Project Gallery dialog to create a new Word notebook file.

Figure 3 A blank Word notebook file.

Figure 4 Here's an example of a document created with Outline view and viewed in Normal view.

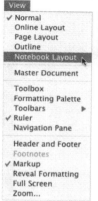

Figure 5 Choose Notebook Layout from the View menu...

Figure 6 ...or click the Notebook Layout view button at the bottom of the document window.

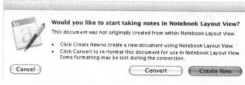

Figure 7 This dialog warns you that formatting may be lost when you convert.

To view any document in Notebook Layout view

1. Open the document you want to view in Notebook Layout view (**Figure 4**).

2. Choose View > Notebook Layout (**Figure 5**).

   or

   Click the Notebook Layout view button at the bottom of the document window (**Figure 6**).

3. A dialog like the one in **Figure 7** may appear. Click Convert to reformat the document for use with Notebook Layout view.

   The document appears in Notebook Layout view (**Figure 8**).

✔ Tip

■ If you click Create New in step 3, Word creates a blank new document in Notebook Layout view (**Figure 3**).

Figure 8 As this example shows, when you convert an existing document for use with Notebook Layout features, much of the formatting is lost.

Entering Notes

Notebook Layout view enables you to enter notes in a number of ways:

◆ Type notes using your keyboard. You can enter paragraphs of notes or take advantage of the outline-like capabilities to enter notes and subnotes.

◆ Draw notes using the Scribble tool. You can use this feature to make simple drawings with your mouse or a graphics tablet.

◆ Record audio notes with your computer's built-in or external microphone.

This part of the chapter explains how to enter notes into a notebook file.

✔ Tip

■ If file size is a concern, use audio notes sparingly. Lengthy notes can greatly increase the size of a Word document file.

To type notes

1. Position the insertion point in the first ruled line of the document (**Figure 9**).

2. Type the note you want to appear (**Figure 10**). It can be as long or short as you like.

3. Press Return to start a new note at the same level.

4. Type another note:

   ▲ To type a note at the same level, repeat steps 2 and 3.

   ▲ To type a note at a lower level, press Tab, then repeat steps 2 and 3.

   ▲ To type a note at a higher level, press Shift Tab and then repeat steps 2 and 3.

5. Repeat this process for all the notes you want to type. **Figure 11** shows an example of some notes.

Figure 9 Position the insertion point on the first ruled line of the document.

Figure 10 Type your note.

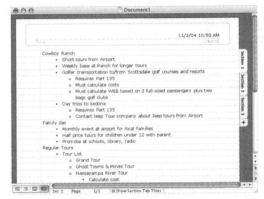

Figure 11 Here's an example with a few notes entered at different levels. Notice that Word automatically places bullets beside notes in lower levels.

Figure 12
In Notebook Layout view, the Formatting Palette includes tools for working with notes.

Figure 13 Position the crosshairs pointer where you want to begin your drawing.

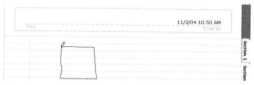

Figure 14 Hold the mouse button down and drag to create your drawing. (I can't even draw a straight line!)

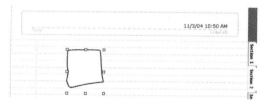

Figure 15 When you release the mouse button, the object is completed and selection handles appear around it.

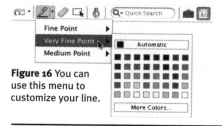

Figure 16 You can use this menu to customize your line.

✔ Tips

- You can change the level and order of notes in Notebook Layout view with toolbar buttons and the Level drop-down list in the Note Levels area of the Formatting Palette (**Figure 12**).

- Typing notes in Notebook Layout view is very much like creating an outline in Outline view. Consult **Chapter 12** for more information about working with hierarchical outlines.

To draw notes

1. Click the Scribble button on the Notebook Layout view Standard toolbar. The mouse pointer turns into a crosshairs pointer.

2. Position the mouse pointer where you want to start drawing (**Figure 13**), press the mouse button down, and drag your mouse to draw. If you have better drawing skills than I do (which is likely), you'll be able to draw something a bit more attractive than what you see in **Figure 14**.

3. Release the mouse button to complete the drawing. Selection handles appear around what you drew (**Figure 15**).

4. Repeat steps 2 and 3 to draw some more.

5. When you are finished drawing, click the Scribble button again or press (Esc) to restore the mouse pointer to normal.

✔ Tips

- You can use the Scribble button's menu and submenus to choose a pen thickness and color (**Figure 16**).

- Once you have drawn an object, you can work with it like any other drawing layer object. I tell you about working with drawn objects in **Chapter 10**.

DRAWING NOTES

To record audio notes

1. Position the insertion point anywhere in the line where you want to link the audio note (**Figure 17**).

2. If necessary, click the Audio Notes Toolbar button in the Notebook Layout view Standard toolbar to display the Audio Notes toolbar (**Figure 18**).

3. Click the Start Recording button on the Audio Notes toolbar. The word *Recording* appears on the left end of the toolbar (**Figure 19**) and whatever sound is picked up by the computer's microphone is recorded.

4. When you are finished recording, click the Stop button on the Audio Notes toolbar. The audio note is saved in your document.

✔ Tip

- You can see an audio note icon by pointing to the text to which the audio note is linked (**Figure 20**).

To play audio notes

Click the audio note icon for the note you want to hear (**Figure 21**). The note plays, followed by whatever notes were recorded after it in the document.

Or

Click the Play button on the Audio Notes toolbar. All audio notes in the document play in the order in which they were recorded.

✔ Tip

- The word *Playing* appears in the Audio Notes toolbar when notes are playing (**Figure 22**).

Figure 17 Position the insertion point in the note you want to link the audio note to.

Figure 18 The Audio Notes toolbar.

Figure 19 The Audio Notes toolbar while recording a note.

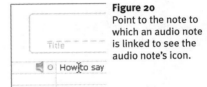

Figure 20
Point to the note to which an audio note is linked to see the audio note's icon.

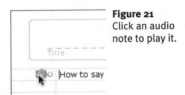

Figure 21
Click an audio note to play it.

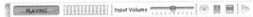

Figure 22 The Audio Notes toolbar while playing back a note.

Figure 23 Position the insertion point in the Title area.

Figure 24 Type in the title.

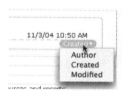

Figure 25
Use a pop-up menu to specify what should appear on the right side of the header.

Figure 26
A newly added section becomes the current section.

Notebook Sections

A Word notebook file is organized into sections. Each section has its own identifying tab on the right side of the document window and a section title in the section header. You can organize the notes in your notebook file by customizing and shuffling section tabs and entering section titles.

To enter a section title

1. Click in the Title area at the top of a section's window to position the insertion point there (**Figure 23**).

2. Type the text you want to appear in the title (**Figure 24**).

✔ Tip

■ You can further customize a section's header by choosing an option from the pop-up menu under the date (**Figure 25**) to change what appears on the right side of the header. If you choose Author, you can type in the name of the author.

To switch to a different section

Click the tab for the section you want to work with. That section's page appears.

To add a section

Click the + button at the bottom of the list of tabs. A new, unnamed section tab appears and its section becomes the current section (**Figure 26**).

To rename a section tab

1. Double-click the tab you want to rename. The tab's text becomes selected (**Figure 27**).

2. Type in the new name (**Figure 28**).

3. Press (Return) to save the name.

To change the order of sections

Drag the tab for the section you want to move into a new position in the list of tabs. When you release the mouse button, the section moves.

To delete a section

1. Hold down (Control) and click on the tab for the section that you want to delete.

2. Choose Delete Section from the shortcut menu that appears (**Figure 29**).

   The section (and its notes) is immediately deleted. Any tabs after it that have not been renamed are renumbered accordingly.

✔ Tip

■ As shown in **Figure 29**, you can also use the contextual menu to add and rename a section.

Figure 27
Double-click a tab name to select it.

Figure 28
Type in a new name.

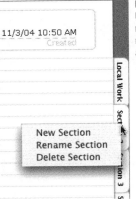

Figure 29
Use a contextual menu to create, rename, or delete a section.

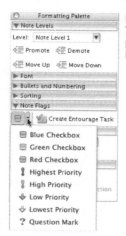

Figure 30
The Note Flags pop-up menu on the Formatting Palette.

Figure 31 Position the insertion point in the note you want to flag.

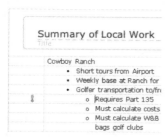

Figure 32 The flag appears in the left margin for the note.

Using Note Flags

Note flags are icons or check boxes you can place in the left margin beside individual notes at any level. You can use these flags to draw attention to specific notes.

You add note flags to items using the Note Flag button or Note Flags pop-up menu in the Formatting Palette (**Figure 30**).

✔ Tips

■ The check boxes are particularly handy since you can use them to check off items that you have finished working with.

■ A note can have up to two flags: one check box and one priority flag.

To add a note flag to a note

1. Position the insertion point anywhere within the note you want to flag (**Figure 31**).

2. To insert the note flag currently displayed on the Note Flag button on the Formatting Palette, click the button.

   or

   To insert a different note flag, choose one from the Note Flags pop-up menu on the Formatting Palette (**Figure 30**).

   The note flag appears in the left margin beside the note (**Figure 32**).

To remove a note flag

1. Position the insertion point anywhere within the note with the flag you want to remove (**Figure 32**).

2. Choose the flag that is assigned to the note from the Note Flags pop-up menu on the Formatting Palette (**Figure 30**).

   The note flag disappears.

Working in Other Views

Although you may create a document in Notebook Layout view, you can switch to other views to work with it. Simply choose the view you want to work in from the View menu or click a view button at the bottom-left of the document window. The document switches to that view.

Figures 33 and **34** show the notebook in **Figure 1** in Normal and Page Layout views.

✔ Tip

■ Although check boxes can appear beside note items in Page Layout view, they do not work like check boxes. Instead, they're just graphic objects.

Figure 33 A notebook in Normal view.

Figure 34 A notebook in Page Layout view.

Envelopes & Labels

Envelopes & Labels

Microsoft Word's Envelopes and Labels features can create and print addressed envelopes and mailing labels based on document contents or other information you provide. This feature makes it easy to print professional-looking envelopes and labels for all of your mailing needs.

✔ Tips

- Word supports a wide variety of standard envelope and label sizes and formats. Settings can also be changed for printing on nonstandard envelopes or labels.

- As discussed in **Chapter 15**, you can use the Data Merge Manager to create envelopes and labels based on database information.

- If you use Microsoft Entourage, you can use the Office Address Book button that appears in the Envelopes and Labels dialogs to insert an Entourage address for an envelope or label. This makes it quicker and easier to create envelopes or labels for people you work with.

Creating an Envelope

In Word, you create an envelope with the Envelope dialog (**Figure 2**). This dialog enables you to provide several pieces of information:

◆ **Delivery address** is the address the envelope will be mailed to.

◆ **Return address** is the address that appears in the upper-left corner of the envelope. You can use your own address, specify another address, or omit the address entirely.

◆ **Printing Options** are the settings your printer uses to print envelopes, including Page Setup options that determine envelope size and feed direction.

Once you have set options for an envelope, you can either print it immediately, create a new document for the envelope, or add it to the currently active document.

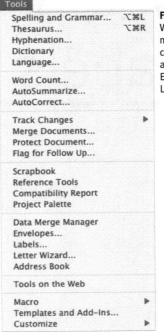

Figure 1
Word's Tools menu includes commands for accessing its Envelopes and Labels features.

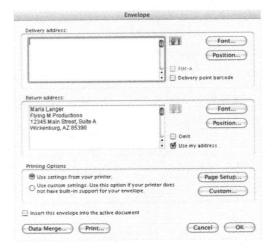

Figure 2 The Envelope dialog.

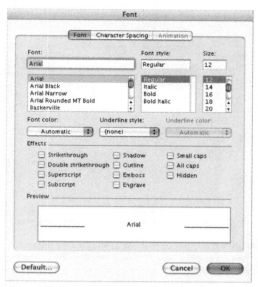

Figure 3 The Font dialog enables you to customize address font settings.

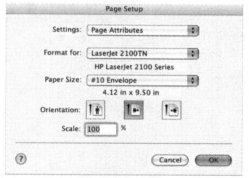

Figure 4 Use the Page Setup dialog to set printer and envelope options.

Figure 5
The Paper Size pop-up menu includes standard envelope sizes.

To set up an envelope

1. Choose Tools > Envelopes (**Figure 1**) to display the Envelope dialog (**Figure 2**).

2. Enter the name and address of the person to whom the envelope should be addressed in the Delivery address box.

3. If desired, enter a return address in the Return address box.

   or

   To create an envelope without a return address, turn on the Omit check box. This omits the return address from the envelope, even if one appears in the Return address box.

4. To modify the font settings for either address, click the Font button beside the address to display the Font dialog (**Figure 3**). Set options as desired and click OK.

5. Click Page Setup to display the Page Setup dialog (**Figure 4**).

6. Choose the printer you will print the envelope on from the Format for pop-up menu. This menu will include all printers you have set up for access by your computer.

7. Choose an envelope size from the Paper Size pop-up menu (**Figure 5**). This menu includes all paper sizes supported by your printer.

8. Click an Orientation option to specify how the envelope will be fed into the printer.

9. Click OK to save Page Setup options and return to the Envelope dialog.

10. Click OK to save your settings and dismiss the Envelope dialog.

Continued on next page...

Continued from previous page.

✔ Tips

■ In step 1, you cannot choose the Envelopes command unless a document window is open.

■ If you are creating an envelope for a letter in the active document window, the Delivery address may be filled in based on the inside address of the letter (**Figure 6**). You can "help" Word enter the correct address by selecting the recipient's address *before* opening the Envelope dialog.

■ In steps 2 and 3, you can click the Address Book button beside the address box to display the Office Address Book dialog (**Figure 7**). Select the name of the person you want to appear in the address box and click Insert to enter the name and address in the box.

■ To include a postal barcode on the envelope, after step 2, turn on the Delivery point barcode check box. You can then turn on the FIM-A check box to add additional postal coding to the envelope.

■ In step 3, turning on the Use my address check box enters your name and address (as recorded in Word's User preferences) in the Return address box. I tell you more about User preferences in **Chapter 20**.

■ To override Word's automatic positioning of addresses, click the Position button beside an address box to display the Address Position dialog (**Figure 8**). Enter measurements in the From left and From top text boxes for the address you want to move and click OK.

■ You can save font formatting changes as default settings by clicking the Default button in the Font dialog (**Figure 3**). Font formatting is covered in detail in **Chapter 3**.

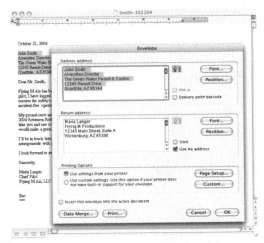

Figure 6 When you create an envelope for a letter, Word is usually "smart" enough to fill in the delivery address for you.

Figure 7 Use the Office Address Book dialog to insert one of your Entourage contacts into an address box.

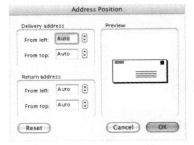

Figure 8 You can fine-tune an address position with this dialog.

SETTING UP ENVELOPES

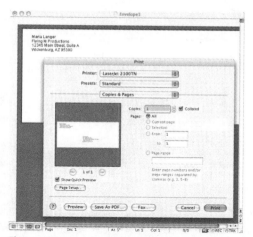

Figure 9 Word creates an envelope document and displays the Print dialog so you can print it.

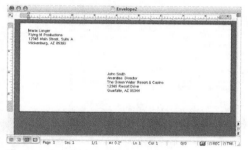

Figure 10 An envelope document.

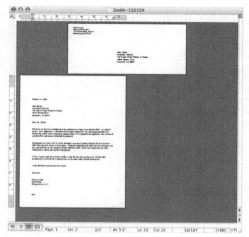

Figure 11 An envelope inserted into a Word document containing a letter.

To print an envelope

1. Set up the envelope as instructed on the previous two pages.

2. Click the Print button in the Envelope dialog (**Figure 2**).

   Word creates a document for the envelope and displays the Print dialog (**Figure 9**).

3. Use the Print dialog to set final print options.

4. Click Print.

   Word prints the envelope.

✔ Tip

- Printing and setting options in the Print dialog are covered in greater detail in **Chapter 6**.

To save the envelope

1. Set up the envelope as instructed on the previous two pages.

2. Click OK.

   Word creates a new document for the envelope (**Figure 10**).

✔ Tip

- If you turn on the Insert this envelope into the active document check box in the Envelope dialog (**Figure 2**) before clicking OK, Word adds a new section to the document with the proper settings to print that section as an envelope (**Figure 11**). I tell you about document sections in **Chapter 5**.

PRINTING & SAVING ENVELOPES

Creating Labels

In Word, you create labels with the Labels dialog (**Figure 12**). This dialog enables you to set up labels by entering the address that should appear on the label and the number of labels that should be printed. You can also use the Label Options dialog to set additional options for the type of label you want to print.

Once you have set options for a label, you can either print it immediately or save it as a new document so it can be printed later.

To set up labels

1. Choose Tools > Labels (**Figure 1**) to display the Labels dialog (**Figure 12**).

2. Enter the name and address for the label in the Address box.

3. To modify the font settings for the address, click the Font button beside the address to display the Font dialog (**Figure 3**). Set options as desired and click OK.

4. Click the Options button to display the Label Options dialog (**Figure 13**).

5. Select one of the Printer information radio buttons to indicate whether your printer is dot matrix, laser, or ink jet.

6. Choose a brand of label from the Label products pop-up menu (**Figure 14**).

7. Select the type of label you will be printing on from the Product number scrolling list.

8. Click OK to save your settings and return to the Labels dialog.

9. Select an option in the Number of labels area:

   ▲ **Full page of the same label** prints the entire page of labels with the name and address that appears in the Address box.

Figure 12 The Labels dialog.

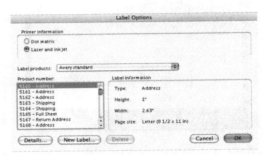

Figure 13 The Label Options dialog.

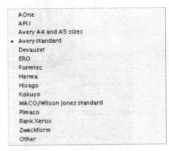

Figure 14
The Label products pop-up menu includes all the major label manufacturers.

SETTING UP LABELS

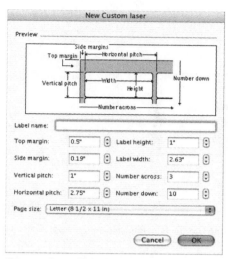

Figure 15 Use a dialog like this one to create your own custom label sizes.

▲ **Single label** prints only one label. If you select this option, be sure to enter the row and column number (if applicable) for the label to print.

✔ Tips

- In step 1, you cannot choose the Labels command unless a document window is open.

- If you are creating a label for a letter in the active document window, the Address may be filled in based on the inside address of the letter. You can "help" Word enter the correct address by selecting the recipient's address *before* opening the Labels dialog.

- In step 2, you can turn on the Use my address check box to enter your address from Word's User preferences into the Address box. (I tell you about User preferences in **Chapter 20**.) This is a handy way to create a sheet of return address labels.

- You can create your own custom label settings. After step 5, click the New Label button to display the New Custom dialog (**Figure 15**). Enter a name and measurements for the label, and click OK. The name of your new labels will appear in the Product number list in the Label Options dialog (**Figure 13**) when Other is selected from the Label products pop-up menu (**Figure 14**).

- If you're not sure which Product number to select in step 7, consult the information on the box of labels.

- After step 7, you can customize the selected label by clicking the Details button. The dialog that appears looks and works very much like the one in **Figure 15**. Make changes as desired and click OK.

To print labels

1. Set up the label as instructed on the previous two pages.

2. Click the Print button in the Labels dialog (**Figure 12**).

3. Word displays the Print dialog (**Figure 16**). Set options in the dialog and click Print to print the labels.

✔ Tips

■ When printing single labels on a laser or inkjet printer, print on the labels at the bottom of the sheet first. This helps prevent printer jamming that could occur when labels at the top of the sheet have been removed.

■ Printing and using the Print dialog are covered in greater detail in **Chapter 6**.

To save the labels as a new document

1. Set up the label as instructed on the previous two pages.

2. In the Labels dialog (**Figure 12**), click OK.

   Word creates a new document containing the labels (**Figure 17**).

✔ Tips

■ Word uses its table feature to create labels. Tables are covered in **Chapter 8**.

■ I use this feature to create return address labels. I create the document and save it. Then, every time I need more labels, I just open the saved document and print off a sheet or two of labels.

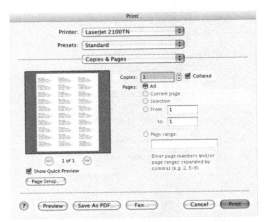

Figure 16 Use the Print dialog to set print options and print the labels.

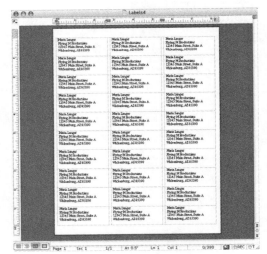

Figure 17 Here's a sheet of return address labels in Page Layout view. You can see the table gridlines (which don't print) separating each label.

Data Merge

Data Merge

Microsoft Word's data merge feature enables you to create mailing labels, form letters, and other documents based on database information. This feature merges fields or categories of information with static text to produce merged documents.

The data merge process uses two special kinds of documents:

◆ A **main document** contains the information that remains the same for each version of the merged document. In a form letter, for example, the main document would consist of the letter text that appears in every letter.

◆ A **data source** contains the information that changes for each version of a merged document. In a form letter, the data source would consist of the names and addresses of the individuals who will receive the letter.

The results of a data merge can be sent directly to the printer or saved as a file.

✔ Tips

■ You can use a single main document with any number of data sources. Similarly, you can use a data source with any number of main documents.

■ You can create a data source with Word as I explain in this chapter or with another application such as Microsoft Excel or FileMaker Pro.

■ Word's data merge feature also includes powerful query and conditional functions. These are advanced features that are beyond the scope of this book.

■ This feature was referred to as Mail Merge in some previous versions of Word and is still referred to as Mail Merge in the Windows version of Word.

The Data Merge Manager

Word's Data Merge Manager (**Figure 1**) is a floating palette that helps you create or identify the main document and data source for a merge and merge the files.

Figure 1
The Data Merge
Manager.

To open the Data Merge Manager

Choose Tools > Data Merge Manager (**Figure 2**).

✔ Tip

- The Data Merge Manager appears automatically when you open a main or data source document.

To use the Data Merge Manager: an overview

1. Open the Data Merge Manager (**Figure 1**).

2. Choose an option from the Create pop-up menu in the Main Document area (**Figure 3**).

3. If desired, edit the main document's static text.

4. Choose an option from the Get Data pop-up menu in the Data Source area (**Figure 4**).

5. If desired, edit the data source's contents.

6. If necessary, edit the main document to include fields from the data source.

7. Click a Merge button to perform the merge.

✔ Tips

- I provide details for all of these steps throughout this chapter.

- To use the Data Merge Manager for an existing main document, open the main document first, then follow these steps.

Figure 2
Choose Data Merge
Manager from the
Tools menu.

Figure 3
The Create
pop-up menu.

Figure 4
The Get Data
pop-up menu.

Figure 5 An example of a main document for a form letter.

Creating a Main Document

A main document (**Figure 5**) has two components:

◆ **Static text** that does not change. In a form letter, for example, static text would be the information that remains the same for each individual who will get the letter.

◆ **Data merge fields** that indicate what data source information should be merged into the document and where it should go. In a form letter, the static text *Dear* might be followed by the field *«First-Name»*. When merged, the contents of the FirstName field are merged into the document after the word *Dear* to result in *Dear Joe*, *Dear Sally*, etc.

Normally, a main document can be created with one or two steps:

◆ Enter the static text first, then insert the fields when the data source is complete. This method is useful when you use an existing document as a main document.

◆ Enter the static text and insert the fields at the same time, when the data source document is complete. This method may save time and prevent confusion when creating a main document from scratch.

✔ Tips

■ You cannot insert fields into a main document until after the data source has been created and associated with the main document.

■ You enter and edit static text in a main document the same way you do in any other Word document.

To create a main document

1. Open a document on which you want to base the main document (**Figure 6**).

   or

   Create a new document.

2. Open the Data Merge Manager (**Figure 1**).

3. Choose an option from the Create pop-up menu (**Figure 3**):

   ▲ **Form Letters** are letters customized for multiple recipients.

   ▲ **Labels** are labels addressed to multiple recipients. If you choose this option, the Label Options dialog appears (**Figure 7**). Use it to specify the type of printer, choose a label product, and select a product number. Then click OK.

   ▲ **Envelopes** are envelopes addressed to multiple recipients. If you choose this option, the Envelope dialog appears (**Figure 8**). Use it to specify return address and printing options for the envelope. Then click OK.

   ▲ **Catalog** is a collection of information about multiple items.

   The name and type of the main document appear in the Data Merge Manager (**Figure 9**).

4. Add or edit static text as desired.

5. Save the document.

✔ Tips

- Do not add any static text at this point for mailing labels or envelopes. These main documents have special formatting needs that must be set up before you can add static text.

- I tell you more about working with envelopes and labels in **Chapter 14**.

Figure 6 A form letter without merge fields.

Figure 7 Use the Label Options dialog to set options for a data merge to mailing labels.

Figure 8 Use the Envelope dialog to set options for a data merge to envelopes.

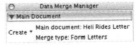

Figure 9 The name and type of the main document appear in the Data Merge Manager.

Figure 10 A data source with three records, created within Microsoft Word.

Figure 11
The data source
in Figure 10
merged into the
main document
in Figure 5.

Creating or Opening a Data Source

A data source (**Figure 10**) has two components:

◆ **Fields** are categories of information. In a form letter, for example, *LastName* and *City* might be two fields. Each field has a unique name which identifies it in both the main document and data source document.

◆ **Records** are collections of information for individual items. In a form letter, the John Smith record would include all fields for John Smith—his name, address, city, state, and postal code.

When you perform a data merge, Word inserts the data from a data source record into a main document, replacing field names with field contents. It repeats the main document for each record in the data source (**Figure 11**).

✔ Tip

■ This chapter explains how to create or open a Word-based data source. You can also use the Office Address Book, a File-Maker Pro database file, or an Excel list as a data source; I tell you more about that in **Chapter 17**.

To create a data source

1. Make sure the main document is the active document window.

2. Choose New Data Source from the Get Data menu on the Data Merge Manager (**Figure 4**) to display the Create Data Source dialog (**Figure 12**). It lists commonly used field names for form letters, mailing labels, and envelopes.

3. Edit the Field names in header row list to include only the field names that you want in your data source document, in the order that you want them to appear:

   ▲ To remove a field name from the list, select it and click the Remove Field Name button.

   ▲ To add a field name, enter it in the Field name text box and click the Add Field Name button.

   ▲ To move a field name up or down in the list, select it and click one of the Move buttons to the right of the list.

4. When you are finished editing the list, click OK.

5. A Save Data Source dialog appears (**Figure 13**). Use it to name and save the data source file.

6. The Data Form dialog appears next (**Figure 14**). Enter information for a specific record into each of the text boxes. You can press Tab to move to the next text box or Shift Tab to move to the previous text box.

7. To add another new record, click the Add New button and repeat step 6.

8. When you are finished adding records, click OK.

   Word displays the name of the data source in the Data Merge Manager (**Figure 15**).

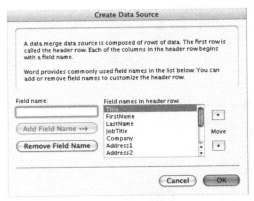

Figure 12 The Create Data Source dialog.

Figure 13 The Save Data Source dialog works just like a standard Save As dialog.

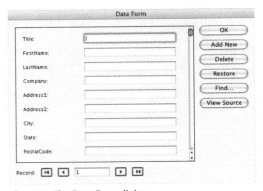

Figure 14 The Data Form dialog.

Figure 15 The name of the data source appears in the Data Merge Manager.

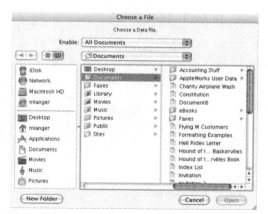

Figure 16 Use the Choose a File dialog to locate and open a data source.

✔ Tips

- Field names cannot include spaces.

- It's a good idea to save the data source in the same folder in which you have saved or will save the main document. This makes it easy to find the data source document when merging.

- You can use other buttons in the Data Form dialog (**Figure 14**) to scroll through, edit, delete, or search for records.

- Clicking the View Source button in the Data Form dialog (**Figure 14**) displays the data source document in a Word document window (**Figure 10**).

- To edit a data source, click the Edit Data Source button in the Data Source area of the Data Merge Manager (**Figure 15**). This displays the Data Form (**Figure 14**), so you can add, modify, or delete records.

To open an existing data source

1. Make sure the main document is the active document window.

2. Choose Open Data Source from the Get Data menu on the Data Merge Manager (**Figure 4**).

3. Use the Choose a File dialog that appears (**Figure 16**) to locate and select the file you want to use as a data source. Click Open.

   Word displays the name of the data source in the Data Merge Manager (**Figure 15**).

✔ Tips

- Use this technique to associate an existing data source with a main document.

- You can also use this technique to change the data source associated with a main document.

Completing a Main Document

Before you can perform a data merge, you must complete the main document by inserting merge fields. How you do this depends on the type of main document you have created.

To complete a form letter or catalog

1. If necessary, open the main document and display the Data Merge Manager (**Figure 17**).

2. Drag a field name from the Merge Field area of the Data Merge Manager into the document window. When the insertion point appears where you want the field (**Figure 18**), release the mouse button. The field appears at the insertion point. As shown in **Figure 19**, it consists of the name of the field surrounded by paired angle brackets («»).

3. Repeat step 2 for each merge field that you want to insert.

   Figure 5 shows an example of a main document with merge fields.

✔ Tips

- Be sure to include proper spacing and punctuation as necessary between merge fields. To do this, position the insertion point where you want the space or punctuation to appear and press the appropriate keyboard key to insert it.

- If you drag a field to the wrong place, simply select it and drag it to the correct position within the document window.

- To remove a field, select it and press Delete .

Figure 17 Display the main document and the Data Merge Manager.

November 4, 2005

Dear,

Flying M Air has been
pilot, I have logged ove

Figure 18 When you drag a field into the document window, a tiny box with the name of the field appears beside the mouse pointer.

November 4, 2005

«Title»

Dear,

Flying M Air has been
pilot, I have logged ove

Figure 19 The field appears at the insertion point.

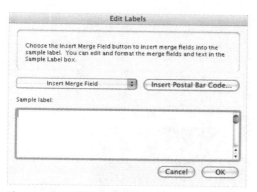

Figure 20 The Edit Labels dialog.

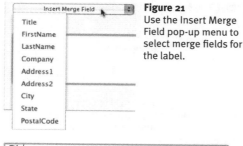

Figure 21
Use the Insert Merge Field pop-up menu to select merge fields for the label.

Figure 22 The field you selected is entered.

Figure 23 Merge fields for a name and address.

Word field

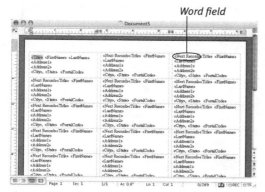

Figure 24 A mailing labels main document.

To complete mailing labels

1. Create or open a data source for a mailing labels main document as instructed earlier in this chapter. The Edit Labels dialog (**Figure 20**) will appear as part of this process.

2. Choose a merge field from the Insert Merge Field menu (**Figure 21**). The field is inserted in the Sample label box (**Figure 22**).

3. Repeat step 2 for each merge field that you want to include on the label. When you're finished, it might look something like **Figure 23**.

4. Click OK to save your settings. The merge fields appear in the main document window (**Figure 24**).

✔ Tips

- If the Edit Labels dialog does not appear, click the Edit Labels for Data Merge button in the Data Source area of the Data Merge Manager.

- Be sure to include proper spacing and punctuation as necessary between merge fields. To do this, position the insertion point in the Sample label box where you want the space or punctuation to appear and press the appropriate keyboard key to insert it.

- Do not change the Word fields included in the mailing labels main document (**Figure 24**). Altering or removing a field can prevent the mailing labels from merging or printing properly.

COMPLETING A MAILING LABELS DOCUMENT

To complete envelopes

1. If necessary, open the main document and display the Data Merge Manager (**Figure 25**).

2. Drag a field name from the Merge Field area of the Data Merge Manager into the address box in the document window. When the insertion point appears where you want the field (**Figure 26**), release the mouse button. The field appears at the insertion point (**Figure 27**).

3. Repeat step 2 for each merge field that you want to insert.

   Figure 28 shows an example of a main document for envelopes with merge fields.

✔ Tip

■ Be sure to include proper spacing and punctuation as necessary between merge fields. To do this, position the insertion point in the document window where you want the space or punctuation to appear and press the appropriate keyboard key to insert it.

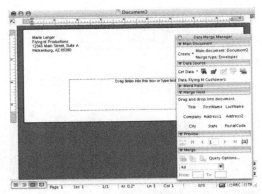

Figure 25 Display the main document and the Data Merge Manager.

Figure 26 When you drag a field into the document window, a tiny box with the name of the field in it appears beside the mouse pointer.

Figure 27 The field appears at the insertion point.

Figure 28 An envelopes main document.

Figure 29
The Data Merge Manager offers several options for merging data.

Merging Documents

The last step in performing a data merge is to merge the main document and data source.

The Data Merge Manager offers several buttons you can use to merge data (**Figure 29**):

◆ **View Merged Data** displays the merged documents onscreen, enabling you to spot potential problems before actually performing the merge.

◆ **Merge to Printer** merges the documents directly to paper, labels, or envelopes to create final output.

◆ **Merge to New Document** creates a file with all of the merged data. The resulting file can be saved, modified, or printed another time.

To view merged data onscreen

1. Display the main document and the Data Merge Manager.

2. Click the View Merged Data button in the Preview area of the Data Merge Manager.

   The merge field names in the main document are replaced with the contents of the first record in the data source (**Figures 11, 30**, and **31**).

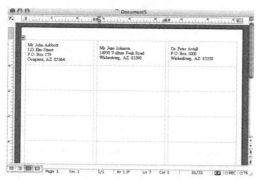

Figure 30 Viewing merged data for a mailing labels main document.

✔ Tip

■ You can scroll through the records in the data source while viewing merged records by clicking the First Record, Previous Record, Next Record, and Last Record buttons in the Preview area of the Data Merge Manager.

Figure 31 Viewing merged data for an envelopes main document.

MERGING DOCUMENTS

To merge to a printer or to a new document

1. Display the main document and the Data Merge Manager.

2. If necessary, choose an option from the pop-up menu in the Merge area of the Data Merge Manager (**Figure 32**):

   ▲ **All** merges all of the records.

   ▲ **Current Record** merges just the record number indicated in the text box in the Preview area of the Data Merge Manager (**Figure 29**).

   ▲ **Custom** enables you to set the starting and ending record number. If you choose this option, enter values in the text boxes beneath the pop-up menu.

3. To merge directly to a printer, click the Merge to Printer button in the Merge area.

   or

   To merge to a new document, click the Merge to New Document button in the Merge area.

4. If you are merging to a printer, Word displays the Print dialog (**Figure 33**). Set print options as desired and click the Print button.

   or

   If you are merging to a new document, Word creates the new document (**Figure 34**) and displays it as the active window. You can edit, save, or print the document.

✔ Tip

■ I tell you more about printing in **Chapter 6**.

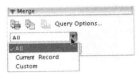

Figure 32
To merge less than all of the records, choose an option from this pop-up menu.

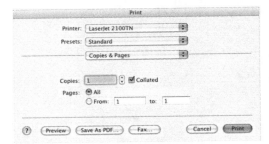

Figure 33 The Print dialog.

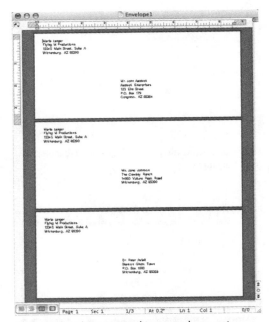

Figure 34 Envelopes merged to a new document.

Working with Others

Collaboration Features

In office environments, a document is often the product of multiple people. In the old days, a draft document would be printed and circulated among reviewers. Along the way, it would be marked up with colored ink and covered with sticky notes full of comments. Some poor soul would have to make sense of all the markups and notes to create a clean document. The process was time consuming and was sometimes repeated through several drafts to fine-tune the document for publication.

Microsoft Word, which is widely used in office environments, includes features that make the collaboration process quicker and easier and help protect documents from unauthorized access and changes:

- ◆ **Properties** stores information about the document's creator and contents.

- ◆ **Comments** enables reviewers to enter notes about the document.

- ◆ **Versions** enables reviewers to save multiple versions of the same document. At any time, you can revert to a previous version.

- ◆ **Change Tracking** enables reviewers to edit the document while keeping the original document intact. Changes can be accepted or rejected to finalize the document.

- ◆ **Document Protection** limits how a document can be changed.

Document Properties

The Properties dialog enables you to view and store information about a document. This information can be viewed by anyone who opens the document.

The Properties dialog has five tabs of information; click a tab to view its contents:

◆ **General** (**Figure 2**) provides general information about a document.

◆ **Summary** (**Figure 3**) enables you to enter additional information about a document.

◆ **Statistics** (**Figure 5**) provides creation and editing information about the document, as well as statistics about its length.

◆ **Contents** (**Figure 6**) displays the document's title or the first line of the document.

◆ **Custom** (**Figure 7**) enables you to specify additional information about the document using a variety of predefined fields.

To open the Properties dialog

1. Open the document for which you want to view or edit properties.

2. Choose File > Properties (**Figure 1**).

Figure 1
Word's File menu.

Figure 2 The General pane of the Properties dialog.

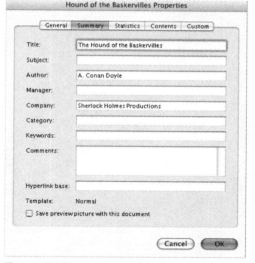

Figure 3 The Summary pane of the Properties dialog.

To view general document information

1. Open the Properties dialog.

2. If necessary, click the General button to display the file's icon, name, and other information (**Figure 2**):
   - ▲ **Type** is the type of document.
   - ▲ **Location** is the complete path to the document.
   - ▲ **Size** is the size, in kilobytes and bytes, of the document.
   - ▲ **Created** is the creation date of the document.
   - ▲ **Modified** is the most recent modification or save date of the document.
   - ▲ **Attributes** are Mac OS file attributes for the file.

3. When you are finished viewing statistics, click OK to dismiss the dialog.

✔ Tip

- ■ Information in the General pane of the Properties dialog (**Figure 2**) cannot be changed.

To enter summary information

1. Open the Properties dialog.

2. If necessary, click the Summary button to display its settings (**Figure 3**).

3. Enter or edit information in each field as desired:
   - ▲ **Title** is the title of the document. This does not have to be the same as the file name. This field may already be filled in based on the first line of the document.
   - ▲ **Subject** is the subject of the document.

Continued on next page...

VIEWING GENERAL & SUMMARY INFORMATION

Continued from previous page.

▲ **Author** is the person who created the document. This field may already be filled in based on information stored in the User Information pane of the Preferences dialog.

▲ **Manager** is the person responsible for the document content.

▲ **Company** is the organization for which the author or manager works.

▲ **Category** is a category name assigned to the document. It can be anything you like.

▲ **Keywords** are important words related to the document.

▲ **Comments** are notes about the document.

▲ **Hyperlink base** is an Internet address or path to a folder on a hard disk or network volume. This option works in conjunction with hyperlinks inserted in the document.

▲ **Template** is the template attached to the document. This information cannot be changed.

4. To create a document preview image that will appear in the preview area of the Open dialog when you select the document (**Figure 4**), turn on the Save preview picture with this document check box.

5. Click OK to save your entries.

✔ Tips

■ It is not necessary to enter information in any of the Summary pane boxes (**Figure 3**).

■ Preview images are automatically created for all new documents you create with Word 2004.

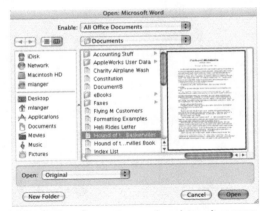

Figure 4 When you create a preview picture, it appears in the Open dialog.

■ I tell you more about the User Information pane of the Preferences dialog in **Chapter 20** and about document templates in **Chapter 2**.

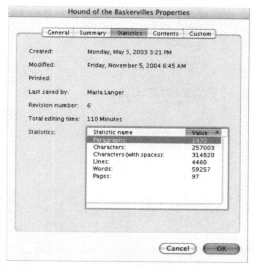

Figure 5 The Statistics pane of the Properties dialog.

To view document statistics

1. Open the Properties dialog.

2. If necessary, click the Statistics button to display its information (**Figure 5**):

   ▲ **Created** is the creation date of the document.

   ▲ **Modified** is the most recent modification or save date of the document.

   ▲ **Printed** is the most recent print date for the document. This field will be blank if the document has never been printed.

   ▲ **Last saved by** is the name of the last person who saved the document. Word gets this name from the User Information pane of the Preferences dialog.

   ▲ **Revision number** is the number of times the document has been revised and saved.

   ▲ **Total editing time** is the total amount of time the document has been worked on.

   ▲ **Statistics** is the number of pages, paragraphs, lines, words, characters excluding spaces, and characters including spaces.

3. When you are finished viewing statistics, click OK to dismiss the dialog.

✔ Tips

■ Information in the Statistics pane (**Figure 5**) cannot be changed.

■ I tell you more about the User Information pane of the Preferences dialog in **Chapter 20**.

VIEWING DOCUMENT STATISTICS

To view document contents

1. Open the Properties dialog.

2. If necessary, click the Contents button to display its information (**Figure 6**). In most cases, this will be the document title or first line of the document and a few paragraphs formatted as headings.

3. When you are finished viewing contents, click OK to dismiss the dialog.

To enter custom information

1. Open the Properties dialog.

2. If necessary, click the Custom button to display its options (**Figure 7**).

3. Select one of the field names in the Name scrolling list.

4. Choose one of the data types from the Type pop-up menu (**Figure 8**).

5. Enter the value you want to record for that field in the Value box.

6. Click Add. The information you entered is added to the Properties list in the bottom of the dialog (**Figure 9**).

7. Repeat steps 3 through 6 for each piece of information you want to add.

8. When you are finished entering information, click OK to dismiss the dialog.

✔ Tip

■ To delete a custom property's information, select its name in the Properties list at the bottom of the Custom pane (**Figure 9**) and click Delete.

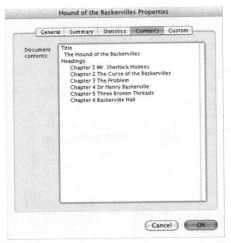

Figure 6 The Contents pane of the Properties dialog.

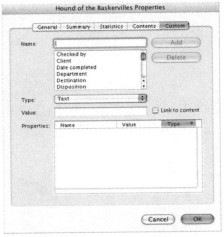

Figure 7 The Custom pane of the Properties dialog.

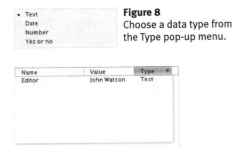

Figure 8
Choose a data type from the Type pop-up menu.

Figure 9 Data you enter appears in the bottom of the Custom pane of the Properties dialog.

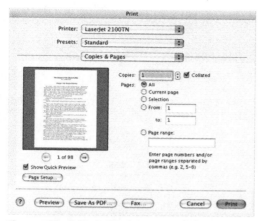

Figure 10 The Print dialog.

To print document properties

1. Choose File > Print (**Figure 1**) or press
   ⌘ ⌘ P to display the Print dialog
   (**Figure 10**).

2. Choose Microsoft Word from the third
   pop-up menu (**Figure 11**) to display
   Microsoft Word Print options (**Figure 12**).

3. Choose Document Properties from the
   Print What pop-up menu (**Figure 13**).

4. Set other options as desired in the Print
   dialog.

5. Click Print.

   Word creates a document containing
   document properties and sends it to your
   printer.

✔ Tip

- Printing and the Print dialog are covered
  in detail in **Chapter 6**.

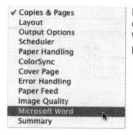

Figure 11
Choose Microsoft
Word from the third
pop-up menu.

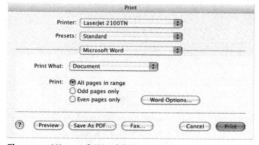

Figure 12 Microsoft Word Print options.

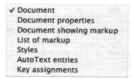

Figure 13
Use the Print What
pop-up menu to
specify what part of
the document you
want to print.

PRINTING DOCUMENT PROPERTIES

Comments

Comments are annotations that you and other document reviewers can add to a document. These notes can be viewed onscreen but don't print unless you want them to.

To insert a comment

1. Select the text for which you want to insert a comment (**Figure 14**).

2. Choose Insert > Comment (**Figure 15**).

   A few things happen: A comment marker (colored parentheses) appears around the selected text, the Reviewing toolbar appears, the window splits, and the insertion point moves to the Reviewing pane at the bottom of the window under a color-coded heading with your name (**Figure 16**).

3. Type in your comment. It can be as long or as short as you like (**Figure 17**).

✔ Tips

- Word gets your name and initials from the User Information pane of the Preferences dialog. I tell you more about that in **Chapter 20**.

- The colored parentheses that appear in the document window (**Figure 16**) do not print.

To close the Reviewing pane

Click the Reviewing Pane button on the Reviewing toolbar.

✔ Tip

- If the Reviewing toolbar is not displayed, choose View > Toolbars > Reviewing to display it.

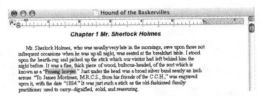

Figure 14 Start by selecting the text you want to enter a comment about.

Figure 15 Choose Comment from the Insert menu.

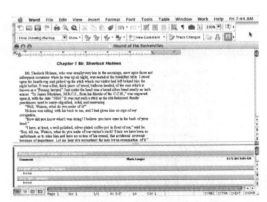

Figure 16 Word prepares to accept your comment.

Figure 17 Enter your comment in the Reviewing pane at the bottom of the window.

Figure 18 In Normal view, a comment appears in a box when you point to marked text.

Figure 19 In Page Layout view, comments appear in "balloons" that point to commented text.

Figure 20 When the Reviewing pane is displayed, it shows all comments entered in a document.

Figure 21 Use the Show pop-up menu to make sure the markup you want to see is displayed.

To view comments

In Normal view, position the mouse pointer over text enclosed in colored parentheses. A box appears. It contains the name of the person who wrote the comment, the date and time the comment was written, and the comment text (**Figure 18**).

Or

In Page Layout view, comments should appear automatically in a "balloon" that points to commented text (**Figure 19**).

Or

Click the Reviewing Pane button on the Reviewing toolbar to display the Reviewing pane and the comments it contains (**Figure 20**).

✔ Tips

- If comments or comment markers do not appear in the document window, choose Comments from the Show pop-up menu on the Reviewing toolbar (**Figure 21**).

- If the Reviewing toolbar is not displayed, choose View > Toolbars > Reviewing to display it.

- You can change the size of the Reviewing pane by dragging the border between it and the main document window.

To delete a comment

1. If necessary, choose View > Toolbars > Reviewing to display the Reviewing toolbar.

2. In the document window, position the insertion point anywhere within the parentheses surrounding commented text.

3. Click the Reject Change/Delete Comment button on the Reviewing toolbar. All traces of the comment disappear.

To print comments

1. Choose File > Print (**Figure 1**) or press ⌃⌘P to display the Print dialog (**Figure 10**).

2. Choose Microsoft Word from the third pop-up menu (**Figure 11**) to display Microsoft Word Print options (**Figure 12**).

3. Choose one of the markup options from the Print What pop-up menu (**Figure 13**):

   ▲ **Document showing markup** prints each page of the document, slightly reduced, with comments in the right margin. **Figure 22** shows what this looks like in Print Preview.

   ▲ **List of markup** prints the contents of the Reviewing pane.

4. Set other options as desired in the Print dialog.

5. Click Print to print the chosen markup option.

✔ Tip

■ Printing and the Print dialog are covered in detail in **Chapter 6**.

Figure 22 Here's the first page of a document printed with markup.

Figure 23 The Versions dialog before any versions have been saved.

Figure 24 Use this dialog to enter comments about the version you are saving.

Versions

Word's Versions feature enables you to save multiple versions of a document. You can then revert to any version to undo editing changes made over time.

To save a version

1. Choose File > Versions (**Figure 1**).

2. In the Versions dialog that appears (**Figure 23**), click Save Now.

3. The Save Version dialog appears (**Figure 24**). If desired, enter comments about the version, then click OK.

   The current state of the document is saved as a version within the document file.

To automatically save a version of the file when you close it

1. Choose File > Versions (**Figure 1**).

2. In the Versions dialog that appears (**Figure 23**), turn on the Automatically save a version on close check box.

3. Click Close.

   From that point forward, every time you close the document, it will be saved as a version.

To open a version

1. With a document that includes multiple versions open and active, choose File > Versions (**Figure 1**).

2. In the Versions dialog that appears (**Figure 25**), select the version you want to open.

3. Click Open.

   The version of the document that you selected opens. Word arranges both document windows—the one that was open in step 1 and the one that you opened in step 3—so you can see them at the same time (**Figure 26**).

✔ Tips

- You can click the View Comments button in the Versions dialog (**Figure 25**) to see the entire text of a comment. It appears in a dialog like the one in **Figure 24**.

- If you save an opened version of a document, it is saved as a separate document.

To delete a version

1. Choose File > Versions (**Figure 1**).

2. In the Versions dialog that appears (**Figure 25**), select the version you want to delete.

3. Click Delete.

4. A confirmation dialog like the one in **Figure 27** appears. Click Yes.

   The version you deleted is removed from the list in the Versions dialog.

✔ Tip

- Each time you save a file version, you increase the size of the file. If your file becomes too large, you can delete early versions to reduce its size.

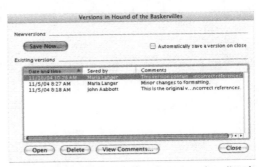

Figure 25 The versions that have been saved are listed in reverse chronological order.

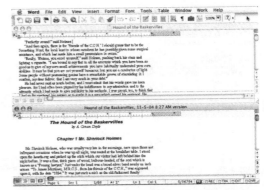

Figure 26 When you open another version of a document, it appears in its own window. Word automatically arranges the windows so you can see them both.

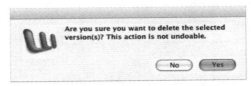

Figure 27 A dialog like this one appears when you delete a version.

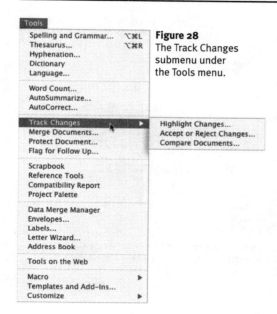

Figure 28
The Track Changes submenu under the Tools menu.

Figure 29 Enable change tracking in the Highlight Changes dialog.

Figure 30 The Reviewing toolbar with change tracking enabled.

Change Tracking

Word's Change Tracking feature makes it possible for multiple reviewers to edit a document without actually changing the document. Instead, each reviewer's markups are displayed in color in the document window.

At the conclusion of the reviewing process, someone with final say over document contents reviews all of the edits and either accepts or rejects each of them. The end result is a final document that incorporates only the accepted changes.

To turn change tracking on or off

1. Choose Tools > Track Changes > Highlight Changes (**Figure 28**).

2. In the Highlight Changes dialog that appears (**Figure 29**), toggle check boxes to set change tracking options:

   ▲ **Track changes while editing** enables the change tracking feature. You must turn this check box on to begin tracking changes.

   ▲ **Highlight changes on screen** displays changes onscreen using revision marks. With this check box turned off, you won't see revision marks when you make changes.

   ▲ **Highlight changes in printed document** prints revision marks.

3. Click OK.

✔ Tip

■ You can tell whether change tracking is enabled by looking at the Track Changes button on the Reviewing toolbar (**Figure 30**). If the button is selected, change tracking is enabled.

To track changes

1. Turn on change tracking as instructed on the previous page.

2. Make changes to the document.

   Your changes appear as colored markups and a vertical line appears in the left margin beside each edit (**Figure 31**).

✔ Tip

■ If the document is edited by more than one person, each person's revision marks appear in a different color. This makes it easy to distinguish one editor's changes from another's.

To view revision information

Point to a revision mark. A colored box with information about the change appears (**Figure 32**).

✔ Tip

■ This is a handy way to see who made a change and when it was made.

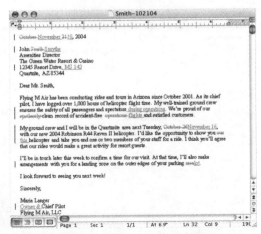

Figure 31 When you edit a document with change tracking enabled, your changes appear as revision marks.

Figure 32 When you point to a revision mark, a box appears with information about the change.

Figure 33 Word selects the change.

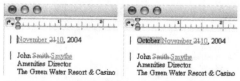

Figures 34a & 34b The change selected in Figure 33 after it has been accepted (left) or rejected (right). As shown here, accepting the change (the deletion of the word *October*) removes the selected text from the document and rejecting the change retains the selected text and removes revision marks from it.

Figure 35 Use this menu to accept all changes in a document.

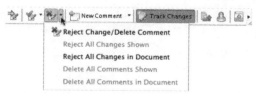

Figure 36 Use this menu to reject all changes in a document.

To accept or reject changes

1. If necessary, choose View > Toolbars > Reviewing to display the Reviewing toolbar (**Figure 30**).

Then:

2. Click the Next or Previous button on the Reviewing toolbar to select the next or previous change (**Figure 33**).

3. Accept or reject the selected change:

   ▲ To accept the change, click the Accept Change button on the Reviewing toolbar. The change is incorporated into the document and its revision mark disappears (**Figure 34a**).

   ▲ To reject the change, click the Reject Change/Delete Comment button on the Reviewing toolbar. The revision mark disappears (**Figure 34b**).

4. Repeat steps 2 and 3 until all changes have been reviewed and either accepted or rejected.

Or then:

2. Accept or reject all changes:

   ▲ To accept all changes, choose Accept All Changes in Document from the Accept Change button's menu on the Reviewing toolbar (**Figure 35**). All revisions are incorporated into the document and the revision marks disappear.

   ▲ To reject all changes, choose Reject All Changes in Document from the Reject Change/Delete Comment button's menu on the Reviewing toolbar (**Figure 36**). The revision marks disappear and the document is returned to the way it was before change tracking was enabled.

ACCEPTING & REJECTING CHANGES

Document Protection

Word's Document Protection feature enables you to limit the types of changes others can make to a document. Specifically, you can limit changes to:

◆ **Tracked changes** enables users to change the document only with the change tracking feature turned on.

◆ **Comments** enables users to add only comments to the document.

◆ **Forms** enables users to enter information only into form fields. (This is an advanced feature of Word that is far beyond the scope of this book.)

To protect a document

1. Choose Tools > Protect Document (**Figure 37**).

2. In the Protect Document dialog that appears (**Figure 38**), select the type of protection you want.

3. If desired, enter a password in the Password text box.

4. Click OK.

5. If you entered a password, the Confirm Password dialog appears (**Figure 39**). Enter the password again and click OK.

✔ Tips

■ Entering a password in the Protect Document dialog (**Figure 38**) is optional. However, if you do not use a password with this feature, the document can be unprotected by anyone.

■ If you enter a password in the Protect Document dialog (**Figure 38**), don't forget it! If you can't remember the password, you can't unprotect the document!

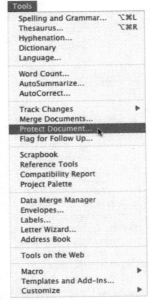

Figure 37
Choose Protect Document from the Tools menu.

Figure 38 The Protect Document dialog.

Figure 39 Confirm that you know the password by typing it in this dialog's box.

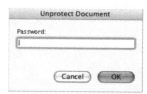

Figure 41 Enter a document's password in this dialog to unprotect it.

To work with a protected document

What you can do with a protected document depends on how you protected it:

◆ If you protected the document for change tracking, the change tracking feature is enabled. Any change you make to the document appears with revision marks.

◆ If you protected the document for comments, you can only insert comments in the document. If you attempt to edit text, an alert sounds.

To unprotect a document

1. Choose Tools > Unprotect Document (**Figure 40**).

2. If protection is enforced with a password, a dialog like the one in **Figure 41** appears. Enter the password and click OK.

WORKING WITH PROTECTED DOCUMENTS

Using Other Applications

Using Word with Other Applications

Word works well with a number of other applications. These programs can expand Word's capabilities:

- ◆ OLE objects created with other Microsoft Office applications can be inserted into Word documents.

- ◆ Word documents can be inserted into documents created with other Microsoft Office applications.

- ◆ Word documents can be e-mailed to others using Entourage.

- ◆ Excel lists and Entourage address book information can be used as data sources for a Word data merge.

- ◆ Word documents can be included as files in Entourage projects.

This chapter explains how you can use Word with some of these other applications.

✔ Tip

- ■ This chapter provides information about applications other than Microsoft Word. To follow instructions for a specific program, that program must be installed on your computer.

OLE Objects

An *object* is all or part of a file created with an OLE-aware application. *OLE*, or *Object Linking and Embedding*, is a Microsoft technology that enables you to insert a file as an object within a document (**Figure 1**)— even if the file was created with a different application. Double-clicking the inserted object launches the application that created it so you can modify its contents.

Word's Object command enables you to insert OLE objects in two different ways:

◆ **Create and insert a new OLE object.** This method launches a specific OLE-aware application so you can create an object. When you are finished, you quit the application to insert the new object in your document.

◆ **Insert an existing OLE object.** This method displays the Insert as Object dialog (**Figure 6**) which you can use to locate, select, and insert an existing file as an object.

✔ Tips

■ All Microsoft applications are OLE-aware. Many software applications created by other developers are also OLE-aware; check the documentation that came with a specific software package for details.

■ Microsoft Word comes with a number of OLE-aware applications that can be used to insert objects. The full Microsoft Office package includes even more of these applications.

■ **Chapter 10** offered a glimpse of OLE objects in its discussion of Microsoft Graph, one of the OLE-aware applications that comes with Word.

■ Double-clicking an inserted object opens the application with which the object was created so you can modify it.

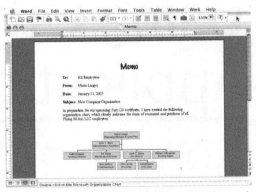

Figure 1 A Microsoft Organization Chart object inserted in a Microsoft Word document.

Figure 2 Choose Object from the Insert menu.

OLE OBJECTS

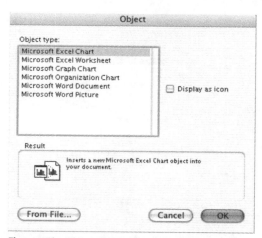

Figure 3 The Object dialog. The options shown here are those that are part of a Microsoft Office X installation.

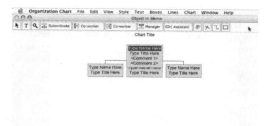

Figure 4 The default Microsoft Organization Chart window.

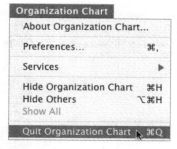

Figure 5
The Quit command on the Organization Chart menu.

To insert a new object

1. Position the insertion point where you want the object to appear.

2. Choose Insert > Object (**Figure** 2) to display the Object dialog (**Figure 3**).

3. Click to select the type of object that you want to insert.

4. Click OK.

   Word launches the application that you selected. It may take a moment for it to appear. **Figure 4** shows the default Microsoft Organization Chart window and toolbar.

5. Use the application to create the object that you want.

6. When you are finished creating the object, choose the Quit command from the *Application Name* menu (**Figure 5**).

7. If a dialog appears, asking whether you want to update the object in the document, click Update.

   The application closes and the object is inserted in the document (**Figure 1**).

✔ Tips

- The exact wording of the Quit command in step 6 varies depending on the application and the name of the document with which you are working.

- For more information about using one of the OLE-aware applications that comes with Word or Office, use the application's Help menu or Office Assistant.

INSERTING OBJECTS

To insert an existing object

1. Position the insertion point where you want the object to appear.

2. Choose Insert > Object (**Figure 2**) to display the Object dialog (**Figure 3**).

3. Click the From File button to display the Insert as Object dialog (**Figure 6**).

4. Locate and select the file that you want to insert.

5. Click Insert. The file is inserted as an object in the document (**Figure 7**).

✔ Tip

■ To insert a file as an object, the application that created the file must be properly installed on your computer or accessible through a network connection. Word displays a dialog if the application is missing.

To customize an inserted object

Follow the instructions in the previous two sections to create and insert a new object or insert an existing object. In the Object (**Figure 3**) or Insert as Object (**Figure 6**) dialog, turn on check boxes as desired:

◆ **Link to File** creates a link to the object's file so that when it changes, the object inserted within the Word document can change. This is similar to inserting a link, which I tell you about in **Chapter 10**. This option is only available when inserting an existing file as an object.

◆ **Display as icon** (**Figure 8**) displays an icon that represents the object rather than the object itself.

Figure 6 Use this dialog to insert an existing file as an object.

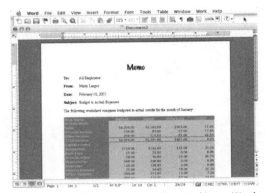

Figure 7 An Excel 2004 worksheet inserted into a Word document.

Figure 8 An Excel 2004 worksheet displayed as an icon.

Figure 9 Spreadsheet software like Excel is most often used to create worksheets full of financial information.

Figure 10 Excel has built-in features for managing lists of information.

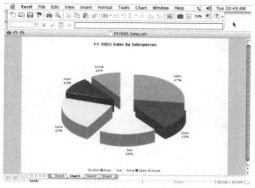

Figure 11 Excel also includes powerful charting capabilities.

Using Excel with Word

Excel is the spreadsheet component of Microsoft Office. A *spreadsheet* (or *worksheet*, in Excel terminology) is like a computerized accountant's worksheet—you enter information and formulas and the software automatically calculates results (**Figure 9**). Best of all, if you change one of the numbers in the worksheet, the results of calculations automatically change as necessary.

You can use Excel with Word to:

◆ Include information from an Excel document in a Word document (**Figure 7**).

◆ Perform a Word data merge with an Excel list as a data source.

✔ Tips

■ Spreadsheet software is especially handy for financial calculations, but it is also often used to maintain lists of data (**Figure 10**).

■ Excel also includes powerful charting capabilities so you can create charts based on spreadsheet information (**Figure 11**).

■ To learn more about using Excel for Mac OS X, pick up a copy of *Excel X for Mac OS X: Visual QuickStart Guide*, a Peachpit Press book by Maria Langer.

To include Excel document content in a Word document

To insert an Excel document as an object in a Word document, consult the section about OLE objects earlier in this chapter.

Or

1. In the Excel document, select the cells (**Figure 12**) or chart (**Figure 13**) that you want to include in the Word document.

2. Choose Edit > Copy (**Figure 14**) or press ⌃ ⌘ C.

3. Switch to Word and position the insertion point in the Word document where you want the Excel content to appear.

4. Choose Edit > Paste (**Figure 15**) or press ⌃ ⌘ V. The selection appears in the Word document (**Figures 16** and **17**).

✔ Tips

- You can also drag-and-drop Excel content into a Word document. I tell you about drag-and-drop in **Chapter 2**.

- Worksheet cells are pasted into Word as a Word table (**Figure 16**). An Excel chart is pasted into Word as a picture (**Figure 17**). I tell you more about tables in **Chapter 8** and working with pictures in **Chapter 10**.

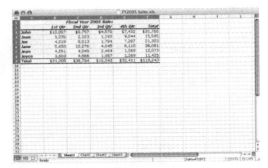

Figure 12 Select the cells...

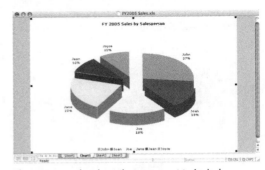

Figure 13 ...or the chart that you want to include.

Figure 14 Choosing Copy from Excel's Edit menu.

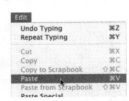

Figure 15 Choosing Paste from Word's Edit menu.

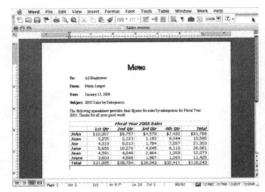

Figure 16 Worksheet cells are pasted into a Word document as a Word table.

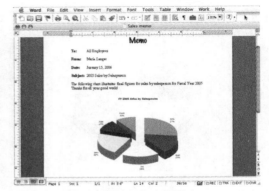

Figure 17 A chart is pasted into a Word document as a picture.

Figure 18
Choose Open Data Source from the Get Data pop-up menu.

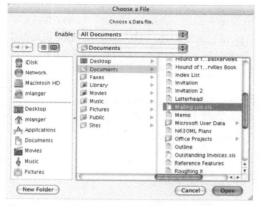

Figure 19 Use the Choose a File dialog to open the file you want to use as the data source.

Figure 20
Set options in the Open Workbook dialog to indicate the worksheet and cells where the data resides.

Figure 21
Field names from the Excel list appear in the Merge Field area of the Data Merge Manager.

To use an Excel list as a data source for a data merge

1. Follow the instructions in **Chapter 15** to display the Data Merge Manager and create a main document.

2. Choose Open Data Source from the Get Data pop-up menu in the Data Source area of the Data Merge Manager (**Figure 18**).

3. Use the Choose a File dialog that appears (**Figure 19**) to locate, select, and open the Excel file you want to use for the data merge.

4. Set options in the Open Workbook dialog (**Figure 20**) to specify which worksheet and cells contain the list you want to use for the merge. Then click OK.

5. Follow the steps in **Chapter 15** to complete the main document with field names that appear in the Merge Field area of the Data Merge Manager (**Figure 21**) and perform the merge.

✔ Tip

■ I explain how to use Word's data merge feature in **Chapter 15**.

Using PowerPoint with Word

PowerPoint is the presentation software component of Microsoft Office. *Presentation software* enables you to create slides for use at meetings and seminars (**Figure 22**). The slides can be printed on paper, output as 35mm slides, saved as a QuickTime movie, or shown directly from the computer.

You can use PowerPoint with Word to:

◆ Create a PowerPoint presentation from a Word outline.

◆ Include a QuickTime movie created with PowerPoint in a Word document.

✔ Tip

■ To learn more about using PowerPoint, consult the documentation that came with the program or its onscreen help feature.

To use a Word outline in a PowerPoint presentation

1. Display the Word outline document you want to use in PowerPoint (**Figure 23**).

2. Choose File > Send To > Microsoft PowerPoint (**Figure 24**).

   The outline is imported into PowerPoint. A new slide is created for each top-level heading (**Figure 22**).

✔ Tip

■ I explain how to use Word's Outline feature in **Chapter 12**.

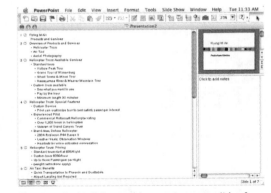

Figure 22 PowerPoint enables you to create slides for presenting information. This is the outline from **Figure 23**, with some formatting applied.

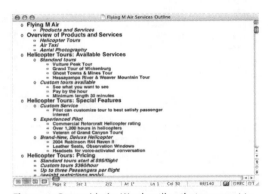

Figure 23 Start with the Word outline that you want to use in PowerPoint.

Figure 24 The Send To submenu offers options for using the active Word document with other Microsoft Office applications.

Figure 25
Choose Make Movie from PowerPoint's File menu.

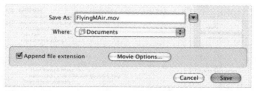

Figure 26 Use this dialog to save the presentation as a movie.

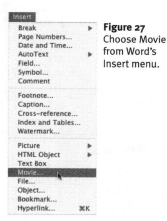

Figure 27
Choose Movie from Word's Insert menu.

To insert a PowerPoint QuickTime movie into a Word document

1. Display the PowerPoint presentation that you want to save as a QuickTime movie (**Figure 22**).

2. Choose File > Make Movie (**Figure 25**).

3. Use the dialog that appears (**Figure 26**) to name and save the current presentation as a movie.

4. Switch to Word and display the document in which you want to insert the movie.

5. Choose Insert > Movie (**Figure 27**).

6. The Insert Movie dialog appears (**Figure 28**). Use it to locate and select the movie you created and then click Choose.

   The movie is inserted into the Word document (**Figure 29**).

✔ Tip

■ I tell you more about inserting movies into Word documents in **Chapter 10**.

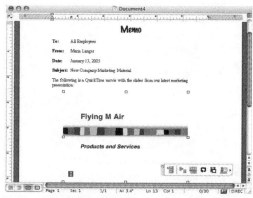

Figure 29 The movie is inserted in the document's drawing layer.

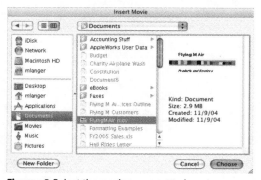

Figure 28 Select the movie you want to insert.

Using Entourage with Word

Entourage is the e-mail, personal information management, and project management software component of Microsoft Office. *E-mail software* enables you to send and receive electronic mail messages (**Figure 30**). *Personal information management software* enables you to store and organize address book (**Figure 31**) and calendar (**Figure 32**) data. *Project management software* enables you to organize files, tasks, and communications for individual projects (**Figure 33**).

You can use Entourage with Word to:

◆ E-mail a Word document to a friend, family member, or co-worker.

◆ Perform a Word data merge with an Entourage address book as the data source.

◆ Flag a document for follow up so Entourage reminds you about it.

◆ Create an Entourage project that includes Word files.

✔ Tip

■ To learn more about using Entourage, consult the documentation that came with the program or its onscreen help feature.

Figure 30 Entourage can handle e-mail...

Figure 31 ...address book information...

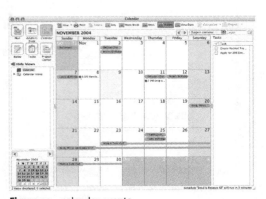

Figure 32 ...calendar events...

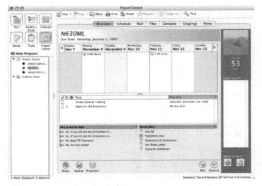

Figure 33 ...and project data.

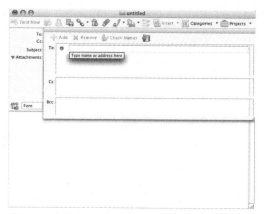

Figure 34 Entourage displays an untitled e-mail form.

Figure 35 Here's what a finished message might look like. Note that the name of the Word document being sent appears in the Attachments area.

To send a Word document as an e-mail attachment

1. Display the Word document you want to send via e-mail.

2. Choose File > Send To > Mail Recipient (as Attachment) (**Figure 24**).

3. Word launches Entourage and displays an empty e-mail window with the To field selected (**Figure 34**). Enter the e-mail address for the person you want to send the document to and press Return.

4. In the Subject field, enter a subject for the message and press Tab.

5. In the message body, enter a message to accompany the file (**Figure 35**).

6. To send the message immediately, click the Send Now button. Entourage connects to the Internet and sends the message.

   or

   To save the message in your outbox so it is sent the next time you send and receive messages, click Send Later.

7. Switch back to Word to continue working with the document or Word.

✔ Tips

■ These instructions assume that Entourage is the default e-mail program as set in the Internet preferences pane. If a different program has been set as the default e-mail program, ignore steps 3 through 6 and send the message as you normally would with your e-mail program.

■ Entourage (or your default e-mail program) must be properly configured to send and receive e-mail messages. Check the program's documentation or onscreen help if you need assistance with setup.

USING ENTOURAGE WITH WORD

To send a Word document as an HTML-formatted e-mail message

1. Display the Word document you want to send via e-mail.

2. Choose File > Send To > Mail Recipient (as HTML) (**Figure 24**).

3. Word launches Entourage and displays an e-mail window containing the document with the To field selected (**Figure 36**). Enter the e-mail address for the person you want to send the document to and press Return.

4. In the Subject field, enter a subject for the message and press Tab.

5. The body of the message should already include your document (**Figure 37**). You can make changes to the document as desired.

6. To send the message immediately, click the Send Now button. Entourage connects to the Internet and sends the message.

   or

   To save the message in your outbox so it is sent the next time you send and receive messages, click Send Later.

7. Switch back to Word to continue working with the document or Word.

✔ Tips

- These instructions assume that Entourage is the default e-mail program as set in the Internet preferences pane. If a different program has been set as the default e-mail program, the Mail Recipient (as HTML) command will not appear on the Send To submenu (**Figure 24**).

- Entourage must be properly configured to send and receive e-mail messages.

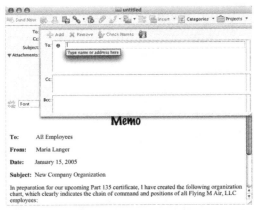

Figure 36 Enter the e-mail address for the person you want to send the file to.

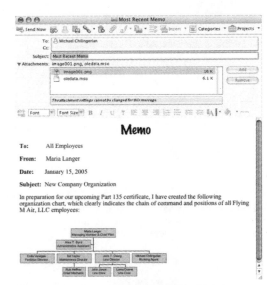

Figure 37 The file appears as an HTML-encoded message. Any images that are part of the file are included as attachments.

Figure 38
Choose Office Address Book from the Get Data pop-up menu.

Figure 39
Field names from the Entourage address book appear in the Merge Field area of the Data Merge Manager.

Figure 40 Use this dialog to enter a date and time to be reminded about a document.

Figure 41 Entourage reminds you with a window like this.

To use an Entourage address book as a data source for a data merge

1. Follow the instructions in **Chapter 15** to display the Data Merge Manager and create a main document.

2. Choose Office Address Book from the Get Data pop-up menu in the Data Source area of the Data Merge Manager (**Figure 38**).

3. Follow the steps in **Chapter 15** to complete the main document with field names that appear in the Merge Field area of the Data Merge Manager (**Figure 39**) and perform the merge.

✔ Tip

■ I explain how to use Word's data merge feature in **Chapter 15**.

To flag a document for follow up

1. Display the Word document you want to flag for follow up.

2. Click the Flag for Follow Up button on the Standard toolbar.

3. In the Flag for Follow Up dialog that appears (**Figure 40**), set the date and time that you want to be reminded to work with the document. Then click OK.

   An entry is added to your Entourage Task list. When the date and time you specified approaches, an Office Notifications window like the one in **Figure 41** appears. You can click the Open Item button to open the document.

✔ Tip

■ The Office Notifications window will only appear at the appropriate time if either Word or Entourage is open.

To add Word documents to an Entourage project

1. In Entourage, switch to the Project Center view.

2. If necessary, double-click the name of the project you want to add the document to to view its calendar and other details (**Figure 33**).

3. Click the Add button at the bottom of the window and choose File from the pop-up menu that appears (**Figure 42**).

4. Use the Add File dialog that appears (**Figure 43**) to locate and select the file you want to add.

5. Click Open.

   The file appears in the Recent Files list (**Figure 44**).

✔ Tips

- In step 4, you can select multiple files. Simply hold down the ⌃ ⌘ key while clicking each file you want to add.

- To open a file in the Project Center's Recent Files list (**Figure 44**), click it.

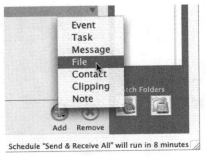

Figure 42 Choose File from the Add pop-up menu.

Figure 43 Use the Add File dialog to select the files you want to add to the project.

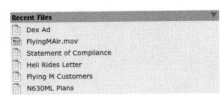

Figure 44 The file you added appears in the Recent Files list.

USING ENTOURAGE WITH WORD

Web Pages

Web Pages

The World Wide Web has had a bigger impact on publishing than any other communication medium introduced in the past fifty years. Web pages, which can include text, graphics, and hyperlinks, can be published on the Internet or an intranet, making them available to audiences 24 hours a day, 7 days a week. They can provide information quickly and inexpensively to anyone who needs it.

Microsoft Word has built-in Web page creation, modification, and interaction tools. With Word, you can build Web pages and open links to other Web pages and sites.

✔ Tips

- This chapter provides enough information to get you started using Word to create Web pages. Complete coverage of Web publishing, however, is beyond the scope of this book.

- Web pages are normally viewed with a special kind of software called a *Web browser*. Internet Explorer and Safari are two examples of Web browsers.

- To access the Internet, you need an Internet connection. Setting up a connection is beyond the scope of this book; consult the documentation that came with Mac OS or your Internet access software for more information.

- To publish a Web page, you need access to a Web server. Contact your organization's Network Administrator or your *Internet Service Provider* (*ISP*) for more information.

- A *hyperlink* (or *link*) is text or a graphic that, when clicked, displays other information from the Web.

- An intranet is like the Internet, but it exists only on the internal network of an organization and is usually closed to outsiders.

- Although Microsoft Word can create Web pages and simple Web sites, it is not the best tool for creating complex Web sites. If you're interested in creating a full-blown Web site, consider Web publishing software such as Macromedia Contribute or Dreamweaver or Adobe GoLive.

Creating a Web Page

Word offers two ways to create a Web page:

◆ The **Web Page** template lets you create a Web page from scratch, using appropriate formatting options.

◆ The **Save as Web Page** command lets you save a regular Word document as a Web page. This encodes the document and saves it as HTML.

✔ Tips

■ *HTML* (or *HyperText Markup Language*) is a system of codes for defining Web pages.

■ I explain how to save a regular Word document as an HTML file near the end of this chapter.

To use the Web Page template

1. Choose File > Project Gallery (**Figure 1**) or press ⇧⌘P to display the Project Gallery dialog.

2. If necessary, click the New button to display icons for new document templates (**Figure 2**).

3. Select the Web page icon.

4. Click Open. A new document appears in Online Layout view (**Figure 3**).

5. Enter and format text in the document window as desired to meet your needs.

Entering & Editing Web Page Text

You can add, edit, or delete text on a Web page the same way you add, edit, or delete text in a regular Word document. Consult **Chapter 2** for details.

Figure 1
Word's File menu.

Figure 2 The Project Gallery enables you to create blank Web pages.

Figure 3 A blank document window for a Web page. Note that Word automatically switches to Online Layout view.

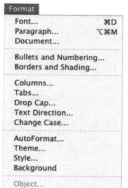

Figure 4
Word's Format menu.

Figure 5
Use the Background palette to select a background color for the page.

Figure 6
Clicking the More Colors button displays a standard Mac OS Colors dialog.

Formatting Web Pages

You format text on a Web page the same way you format text in any other Word document: by using the Formatting Palette, Format menu commands with their related dialogs, and shortcut keys. **Chapters 3** and **4** provide details about Word's formatting features.

Although the font and paragraph formatting techniques are the same for Web pages as they are for regular Word documents, there are two options that are especially useful for Web pages:

◆ **Background** enables you to set the background color, pattern, or image for the page.

◆ **Theme** enables you to set background patterns, graphic elements, and color schemes for an entire page all at once.

✔ Tip

■ Formatting and multimedia element insertion techniques that are not specifically covered in this chapter either work exactly as they do for regular Word documents or they do not apply to Web pages.

To set the page background color

1. Choose Format > Background (**Figure 4**) to display the Background palette (**Figure 5**).

2. Click to select a color in the palette.

   or

   Click the More Colors button, use the standard Colors dialog that appears (**Figure 6**) to select a color, and click OK.

   The page background changes color immediately.

3. Click the Background palette's close button to dismiss it.

To set the page background pattern or picture

1. Choose Format > Background (**Figure 4**) to display the Background palette (**Figure 5**).

2. Click the Fill Effects button.

3. Set options on one of the four panes of the Fill Effects dialog that appears:

   ▲ **Gradient** (**Figure 7**) enables you to set a gradient fill pattern for the background. Set Shading styles, Variants, Colors, and Transparency options to create the gradient you want. Other options appear in the pane depending on the options you select.

   ▲ **Texture** (**Figure 8**) enables you to set a texture for the background. Click a texture button to select it.

   ▲ **Pattern** (**Figure 9**) enables you to set a standard fill pattern for the background. Select the pattern you want, then choose Foreground and Background colors from the pop-up menus.

   ▲ **Picture** (**Figure 10**) enables you to use an image as a background. The image is repeated to fill the page. Click the Select Picture button to locate and select a picture file on disk.

4. Click OK. The page background changes immediately.

5. Click the Background palette's close button to dismiss it.

✔ Tip

■ Use care when setting a background pattern or picture. If the background has too much contrast, text that appears on it may not be legible.

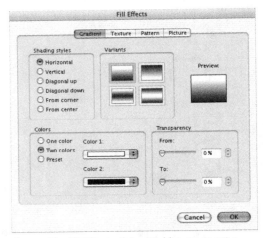

Figure 7 The Fill Effects dialog enables you to set a background gradient pattern...

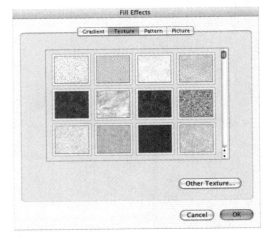

Figure 8 ...texture...

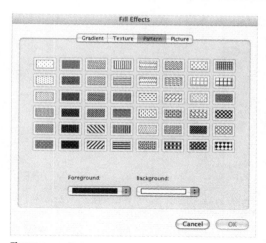

Figure 9 ...pattern...

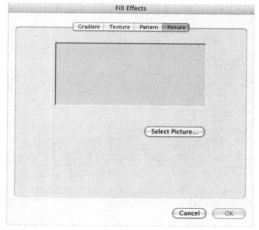

Figure 10 ...or picture.

To remove a page background color, pattern, or picture

1. Choose Format > Background (**Figure 4**) to display the Background palette (**Figure 5**).

2. Click the No Fill button.

   The background color or pattern changes back to white.

3. Click the Background palette's close button to dismiss it.

REMOVING BACKGROUND COLOR OR PATTERN

To set the page theme

1. Choose Format > Theme (**Figure 4**) to display the Theme dialog (**Figure 11**).

2. In the Theme scrolling list, select the name of the theme you want to apply to the page. The Sample area changes to show what the theme looks like.

3. Set other options by toggling check boxes near the bottom of the Theme dialog:

   ▲ **Vivid Colors** makes styles and borders a brighter color and changes the document background color.

   ▲ **Active Graphics** displays animated graphics in the Web browser window when the theme includes them.

   ▲ **Background Image** displays the background image for the theme as the page background. Turning off this check box enables you to use a plain background color with a theme.

4. Click OK to save your settings.

   The page's colors and background change to match the theme (**Figure 12**).

✔ Tip

■ Themes are a great way to apply consistent formatting to multiple Web pages.

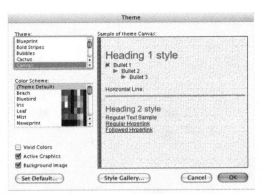

Figure 11 The Theme dialog with one of my favorite themes selected.

Figure 12 A Web page document with the Canvas theme applied.

Maria Langer
12345 Main Street, Suite A, Wickenburg, AZ 85390
H: 928/684-1212 • W: 928/684-1313 • C: 928/555-5555
maria@theflyingm.com • www.marialanger.com
OBJECTIVE
To obtain part-time work as a helicopter tour/charter pilot and/or Robinson helicopter ferry pilot.

Figure 13 This portion of a Web page includes three links. By default, they're underlined and appear in a different color text.

FLIGHT TRAINING & RATINGS
✖ **Papillon Airways**, Grand Canyon, AZ
  Turbine Transition Training (Bell 206L-C30P), April 2004
✖ **Robinson Helicopter Company**, Torrance, CA
  Factory Safety Course, October 2002 & December 2000

Figure 14 Select the text you want to turn into a link.

Figure 15 Choose Hyperlink from the Insert menu.

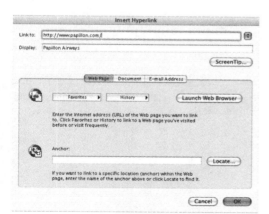

Figure 16 The Insert Hyperlink dialog for inserting a link to a Web page.

Hyperlinks

A *hyperlink* is text or a graphic that, when clicked, displays other information. Word enables you to create two kinds of hyperlinks:

◆ A link to a *URL* (*Uniform Resource Locator*), which is the Internet address of a document or individual. Word makes it easy to create links to two types of URLs:

   ▲ **http://** links to a Web page on a Web server.

   ▲ **mailto:** links to an e-mail address.

◆ A link to a Word document on your hard disk or network.

By default, hyperlinks appear as colored, underlined text (**Figure 13**).

✔ Tip

■ Word can automatically format URLs as hyperlinks. Simply type the complete URL; when you press [Spacebar] or [Return], Word turns the URL into a hyperlink. You can set this option in the AutoFormat tab of the AutoCorrect dialog, which I tell you about in **Chapter 4**.

To insert a hyperlink

1. Position the insertion point where you want the hyperlink to appear.

   or

   Select the text or picture that you want to convert to a hyperlink (**Figure 14**).

2. Choose Insert > Hyperlink (**Figure 15**), press ⌃⌘K, or click the Insert Hyperlink button on the Standard toolbar.

   The Insert Hyperlink dialog appears (**Figure 16**).

Continued on next page...

INSERTING HYPERLINKS

Continued from previous page.

3. To link to a Web page, enter the complete URL of the page you want to link to in the Link to box (**Figure 16**).

   or

   To link to a document on your hard disk or another computer on your network, click the Document button to display Document pane options (**Figure 17**). Click the Select button and use the Choose a File dialog that appears (**Figure 18**) to locate and select the document. When you click Open, Word automatically fills in the Link to box (**Figure 19**).

   or

   To link to an e-mail address, click the E-mail Address button to display E-mail Address pane options. Enter an e-mail address in the To box and a message subject in the Subject box. Word automatically fills in the Link to box. You can see all this in **Figure 20**.

4. If necessary, enter the text you want to appear in the document in the Display box.

5. To create a custom ScreenTip for the hyperlink, click the ScreenTip button. Then enter the ScreenTip text in the Set Hyperlink ScreenTip dialog that appears (**Figure 21**) and click OK.

6. Click OK to save your settings and dismiss the Insert Hyperlink dialog.

   The hyperlink is inserted.

   or

   The selected text turns into a hyperlink (**Figure 22**).

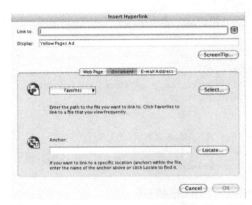

Figure 17 The Document pane of the Insert Hyperlink dialog enables you to create a link to a document on disk.

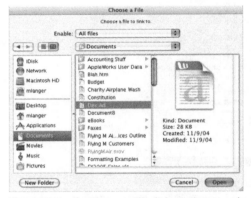

Figure 18 Use the Choose a File dialog to locate and select the file you want to link to.

Figure 19 Word enters the URL for the document in the Link to box.

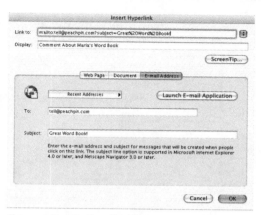

Figure 20 Use the E-mail Address pane to enter an e-mail address and subject. Word enters the URL for the link.

Figure 21 Use the Set Hyperlink ScreenTip dialog to create a custom ScreenTip for a hyperlink.

FLIGHT TRAINING & RATINGS
* **Papillon Airways**, Grand Canyon, AZ
  Turbine Transition Training (Bell 206L-C30P), April 2004
* **Robinson Helicopter Company**, Torrance, CA
  Factory Safety Course, October 2002 & December 2000

Figure 22 The text you originally selected turns into a hyperlink.

Figures 23 & 24 When you position the mouse pointer on a hyperlink, a box containing either the link's URL (above) or ScreenTip (below) appears.

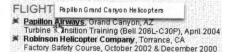

✔ Tip

■ In step 3, you can use pop-up menus in the Web Page, Document, or E-mail Address pane to quickly enter a bookmarked Web site, recently accessed Web site, or recently used e-mail address.

To follow a hyperlink

1. Position the mouse pointer on the hyperlink. The mouse pointer turns into a hand with a pointing finger and a box containing the URL (**Figure 23**) or Screen-Tip (**Figure 24**) for the link appears.

2. Click the link.

   If the hyperlink points to an Internet URL, Word starts your default Web browser, connects to the Internet, and displays the URL.

   or

   If the hyperlink points to a file on your hard disk or another computer on the network, the file opens.

   or

   If the hyperlink points to an e-mail address, Word starts your default e-mail program and displays a new message form with the address included in the link.

INSERTING & FOLLOWING HYPERLINKS

To remove a hyperlink

1. Position the insertion point anywhere within the hyperlink.

2. Choose Insert > Hyperlink (**Figure 15**) or press ⌃ ⌘ K.

   or

   Click the Insert Hyperlink button on the Standard toolbar.

3. In the Edit Hyperlink dialog that appears (**Figure 25**), click the Remove Link button.

4. Click OK.

   The link is removed from the text, but the text remains. All hyperlink formatting is removed.

Or

1. Drag to select the hyperlink.

2. Press Delete.

   Both the text and its hyperlink are removed from the document.

✔ Tip

- You can also use the Edit Hyperlink dialog (**Figure 25**) to modify the link, as discussed earlier in this section.

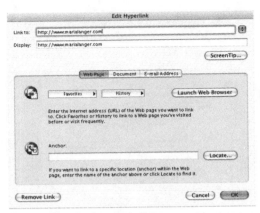

Figure 25 The Edit Hyperlink dialog.

Figure 26 The Web page appears in your default Web browser's window.

Previewing Web Page Files

Not all Word formatting appears the same in a Web browser window as it does in Word. This means that a Web page you create in Word may look different when published on the Internet or a corporate intranet.

The Web Page Preview command on Word's File menu (**Figure 1**) enables you to see what a Web page you created in Word looks like when viewed with a Web browser. Previewing a Web page helps you ensure that its appearance is acceptable when viewed by others.

To preview a Web page

1. Choose File > Web Page Preview (**Figure 1**).

   Word launches your default Web browser. The Web page appears in the browser window (**Figure 26**).

2. When you are finished viewing the document in your Web browser, choose *Application menu name* > Quit *Application* or press ⌘ Q to quit the program and return to Word.

Saving Web Page Files

Word offers two options for saving Web page files:

◆ Save a Word document—either created with a Web page template or as a regular Word document—as a Web page.

◆ Save a Web page as a regular Word document.

✔ Tip

■ Detailed instructions for using the Save As dialog are provided in **Chapter 2**.

To save a document as a Web page

1. Choose File > Save as Web Page (**Figure 1**) to display the Save As dialog (**Figure 27**).

2. Use the dialog to enter a name and select a disk location for the file.

3. Make sure Web Page (HTML) is chosen from the Format pop-up menu.

4. Select one of the radio buttons to specify how the Web page should be saved:

   ▲ **Save entire file into HTML** saves all properties of the document, including Word-specific elements that don't display on the Web. Use this option if the document contains headers, comments, footnotes, or other elements you want to retain.

   ▲ **Save only display information into HTML** saves only the information that will display on the Web. This discards all Word-specific elements.

5. To specify a page title for the Web page, click the Web Options button. Then enter a page title and keywords in the General pane of the Web Options dialog that appears (**Figure 28**) and click OK.

6. Click Save.

Figure 27 The Save As dialog when saving a document as a Web page.

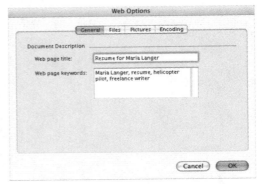

Figure 28 Use this dialog to enter a page title and keywords for the Web page.

Figure 29 Word saves not only the document, but all image files embedded in it. All of these files must be copied to the Web server for the page to appear properly.

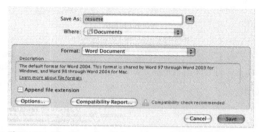

Figure 30 The Save As dialog when saving a file as a Word document.

✔ Tips

- A Web page *title* is the text that appears in the title bar of a Web browser.

- When Word saves a document as a Web page, it creates a folder named *filename_* files (**Figure 29**) that contains image files that are part of the Web page. When copying Web pages to a directory on a Web server to make them available on the Internet or an intranet, be sure to include the Web page file and this folder of associated image files.

To save a Web page as a Word document

1. With a Web page open, choose File > Save As (**Figure 1**) to display the Save As dialog (**Figure 30**).

2. Use the dialog to enter a name and select a disk location for the file.

3. Make sure Word Document is chosen from the Format pop-up menu.

4. Click Save.

Viewing Web Pages with Word

Word can also open Web pages stored on your computer or on another computer on the network. This makes it possible to view and edit Web pages within Word, even if they were not created with Word.

To open a Web page

1. Choose File > Open (**Figure 1**) to display the Open dialog (**Figure 31**).

2. Choose Web Pages from the Enable pop-up menu.

3. Use the dialog to locate and select the file you want to open.

4. Click Open.

   Word opens the Web page you indicated (**Figure 32**).

✔ Tip

- Double-clicking the icon for a Web page created with Word will open it in your default Web browser—*not* Microsoft Word.

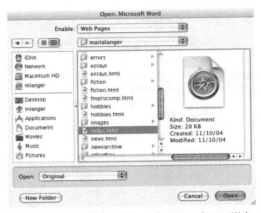

Figure 31 Use the Open dialog to locate and open Web page files.

Figure 32 In this example, I've used Word to open a Web page I created and maintain with Macromedia Dreamweaver. Word has done a pretty good job of displaying the page's complex layout and graphics.

Macros

Macros

Microsoft Word's macro feature enables you to automate repetitive tasks within Word. For example, suppose you often insert a table, with specific size and formatting settings, in your Word documents. You can turn on Word's macro recorder and perform the steps to insert the table. Word records each step as you work. You then save the resulting macro so you can run it at any time. This can be a real timesaver because not only will Word faithfully repeat all the steps you included in the macro, but it will do it much quicker than you could do it manually.

Word's macro feature uses Microsoft Visual Basic for Applications (VBA), a programming language that makes it possible to create complex macro routines for Word. Wizards, for example, which I discuss in **Chapter 2**, are created with VBA. VBA is extremely powerful. Unfortunately, however, it requires a solid understanding of the VBA programming language. It has also become a popular tool for virus programmers who unleash their creations on unsuspecting Office users.

This chapter tells you how you can get started using Word's macro feature. It explains how you can record, run, and modify macros. It introduces the VBA programming environment and tells you how you can access VBA-specific help. It also covers Word's built-in macro virus protection feature and explains how you can use it to prevent Word viruses from infecting your computer.

Using Word's Macro Recorder

The quickest and easiest way to get started using Word's macro feature is to use its macro recorder. The macro recorder records the steps you perform within Word, automatically writing the VBA code that makes up the macro. You can then run the macro to repeat the steps.

There are two potential "gotchas" that you may encounter when using the macro recorder:

◆ The macro recorder cannot record mouse movements within the document window. So if you want to select text or reposition the insertion point as part of a macro, you must use shortcut keys to do it.

◆ The macro recorder will record *every* keystroke and menu choice you make. So if you make a mistake, it's recorded as part of the macro, too.

To make the most of the macro recorder and record a macro correctly the first time, you should have a solid understanding of what you want the macro to do and what steps are required to complete the task. Don't be afraid to jot down a few notes before starting the recorder. A little advance preparation may save you time in the long run.

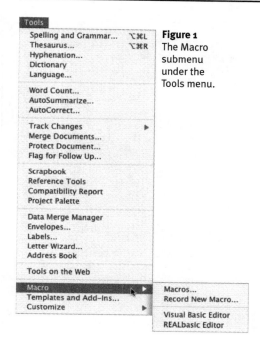

Figure 1
The Macro submenu under the Tools menu.

Figure 2 The Record Macro dialog.

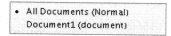

Figure 3 The Store macro in pop-up menu.

Figure 4 The tiny Stop Recording toolbar.

To record a macro

1. If necessary, open the document you want to have open when recording the macro steps and position the insertion point or select text as desired.

2. Choose Tools > Macro > Record New Macro (**Figure 1**) to display the Record Macro dialog (**Figure 2**).

3. Enter a name for the macro in the Macro name box. The name cannot contain any spaces or special characters.

4. Choose a location to store the macro from the Store macro in pop-up menu (**Figure 3**).

5. If desired, enter a description for the macro by editing the contents of the Description box.

6. Click OK. The tiny Stop Recording toolbar appears (**Figure 4**).

7. Perform the steps you want to record. (Remember that the macro recorder won't record mouse movements or clicks within the document window.)

8. When you are finished performing all of the steps you want to include in the macro, click the Stop Recording button on the Stop Recording toolbar. The Stop Recording toolbar disappears and your macro steps are saved.

Continued on next page...

RECORDING MACROS

Continued from previous page.

✔ Tips

- In step 4, if you want to store the macro in a specific template or document, make sure that template or document is open before you open the Record Macro dialog.

- After step 5, you can click the Toolbars button or Keyboard button to display the Commands pane of the Customize Toolbars/Menus dialog (**Figure 5**) or the Customize Keyboard dialog (**Figure 6**). I explain how to use these dialogs to assign toolbar buttons and shortcut keys to commands, including macros, in **Chapter 20**. Clicking OK in either of these dialogs starts the macro recorder.

- In step 3, if you enter the name of an existing macro, when you click OK to begin recording the macro a dialog like the one in **Figure 7** will appear. Click Yes to overwrite the macro; click No to return to the Record Macro dialog so you can rename the macro you want to record.

- In step 7, you can pause macro recording at any time by clicking the Pause Recording button on the Stop Recording toolbar. The button looks pushed in (**Figure 8**) or selected until you click it again to resume recording.

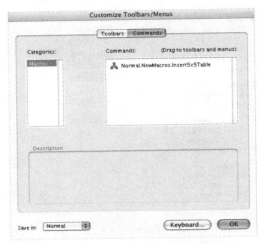

Figure 5 The Commands tab of the Customize Toolbars/Menus dialog. Use this dialog to assign a macro to a toolbar button.

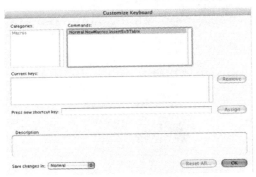

Figure 6 The Customize Keyboard dialog. Use this dialog to assign a shortcut key to a macro.

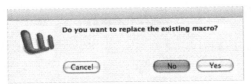

Figure 7 A dialog like this appears when you attempt to record a macro with the same name as an existing macro.

Figure 8 The Stop Recording toolbar with the Pause Recording button selected.

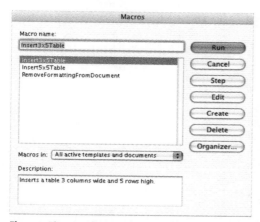

Figure 9 The Macros dialog with three macros defined.

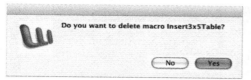

Figure 10 This dialog confirms that you really do want to delete a macro.

To run a macro

1. If necessary, open the document you want to have open when running the macro and position the insertion point or select text as desired.

2. Choose Tools > Macro > Macros to display the Macros dialog.

3. Select the name of the macro you want to run (**Figure 9**).

4. Click Run. The macro steps are performed, just the way they were recorded (but a heck of a lot quicker).

✔ Tip

■ If this is the first time you're running a macro that modifies the contents of a document, you might want to save the document before running the macro. This way you can revert to the saved copy if something goes wrong during macro execution.

To delete a macro

1. Choose Tools > Macro > Macros to display the Macros dialog.

2. Select the name of the macro you want to delete (**Figure 9**).

3. Click Delete.

4. A confirmation dialog like the one in **Figure 10** appears. Click Yes.

Working with the Visual Basic Editor

Microsoft Word comes with the Microsoft Visual Basic Editor (**Figure 11**). This program enables you to write macros from scratch and edit macros that were either manually written or written using the macro recorder. The Visual Basic Editor is a true programming environment that includes a variety of windows, commands, and buttons designed for programmers.

To take full advantage of the Visual Basic Editor, you need to know how to program in the VBA languge. But even without a full understanding of VBA, you may be able to edit macros you recorded to remove or modify macro steps. For example, suppose you made and fixed a mistake while recording a macro. You can edit the macro code to remove the step where you made the mistake and the step where you fixed it.

In this part of the chapter, I explain how you can use the Microsoft Visual Basic Editor to edit a macro. I also tell you how you can get started writing macros from scratch and where you can find more information about programming in VBA.

✔ Tip

■ One way to learn more about VBA is to use the Visual Basic Editor to examine macros written by others, including Microsoft Corporation.

Menu bar   Standard toolbar

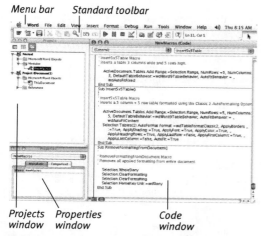

Projects   Properties   Code
window   window   window

Figure 11 The Microsoft Visual Basic Editor programming environment for Word.

To edit a macro

1. Choose Tools > Macro > Macros to display the Macros dialog (**Figure 9**).

2. Select the macro you want to edit.

3. Click Edit. Microsoft Visual Basic Editor launches and displays its windows (**Figure 11**).

4. Edit the macro code in the Code window.

5. Choose File > Save *Template Name*, or press ⌃⌘Ｓ.

6. Choose Word > Close and Return to Microsoft Word, or press ⌃⌘Ｑ.

✔ Tip

■ If you don't know a thing about VBA, in step 4, limit yourself to modifying commands that you can recognize. For example, in the macro shown in **Figure 11**, I could change the AutoFormatting options by changing some True settings to False or remove AutoFormatting completely by deleting the step that begins with Selection.Tables(1) AutoFormat. This is pretty easy to figure out, even without VBA programming experience.

To write a macro from scratch

1. Choose Tools > Macro > Macros to display the Macros dialog (**Figure 9**).

2. Enter a name for the macro in the Macro name box.

3. Choose a location to store the macro from the Macros in pop-up menu (**Figure 12**).

4. If desired, enter a description for the macro by editing the contents of the Description box.

5. Click Create. Microsoft Visual Basic Editor launches and displays its windows. The Code window includes a new Sub procedure named for the macro (**Figure 13**).

6. Enter the macro code in the Code window for the new Sub procedure.

7. If desired, use commands under the Debug menu (**Figure 14**) to compile or step through your macro statements.

8. Choose File > Save *Template Name*, or press ⌃ ⌘ S.

9. Choose File > Close and Return to Microsoft Word, or press ⌃ ⌘ Q.

✔ Tips

■ As you can see in **Figure 13**, the clean slate approach to writing macros requires an intimate knowledge of VBA.

■ Using Debug menu commands (**Figure 14**) can help identify syntax errors (**Figure 15**) that will prevent the macro from running properly. These commands can't, however, fix errors. That's up to you. (And please don't ask me for help—I just told you everything I know about VBA!)

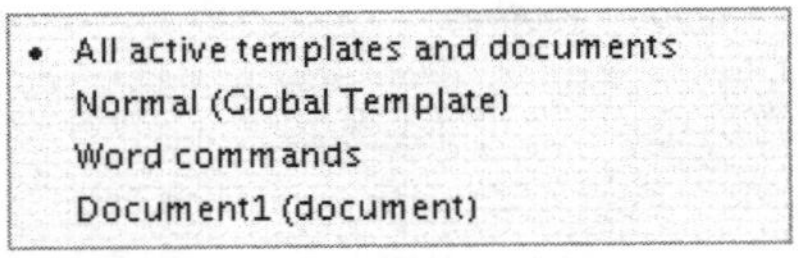

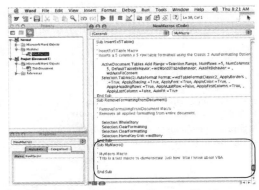

- All active templates and documents
  Normal (Global Template)
  Word commands
  Document1 (document)

Figure 12 The Macros in pop-up menu.

Figure 13 A new Sub procedure is created for the macro in the Code window.

Figure 14
The Debug menu in the Visual Basic Editor. These commands help programmers find errors in VBA code.

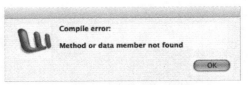

Figure 15 If you use the Compile command on the Debug menu to check VBA code that contains an error, a dialog like this appears. When you click OK, the offending code is highlighted in the Code window.

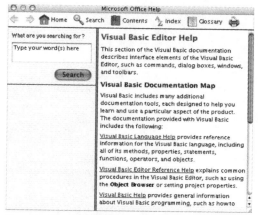

Figure 16 The Microsoft Visual Basic Editor's Help menu.

Figure 17 Visual Basic Help appears in a familiar-looking Microsoft Office Help window.

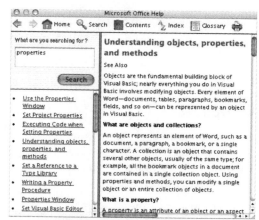

Figure 18 Clicking a topic link displays information about the topic in the right side of the window.

Getting VBA Help

The Microsoft Visual Basic Editor's Help menu offers commands for accessing an extensive onscreen help system. This help system provides a wealth of information about using the editor. It also provides valuable information about the VBA language to help you write, edit, or debug macros.

In this part of the chapter, I explain how to access Visual Basic Help and tell you what you can expect to find within it.

To access Visual Basic Help

1. While using the Visual Basic Editor (**Figure 11**), choose Help > Visual Basic Help (**Figure 16**). A Microsoft Office Help window appears (**Figure 17**).

2. Enter a Search word or phrase in the box on the left side of the window and click Search.

   or

   In the right side of the window, click the link for the help topic you want to browse.

3. Click links in the Microsoft Office Help window to browse Help topics (**Figure 18**).

✔ Tip

■ As you can see, Visual Basic Help is very similar to Word Help. I discuss Word Help in more detail in **Chapter 2**; consult that chapter for instructions and tips for using Help.

Macro Virus Protection

VBA is a powerful programming language that can be used to create applications that work within Microsoft Office. Unfortunately, virus programmers have embraced it as a perfect programming and distribution environment for creating and spreading their dirty deeds.

One of the benefits of Word's macro feature—from the programmer and user points of view—is that macros are stored in template files. This makes them easy to distribute. Send someone a Word file that contains a macro and that person can use the macro on his computer. He can even copy the macro to other templates and share them with others.

It's this feature that also makes macros dangerous to users. Opening a Word file that contains a malicious macro—one designed to do something annoying or damaging—can trigger its functions. Macros like this are known as *macro viruses*.

One particularly widespread example of a Word Macro virus appeared in March 2002. Dubbed "Melissa," it spread in a Word file that, once opened, sent e-mail messages to the first 50 people in the user's Outlook address book. The e-mail message included the infected file as an attachment, thus spreading the virus to other users.

Fortunately, the folks at Microsoft have developed a strategy for protecting Word users from unsuspectingly opening a Word file that includes a macro virus. In this part of the chapter, I explain how you enable macro virus protection and how you can use it to protect your computer from macro viruses.

✔ Tips

- You can protect your computer from all kinds of viruses by installing virus protection software, keeping it up to date, and using it regularly.

- You can learn more about macro viruses on the Microsoft Web site, www.microsoft.com; search for the phrase "macro virus".

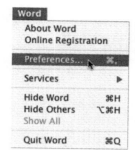

Figure 19
Choose Preferences from the Word menu.

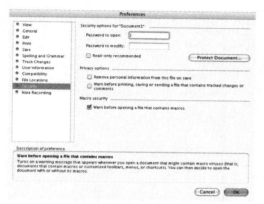

Figure 20 You enable macro virus protection in the Security pane of the Preferences dialog.

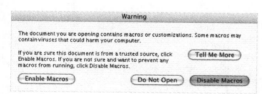

Figure 21 This Warning dialog appears when you open a file containing macros and macro virus protection is enabled.

To enable macro virus protection

1. Choose Word > Preferences (**Figure 19**) or press ⌥ ⌘ , to display the Preferences dialog.

2. Click Security on the left side of the dialog to display the Security Preferences pane (**Figure 20**).

3. Turn on the Warn before opening a file that contains macros check box.

4. Click OK.

✔ Tips

- With macro virus protection enabled, a dialog like the one in **Figure 21** appears each time you open a file that contains a macro. Click a button to proceed:

  ▲ **Enable Macros** opens the files and enables the macros. Click this button only if you're sure the macros in the file are not harmful.

  ▲ **Do Not Open** does not open the file at all. Click this button if you have serious doubts about the macros in the file.

  ▲ **Disable Macros** opens the file but disables all of its macros. Click this button if you need to open the file but don't need the macros, especially if you're not sure whether the macros could be harmful.

- I tell you more about options in the Security pane of the Preferences dialog in **Chapter 20**.

ENABLING MACRO VIRUS PROTECTION

Customizing Word

Setting Word Preferences

Microsoft Word's Preferences dialog offers twelve categories of preferences that you can set to customize the way Word works for you:

- ◆ **View** preferences control Word's onscreen appearance.

- ◆ **General** preferences control general Word operations.

- ◆ **Edit** preferences control editing.

- ◆ **Print** preferences control document printing.

- ◆ **Save** preferences control file saving.

- ◆ **Spelling and Grammar** preferences control spelling and grammar checker operations.

- ◆ **Track Changes** preferences control the track changes feature.

- ◆ **User Information** preferences contain information about the primary user.

- ◆ **Compatibility** preferences control a document's compatibility with other applications or versions of Word.

- ◆ **File Locations** preferences specify where certain Word files are stored on disk.

- ◆ **Security** preferences enable you to set file encryption, file sharing, and privacy options for a file.

- ◆ **Note Recording** preferences control the recording quality of audio notes.

✔ Tip

- ■ Word's default preference settings are discussed and illustrated throughout this book.

To set preferences

1. Choose Word > Preferences (**Figure 1**) or press ⌃⌘, to display the Preferences dialog (**Figure 3**).

2. In the list on the left side of the dialog, click the category of preferences that you want to set.

3. Set options as desired.

4. Repeat steps 2 and 3 for other categories of preferences that you want to set.

5. Click OK to save your settings.

✔ Tip

■ I illustrate and discuss all Preferences dialog options throughout this chapter.

To restore preferences to the default settings

1. If Word is running, choose Word > Quit Word (**Figure 1**) to quit it.

2. In the Finder, open the folder at this path: ~/Library/Preferences/Microsoft/ (where ~/ represents your Home folder).

3. Locate the file named *com.microsoft. Word.prefs.plist* (**Figure 2**) and drag it to the Trash.

4. Choose Finder > Empty Trash.

5. Open Word.

✔ Tips

■ When the com.microsoft.Word.prefs.plist file is deleted, Word automatically creates a new file with the same name, using default preference settings.

■ As you may have guessed, Word creates a com.microsoft.Word.prefs.plist file for each user.

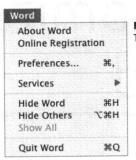

Figure 1
The Word menu.

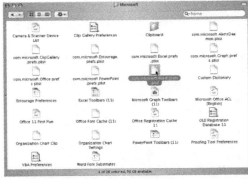

Figure 2 The Word preferences file is buried deep within your Library folder, in the Microsoft folder.

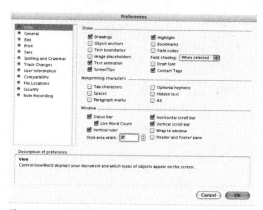

Figure 3 The default settings in the View pane of the Preferences dialog when in Normal view.

View Preferences

The View pane of the Preferences dialog **(Figure 3)** offers options in three categories: Show, Nonprinting characters, and Window.

Show

Show options determine what Word interface elements appear onscreen:

◆ **Drawings** displays objects created with Word's drawing tools. Turning off this option can speed up the display and scrolling of documents with many drawings. This option only applies to Online and Page Layout views.

◆ **Object anchors** displays an anchor marker indicating that an object is attached to text. An object's anchor can only appear when the object is selected, this check box is turned on, and non-printing characters are displayed. You must turn on this option to move an anchor. This option only applies to Online and Page Layout views.

◆ **Text boundaries** displays dotted lines around page margins, text columns, and objects. This option only applies to Online and Page Layout views.

◆ **Image placeholders** displays graphics as empty boxes. Turning on this option can speed up the display of documents with a lot of graphics.

◆ **Text animation** displays animation applied to text. Turning off this option displays animated text the way it will print.

◆ **ScreenTips** displays information or comments in boxes when you point to buttons or annotated text.

Continued on next page...

VIEW PREFERENCES

Continued from previous page.

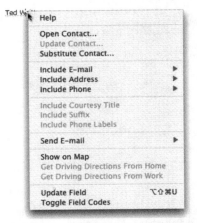

- ◆ **Highlight** displays text highlighting.

- ◆ **Bookmarks** displays document book-marks by enclosing their names in square brackets. If displayed, the bookmarks do not print.

- ◆ **Field codes** displays field codes instead of results.

- ◆ **Field shading** enables you to specify how you want fields shaded. The options are:

  - ▲ **Never** never shades fields.

  - ▲ **Always** always shades fields.

  - ▲ **When selected** only shades a field when it is selected.

- ◆ **Draft font** displays most character for-matting as bold or underlined and displays graphics as empty boxes. This option only applies to Normal and Out-line views.

- ◆ **Contact Tags** displays purple dotted underlines beneath contacts inserted from your Entourage contacts database. Hold down Control and click a contact tag to display a menu of options (**Figure 4**).

Figure 4 When you display the contextual menu for a contact tag, you see additional options not available for regular text.

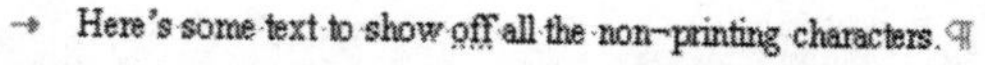

→ Here's some text to show off all the non-printing characters. ¶

Figure 5 Nonprinting characters revealed!

Nonprinting characters

Nonprinting characters options determine which (if any) nonprinting characters appear onscreen (**Figure 5**).

◆ **Tab characters** displays gray right-pointing arrows for tab characters.

◆ **Spaces** displays tiny gray dots for space characters.

◆ **Paragraph marks** displays gray backwards Ps (like this: ¶) for return characters.

◆ **Optional hyphens** displays L-shaped hyphens for optional hyphen characters.

◆ **Hidden text** displays text formatted as hidden with a dotted underline.

◆ **All** displays all nonprinting characters. Turning on this option is the same as turning on the Show/Hide ¶ button on the Standard toolbar.

VIEW PREFERENCES

Window

Window options determine what interface elements appear on Word document windows.

- ◆ **Status bar** displays the status bar at the bottom of the window.

- ◆ **Live Word Count** displays word count information in the status bar. The Status bar option must be turned on to enable this option.

- ◆ **Vertical ruler** displays a ruler down the left side of the window in Page Layout view. This option only applies to Page Layout view.

- ◆ **Style area width** enables you to specify a width for the style area. When set to a value greater than 0, the style area appears along the left side of the window and indicates the style applied to each paragraph in the document (**Figure 6**). This option only applies to Normal and Outline views.

- ◆ **Horizontal scroll bar** displays a scroll bar along the bottom of the window.

- ◆ **Vertical scroll bar** displays a scroll bar along the right side of the window.

- ◆ **Wrap to window** wraps text to the width of the window rather than to the right indent or margin.

- ◆ **Header and Footer pane** displays a document's header or footer in a special pane within the window (**Figure 7**). This option only applies to Normal and Outline views.

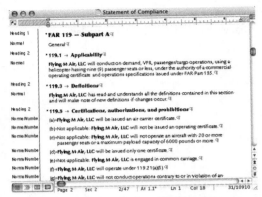

Figure 6 The Style area displayed in Normal view.

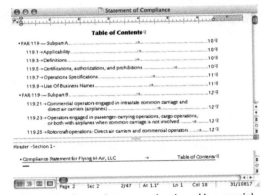

Figure 7 Headers or footers can be viewed in a special pane in Normal view.

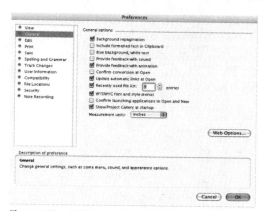

Figure 8 The default settings in the General pane of the Preferences dialog.

Figure 9
You can include a list of recently opened files at the bottom of the File menu.

General Preferences

General options (**Figure 8**) control the general operation of Word:

◆ **Background repagination** paginates documents automatically as you work. (This option cannot be turned off in Page Layout view.)

◆ **Include formatted text in Clipboard** includes text formatting when you copy text to the Clipboard.

◆ **Blue background, white text** displays the document as white text on a blue background—like the old WordPerfect software. (Why you'd want to do this is beyond me. Not only is it hard to read, but it's downright ugly!)

◆ **Provide feedback with sound** plays sound effects at the conclusion of certain actions or with the appearance of alerts.

◆ **Provide feedback with animation** displays special animated cursors while waiting for certain actions to complete.

◆ **Confirm conversion at Open** displays a dialog that you can use to select a converter when you open a file created with another application.

◆ **Update automatic links at Open** automatically updates linked information when you open a document containing links to other files.

◆ **Recently used file list** enables you to specify the number of recently opened files that should appear near the bottom of the File menu (**Figure 9**). This feature is handy for quickly reopening recently accessed files.

Continued on next page...

GENERAL PREFERENCES

Continued from previous page.

- ◆ **WYSIWYG font and style menus** displays the characters in font and style menus with the corresponding font and styles applied (**Figures 10** and **11**).

- ◆ **Confirm launching applications in Open and New** displays a confirmation dialog when you use the Open dialog or Project Gallery to open or create a non-Word document.

- ◆ **Show Project Gallery at startup** always displays the Project Gallery dialog when you launch Word by opening its application icon.

- ◆ **Measurement units** enables you to select the measurement unit used throughout Word. Options are Inches, Centimeters, Millimeters, Points, and Picas.

Figure 10
Fonts listed on the Font menu can display in their typefaces.

Figure 11
The Styles area of the Formatting Palette can display a list of styles with the styles applied.

GENERAL PREFERENCES

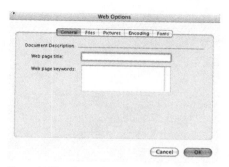

Figure 12 The General pane of the Web Options dialog.

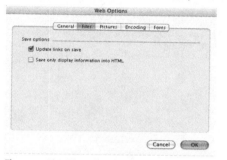

Figure 13 The Files pane of the Web Options dialog.

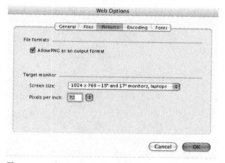

Figure 14 The Pictures pane of the Web Options dialog.

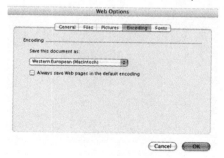

Figure 15 The Encoding pane of the Web Options dialog.

Web Options

Clicking the Web Options button displays the Web Options dialog (**Figures 12** through **16**), which has five different panes of options for creating and working with Web pages. Although these options are advanced and far beyond the scope of this book, here's a quick overview of each.

◆ **General** options (**Figure 12**) enable you to set a Web page title and keywords for the current document.

◆ **Files** options (**Figure 13**) control file saving options for Web pages.

◆ **Pictures** options (**Figure 14**) control the file formats of images and the resolution of the target monitor.

◆ **Encoding** options (**Figure 15**) control how a Web page is coded when saved.

◆ **Fonts** options (**Figure 16**) control the character set and default fonts for Web pages.

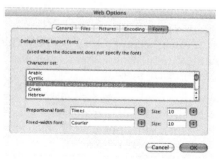

Figure 16 The Fonts pane of the Web Options dialog.

Edit Preferences

Edit preferences (**Figure 17**) control the way certain editing tasks work. There are three categories: Editing options, Cut and paste options, and Click and type.

Editing options

Editing options set the way text is edited:

◆ **Typing replaces selection** deletes selected text when you start typing. If you turn this check box off, Word inserts typed text to the left of any text selected before you began typing.

◆ **Drag-and-drop text editing** allows you to move or copy selected text by dragging it.

◆ **Include paragraph mark when selecting paragraphs** includes the paragraph mark when you select a paragraph.

◆ **When selecting, automatically select entire word** selects entire words when your selection includes the spaces after words. This feature makes it impossible to use the mouse to select multiple word fragments.

◆ **Use the INS key for paste** enables you to press [Ins] to use the Paste command.

◆ **Overtype mode** replaces characters, one at a time, as you type. This is the opposite of Insert mode.

◆ **Tabs and backspace set left indent** increases or decreases the left indent when you press the [Tab] or [Delete] key. This feature can cause undesired paragraph formatting changes.

◆ **Allow accented uppercase in French** enables Word's proofing tools to suggest accent marks for uppercase characters for text formatted as French.

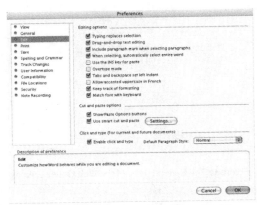

Figure 17 The default settings in the Edit pane of the Preferences dialog.

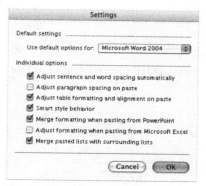

Figure 18 Clicking the Paste Options button displays a menu of options for pasted text.

Figure 19 Use this Settings dialog to fine-tune the way smart cut and paste works.

◆ **Keep track of formatting** tells Word to record formatting commands as you type so you can apply the formatting again.

◆ **Match font with keyboard** automatically switches the keyboard layout to match the language of another character set, such as Russian or Greek.

Cut and paste options

Cut and paste options set the way the cut, copy, and paste commands work.

◆ **Show Paste Options buttons** displays a button beneath pasted text that offers additional options for the text (**Figure 18**).

◆ **Use smart cut and paste** adds or removes spaces as necessary when you delete, drag, or paste text. This feature can save time when editing text.

◆ **Settings** displays the Settings dialog (**Figure 19**), which you can use to fine-tune the way the smart cut and paste feature works.

Click and type

Click and type options control the way the click and type feature works:

◆ **Enable click and type** turns on the click and type feature.

◆ **Default Paragraph Style** enables you to select the default style for click and type entries in a document.

EDIT PREFERENCES

Print Preferences

Print preferences (**Figure 20**) control the way documents print. There are three categories: Printing options, Include with document, and Options for current document only.

Printing options

Printing options let you specify how the document content is updated and printed:

◆ **Update fields** automatically updates Word fields before you print. This feature prevents you from printing a document with outdated field contents.

◆ **Update links** automatically updates information in linked files before you print. This feature prevents you from printing a file with outdated linked file contents.

◆ **Reverse print order** prints documents in reverse order—last page first. This might be useful if your printer stacks output face up.

Include with document

Include with document options enable you to print or suppress specific information from the document:

◆ **Document properties** prints the document's summary information on a separate page after the document. This information is stored in the Summary tab of the Properties dialog (**Figure 21**).

◆ **Field codes** prints field codes instead of field contents.

◆ **Drawing objects** prints objects drawn with Word's drawing tools.

◆ **Hidden text** prints text formatted as hidden.

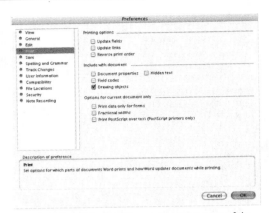

Figure 20 The default settings in the Print pane of the Preferences dialog.

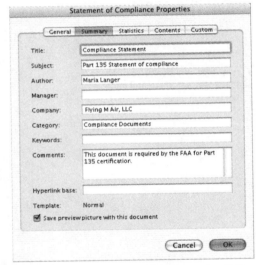

Figure 21 The Summary pane of the Properties dialog.

Options for current document only

As the name implies, Options for current document only affect the way the active document prints:

◆ **Print data only for forms** prints just the information entered in fill-in forms—not the form itself.

◆ **Fractional widths** adjusts the spacing of proportionally spaced fonts like Helvetica and Times. This may improve the appearance of these fonts when printed.

◆ **Print PostScript over text** prints any PostScript code in a converted Word for Macintosh document (such as a digital watermark) on top of document text instead of underneath it. This option only works with PostScript printers.

PRINT PREFERENCES

Save Preferences

Save preferences (**Figure 22**) control the way files are saved to disk.

◆ **Always create backup copy** saves the previous version of a file as a backup copy in the same folder as the original. Each time the file is saved, the new backup copy replaces the old one.

◆ **Save preview picture with new documents** automatically creates a preview picture for all new documents you save.

◆ **Allow fast saves** speeds up saving by saving only the changes to an existing file. If you turn off this check box, Word saves the entire file; this takes longer but results in slightly smaller files that are less likely to suffer from file corruption problems. This option is not available when the Always create backup copy option is enabled.

◆ **Prompt for document properties** displays the Summary tab of the Properties dialog (**Figure 21**) when you save a file for the first time. You can use this dialog to enter and store information about the file.

◆ **Prompt to save Normal template** displays a dialog that enables you to save or discard changes you made to the default settings in the Normal template. With this check box turned off, Word automatically saves changes to the Normal template.

◆ **Save data only for forms** saves the data entered into a form as a single, tab-delimited record that you can import into a database. This option applies to the currently active document only.

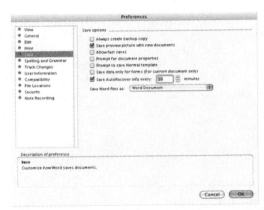

Figure 22 The default settings in the Save pane of the Preferences dialog.

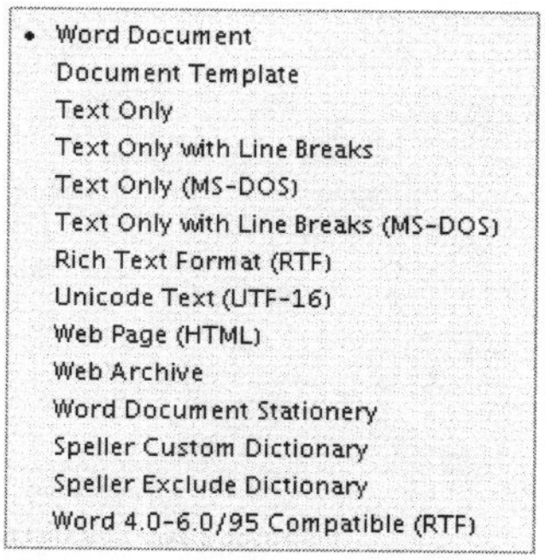

```
•  Word Document
   Document Template
   Text Only
   Text Only with Line Breaks
   Text Only (MS-DOS)
   Text Only with Line Breaks (MS-DOS)
   Rich Text Format (RTF)
   Unicode Text (UTF-16)
   Web Page (HTML)
   Web Archive
   Word Document Stationery
   Speller Custom Dictionary
   Speller Exclude Dictionary
   Word 4.0-6.0/95 Compatible (RTF)
```

Figure 23 Use this pop-up menu to specify a default file format for Word files that you save.

◆ **Save AutoRecover info every** enables you to set a frequency for automatically saving a special document recovery file. Word can use the AutoRecover file to recreate the document if your computer crashes or loses power before you get a chance to save changes.

◆ **Save Word files as** enables you to choose a default format for saving Word files. The pop-up menu (**Figure 23**) offers the same options found in the Save As dialog.

Spelling and Grammar Preferences

Spelling and Grammar preferences (**Figure 24**) control the way the spelling and grammar checkers work. There are two categories of options: Spelling and Grammar.

Spelling

Spelling options control the way the spelling checker works:

◆ **Check spelling as you type** turns on the automatic spelling check feature.

◆ **Hide spelling errors in this document** hides the red wavy lines that Word uses to identify possible spelling errors when the automatic spelling check feature is turned on. This option is only available with Check spelling as you type enabled.

◆ **Always suggest corrections** tells Word to automatically display a list of suggested replacements for a misspelled word during a manual spelling check.

◆ **Suggest from main dictionary only** tells Word to suggest replacement words from the main dictionary—not from your custom dictionaries.

◆ **Ignore words in UPPERCASE** tells Word not to check words in all uppercase characters, such as acronyms.

◆ **Ignore words with numbers** tells Word not to check words that include numbers, such as *MariaL1*.

◆ **Ignore Internet and file addresses** tells Word not to check words that appear to be URLs, e-mail addresses, or file pathnames.

◆ **Use German post-reform rules** tells Word to use German post-reform rules rather than traditional rules when the language is set to German.

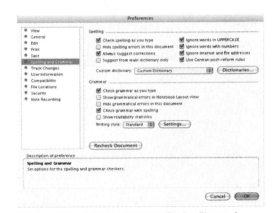

Figure 24 The default settings in the Spelling and Grammar pane of the Preferences dialog.

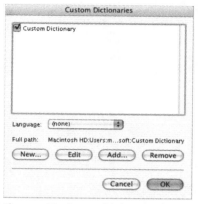

Figure 25 The Custom Dictionaries dialog.

◆ **Custom dictionary** enables you to create, edit, add, and remove custom dictionaries. Click the Dictionaries button to display the Custom Dictionaries dialog (**Figure 25**), which lists all the dictionary files open in Word. Then:

▲ To activate a dictionary file so it can be used by the spelling checker, turn on the check box to the left of its name in the Custom dictionaries list.

▲ To change the language of the selected dictionary file, choose a language from the Language pop-up menu.

▲ To create a new custom dictionary, click the New button and use the dialog that appears to name and save the new dictionary file.

▲ To edit the selected dictionary, click the Edit button to open it in Word. Then make changes and save it. Keep in mind that using this feature will turn off the automatic spelling check feature, so you'll have to turn it back on to use it again when you're done.

▲ To add a dictionary to the Custom dictionaries list, click the Add button and use the dialog that appears to locate and open the dictionary file. This feature makes it possible to share dictionary files that contain company- or industry-specific terms with other Word users in your workplace.

▲ To remove a dictionary from Word, select the dictionary and click the Remove button. This does not delete the dictionary file from disk.

When you are finished making changes in the Custom Dictionaries dialog, click OK.

SPELLING AND GRAMMAR PREFERENCES

Grammar

Grammar options control the way the grammar checker works:

◆ **Check grammar as you type** turns on the automatic grammar check feature.

◆ **Show grammatical errors in Notebook Layout view** indicates possible grammar errors in Notebook Layout view. You may prefer to keep this option turned off if you often take notes with informal writing styles that could be flagged as errors.

◆ **Hide grammatical errors in this document** hides the green wavy lines that Word uses to identify possible grammar errors when the automatic grammar check feature is turned on. This option is only available when the Check grammar as you type option is enabled.

◆ **Check grammar with spelling** performs a grammar check as part of a manual spelling check.

◆ **Show readability statistics** displays readability statistics (**Figure 26**) for a document at the conclusion of a manual spelling and grammar check. This option is only available when the Check grammar with spelling option is enabled.

◆ **Writing style** enables you to select a set of rules for the grammar checker. Use the pop-up menu to select an option (**Figure 27**).

◆ **Settings** enables you to customize the rules for the grammar checker. Click this button to display the Grammar Settings dialog (**Figure 28**). Choose the set of rules that you want to modify from the Writing style drop-down list (**Figure 27**), then use the options in the dialog to set the style's rules. You can use the Reset All button to reset all writing style rule sets to the default settings.

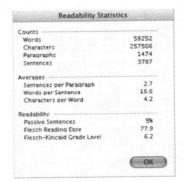

Figure 26 Readability statistics for *Hound of the Baskervilles* by Sir Arthur Conan Doyle.

Figure 27
Choose a writing style for your documents from this pop-up menu.

Figure 28 The Grammar Settings dialog enables you to fine-tune the way the grammar checker works.

◆ **Recheck Document** clears the list of ignored problems so you can recheck a document for errors.

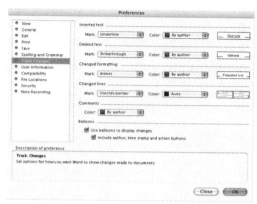

Figure 29 The default settings in the Track Changes pane of the Preferences dialog.

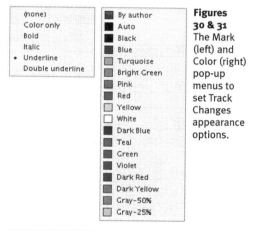

(none)
Color only
Bold
Italic
• Underline
Double underline

By author
Auto
Black
Blue
Turquoise
Bright Green
Pink
Red
Yellow
White
Dark Blue
Teal
Green
Violet
Dark Red
Dark Yellow
Gray-50%
Gray-25%

Figures 30 & 31 The Mark (left) and Color (right) pop-up menus to set Track Changes appearance options.

(none)
Left border
Right border
• Outside border

Figure 32 The Mark pop-up menu for setting the location of changed lines markers.

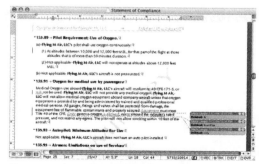

Figure 33 An example of change balloons in a document's margins.

Track Changes Preferences

The Track Changes preferences (**Figure** 29) control the way the track changes feature works.

◆ **Inserted text** controls the appearance of text that is inserted into the document. Choose options from the Mark and Color pop-up menus (**Figures 30** and **31**).

◆ **Deleted text** controls the appearance of text that is deleted from the document. Choose options from the Mark and Color pop-up menus (**Figures 30** and **31**).

◆ **Changed formatting** controls the appearance of text that has been reformatted. Choose options from the Mark and Color pop-up menus (**Figures 30** and **31**).

◆ **Changed lines** controls the location and appearance of the changed lines marker. Choose options from the Mark and Color pop-up menus (**Figures 32** and **31**).

◆ **Comments** controls the color of comment balloons for changes. Choose an option from the Color pop-up menu (**Figure 31**).

◆ **Use balloons to display changes** displays changes in balloons in the margin of the document (**Figure 33**).

◆ **Include author, time stamp and action buttons** includes the author name, the date and time the change was made, and action buttons for the change in the balloon (**Figure 33**). The Use balloons to display changes option must be enabled to change this option.

User Information Preferences

The User Information options (**Figure 34**) store information about the primary user of that copy of Word. This information is used by a variety of features throughout Word. The fields of information here are self-explanatory, so I won't go into them in detail. Clicking the More button displays a window with your information from Entourage's contact database, so you can add or change additional information for yourself.

Figure 34 The User Information pane of the Preferences dialog.

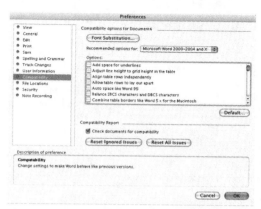

Figure 35 The default settings in the Compatibility pane of the Preferences dialog.

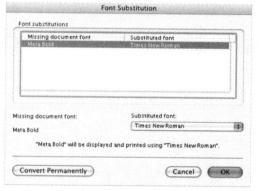

Figure 36 The Font Substitution dialog.

- Microsoft Word 2000-2004 and X
  Microsoft Word 97-98
  Microsoft Word 6.0/95
  Word for Windows 1.0
  Word for Windows 2.0
  Word for the Macintosh 5.x
  Word for MS-DOS
  WordPerfect 5.x
  WordPerfect 6.x for Windows
  WordPerfect 6.0 for DOS
  Custom

Figure 37
The Recommended options for pop-up menu.

Compatibility Preferences

Compatibility options (**Figure 35**) control the internal formatting of the current Word document for compatibility with other applications or versions of Word. Settings are divided into two categories: Compatibility options for the current document and Compatibility Report.

Compatibility options for the current document

Compatibility options enable you to set options for the currently active document:

◆ **Font Substitution** enables you to specify a font to be used in place of a missing font. (This happens most often when you open a file that was created on someone else's computer.) Click this button to display the Font Substitution dialog (**Figure 36**). You can then select the missing font name and choose a substitution font from the Substituted font pop-up menu, which includes all fonts installed on your computer. To reformat text by applying the substituted font, click the Convert Permanently button. If the document does not contain any missing fonts, Word will not display the Font Substitution dialog.

◆ **Recommended options for** enables you to select a collection of compatibility rules for a specific application. Choose an option from the pop-up menu (**Figure 37**).

◆ **Options** enables you to toggle check boxes for a variety of internal formatting options. These options are automatically set when you choose one of the rule sets from the Recommended options for pop-up menu, but you can override them as desired.

◆ **Default** applies the current dialog settings to all documents created with the current template from that point forward.

Compatibility Report

Compatibility Report options enable you to set up the compatibility report feature. This feature checks a document and displays a list of possible incompatibilities with specific versions of Word (**Figure 38**).

◆ **Check documents for compatibility** enables the compatibility report feature.

◆ **Reset Ignored Issues** allows the compatibility report feature to recheck the current document for previously ignored issues.

◆ **Reset All Issues** allows the compatibility report feature to recheck all documents for previously ignored issues.

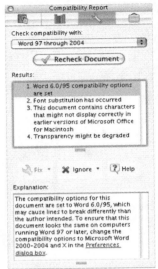

Figure 38
An example of a compatibility report created by Word. To check a document's compatibility, choose Tools > Compatibility Report.

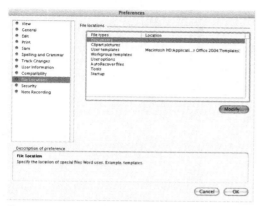

Figure 39 The File Locations pane of the Preferences dialog.

Figure 40 Use this dialog to set the location of a specific type of file.

Figure 41 The pathname for the folder you selected appears in the dialog.

File Locations Preferences

File Locations preferences (**Figure 39**) enable you to set the default disk location for certain types of files. This makes it easier for Word (and you) to find these files.

To set or change a default file location

1. Click to select the name of the file type for which you want to set or change the file location (**Figure 39**).

2. Click the Modify button.

3. Use the Choose a Folder dialog that appears (**Figure 40**) to locate and select the folder in which the files are or will be stored.

4. Click Choose.

   The pathname for the location appears to the right of the name of the file type (**Figure 41**).

Security Preferences

Security preferences (**Figure 42**) help keep your documents and system secure. There are three categories of options: Security options for the current document, Privacy options, and Macro security.

Security options for the current document

Security options enable you to password-protect a document so it's impossible to open or modify without entering a correct password.

◆ **Password to open** enables you to specify a password that must be entered to open the file. When you click OK to save your settings and close the Preferences dialog, Word displays a dialog that prompts you to enter this password again (**Figure 43**). Later, when you reopen the document, Word displays a dialog that prompts you to enter the password (**Figure 44**). If you fail to enter the correct password, the file will not open.

◆ **Password to modify** enables you to specify a password that must be entered to save modifications to the file. When you click OK to save your settings and close the Preferences dialog, Word displays a dialog similar to the one in **Figure 43** that prompts you to enter this password again. Later, when you reopen the document, Word displays a dialog that prompts you to enter the password (**Figure 45**). If you cannot enter the correct password, you can open the file as a read-only file.

Figure 42 The default settings in the Security pane of the Preferences dialog.

Figure 43
Use this dialog to confirm that you know the password to open the file.

Figure 44 Use this dialog to enter a file's password when opening it.

Figure 45 This dialog appears when you open a document that has a password to modify it.

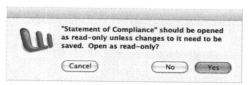

Figure 46 This dialog appears when you open a document that is set as Read-only recommended.

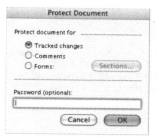

Figure 47
Use the Protect Document dialog to limit the types of modifications a user can make to a document.

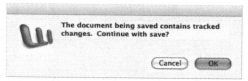

Figure 48 Word can warn you when you save, print, or e-mail a file that contains tracked changes or comments.

Figure 49 Word can display a dialog like this one to warn you when you open a file containing macros.

◆ **Read-only recommended** displays a dialog that recommends that the file be opened as a read-only file (**Figure 46**) each time the file is opened. If the file is opened as read-only, changes to the file must be saved in a file with a different name or in a different disk location.

◆ **Protect Document** displays the Protect Document dialog (**Figure 47**), which you can use to limit the types of changes that can be made to the document. (This feature is covered in **Chapter 16**.)

Privacy options

Privacy options help protect your privacy.

◆ **Remove personal information from this file on save** removes user information from the file when you save it.

◆ **Warn before printing, saving or sending a file that contains tracked changes or comments** displays a warning dialog (**Figure 48**) when you print, save, or e-mail a file that contains tracked changes or comments. This helps prevent you from sending draft files that may include confidential information.

Macro security

The Macro security option enables you to protect your computer from viruses attached to macros that work with Word or other Microsoft Office products. (Macro security is discussed in **Chapter 19**.)

◆ **Warn before opening a file that contains macros** displays a dialog like the one in **Figure 49** when you open a Word file that contains macros.

Note Recording Preferences

Note Recording preferences (**Figure 50**) control how audio notes are recorded. The options in this pane will determine how audio notes sound as well as how much space they take in a Word file.

◆ **Quality** is the overall quality of the recording. Your options are Low, Medium, Medium-High, High, and Custom. The higher the quality, the more disk space is required for a recording. Changes you make to this pop-up menu affect settings in the other pop-up menus.

◆ **Audio Type** is the format for the recording. Your options are Advanced Audio Coding (MP4), AIFF, and WAV. AIFF and WAV require more disk space than MP4.

◆ **Channels** enables you to record in one channel (Mono) or two channels (Stereo). Stereo requires more disk space than Mono.

◆ **Sample Size** is the bit rate for recording. Your choices are 8 bit and 16 bit. The more bits, the more disk space required. This option is only available if you choose AIFF or WAV from the Audio Type pop-up menu.

◆ **Sampling Rate** is the digital audio frequency for capture. A higher sampling rate requires more disk space.

Figure 50 The default settings in the Note Recording pane of the Preferences dialog.

Figure 51
The Customize sub-menu at the bottom of the Tools menu offers several options for customizing Word.

Customizing Word's Toolbars & Menus

Word's toolbars and menus enable you to access commands by clicking a toolbar button or choosing a menu command. This is pretty standard stuff that's available in many applications. But what isn't standard is your ability to customize Word's menus and toolbars as follows:

◆ Create new toolbars with any combination of buttons.

◆ Display any combination of toolbars.

◆ Show or hide ScreenTips with or without shortcut keys on toolbars.

◆ Display font names in plain text or font typefaces on font menus.

◆ Add and remove toolbar buttons, menu commands, and menus.

You customize Word's toolbars and menus with its Customize Toolbars/Menus dialog. This part of the chapter explains how—and how to restore toolbars and menus to default settings when you need to.

To open the Customize Toolbars/Menus dialog

Choose Tools > Customize > Customize Toolbars/Menus (**Figure 51**).

CUSTOMIZING TOOLBARS & MENUS

To modify the appearance of toolbars & menus

1. In the Customize Toolbars/Menus dialog, click the Toolbars button to display its options (**Figure 52**).

2. Toggle check boxes as desired in the bottom-right corner of the dialog:

   ▲ **Show ScreenTips on toolbars** displays the name of a button in a small box when you point to the button (**Figure 53**).

   ▲ **Show shortcut keys in ScreenTips** displays a command's shortcut key in the ScreenTip box when you point to its button (**Figure 54**).

   ▲ **WYSIWYG font menus** displays font menus and lists in their typeface (**Figure 10**).

3. Click OK to save your settings.

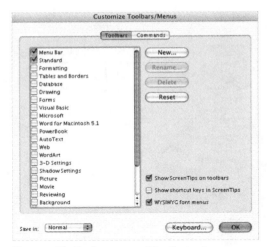

Figure 52 The Toolbars pane of the Customize Toolbars/Menus dialog.

Figure 53 A ScreenTip for a toolbar button.

Figure 54 A shortcut key displayed in a ScreenTip.

Figure 55
Use this dialog to set options and create a new toolbar.

Figure 56
An empty toolbar. As you can see, it isn't much to look at.

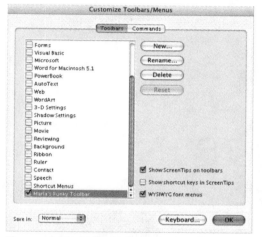

Figure 57 A new toolbar's name appears at the bottom of the Toolbars list.

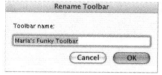

Figure 58
Use this dialog to rename a toolbar you created.

To create a new toolbar

1. In the Customize Toolbars/Menus dialog, click the Toolbars button to display its options (**Figure 52**).

2. Choose a template or document name from the Save in pop-up menu to specify where the toolbar should be saved.

3. Click the New button to display the New Toolbar dialog (**Figure 55**).

4. Enter a name for the toolbar in the Toolbar name box and click OK.

   A tiny empty toolbar appears onscreen (**Figure 56**) and the name of the toolbar you created appears at the bottom of the list in the Toolbars pane of the dialog (**Figure 57**).

✔ Tip

- I explain how to add buttons to a custom toolbar later in this chapter.

To rename a toolbar

1. In the Customize Toolbars/Menus dialog, click the Toolbars button to display its options.

2. Select the name of the toolbar you want to rename (**Figure 57**).

3. Click the Rename button to display the Rename Toolbar dialog (**Figure 58**).

4. Enter a new name for the toolbar in the Toolbar name box and click OK.

   The name of the toolbar changes in the list in the Toolbars tab of the dialog.

✔ Tip

- You can only rename a toolbar you created. You cannot rename Word's built-in toolbars.

CREATING & RENAMING TOOLBARS

To delete a toolbar

1. In the Customize Toolbars/Menus dialog, click the Toolbars button to display its options.

2. Select the name of the toolbar you want to delete (**Figure 57**).

3. Click the Delete button.

4. Click OK in the confirmation dialog that appears (**Figure 59**).

   The name of the toolbar is removed from the list in the Toolbars tab of the dialog.

✔ Tip

■ You can only delete a toolbar you created. You cannot delete Word's built-in toolbars.

To show or hide toolbars

1. In the Customize Toolbars/Menus dialog, click the Toolbars button to display its options (**Figure 52**).

2. To display a toolbar, turn on the check box beside the toolbar name.

   or

   To hide a toolbar, turn off the check box beside the toolbar name.

✔ Tips

■ You can also display or hide most toolbars by choosing the toolbar's name from the Toolbars submenu under the View menu (**Figure 60**), as discussed in **Chapter 1**. This submenu also includes the Customize Toolbars/Menus command, which opens the Toolbars pane of the Customize Toolbars/Menus dialog (**Figure 52**).

■ You must display a toolbar to make changes to its buttons as discussed on the following pages.

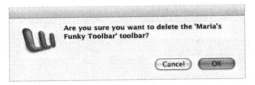

Figure 59 A dialog box like this appears to confirm that you really do want to delete the toolbar.

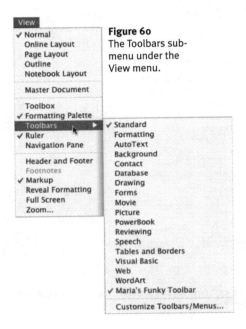

Figure 60 The Toolbars sub-menu under the View menu.

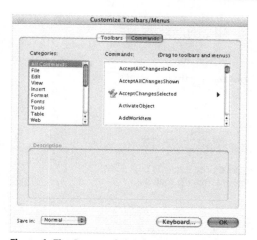

Figure 61 The Commands button of the Customize Toolbars/Menus dialog.

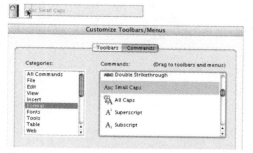

Figure 62a You can add a button to a new toolbar...

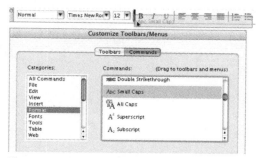

Figure 62b ...or an existing one.

To add buttons to a toolbar

1. In the Customize Toolbars/Menus dialog, click the Toolbars button to display its options (**Figure 52**).

2. Make sure the check box for the toolbar you want to change is turned on so the toolbar appears onscreen.

3. Click the Commands button to display its options (**Figure 61**).

4. Select a command category in the Categories list. The commands that appear in the Commands list change.

5. Scroll through the Commands list to find the command you want to add to the toolbar.

6. Drag the command from the Commands list to the toolbar you want to add it to. A vertical bar appears where the button will be inserted (**Figures 62a** and **62b**). When the bar is in the desired location, release the mouse button. The toolbar button appears (**Figures 63a** and **63b**).

7. Repeat steps 4 through 6 for each button you want to add to a toolbar.

8. When you are finished adding buttons, click OK to dismiss the Customize Toolbars/Menus dialog.

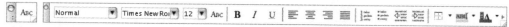

Figures 63a & 63b The toolbars from Figures 62a and 62b after adding a button.

ADDING TOOLBAR BUTTONS

To remove buttons from a toolbar

1. In the Customize Toolbars/Menus dialog, click the Toolbars button to display its options (**Figure 52**).

2. Make sure the check box for the toolbar you want to change is turned on so the toolbar appears onscreen.

3. Drag a button off the toolbar (**Figure 64**). When you release the mouse button, the button disappears (**Figure 65**).

4. Repeat step 3 for each button you want to remove from the toolbar.

5. When you are finished removing buttons, click OK to dismiss the Customize Toolbars/Menus dialog.

To restore a toolbar to default settings

1. In the Customize Toolbars/Menus dialog, click the Toolbars button to display its options (**Figure 52**).

2. Select the name of the toolbar you want to restore to its default settings.

3. Click the Reset button. A warning dialog appears (**Figure 66**).

4. Click OK. The toolbar is restored to its default settings.

✔ Tip

■ You can only restore Word's built-in tool-bars. You cannot restore a toolbar that you created.

Figure 64 Drag the button off the toolbar.

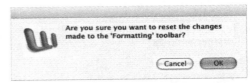

Figure 65 The button is removed from the toolbar.

Figure 66 A dialog like this one confirms that you really do want to reset the toolbar.

Are you sure you want to reset the changes made to the 'Formatting' toolbar?

Cancel   OK

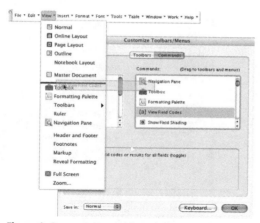

Figure 67 Drag a command from the Customize Toolbars/Menus dialog to a menu.

Figure 68
The command is added to the menu.

To add commands to a menu

1. In the Customize Toolbars/Menus dialog, click the Toolbars button to display its options (**Figure 52**).

2. Make sure the check box beside Menu Bar is turned on so the customizable menu bar appears onscreen.

3. Click the Commands button to display its options (**Figure 61**).

4. Select a command category in the Categories list. The commands that appear in the Commands list change.

5. Scroll through the Commands list to find the command you want to add to the menu.

6. Drag the command from the Commands list to the menu you want to add it to. The menu opens and a horizontal bar appears where the command will be inserted (**Figure 67**). When the bar is in the desired location, release the mouse button. If you click the menu to display it again, you'll see that the command has been added (**Figure 68**).

7. Repeat steps 4 through 6 for each command you want to add to a menu.

8. When you are finished adding commands, click OK.

✔ Tip

- In step 6, if you drag the command over a submenu name, the submenu opens so you can insert the command on it.

To remove a command from a menu

1. In the Customize Toolbars/Menus dialog, click the Toolbars button to display its options (**Figure 52**).

2. Make sure the check box beside Menu Bar is turned on so the customizable menu bar appears onscreen.

3. Click the name of the menu containing the command you want to remove to display the menu (**Figure 68**).

4. Drag the command off the menu (**Figure 69**). When you release the mouse button, the command is removed (**Figure 70**).

5. Repeat steps 3 and 4 for each command you want to remove from a menu.

6. When you are finished removing commands, click OK.

To remove a menu

1. In the Customize Toolbars/Menus dialog, click the Toolbars button to display its options (**Figure 52**).

2. Make sure the check box beside Menu Bar is turned on so the customizable menu bar appears onscreen.

3. Drag the name of the menu you want to remove off the Menu toolbar. When you release the mouse button, the menu is removed.

4. Repeat step 3 for each menu you want to remove.

5. When you are finished removing menus, click OK.

✖ Warning!

■ Removing menu commands and menus can make Word commands inaccessible!

Figure 69
To remove a command from a menu, simply drag it off.

Figure 70
The command is removed from the menu.

REMOVING COMMANDS & MENUS

To restore menus to default settings

1. In the Customize Toolbars/Menus dialog, click the Toolbars button to display its options (**Figure 52**).

2. Select Menu Bar in the scrolling list.

3. Click the Reset button. A warning dialog appears (**Figure 66**).

4. Click OK. The menu bar is restored to its default settings.

✔ Tip

- Use this technique to recover menus you removed from the menu bar in error.

Customizing the Formatting Palette

You can also customize the Formatting Palette to adjust its appearance—whether it fades or minimizes and how it does it—and contents. You do this with the Customize Formatting Palette dialog (**Figure 71**).

To customize the Formatting Palette

1. Choose Tools > Customize > Customize Formatting Palette (**Figure 51**) to display the Customize Formatting Palette dialog (**Figure 71**).

2. Set Behavior options as desired:
   - ▲ **If inactive for** enables you to specify how long the Formatting Palette should be inactive before it either fades or minimizes. Drag the slider to set the amount of time from 0 to 60 seconds. Turning on the **Never** check box prevents the Formatting Palette from either fading or minimizing due to inactivity.
   - ▲ **Make it** enables you to specify whether the Formatting Palette should fade or minimize when inactive. Select one of the radio buttons.

3. Set Effects options as desired:
   - ▲ **Fade** enables you to specify how transparent the Formatting Palette should get when it fades. Drag the slider to set the transparency from 10 to 100 percent or enter a value in the box beside the slider.
   - ▲ **Minimize** lets you specify whether the Formatting Palette should minimize with a genie effect, scale effect, or no effect at all. Choose an option from the pop-up menu.

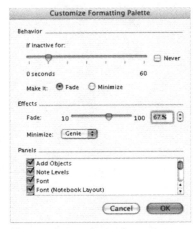

Figure 71 The Customize Formatting Palette dialog.

4. Toggle the check boxes in the Panels area to determine which categories of options appear in the Formatting Palette.

5. Click OK to save your settings.

✔ Tips

■ If you often use the Formatting Palette, you may find it annoying that it fades or minimizes. If so, turn on the Never check box in step 2 and it will never fade or disappear on its own again.

■ The options that appear in the Formatting Palette vary depending on the document view and text or objects selected in the document window.

CUSTOMIZING THE FORMATTING PALETTE

Customizing Word's Shortcut Keys

Word comes preconfigured with a surprising number of shortcut keys assigned to menu commands and other options. This enables you to perform many commands without menus or dialogs.

Word's Customize Keyboard dialog enables you to modify existing shortcut keys or add new ones.

This part of the chapter tells you how you can create a list of assigned shortcut keys, and then explains how you can modify them.

To create a list of existing shortcut keys

1. Choose Tools > Macro > Macros to display the Macros dialog.

2. Choose Word commands from the Macros in pop-up menu (**Figure 72**).

3. Select ListCommands from the list of macros (**Figure 73**).

4. Click Run.

5. In the List Commands dialog that appears (**Figure 74**), select the Current menu and keyboard settings option.

6. Click OK. Word creates a document that lists all commands that appear on menus or have shortcut keys assigned to them (**Figure 75**).

✔ Tips

- You can print or save the command list document Word creates (**Figure 75**).

- If you make changes to keyboard or menu settings, recreate this document to get an updated list.

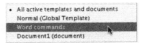

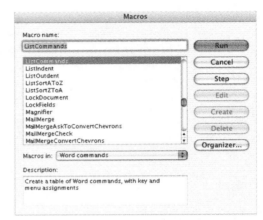

Figure 72 Choose Word commands from the Macros in pop-up menu in the Macros dialog.

Figure 73 Select the ListCommands macro.

Figure 74 The List Commands dialog.

Figure 75 Word creates a document that lists all commands that appear on menus or have shortcut keys.

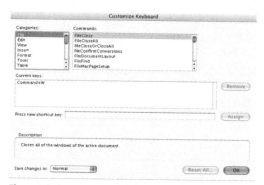

Figure 76 The Customize Keyboard dialog.

Figure 77 The keystroke you type appears in the box and the status of that keystroke appears beneath it.

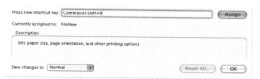

Figure 78 In this example, the keystroke I typed is already assigned to another command.

Figure 79 Shortcut keys can be a series of keystrokes.

To customize shortcut keys

1. Choose Tools > Customize > Customize Keyboard (**Figure 51**) to display the Customize Keyboard dialog (**Figure 76**).

2. Select a command category in the Categories list.

3. Select the command you want to modify in the Commands list.

4. Customize the shortcut key as follows:
   ▲ To remove an existing shortcut key, select the keystroke in the Current keys box and click Remove.
   ▲ To add a shortcut key, position the insertion point in the Press new shortcut key box and press the keystroke you want to assign. The keystroke status appears (**Figure 77**). If the keystroke is unassigned, click Assign to assign it to the current command.

5. Repeat steps 2 through 4 to add or remove as many shortcut keys as you like.

6. If desired, choose a template or document to save customized shortcut keys into from the Save changes in pop-up menu.

7. Click OK to save your changes and dismiss the Customize Keyboard dialog.

✔ Tips

■ In step 4, if the keystroke is already assigned to another command (**Figure 78**), remove it from that other command before assigning it to the current command.

■ In step 4, you can enter a series of keystrokes to invoke a command. For example, pressing ⌃ ⌘ Shift P and then P (**Figure 79**) creates a shortcut key that requires you to press that series of keystrokes.

■ A command can have more than one shortcut key.

To restore all shortcut keys

1. Choose Tools > Customize > Customize Keyboard (**Figure 51**) to display the Customize Keyboard dialog (**Figure 76**).

2. Click the Reset All button.

3. Click Yes in the confirmation dialog that appears (**Figure 80**).

4. Click OK to dismiss the Customize Keyboard dialog.

✔ Tip

■ The Reset All button can only be clicked if there have been changes to shortcut keys.

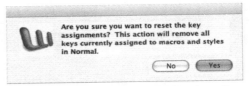

Figure 80 Use this dialog to confirm that you really do want to reset shortcut keys.

Menus & Shortcut Keys

Menus & Shortcut Keys

This appendix illustrates all of Microsoft Word's standard menus and provides a list of shortcut keys—including many that don't appear on menus.

To use a shortcut key, hold down the modifier key (usually ⌃ ⌘) and press the keyboard key corresponding to the command. For example, to use the Save command's shortcut key, hold down ⌃ ⌘ and press Ⓢ.

✔ Tips

- ■ I explain how to use menus and shortcut keys in **Chapter 1**.

- ■ I tell you how you can customize menus and shortcut keys in **Chapter 20**.

Word Menu

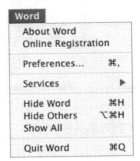

Word	
About Word	
Online Registration	
Preferences...	⌘,
Services	▶
Hide Word	⌘H
Hide Others	⌥⌘H
Show All	
Quit Word	⌘Q

⌘ ,	Preferences
⌘ H	Hide
Option ⌘ H	Hide Others
⌘ Q	Quit Word

File Menu

File	
Project Gallery...	⇧⌘P
New Blank Document	⌘N
Open...	⌘O
Close	⌘W
Save	⌘S
Save As...	
Save as Web Page...	
Versions...	
Web Page Preview	
Page Setup...	
Print Preview	
Print...	⌘P
Send To	▶
Properties...	
1 Statement of Compliance	
2 Hound of the Baskervilles	
3 Flying M Customers	
4 Charity Airplane Wash	

Shift ⌘ P	Project Gallery
⌘ N	New Blank Document
⌘ O	Open
⌘ W	Close
Option ⌘ W	Close All
⌘ S	Save
F12	Save As
⌘ F2	Print Preview
⌘ P	Print

Send To submenu

Mail Recipient (as HTML)...
Mail Recipient (as Attachment)...
Microsoft PowerPoint

(no shortcut keys)

Edit Menu

Edit	
Undo Paste	⌘Z
Repeat Copy	⌘Y
Cut	⌘X
Copy	⌘C
Copy to Scrapbook	⇧⌘C
Paste	⌘V
Paste from Scrapbook	⇧⌘V
Paste Special...	
Paste as Hyperlink	
Clear	▶
Select All	⌘A
Find...	⌘F
Replace...	⇧⌘H
Go To...	⌘G
Links...	
Object	

⌘ Z	Undo
⌘ Y	Redo or Repeat
⌘ X	Cut
⌘ C	Copy
Shift F2	Copy Text
Shift ⌘ C	Copy to Scrapbook
Ctrl V	Paste
Shift ⌘ V	Paste from Scrapbook
⌘ A	Select All
⌘ F	Find
Shift F4	Repeat Find
Shift ⌘ H	Replace
⌘ G	Go To
Shift F5	Go Back

Clear submenu

Clear Formatting
Contents

Del	Contents

View Menu

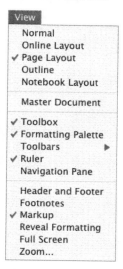

⌃ ⌘ N   Normal

Option ⌃ ⌘ P   Page Layout

Option ⌃ ⌘ O   Outline

Option ⌃ ⌘ B   Notebook
Layout

Toolbars submenu

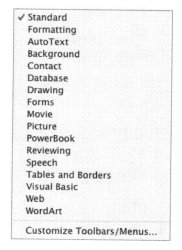

(no shortcut keys)

Insert Menu

Ctrl Shift D   Date Field

Ctrl Shift T   Time Field

Option ⌃ ⌘ A   Comment

Option ⌃ ⌘ F   Footnote

Option ⌃ ⌘ E   Endnote

Shift ⌃ ⌘ F5   Bookmark

⌃ ⌘ K   Hyperlink

Break submenu

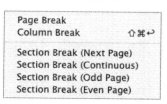

Shift Enter   Page Break

Shift ⌃ ⌘ Return Column Break

⌃ ⌘ Enter   Section Break

AutoText submenu

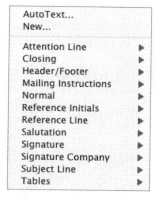

Option ⌃ ⌘ V   AutoText

Option F3   New

Picture submenu

Clip Art...
From File...

Horizontal Line...
AutoShapes
WordArt...
From Scanner or Camera...
Chart

(no shortcut keys)

HTML Object submenu

Background Sound...
Scrolling Text...

Checkbox...
Option Button...
List Box...
Textbox...
Submit...
Reset...
Hidden...

(no shortcut keys)

Format Menu

FORMAT MENU

Format	
Font...	⌘D
Paragraph...	⌥⌘M
Document...	
Bullets and Numbering...	
Borders and Shading...	
Columns...	
Tabs...	
Drop Cap...	
Text Direction...	
Change Case...	
AutoFormat...	
Theme...	
Style...	
Background	
Insert Text Box	

⌘D	Font
⌘B	Bold
⌘I	Italic
⌘U	Underline
Shift ⌘W	Word Underline
Shift ⌘D	Double Underline
Shift Ctrl H	Hidden
Shift ⌘A	All Caps
Shift ⌘K	Small Caps
⌘=	Subscript
Shift ⌘=	Superscript
Shift ⌘.	Grow Font
⌘]	Grow Font One Point
Shift ⌘,	Shrink Font
⌘[	Shrink Font One Point
Option ⌘M	Paragraph
Shift Ctrl M	Indent
Shift ⌘M	Unindent
⌘T	Hanging Indent
Shift ⌘T	Unhang Indent
⌘L	Left Align Paragraph
⌘E	Center Paragraph
⌘R	Right Align Paragraph
⌘J	Justify Paragraph
⌘1	Single Space Paragraph
⌘5	1.5 Space Paragraph
⌘2	Double Space Paragraph
⌘0	Open or Close Up Paragraph
Shift ⌘L	Bulleted List
Shift F3	Change Case
Option ⌘K	AutoFormat
Shift ⌘S	Style
Shift ⌘N	Normal Style
Option ⌘1	Apply Heading 1
Option ⌘2	Apply Heading 2
Option ⌘3	Apply Heading 3

Font Menu

Font

American Typewriter
American Typewriter Condensed
American Typewriter Light
Apple Chancery
Arial
Arial Black
Arial Narrow
Arial Rounded MT Bold
Baskerville
Baskerville Semibold
Big Caslon
Brush Script MT
Calisto MT
Century
Century Gothic
Chalkboard
Cochin
Colonna MT
Comic Sans MS
COPPERPLATE
COPPERPLATE GOTHIC BOLD
COPPERPLATE GOTHIC LIGHT
COPPERPLATE LIGHT
Courier
Courier New
Curlz MT
Didot
▼

(no shortcut keys)

Tools Menu

Tools

Spelling and Grammar...   ⌥⌘L
Thesaurus...   ⌥⌘R
Hyphenation...
Dictionary
Language...

Word Count...
AutoSummarize...
AutoCorrect...

Track Changes   ▶
Merge Documents...
Protect Document...
Flag for Follow Up...

Scrapbook
Reference Tools
Compatibility Report
Project Palette

Data Merge Manager
Envelopes...
Labels...
Letter Wizard...
Address Book

Tools on the Web

Macro   ▶
Templates and Add-Ins...
Customize   ▶

Option ⌃ ⌘ L	Spelling and Grammar
Option F7	Next Misspelling
Option ⌃ ⌘ R	Thesaurus
Ctrl Shift F	Merge Field
Ctrl Shift K	Mail Merge Check
Ctrl Shift E	Mail Merge Edit Data Source
Ctrl Shift N	Mail Merge to Document

Track Changes submenu

Highlight Changes...
Accept or Reject Changes...
Compare Documents...

(no shortcut keys)

Macro submenu

Macros...
Record New Macro...

Visual Basic Editor
REALbasic Editor

Option F8	Macros
Option F11	Visual Basic Editor

Customize submenu

Customize Toolbars/Menus...
Customize Formatting Palette...
Customize Keyboard...

(no shortcut keys)

FONT & TOOLS MENUS

Table Menu

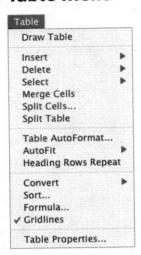

(no shortcut keys)

Insert submenu

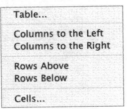

| Ctrl ⌃ ⌘ V | Insert Row |

Delete submenu

Table
Columns
Rows
Cells...

| Ctrl ⌃ ⌘ X | Delete Rows |

Select submenu

Table
Column
Row
Cell

| Option ⌃ ⌘ T | Select Table |

AutoFit submenu

AutoFit to Contents
AutoFit to Window
Fixed Column Width
Distribute Rows Evenly
Distribute Columns Evenly

(no shortcut keys)

Convert submenu

Convert Text to Table...
Convert Table to Text...

(no shortcut keys)

Window Menu

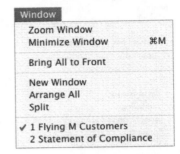

⌃ ⌘ M	Minimize Window
Option ⌃ ⌘ S	Split/Remove Split
F6	Other Pane
⌃ ⌘ F6	Next Window
Shift ⌃ ⌘ F6	Previous Window

Work Menu

Work
Add to Work Menu

(no shortcut keys)

Help Menu

Help
Word Help
Sample Documents
Use the Office Assistant
Check for Updates
Downloads and Updates
Visit the Product Website
Send Feedback on Word

| ⌃ ⌘ / | Word Help |

Index

INDEX

INDEX

INDEX

THIS BOOK IS SAFARI ENABLED

INCLUDES FREE 45-DAY ACCESS TO THE ONLINE EDITION

The Safari® Enabled icon on the cover of your favorite technology book means the book is available through Safari Bookshelf. When you buy this book, you get free access to the online edition for 45 days.

Safari Bookshelf is an electronic reference library that lets you easily search thousands of technical books, find code samples, download chapters, and access technical information whenever and wherever you need it.

TO GAIN 45-DAY SAFARI ENABLED ACCESS TO THIS BOOK:

● Go to **http://www.peachpit.com/safarienabled**

● Complete the brief registration form

● Enter the coupon code found in the front of this book before the Table of Contents

If you have difficulty registering on Safari Bookshelf or accessing the online edition, please e-mail customer-service@safaribooksonline.com.